ESTATES ON THE EDGE

Estates on the Edge

The Social Consequences of Mass Housing in Northern Europe

Anne Power
Professor of Social Policy and Administration
London School of Economics and Political Science

Published by
MACMILLAN PRESS LTD
Houndmills, Basingstoke, Hampshire RG21 6XS
and London
Companies and representatives
throughout the world

First edition 1997
Reprinted 1998, (with new preface and minor alterations) 1999

ISBN 0–333–67463–4 hardcover
ISBN 0–333–74603–1 paperback

A catalogue record for this book is available
from the British Library.

This book is printed on paper suitable for recycling and
made from fully managed and sustained forest sources.

10 9 8 7 6 5 4 3 2
08 07 06 05 04 03 02 01 00 99

Printed and bound in Great Britain by
Antony Rowe Ltd, Chippenham, Wiltshire

Contents

PART II   A SURVEY OF TWENTY EUROPEAN ESTATES

PART IV   CHAOS OR COMMUNITY?

Contents   xi

List of Tables

List of Figures

Acknowledgements

This study of European estates was made possible through a grant from the Nuffield Foundation and Research Initiative Funding from the London School of Economics. I would first like to thank all those who participated in the LSE European Workshop on extreme estates at Cumberland Lodge, Windsor Great Park, in April 1991. The questionnaires, reports and presentations of the five country representatives made it possible to write this book.

The following participants were particularly important: Yves Bourgeat, Pierre Peillon, Stefan Schmidt, Rudiger Rahs, Jesper Nygaard, Henning Anderson, Peter Whelan, John Heagney, Ina Gould, Alicia Francis, Monica Zulauf, Alistair Jackson, Wendy Lewsey. In addition, I would like to thank the many housing organisations and staff whose co-operation made it possible to learn about European estates, including: *France* – the Association des HLMs, Île de France; OPACs of Val Fourré, Val de Marne, Rhône, Logirel; La SCIC; the Caîsse des Dépots et Consignations; Villes et Banlieues; UNFOHLM; CREPAH; *Germany* – Institut Wohnung und Umwelt; Empirica; Büro Sachs – Pfeiffer; German Federal Ministry of Housing; LEG Wohnen; Gesamtverband für Wohnungsunternehmen; Hillebrand management company; Cologne City Council; Cologne Adult Education Institute; Cologne social services dept; *Denmark* – AKB, KAB, AAB housing companies; Braband housing company, Haraldskaer National Tenant Training centre; National Federation of Non-profit Housing Companies; National Urban Renewal Unit; Jorgen Moeller; Danish Ministry of Housing; Building Research Institute; Hedwig Vestergaard; Hans Kristensen; *Ireland* – Department of the Environment; Institute of Public Administration; Dublin Corporation; Cork City Council; Ballymun Task Force; Ballymun Credit Union; Ballymun concierge co-operative; Sean O'Cuinn; Frank Fallon; John Blackwell; Eithne Fitzgerald; *Britain* – Haringey Council; Rhondda Borough Council; Hull City Council; Glasgow City Council; Department of the Environment; Welsh Office; Scottish Office; Scottish Homes; Priority Estates Project.

Many individuals have advised and helped in carrying out this study. I would particularly like to thank Marie-Christine LeRoy, Jean-Michel Guenod, Giles Renaudin, Jean-Claude Toubon, Ulli and Toni Pfeiffer, Soeren Villadsen, Judy O'Mahoney, Michael Burbidge, Volker Kreibich, Rebecca Tunstall and Carol Jenkins. Hilde Gage played a particularly vital role in preparing the manuscript, figures and references, keeping track of detailed records in four languages.

The following colleagues read drafts of the text and made helpful comments and suggestions: Alan Holmans, David Piachaud, Howard Glennerster, John Hills, Alan Murie, Julian Le Grand and Albert Martens. I have tried to take on board as many as possible of their comments but of course take full responsiblity for errors, misinterpretations and failures of clarity. Finally I must give very special recognition to Brian Abel-Smith who advised me throughout this long project, read and commented on many versions, and talked through the central themes. His sudden death in April 1996 was a great loss.

ANNE POWER

Definitions and Explanatory Notes

Mass housing refers to postwar, publicly sponsored and subsidised housing estates built on a large scale using mass-production industrial techniques and targeted at housing 'the masses' – a broad band of moderate to low-income city dwellers.

Social landlords include all those owners of rented housing that receive direct government subsidies for the production and maintenance of their stock and who are subject to regulation in their operations, to ensure that public money is properly invested with an adequate return for the government. Social landlords normally regulate their access to perform a *social* function according to government priorities and conform to certain publicly agreed standards in the conditions they provide.

Social landlords differ widely in their size, style and structure. Generally they fall into four categories:

- public bodies, such as local authorities in Britain and Ireland;
- publicly sponsored bodies, such as the *offices publics* of HLMs in France or the local authority-sponsored limited dividend companies in Germany and Denmark;
- privately sponsored but publicly subsidised non-profit housing associations and companies;
- member-based, co-operative-style or resident-controlled landlords.

In addition, private landlords can play a social role through at least partial public subsidy.

Social normally describes relations and links between people and groups within society in ways which connect them together, helping them interact. In the context of housing it describes housing built for a social purpose, i.e. to help people.

Non-profit housing organisations are legally autonomous housing bodies that operate for the good of people in need of housing who are unable to provide it for themselves. Any surpluses are used to further the aim of helping households in need.

Estates are groups of housing built in a defined geographical area, that are recognised as distinct and discrete entities. Estates can be high- or low-income, privately or publicly owned, rented or individually owned. A majority of estates, public and private, provide satisfactory housing.

Estate-level organisations include all those organisations and their employees operating at *estate* level, sometimes described as front line.

Unpopular estates are separate areas of housing which are difficult to let and to manage, and disproportionately house people with little choice, often people dependent on state support.

Rescue programmes describe special, publicly funded initiatives targeted at unpopular estates, with the aim of arresting their decline and upgrading physical conditions. All rescue programmes rely on central or local government support, although they also draw in other support.

Dumping is housing shorthand for pushing households with special support needs and often behaviour and 'coping' problems into unpopular areas or estates where there are vacancies.

Ghetto refers to an area, housing predominantly disadvantaged people who suffer discrimination in the wider society. This discrimination both pushes them into marginal, unpopular areas and makes it difficult for them to move out. The term 'ghetto' suggests extreme social decline, isolation and failure. Historically and in the US, the term 'ghetto' is applied where a particular racial or ethnic group is forced into a segregated area. In Europe today, the term 'social ghetto' or 'welfare ghetto' is increasingly applied to unpopular housing areas suffering steep decline and acute problems in which marginal groups become isolated and trapped.

Ghettoisation describes the processes that push disadvantaged groups into the most unpopular and disadvantaged areas through many hidden, as well as explicit, approaches to allocations and access.

Grands ensembles are large French outer estates·of high-rise flats.

HLM – Habitations à Loyer Modéré – stands for French housing associations.

ZUPs – the French *Zones à urbanisation prioritaire* – are large, designated green-field developments of high-rise, high-density social housing, built under state-subsidised programmes of the 1950s and 1960s. Around 1 000 000 social flats in ZUPs pose the most serious urban social problems in France.

CNDSQ – stands for Commission Nationale pour le Développement Social des Quartiers (National Commission for the Social Development of Neighbourhoods).

Quartiers en Crise – 'neighbourhoods in crisis – is the title given to the EU exchange programme for estates and areas experimenting with rescue programmes.

BRBS – stands for Bundesministerium für Raumordnung, Bauwesen und Städtebau – German Ministry of Planning, Building and Urban Development.

The Continent refers to mainland Europe, excluding Britain and Eire (also referred to as Ireland); the European Union refers to the 16 Member States, including Britain and Ireland.

Social polarisation describes the process of growing inequality between the majority, enjoying the benefits of economic growth and development, and the minority in most industrial economies of people who are largely excluded from those benefits through lack of jobs, family breakdown, discrimination and dependence on state support.

Marginalisation and residualisation refer to the processes which push disadvantaged groups into disadvantaged areas on the margins of society, further away from the mainstream or further down the social hierarchy to lower status, less power and greater disadvantage.

Industrial building is a method of building involving large-scale, factory-produced units that can be mechanically assembled and that involve simplified, uniform and repetitive techniques that are supposed to speed up building processes. These techniques usually involve concrete and steel, with parts too big to be handled without heavy machinery.

High-rise applies to multistorey buildings, over five storeys high, accessible by common entrances and lifts. Different countries in the study apply the term differently. We have followed the definition set out by Dunleavy (Dunleavy, 1981).

Welfare refers to state-organised and state-funded support for social needs. In the housing context it refers to the obligation placed on social landlords to give overriding priority to applicants with the greatest social needs.

Preface to the 1999 Reprint

When *Estates on the Edge* appeared in 1997 Britain was basking in the euphoria of a new government, a new social agenda and rising prosperity. The mood today is different. Most European countries are in social and political ferment as they scramble to reduce public debt and the costs of their welfare state. A determination to avoid American-style ghettos is diluted by a fear of taxing voters, a distrust of big government and a search for flexible job markets. Galloping change in the world order, driven by the international market for goods, services and labour, has created growing tensions throughout the European Union. This puts intense pressure on the already poor, but it affects most people in some way.

People under pressure – the less skilled, less stable, less prosperous – are often concentrated in less successful areas, particularly the unpopular social housing of the 1960s and 1970s. This area-based form of social exclusion provides the central theme of the book. As Europeans straddle two worlds – the postwar world of underpinning and cohesion and the post-industrial world of incipient ghettos and breakdown, the fate of people at the bottom in the new order is deeply uncertain.

For these reasons, *Estates on the Edge* reflects a strong sense of drama on the European stage – 'Le feu qui couve sous les cendres – the fire which smoulders under the ashes'. The large outer estates described in the book house a potentially explosive mix of the young, the unemployed, racial minorities and the politically alienated. Attempts at control, order and improvement can seem insignificant, even counterproductive. 'Targeting estates only enhances their stigma' as a senior French civil servant recently stated. To avert conflict, rebellion and breakdown of order, the state is searching for a new political framework, stressing citizenship, unity, inclusion and above all greater 'flexibility'. In each of the five countries examined, this new agenda is reshaping estates on the edge.

The British problem of the 'worst estates' is closely aligned with 'poor co-ordination of services', and concentrations of work-less households exacerbated by 'anti-social behaviour', 'neighbour nuisance', crime and family breakdown. The strongest policy initiatives to tackle the problem are Welfare to Work programmes for unemployed young and disadvantaged people, proposed new criminal powers to enforce behaviour standards and a plethora of Action Zones – targeting education, health and work. The creation of a special Social Exclusion Unit at the heart of the new British government, whose remit is to make spending departments work together to tackle difficult estates is focusing minds on the unexpectedly voguish French concept of social exclusion.

The French Government takes a more grandiose position – against exclusion, for cities, for work and education, certainly not against welfare *per se*. 'We must include people in society, not ghettoise them'. But the practical measures are inevitably small scale, participatory, fragmented and localised. Bit by bit France is changing its once 'kingly state' into something more flexible, adaptive, even 'Blairite'. Prime Minister Jospin's newly announced 'right to inclusion' and proposed 'law for cities' will be as problematic to deliver as his promise of half a million state subsidised jobs. But they do reflect a strong underlying commitment to action and a sense of urgency about worsening social conditions. Some see greater flexibility as a danger; most see it as essential.

Britain and France are battling with dramatic change from top to bottom of their societies. Poorly educated, low-skilled young men have been especially heavily affected by social and technological change. The tensions have often spilled over into social unrest and disorder. Police action intended to stem lawlessness, but too often heavy-handed, can lead to violent confrontations. My 1997 report *Dangerous Disorders* with Rebecca Tunstall addressed this problem in more detail.

Germany faces a different but related set of problems. The extraordinary effort and huge burden of reunification of the two Germanies has transformed the pressures of change into a pressure cooker of conflicts. The emergence of new leaders challenging the stable, wealth driven consensus of the last generation suddenly makes German politics and German society more fluid, more volatile, potentially more flexible. Once unpopular, outer estates are packed tight with newcomers in western regions, but giant concrete blocks are often under-occupied in under-employed Eastern regions. The new

'German Giant' is diverting huge resources into equalisation, urban upgrading, rent subsidies, cohesion. German welfare and labour costs continue to outstrip most other developed economies, but the German welfare system is strongly defended at all levels of German society since it results in less inequality, higher productivity and so far more stability. Nonetheless the hugely dominating problems of unemployment, immigration, globalised investment and pressures eastwards make some flexibilisation inevitable and imminent.

Denmark and Ireland as smaller economies are transforming themselves more easily than their larger EU partners. Denmark has recovered far more successfully than France or Germany from the deep recession of the early 1990s, but is increasingly pressured by the costs of its all-encompassing welfare system. Denmark is also struggling with the integration of its growing ethnic minority population. In order to facilitate integration the Danish Government is funding a new renewal programme in the difficult concrete estates of the 1960s and 1970s, while supporting tenant advisors and community organisers through the Mayors' programmes. This Danish initiative underlines one route out of exclusion for other countries. Marginal communities can only be linked if there are human bridges, people whose job it is to build and maintain such bridges over time. As the Danish programme shows, reinforcing French, German and British experience, it is a slow, painstaking and essentially small-scale process. NO other mechanism works without this human link.

The 'Celtic Tiger', a decade ago one of the poorest of European Union member-states, now overtakes Britain on some wealth counts and grows faster than any other member-state. Competitive Ireland experiences growing divisions and tensions as it accommodates its new wealth with its old poverty. The Irish Government's dramatically expensive and elaborate plans to demolish its only major high rise estate may yet be tempered by the need for cheap housing as Irish society copes with reverse migration, escalating family breakdown, crime and drug abuse in the wake of the new internationalism.

Difficult estates epitomise the most extreme elements of change – rapid migration across continents, poverty and job change, political alienation and community disintegration. System failure has become a reality. Governments have no magic wand but if they want to retain power they have no choice but to change. For social breakdown represents not just the absence of control, the lack of links, the failure of existing systems, but the violent eruption through the weakest seams in society of smouldering conflicts – a sharp reminder that societies, like the earth's crust, are never static or inherently stable.

Here the European experience of marginal estates comes into play. The heavy-handed approach to cities of the postwar interventionist era broke down, but it was not replaced with the hands-off abandon that characterises urban change in newer cities around the world. The European pattern of underpinning and intervention is battling at the faultlines of the ferment for change. Weaving together new supports at the point of greatest weakness relies on the stronger and more cohesive surrounding areas to buttress and manage the links. Thus the whole remains intact and fragile communities, such as estates on the edge, are specially nurtured back into the mainstream.

The ability of people living in volatile, precarious, explosive areas to control conditions is limited by the upheavals beyond the boundaries of their lives. Europe provides a model of city development – more public spirited, more inclusive, more inter-racial, more managed than in other less densely urbanised cultures including America. For the half of the world already in cities, the European battle against social exclusion based in its most difficult estates is a life and death experiment.

Part I
The Social and Political Problems of Mass Housing in Europe

1 Introduction

WHY UNPOPULAR HOUSING ESTATES IN EUROPE?

European governments became enmeshed in urban housing problems through economic, social and electoral pressures. The war pushed that involvement to new limits, as chronic housing shortages swamped other issues. Governments ended up financing the building of thousands of large, concrete estates in cellular form over the postwar era to cope with crude homelessness and an unforeseen explosion in urban populations. Rural to urban migration, slum redevelopment, public aspirations, and the development of industrialised building systems led to a belief in gigantism and mass solutions, which in turn created unwieldy, heavily subsidised, separate housing areas that were designed for those in need. Gradually as overall shortages diminished, the populations that could not realistically aspire to ever more popular, owner-occupied houses of a very different style and smaller-scale ended up often feeling trapped in, or coerced into, estates which were marginalised, stigmatised and rejected by mainstream society.

The questions that this book addresses are new. In Britain, it became clear by the 1980s that the problems facing social housing showed up most acutely and most prominently in the third of the public rented stock that comprised large estates of flats in inner cities or impoverished, peripheral estates around the urban fringe (Power, 1993). Maybe the experiences of similar estates in similar locations in other countries would shed light on the problems. If the conditions were similar, what were the problems that made for similar outcomes? If they were different, what pressures and practices had made them different? Were conditions better or worse? Did the estates in different countries house similar people? To what extent were they owned and managed under similar regulations and incentives? How many estates were there? What was the direction of change? What was the pace of change? And why? Were problems and decline endemic and inevitable in

3

poor housing areas, however built, owned or managed? Had all the attempts at 'mass housing' solutions failed? It was unlikely that a single or simple answer would be found to these questions since, in Britain, they had provoked bitter argument for over a decade, a debate that was still unresolved (Coleman, 1985; Teymur, 1988; Power, 1993).

The five countries of the study, France, Germany, Britain, Denmark, Ireland, have important things in common. They are all part of the European Union. They belong to the northern rather than the southern belt of the continent. In world terms they are highly developed. They enjoy a level of human development – in life expectancy, literacy and basic income – that makes them privileged, even allowing for the poverty of some groups and the lower though fast accelerating development of Ireland (UN, 1994). The five countries also reflect sharp differences within the community. They stretch from the Mediterranean to the North Sea, from the Atlantic to the Baltic. They include the largest and one of the smallest countries in the European Union, the richest and one of the poorest. Their religious and cultural histories also offer stark contrasts: strict, near universal, Catholicism in Ireland, intense secularism in Denmark and parts of France; the cradle of Protestantism in parts of Germany and Britain. They also now combine the experiences of eastern-style Communism, with welfare statism and 'social' capitalism. The cities are as varied as the people – some almost entirely low-rise, like Dublin, Copenhagen and Bonn, some scattered with skyscrapers, like Paris, Berlin and London. The dominance of conspicuously large, government-created housing estates, across frontiers of history, language, climate and politics, raised questions about housing policy that could be important for other developing parts of the world that are beginning to follow that same all-too-obvious road.

This book examines the ground-level experiences of 20 estates spread across France, Germany, Britain, Denmark and Ireland, based on visits to the estates and drawing on extensive research into the problem within each country. It catalogues the nature of their difficulties, their decline and their rescue. It draws together evidence for and against the prospect of long-lasting reversal in conditions by examining closely five estates, one from each country, and tracing their history and development up to 1993.

The decline of mass estates has significant impact on national economies and on urban conditions, for there are between 3 500 000 and 5 500 000 social housing dwellings on unpopular and difficult to manage estates in the five countries (Power, 1993). Most of these units are desperately needed, as each country faces a shortage of low-cost, subsidised homes and acute social tensions over economic change, homelessness, joblessness, continuing migration and youth disorder (IWU, 1992). The estates are an important asset in a situation of combined budgetary and welfare pressures. The estates are also clearly in many senses a liability, since they are expensive to manage and maintain, subject to major building and design problems, unpopular with more economically stable households, and prone to serious social problems. As a result, their continued existence is frequently called into question and the direct costs to society are great. This leads to inadequate funding for full-scale maintenance and a consequent marginalisation of the communities that live in them. Residents are, on the one hand, unusually dependent on the wider system and, on the other hand, frequently excluded, in conditions that are unacceptable to the majority with choice. These contradictions pose new questions for governments about the meaning of citizenship and the role of government in building a more responsible and cohesive urban social order (Delarue, 1993).

The story that unfolds is surprising. Not only are the problems in mass housing estates often of overwhelming proportions, posing a real threat to established social order, but the scale of government intervention, the arduous detail of each improvement scheme, belie the glib assumptions of media commentators and tired bureaucrats that people do not care: that high-rise is inevitably unpopular, that marginal communities house a 'feckless underclass', that race is a root cause and explanation of current problems, or that there are no workable solutions. The story is both harrowing and hopeful (Élie *et al.*, 1989).

GROWING GAP

The experience of marginal areas is of great importance because it reflects large-scale changes in society as a whole, the most important of which is the growing gap between the affluent majority – in work, well-housed, well-educated – and the increasing minority of unemployed people, of one-parent families, of non-white minorities, many of whom are disproportionately concentrated in the worst estates in all countries. This is a dominant concern within the European Union (EC, 1991). Increasingly, it is the social housing estates that are becoming the most deprived communities. According to the German Ministry of Housing, 'a few are developing a ghetto character' (BRBS, 1990). This is both a cause and a product of cutbacks in public housing programmes in favour of alternative housing subsidies (Ghekiere, 1988).

Concerns are growing among the 'haves' over high taxes, rising welfare costs, the liabilities of previous growth, and the phenomenon of street homelessness. Europe is becoming increasingly defensive and overtly anxious over new, large-scale immigration, racial violence and social polarisation (*Le Monde*, 1995). Yet 'Fortress Europe' is a misnomer of absurd proportions, as Germany's borders were crossed by at least 2000 immigrants, refugees and asylum-seekers each day in the late 1980s, and Southern Europe plays informal host to visible waves of sea-borne, illegal immigrants (Pfeiffer *et al.*, 1994).

Unemployment, as it lengthens its shadow across society, becomes confused with the bitter American-led debate over the 'underclass' (Jencks and Peterson, 1991). Rising crime, much of it drug-related, undermines stability and enhances the fear that city streets in Europe may become as unsafe and barren as they often are across the Atlantic (Peillon, 1991). Unpopular estates are often conspicuous enclaves of societal problems.

The 'long-running consensus that the rich would subsidise the poor in return for social peace' (Münchau, 1992) had been broken by the 1980s, a decade of crumbling agreement over social harmony and of serious urban disorders in France and Britain. The electoral rejection of the tax costs of social welfare and of integrationist policies pushed marginal groups faster and further down the road towards social conflict (Galbraith, 1992). The riots in France, Germany and Britain in the early 1990s drew attention to the shared experience of estate decline, racial tension and urban unrest, accompanied by rising housing demand. Urban unrest had a disturbing effect on governments in spite of, or maybe because of the growing 'toughness' of welfare policies.

The new problems encouraged programmes to rescue the most marginal estates (Jacquier, 1991). The French Minister for cities, Bernard Tapie, explained the response after the disorders of 1991 in France:

> When at the beginning of the 1980s the first incidents [of disorder] occurred at Les Minguettes, no-one had a ready solution. The reason was, suburban estates posed a totally new and unfamiliar problem.... It was a matter of reacting on many fronts together, over integration, urban renovation, education, housing, security and the family. It was easy to see that all centralising strategies were certain to fail. (Tapie, 1993, p. 10)

The new programmes that resulted, not only in France but across all the countries of the study, are the main focus of this book.

Problems were building up on urban edges. The central question was whether there were common threads underlying the changes in urban social and housing conditions. It was certainly true that these were not new problems. They evoked conditions and pressures that were common in Victorian times (Stedman-Jones, 1976).

Visits to housing developments around Europe confirmed the existence of many marginal estates facing accelerating decline – 'dwelling silos in green meadows', as the German Government report described them (BRBS, 1988). The methods of managing, handling or controlling these estates were puzzling. In spite of the parallels and similarities, there was a clear contrast in superficial building and environmental conditions between the continental estates on the one hand, and the British and Irish estates on the other. The privately-oriented, efficiency and up-market emphasis of the autonomous continental housing bodies stood out against the public welfare emphasis of council landlords in Britain and Ireland (Power, 1993). This gave rise to questions about the social conditions on estates, questions that were not fully answered by the different patterns of social housing provision.

The contrast in ownership and management was producing different shifts in government policy. On the one hand, continental landlords were being pushed somewhat reluctantly towards a stronger social welfare role, even though the objective of a social mix was clear; on the other hand, British – and to a lesser extent Irish – social landlords were being pushed relentlessly towards more private patterns, while playing an increasingly welfare role (Dublin Corporation, 1993). In Ireland, the idea of screening incoming tenants to reduce the social stigma of 'welfare dumping' was gaining ground (Ballymun Task Force, 1987).

Would the two patterns cross in the middle? What would happen to the poor? Was there a way out of marginalisation? What management system worked best for the wide social role estates were expected to play? These questions seemed vitally important to every major European city in the study – London, Paris, Copenhagen, Dublin, Cork, Glasgow, Lyons, Cologne, Düsseldorf, Aarhus. One third to one half of all social rented housing in major cities – more in some cases – was on large, hard-to-manage estates. One thing was clear to every government – most of it could not be replaced in the foreseeable future. There was too much of it for this to be thinkable in the current climate of cash shortages, welfare malaise and pressing housing needs at the bottom of society. It had to be saved and managed somehow (BRBS, 1988).

LIABILITIES OF MASS HOUSING

Mass housing, having been heralded in the 1960s as a far-seeing solution to urban pressures and slum conditions, generously funded by all governments, had become a major liability of financial, organisational, physical and social disarray (Dubedout, 1983; BRBS, 1990; SBI, 1991). The crisis in mass housing had deep repercussions on social housing organisations, threatening bankruptcy under the more autonomous continental system, creating social unrest and deep, visible polarisation in Ireland and Britain (Scarman, 1986; Dublin Corporation, 1993). Both the financial and the social problems drew governments closer to the estates and eventually engaged them in expensive attempts at solutions. From the mid-1970s, governments began to express their fears, which gradually mounted until major rescue programmes became a political inevitability. In the end, no government was willing to allow its most conspicuous housing legacy to fail, even if the public consensus had shifted completely away from support for mass estates (Burbidge *et al.*, 1981; Dunleavy, 1981; Dubedout, 1983).

The mass estates overshadowed all other forms of social housing by their sheer scale and dominant problems. But they were not in fact the only marginal areas. Nor did they represent the majority of social housing in most countries. This study focuses on them because they were invariably the most conspicuous and the most difficult. They had come to symbolise the failure of public housing policies (Castro, 1994). The Lord Mayor's Commission on Housing in Dublin singled out the social problems of estates as overshadowing the potential housing gain:

> The concentration of social deprivation and low-income households in these estates exacerbates social problems to the detriment of tenants and of households in neighbouring areas ... [It leads to] a ghettoisation of public housing tenants ... by addressing only one of the symptoms of poverty. A policy of providing local authority dwellings may divert significant resources from a more fundamental objective, namely the relief of poverty. (Dublin Corporation, 1993, p. 52)

The role of governments in the quest for solutions to these problems was contradictory. The rhetoric of privatisation, the disenchantment with some aspects of welfare, seemed to run counter to the commitment to avoiding ghettos, dependency, and the 'underclass' problems of America. There appeared no alternative to government intervention, if social landlords were to play that crucial 'buffer' role between the wider society and destitution (Wilson, 1987). But the nature of government intervention was becoming far more cautious and incremental than in the original creation of estates. It had a stronger social or 'community' focus. Danish social housing bodies understood and emphasised the social, as well as the building, requirements:

It is difficult to build for social intercourse. The right physical framework is not enough to get people to function together. Organisation, social and educational know-how are also needed. (SBI, 1993)

This study examines two sides of a single issue – estates at the centre of urban social and economic decline; and estates as the focus for alternative, social and management experiments. Five aspects of the story were particularly intriguing:

– first, the real conditions on problem estates, not the local press version, and their relation to wider problems;
– second, the contrasting management styles, systems and practices of different countries with their different impacts;
– third, the growing social and welfare role of older mass housing and the effect of concentrating social need in specific areas;
– fourth, the re-engagement of government in social housing estates as they became both a major liability and an irreplaceable resource. This appeared to apply even where the estates were privately-owned;
– fifth, political fears about ghettos and the consolidation of an 'underclass'.

Many social problems and their connection with housing policies are highlighted by the experience of unpopular social housing estates and are shared by all the countries in this study: the conflict between targeting help on those who most need it and retaining a level of social integration between people of different backgrounds, avoiding the creation of ghettos; the problems of access to cheap housing for groups and individuals who might otherwise be excluded but who cannot afford reasonable standards accommodation; the support needs of households that cannot cope with normal living pressures and yet often end up in far more difficult conditions than average; and the extreme exclusion that can result from concentrating need in peripheral and unpopular areas. The whole shape of postindustrial civilisation may be determined by our ability to solve these most extreme problems (Dahrendorf, 1992).

There is the beginning of a consensus between experts and operators that as a combination of elements causes the problems of exclusion, so a combination of strategies may be the only way to address the problems (Élie *et al.*, 1989). This study examines a new approach to area-based problems. There are three propositions:

- combined strategies are needed to tackle estate problems as there are no single, simple solutions;
- localised operations are needed to reverse poor conditions;
- creating a sense of community by involving residents and building confidence in an area will enhance conditions and prospects, reducing the threat of breakdown.

We wanted to find out whether a patchwork approach to renewal, involving many actors on the ground in flexible and evolutionary strategies might work better than a single, imposed strategic plan, such as those which created mass housing in the early postwar period. For according to the German Housing Ministry, 'There is too rigid a framework for running and improving estates' (BRBS, 1990).

It does not mean that co-ordination and overall strategy are unimportant. But the workable point of control may be local and multiple rather than single and central. The pattern of a well-designed patchwork quilt is complex and unifying. The many small pieces are carefully joined together. The combined strength and impact are dramatic. But the aims, the process and the effect are radically different from a single, large, all-embracing design, such as was used to create estates. German government researchers used the term 'cast-iron cities', which vividly captures the point (BRBS, 1991). The French Government strongly advocated an alternative approach after the riots around Paris and Lyons in 1990 and 1991 had highlighted the failure of the centralist approach:

For the first time, they [Government and city officials] are able to carry out programmes where everything is decided locally...traditional methods in these situations failed because they were too rigid. Municipal services, state administration, tenants and local associations must all communicate with each other and invent new ways of working. (Tapie in Delarue, 1993, p. 233)

It is this alternative approach to mass estates that the study led us to examine.

GAINS OF INTERNATIONALISM

What do we gain from studying such local problems on a Europe-wide basis? Britain is part of the European Union, even though it may retain a strong national identity and an island heritage. Inescapably, we are involved in each other's problems in a shrinking and interdependent world. Therefore, as Europe's problems will be increasingly interconnected, Europeans need to know more about each other's social and housing dilemmas (Kleinman and Piachaud, 1993). The similarities and differences help clarify national and European-level thinking on this subject.

As the story of unpopular social housing estates unfolds in the five countries, we will discover strengths and weaknesses, experiments and innovations in each country that are bound to excite new debate about ownership and tenure, about social problems and housing solutions, housing problems and social solutions. A common understanding of problems, their roots, their growth and their resolution, introduces light which enables us to see more clearly where we are, what ways lie around us and how we might follow them, offering the possibility of a change of direction if necessary. Finding new directions based on common experiences is the point of this study of a common European problem.

European housing developments help shed light on insular debates about policy directions in Britain (OECD, 1987), many of which affect marginal areas disproportionately. Firstly, all governments, socialist, social democratic or conservative, have adopted tougher economic and social policies. For example, many benefits are now narrowly targeted towards low-income households rather than provided as a right to all. This applies particularly strongly to social housing where 'bricks and mortar' subsidies have been increasingly reduced in favour of housing allowances to individuals, depending on income levels. As a result, rents, including social housing rents, have risen steeply across Europe and so in parallel, iron-ically, have the costs of benefits. This makes for unexpected outcomes – for example, the impact of rising rents and tar-geted housing allowances on who lives in social housing. In many cases, only the very poor can afford it. Having shifted housing policy heavily in favour of targeting, governments are anxious over rising costs, as more and more people fall within the net and it becomes increasingly difficult to climb out.

Secondly, the private landlord tradition has survived on the Continent, whereas it has been virtually wiped out in Britain and Ireland. Private landlords are still a major force in Europe, in spite of suffering from serious decline in most countries. Their survival and relative strength is important as a housing resource and greatly influences the role of social landlords, often reducing the concentration of the poorest households in mass estates.

Thirdly, the non-profit housing tradition, usually taking the form of housing associations or co-operatives, is much stronger on the Continent than in Britain or in Ireland, with Government-sponsored housing provided almost entirely through autonomous non-profit housing organisations rather than through local authorities directly. Government reliance on non-government agencies for carrying out many of its poli-cies offers useful insights into the radical changes under way in Britain. Britain is increasingly adopting the Continental model but with a heavy restraining legacy of earlier state systems.

Fourthly, there have been no major slum clearance pro-grammes comparable to Britain's elsewhere in Europe. Therefore a majority of 'mass housing' developments have been built on the edge of cities, and inner areas have con-tinued to house very poor people in old and run-down, pri-vately-owned housing, although urban renewal and gentrification have created growing pressures, pushing more of the very poor outwards into the peripheral estates.

Fifthly, urban housing on the Continent is invariably in blocks of flats, regardless of owner or income group. A closely supervised system of custodial caretaking maintains order and enforces common standards in a way that would be considered unusual in Britain and Ireland.

Sixthly, all other countries in the European Union indus-trialised and urbanised later than Britain. This difference, when examined, helps to explain why the British experience often seems out of step and why Britain is likely to be under increasing pressure to adapt its systems to more flexible and up-to-date models. However in some important respects, British social legislation is ahead of and more progressive than some European partners, for example, race relations legislation and the enforcement of equal opportunities, inadequate though those measures are in the face of serious racial problems.

Outmoded and clumsy as large-scale state landlords seem to Continental housing experts, they are extremely hard to dismantle since they tend to be strongly bedded in state-run institutions and part of Britain's 'national' culture. It is hard even to adapt their structure significantly without massive public protest. While state intervention has not always proved popular, state withdrawal is often seen as menacing and irresponsible (Cole and Furbey, 1994).

The growing emphasis across Europe on market solutions for public and social problems faced severe limitations, as levels of unemployment soared in the 1980s. This in turn was affected by, and even possibly affected the rapid growth in lone parenthood and family break-up, leaving many single parents – most commonly women and dependent children – in poverty and on isolated estates (SBI, 1993). The growth in elderly populations was another taxing problem that could not simply be left to market forces. The 'grey' movement in Germany underlines the sense of vulnerability and need for a 'social shield'.

The outbreaks of violence among young people in French and British outer estates created almost a panic sense of having to change the urban order (Delarue, 1993). Serious clashes between Germans, the police and refugees in large housing estates in the new *Länder* highlighted similar tensions (Wullkopf, 1992; Kirchner and Sautter, 1990). Therefore, social solutions regained prominence, regardless of the political complexion of governments. The shifts applied in varying degrees to all five countries in the study (Power, 1993).

EXTREME CONDITIONS

The social changes and growing tensions were at their most extreme in some of the peripheral housing estates we visited.

The examination of extreme conditions often helps clarify more general problems. In this sense, the problems of 'estates on the edge' and the 'underclass' are not separate from wider societal problems, only more concentrated and more defined because of being area-based. Sir Ralph Dahrendorf explains how the whole fabric of society may be undermined by the exclusion of some groups.

> Professing values like those of work and family means that one tolerates a not insignificant group which has no stake in accepted general values... and the values themselves begin to become much more tenuous and precarious than is sustainable for any length of time... The underclass is the living doubt in the prevailing values which will eat into the texture of the societies in which we are living. In fact it has already done so. (Dahrendorf, 1991, p. 57)

The weakening in family ties, the speed of economic change and high levels of unemployment, the evidence of social breakdown in some urban areas, undermine Western society at every level. We are all affected by these pressures and therefore need at least to know the depth and extent of the problems. It may be that we no longer fully grasp what is happening within our cities (McGregor, 1993). The areas under study here cannot be isolated from the bigger social, economic and organisational problems that could engulf whole societies (Rogers and Fisher, 1992). As the elected head of the Danish non-profit housing movement expressed it, 'It is not possible for a non-profit housing organisation to change social segregation in society' (Nygaard, 1995). Table 1.1 summarises the broad evolution of conditions and policies that underpin this study.

STRUCTURE OF THE BOOK

The five parts of the book allow the reader to approach the study as a whole, with each subsequent part probing more deeply into the subject. Alternatively, the reader can select parts that provide the level of detail that is most useful. Part I outlines the background to the study, the nature and role of

Table 1.1 Social change and social breakdown in Europe

Historic legacy	New patterns	Emerging forms	Signs of breakdown
Urban infrastructure	*Family* Smaller households	Unstable family and community patterns	Crime/violence
Social/cultural forms	Older	Mobility	Reduced social cohesion
External relations	Divorce Lone parenthood	Job insecurity Short-term Part-time High-tec	Government fears
Expectations about work, family and community	*Migration* Rural/urban Ethnic change		Extremism
Traditional economies	Multicultural communities	Job losses for low-skilled	New interventions
Role of state	*Economy* Technology Globalisation Privatisation High skill Unemployment Women's employment	Tax resistance and welfare funding problems Fierce international competition New nationalism	
	Cities Growth centres Urban sprawl Transport Employment change Neighbourhood decline		
	Housing Mass/single family Quantity/quality New-build/renovation Public/private Supply/demand/cost		

Source. Author's research.

mass social housing, the interaction of social change and the marginalisation of unpopular mass housing estates. It explains the method of carrying out the research and the collaborative links with research, housing and government organisations in each country. It details how five national governments came to drive the programmes of mass housing forward in each country; how an almost uniform structure and style of development created near universal social and management problems; how residualisation and polarisation acutely affected the least popular areas in every country; and how these problems provoked a financial and organisational crisis for landlords. Part I ends by tracing the chronological development of rescue programmes, sponsored by governments in each country, to attempt the reversal of steep decline and threatened disorder on mass estates.

Part II presents the findings from a survey of 20 European estates. It reveals a consistent and clear pattern of decline with strong physical, organisational and social trends in common between countries in the most difficult, modern, publicly-sponsored estates. It examines the obstacles to restoring the estates but shows how the government emphasis on physical solutions for the benefit of existing populations led to landlords involving residents, localising their services and addressing wider social problems. No single problem or solution operated in isolation. The estates, like cities, were made of many living parts, and only an approach that responded in a live, integrated and flexible way could work.

Part III tells the story of five of the most extreme cases in the survey, one from each country. The five portraits aim to bring to life the sequence of events within each national context that led to certain estates experiencing chaotic decline and a threatened collapse of order. All the estates experienced such serious social disarray in a deeply alienating physical environment that their future was in doubt. Yet in every case, they were pulled back from demolition by intense, committed and locally structured intervention. The most striking aspect of this part of the study was the strong similarity in trends between countries in spite of the highly original history and experience of each estate.

Part IV draws together the detailed events on the five extreme or 'symbolic' estates in order to present an overview of the acute decline and the unexpected reinstatement of liveable conditions. Part IV parallels the sequence of Part II, but it analyses in much greater detail and depth the roles of landlords, governments, residents and social agencies in changing the fate of estates. Based on the case studies, it reveals an evolving pattern of change and renewal.

Part V links the marginalisation of mass estates with the wider economic and social problems they reflect. The conclusions highlight strong negative pressures on poor housing areas, which almost by definition over time become obsolete, and yet are increasingly necessary to house Europe's more marginal communities.

CROSSROADS

Europe is at a crossroads on many social and economic issues. Housing is central to the changes under way. The political dynamics surrounding housing, and particularly social housing, are conflictual. In Britain homelessness and polarisation are highly charged issues, with deep social consequences. Elsewhere a more open debate rages around social exclusion, poverty, unemployment, family break-up and the consequences of large-scale immigration, all linked to growing social problems on unpopular estates. The role of government in this context is controversial and sometimes provocative. The French Prime Minister, Raymond Barre, described social housing estates as 'ghettos at the gates of our cities' (Toubon and Renaudin, 1987).

The book explores the process of mass housing creation, decline and rescue in order to assess whether mass housing of itself led to decay – sometimes bordering on chaos – or whether the structure, style and scale of mass housing only exacerbated deeper underlying trends and problems in cities; whether the social role of mass housing programmes led to growing polarisation on estates; whether social housing was less problematic in continental Europe because it housed less disadvantaged tenants or was differently managed; whether the social problems that emerged were the overriding factors in acute physical decline; and whether the mix of incomes, class and race in housing areas was a determining factor in the reversal of declining conditions. Was the welfare role of social housing the critical variable?

SUMMARY: THE SIGNIFICANCE OF ESTATES

This book about unpopular estates in Europe looks at the experience of mass housing decline in five northern countries. These countries have 5 500 000 social housing units on large, modern flatted estates, housing increasingly poor people. The study aims to uncover the underlying social problems of estates and examine the progress of common rescue programmes.

Conditions on some very difficult estates plummeted in the 1970s and 1980s. Governments intervened to rescue them, advocating localised strategies in different settings. The ownership, management and lettings patterns diverged between council landlords and non-profit, independent landlords. The social welfare role of public landlords contrasted with the more private role of non-profit landlords. But their estate problems revealed similar trends towards decline and polarisation. The problems of estates reflected and affected wider urban and societal problems.

2 Collecting the Evidence

ORIGINS OF THE STUDY

In 1987, the French Commission nationale pour le Développement Sociale des Quartiers (CNDSQ), which was created in 1983 under the Prime Minister's office to orchestrate the rescue of large, distressed peripheral estates, organised an international conference in Paris with a twin focus on the experience of rescue programmes in poor housing areas and the importance of resident involvement in tackling these conditions. The conference brought together 11 European countries, including Hungary and the former Yugoslavia; and in addition, the United States and Israel. First-hand information demonstrated how pervasive and ill-understood the problems of marginal estates were in many countries (CNDSQ, 1987).

The conference procedures and documents, including films and slides as well as reports and personal accounts, provided a wealth of insights into a devastating failure of public intervention. It confirmed that the problem of marginal estates was common to many industrial societies; and that the social dimension was at least as significant as the physical and housing aspects of the problem.

The problems of 'socially segregated estates' attracted the attention of the European Union following this conference. A special information and exchange programme was set up in 1989, funded by the EU, including four of the countries in this study. It was called the 'Quartiers en Crise Programme' and was funded by the Social Affairs Commission of the EU. It brought together ten neighbourhoods in severe decline and traced their experience of renewal (Jacquier, 1991). In 1990 and 1991, European Union representatives discussed the theme of social exclusion based on the experience of peripheral housing estates (CECODHAS, 1990). These studies and meetings provided a great deal of information on the problem, while revealing a gap in detailed ground-level international inquiry.

Visits by the author to continental estates began in 1987 with Mantes-La-Jolie, which was to attract international publicity in 1991 after serious riots tore open the uneasy progress of the rescue programme. The French government then extended its target programme from 140 to 400 estates or areas.

The German government in 1985 organised a special international meeting in Bonn to discuss the problems facing its unpopular outer estates. This highlighted the existence of serious problems in Germany. Reunification in 1990 brought with it the additional burden of nearly 2 500 000 additional state-owned homes, a majority on giant estates of up to 30 000.

Danish housing researchers and non-profit directors made several visits to Britain in the mid- to late-1980s, after establishing an ambitious rescue programme for their own estates aimed at tackling social, economic and organisational, as well as physical problems. Other Scandinavian countries came too.

The Irish government, disturbed by extreme social problems on estates, sent parties of tenants and local authority officials to visit estates in Britain. Tenants' groups also came from priority estates in Northern Ireland. All these movements coincided with intense anxiety and activity around the subject in Britain.

France, Germany, Denmark, Ireland and Britain therefore appeared to offer useful comparative experience in a study of European difficult-to-let estates. They all had many problem estates of social rented housing; their governments were funding rescue initiatives; they were clear about the social as well as the physical nature of the decline; housing organisations agreed to collaborate in an international investigation of a major urban problem.

Based on this, the specific goals of the study became:

- to uncover the nature and extent of unpopular estates and the problems facing social landlords in their management;
- to see how the problems manifested themselves and identify possible causes;
- to single out elements in decline that led to some estates becoming extremely difficult, while other similar areas appeared to survive without such serious problems;
- to look at the degree of population change and the links between population change and declining conditions;
- to examine the relationship between estates and the wider urban structure;

- to assess the prospects for the worst estates and for social landlords in the light of the extensive problems they faced and the expensive rescue programmes under way.

Within each country, between 15 and 35 per cent of the social housing stock was identified by governments and housing organisations as having severe physical, social and management problems. The proportion was far higher in the eastern regions of reunified Germany. Housing experts and politicians were aware of the seriousness of the problem but often defended themselves against media attacks with the fact that only a minority of social housing estates were in deep trouble.

The problem commanded disproportionate attention in the local press, in spite of limited space in international studies. This suggested an underlying and simmering layer of anxiety. The obvious way to find out what was really happening was to go into the troubled areas and find out at first hand. This study originated in those visits.

The information about the estates was gathered between 1987 and 1995. None of the Continental visits were made while the estates were in their most serious decline, whereas many British and Irish estates had been known and visited during their most difficult phases in the early 1980s. This was because the Continental exchanges and visits began after governments had recognised the problems and developed programmes to address them. The estates in the study were in various stages of decline and rescue over the eight-year period of study; their conditions evolved significantly over that period.

METHODS OF STUDY

There were two main methods in the conduct of this research: direct fieldwork visits to all the estates; and indirect research. The indirect research drew on two main sources – documentary and research findings within each country about the estates, and collaborative exchanges with academic research bodies and specialist housing organisations involved in the estates under study.

The aims of the estate visits were to collect first-hand information; to observe conditions; to understand the relationships between organisations within each community; to examine the processes of decline and rescue and the interaction of different elements in the process. Only by visiting the estates was it possible to understand the dynamics and the problems of the estates directly. Such a localised international study of mass estates had not been carried out previously. The only effective method seemed to be a small-scale local exploration of each community with its own history, set of conditions, programmes, developments, people and organisations.

The approach to the study owes much to social anthropology, where the essential tools are observation, inquiry at close quarters, interviews with the main local actors, and careful recordings and analysis of findings. The areas under study also share the characteristics of areas lending themselves to an anthropological approach – small-scale communities and distinct cultural and social patterns which are hard to interpret without moving out towards the community. Dynamic, interactive processes, many unrecorded, are only discernable on the ground and not through remote sources (Beattie, 1993). In living communities, briefly visited by an outsider, we can hope only to begin the process of understanding. But without direct contact, the main point of this study would have been lost: to 'get under the skin of' what was happening and try to understand the human and social processes at work.

The focus of much of the study was the organisation and management of social housing in the particular form of mass estates. This too had to be examined at close quarters through visits and interviews with the people directly involved, for as Howard Glennerster argued in his book, *Planning for Priority Groups*, 'Social administration can be seen as the anthropological study of modern social welfare institutions' (Glennerster, 1983). Therefore, the approach of this study shares many methods and systems of analysis with the study of human society at a local scale in order to help our understanding of bigger, overarching problems.

Fifty-eight people from the 20 estates helped directly with the study. Contact was made with residents on 14 estates, either in their own clubs and centres, in the offices, or around the estate. The account of estate conditions in Part II relies on the views of local staff working on the estate, supplemented by senior managers, residents, and documented evidence. Direct observations were recorded during each visit and later analysed.

Although much of the evidence was drawn from the subjective judgements of people on the ground, the findings were compared with government research reports and information from other more objective sources. Detailed official reports on estate problems were available in all five countries from governments, landlords and research bodies. The combination of outside and inside evidence provided a clear pattern of information covering a wide range of estates in different countries. The method of collecting estate-level information drew on experience of research in unpopular estates in Britain, using a combination of eye-witness accounts and official reports (Power, 1984, 1991; Power and Tunstall, 1995).

NATIONAL RESEARCH

In all countries, long-term research into difficult estates was being carried out at the same time as this study. The severity of the problems was provoking intense public debate. The government programmes to rescue estates created a need for careful documentation of the preconditions, process of renewal and impact of programmes. Therefore there was a great deal of government information within each country on the problem of estates.

The most important research and evaluation studies on difficult-to-manage social housing estates were used as a baseline for the fieldwork visits and evaluation of programmes. They are listed country by country below. Other national and local reports are listed in the bibliography. The reports from each country provided evidence for the main thesis of this book: that difficult-to-manage, publicly subsidised estates were built under mass housing programmes on a large scale in each country; that certain of the most unpopular estates declined rapidly after initial occupation; that physical problems alone did not cause the decline but interacted with social and management problems; that governments undertook varied rescue programmes in partnership with landlords and local authori-

ties (where distinct from landlords); that the impact of these
programmes was significant but the estates continued to house
mainly low-income people and continued to require special
localised care and control; that intense concentrations of socially marginal households in separate estates continued to
make areas unstable, deprived and polarised, even after the
renewal programmes were complete.

The following are the main studies that provided independent information on the problem of mass estates:

France: *Ensemble Refaire La Ville* (Dubedout, 1983); *148
Quartiers* (CNVDSU, 1988); *Le Roman de la ZUP* (Élie,
Soubeyran, Blery, 1989); *Banlieues en difficultés – la Rélégation*
(Delarue, 1991); *Voyage dans dix quartiers Européens en Crise*
(Jacquier, 1991).

Germany: *Der Wohnungsbestand in Grosssiedlungen in der
Bundesrepublik Deutschland* (BRBS, 1986), *Städtebaulicher Bericht,
Neubausiedlungen der 60er und 70er Jahre.* *Probleme und
Lösungswege* (BRBS, 1988), *Städtebauliche Lösungen für die
Nachbesserung von Grosssiedlungen der 50er bis 70er Jähre* (BRBS,
1990), *Grosssiedlungen Bericht* (BRBS, 1994); *Grosssiedlungen,
Bestandspflege und Weiterentwicklung* (Gibbins, 1988); *Report on
the problems of Kölnberg* (City of Cologne, 1989).

Britain: *An Investigation of Difficult to Let Housing,* vols 1, 2, 3
(Burbidge *et al.,* 1981); *Inquiry into Glasgow's Housing* (Glasgow
City Council, 1985); *The Broadwater Farm Inquiry Report*
(Gifford, 1986); *Priority Estates Project Cost-Effectiveness Study*
(Capita, 1993); *Estate Based Housing Management* (Glennerster
and Turner, 1993).

Denmark: *Boligomraader i Krise* (SBI, 1986), *Did the buildings
become better?* (SBI, 1991), *Bedre Bebyggelser – bedre liv?* (Better
housing estates – quality of life?), Town Planning Report (SBI,
1993); *Social rehabilitation in Danish social housing areas* (KAB,
1994a).

Ireland: *A Programme of Renewal for Ballymun – An Integrated
Housing Policy* (Ballymun Task Force, 1988); *A Plan for Social
Housing* (DoE Ireland, 1991); *Lord Mayor's Commission on*

Housing (Dublin Housing Corporation, 1993); *An Evaluation of the Ballymun Refurbishment* (Craig Gardner, August 1993). The bibliography provides fuller details of these and other sources.

The following organisations helped directly with the study:

France: Commission Nationale pour le Développement Social des Quartiers, CREPA H, Délégation Interministérielle à la Ville, La SCIC, Union Nationale des Fédérations d'Organismes d'Habitations à Loyer Modéré.

Germany: Bundesministerium für Raumordnung, Bauwesen und Städtebau, City of Cologne, Empirica, Institut Wohnen und Umwelt, LEG Wohnen, University of Dortmund.

Britain: Department of the Environment, Home Office, Priority Estates Project, Scottish Office, Welsh Office, Glasgow City Council, Haringey Borough Council.

Denmark: Arbejdernes Kooperative Byggeforening (AKB), Kooperative Arbejdernes Byggeforening (KAB), Statens Byggeforskningsinstitut, Boligministeriet, University of Roskilde, Danish National Federation of Non-profit Housing Companies.

Ireland: Department of the Environment (Ireland), Dublin Corporation, Institute of Public Administration, Cork City Council, Ballymun Task Force.

STAGES OF THE RESEARCH

The study involved five distinct stages, each of which had to be applied in all five countries. The author carried out all stages of the research in all five countries, ensuring continuity and consistency.

Stage 1 – identifying sources of information

The first step was to identify social housing organisations at national and local levels, government bodies involved in social housing, research organisations concerned with difficult estates, city governments and other landlords. Through them, it was possible to trace the development and structure of social housing in fice European countries, the location and character of estates, the emergence and scale of problems, the nature and extent of government programmes. The early findings from this stage were written up in *Hovels to High Rise* (Power, 1993).

Stage 2 – visits to estates

When organisations and estates had been identified, visits to 50 estates across Northern Europe provided direct evidence of the problems. Observations were recorded at each visit. Information was collected over eight years, in the course of which estate conditions and government programmes evolved, allowing greater understanding of the process of decline and renewal.

Stage 3 – selection of estates

Sixteen estates were selected from among the 50 estates visited outside Britain. In order to be included, they had to meet the following conditions:

- they formed part of a major urban area;
- they were considered unpopular, based on local feedback;
- they were difficult to manage, meaning that rent collection, repair, lettings and tenant relations, all posed above average difficulties for the landlord;
- they exhibited a range of social problems that made the outcome of improvement measures uncertain and made their difficulties long-lasting, in spite of efforts to reverse them;
- their problems were serious enough to warrant special government funding;
- they took part in government rescue programmes, involving a redirection in the approach to the estates;
- there was authenticated information on their experience of decline and rescue.

Within each country, the detailed government studies on a large number of the most difficult estates highlighted the most striking characteristics, such as size, type of building, nature of the problems and of rescue attempts. It was therefore possible to select four estates per country, from the larger number visited, on the basis that they reflected as far as possible the dominant problems identified within each country.

There was a danger that the main actors – politicians and landlords – might either want to underplay or overplay the problems. However, visits to more popular and satisfactory social housing as well as estates with the most dramatic problems ensured a balanced perspective. In all countries, the majority of the social rented stock appeared to satisfy both residents and landlords. The sharp contrast between satisfactory social housing and the worst estates was a clear measure of how serious the problems were in these extreme areas.

The criterion of inclusion in a publicly supported rescue programme may have biassed the findings in favour of government priorities. As the major funders of social housing, the governments' influence was disproportionate. But a compelling argument for the selection of these estates is that governments prioritised these marginal areas in a period of great funding difficulty, precisely because their problems had become inescapably serious.

Rescue initiatives had been going on for at least eight years in Britain and France, five years in Ireland, and three years in Germany and Denmark when the study began. By 1994 when the study ended, all countries had at least 10 years of experience in estate rescue. Governments had changed, funding programmes had ended or been reformulated, and landlords had reformed their systems. Therefore there was a long and varied experience to draw on and little chance that a particular political perspective would dominate.

There was an important benchmark against which the 20 estates in this survey could be measured. Each country was analysing the problem and the impact of the rescue programmes through government-funded research and evaluation projects. The findings of this study across five countries could be compared country by country with, and to a large extent drew on, the internal research going on in each country. The main research organisations and the reports they produced about the problems and lessons of mass estates have already been listed in the earlier section on national research.

Stage 4 – analysing the information

Following the visits, information on the 20 estates was broken down under four main headings – physical, social, management and financial issues. The impact of the programmes was assessed, based on evidence collected during visits, the evaluations carried out by research bodies, the landlords' experience, the views of the government and other funding bodies. Tenants on six Danish, British and Irish estates had been surveyed as part of government-supported evaluations of renewal programmes. The findings from tenants' surveys were among the most interesting findings from official research.

Stage 5 – examining the case studies

Stage 5 involved a detailed examination of one extreme example from each country. Representatives from the chosen estate in each country took part in a three-day European workshop in 1991 to analyse the problems and to discuss the programmes to reverse the extreme conditions. The owners of the five estates provided exact and detailed material of common social and organisational problems. On the basis of this exchange, detailed comparison became possible.

The information and ideas from the workshop were backed by questionnaires, photographs, development plans, local reports and studies. Additional information for the five case studies came from additional visits, press coverage and ongoing contact with the main organisations involved. Local managers, city officials, researchers and residents all contributed to the case studies.

PATTERNS OF PROBLEMS

Cross-national studies pose many difficulties. The most important is the fact that each national context, institutional framework, and evolving culture is different (Oxley, 1991;

Harloe, 1995). Superficial similarities and differences can be very misleading, but consistent and deeply entrenched patterns are enlightening. They suggest some common and important explanations and they lend themselves to wider investigation and interpretation.

The clear contrast in histories, housing institutions, patterns of ownership and management between the countries, offered fertile ground for interpreting the relationship of structures to social housing decline. The common patterns of problems and reform indicated the emergence of a European-wide phenomenon, overriding national differences. Findings are presented country by country, as well as across all five countries. In this way, national differences and international patterns become clear. Figures and diagrams are used to attempt to capture the patterns of findings.

This is a study at the micro level about a problem that both reflects and affects governments. Its international relevance is underlined by the common trends, policies and approaches this study uncovered. The method was specially oriented to filling a gap in understanding through lack of local detail at an international level.

BACKGROUND TABLES

To help readers understand the background against which this study is presented, we include here a brief summary of central facts about the five countries. Populations in the five countries are more or less stable, with low birth and death rates, a growing elderly and shrinking younger population. The countries are largely urbanised, have a large and still expanding housing stock with high amenities, low sharing and overcrowding. Tenure and ownership patterns are varied but owner occupation has been growing; social housing is still important; private renting is under pressure and declining proportionately in all countries except Germany. Although Ireland has a somewhat different pattern, it is moving rapidly in a common direction with the rest of Europe (Blackwell, 1989). Tables 2.1 and 2.2 summarise conditions.

Table 2.1   Population

	France	Germany	UK	Denmark	Ireland
Population	57.3m	80.5m	57.7m	5.1m	3.5m
Annual rate of growth	0.6%	0.5%	0.3%	0.1%	0.1%[a]
Density (per sq. km)	105	226	234	121	49
Per cent of population in urban areas	74%	84%	89%	87%	57%
Main cities	Paris Lyons Marseilles Lille	Berlin Hamburg München Cologne	London Manchester Birmingham Glasgow	Copenhagen Aarhus	Dublin[b] Cork
Population of capital	8.7m	3.3m	6.8m	1.4m	1.0m
Average size of households	2.5	2.1	2.6	2.2	3.8
Births per 1000	14	11	14	13	14
Deaths per 1000	10	11	12	12	9
Percentage under 15	20%	17%	19.7%	17%	24.7%
Percentage over 65	15%	15%	15.6%	15.4%	11.6%

Notes: [a]Growth rate 1985–92.
  [b]Greater Dublin has a population of over 1 million, but the city has only 500 000 inhabitants.

Sources: *The Economist Pocket Europe* (1994); EU (1993); *Times Atlas* (1988).

SUMMARY

The main method of investigation was to visit as many estates as possible in the five countries, to collect ground-level evidence of decline and renewal, to uncover problems, performance and initiatives, to explore the roles of local staff and residents, agencies and government, both local and central. The method of research drew on anthropological techniques

8420

Table 2.2   Housing

	France	Germany	UK	Denmark	Ireland
Housing stock					
Total no. of dwellings	26.2m (1991)	34.2m (1991)	23.8m (1991)	2.4m (1991)	1.039m (1991)
Dwellings per 1,000 inhabitants 1991	463	421 West 422 East	411	465	286
Flats as percentage of total	44%	51% West	10%	39%	8%
Flats as percentage of new dwellings 1988	47%	30% West 69% East	21%	31%	2%
Source: Ibid.					
Tenure					
Owner-occupation	54%	37%	65%	51%	81%
Private Rent	21%	38%	10%	16%	9%
Non-profit Housing Association	16%	25%[a]	4%	18%	0.5%
Local Authority	1%	0%	21%	3%	13.5%
Social housing organisations					
Number of non-profit landlords	600	1 200	2 500	500	—[b]
Average size (number of units)	4 000	3 700 for limited dividend; 1 200 for co-operatives	200[c]	600	
Number of local authority landlords[d]	—	—	365	—	45
Average size			13 000		3 000

Notes: [a]Some, formerly public in East, now owned by local authority-sponsored housing associations.
[b]Ireland has a very small non-profit sector which is now receiving government support.
[c]There are many very small housing associations and only 186 with over 1 000 units.
[d]There is a small stock of emergency public housing on the Continent, under 3 per cent of the total.

Sources: Power (1993); Gardiner *et al.* (1995).

and approaches, by examining small-scale, local neighbourhoods, identifying key local actors and external influences, and tracing the rapid evolution of estates from success through decline to renewal. The main focus was on processes of change within local communities in the course of external intervention.

It was possible, using detailed government research within each country to compare information from the survey with wider evidence. The study reflects direct experience, as well as national and local documentation. On the basis of as full a picture as possible, 20 estates were selected for the survey. Out of them, five were chosen as case studies.

3 The Die is Cast

There are several reasons for providing social housing:

- to increase the total supply quickly;
- to raise and equalise housing and urban standards;
- to help the economy;
- to ensure enough low-cost housing for those who cannot afford to pay full costs;
- to guarantee that low-income groups gain access.

The first three were dominant in the 30 years after the Second World War. Private housing became more popular and more common when once the crudest mass shortages were over. As a result, private housing rather than public or social housing became an economic motor, while higher general standards led to a desire for privately-owned, individual and better quality housing than the state could provide. But the social aim of building cheap housing for the needy remained important. The state retained the central role of trying to ensure an adequate supply of low-cost, and therefore lower-than-average quality housing for the needs of growing groups of dependent households. To achieve this, it had to be able to ensure not only supply, but access.

Social housing was the only vehicle governments could directly control, although private landlords continued to play a relatively important role on the Continent. But it was a declining role, particularly for the poorest groups, as rising standards progressively eliminated older slum conditions. Social housing estates were needed to house the poorest groups to fulfil the central social housing goals of an affordable supply and access for the poor and potentially excluded.

THE ROLE OF GOVERNMENTS

Without government funding, mass housing – as the large, publicly subsidised housing estates came to be called – would simply not have been built (Dunleavy, 1981). Governments were induced to support social house-building on a large scale for many reasons:

- the ravages of the Second World War, leaving many homeless;
- rapid postwar urban migration both internally from rural areas and externally from ex-colonies and other countries;
- the decay of private urban housing built in the Industrial Revolution and the difficulty of upgrading and modernising it without displacing significant numbers of residents;
- the desire for modernity;
- the belief in corporate, technocratic solutions in the postwar economic boom;
- a general growth in tax income due to economic success and a rapid growth in publicly-sponsored services;
- a postwar belief in 'welfare' solutions.

Private-sector, non-profit housing bodies and local authorities, were quick to seize on the opportunities offered by governments' willingness and ability to fund 'mass' social housing. These social landlords, as they came to be called, became infected with the desire for power and prestige that mass housing offered, with its strong imprint on the landscape, its visible modernity and its expected contribution to social betterment (Salicath, 1987; Quilliot and Guerrand, 1989). Building firms, architects, planners, engineers, and suppliers, could all see the scope for profit, the political mileage and the publicity that would accrue from such a sharp break with urban social traditions.

Cities were much maligned after the war. They had been bombed, occupied and ransacked; their inhabitants had suffered incredible hardships; supplies were scarce and poverty was rife; repairs were seriously neglected and traffic was beginning to pile up in the early car boom. People who had little connection with existing networks were pouring into inner areas, crowding the oldest and worst neighbourhoods, leading to internal tensions, exploitation and disrepute (Holland, 1965).

The notion of beautifully ordered, scientifically planned environments, with a form that clearly broke the mould, held a certain magic for everyone. Thus, in its early years, mass housing was not simply tolerated, but embraced with jubilation. Politicians led the charge towards mass housing solutions because they had hit upon a running sore – urban squalor – that everyone wanted eradicated. People had an extraordinary confidence in the power of government and a belief in its extensive responsibility following the hardships of the war. The French Reconstruction Minister captured the postwar mood:

> We must not look back and reconstruct. We must do something new. (French Reconstruction Minister, 1949, in Quilliot and Guerrand, 1989)

Governments used whichever vehicle was most pliable for the publicly-funded housing drive. In Britain and Ireland, local authorities were already the major social landlords. They were directly under political control. They became the central housing developers and in Britain, they built 5 000 000 units in 30 years, an extraordinary 'Rolls Royce' achievement (Donnison, 1980).

On the Continent, non-profit organisations had led the social housing movement up till the war. They were small, pliable, business-like companies, relying on private and charitable support. This made them cheap and responsive. Governments seized the model and with strong subsidies converted many of these independent landlords into mass developers. Local authorities and regional governments were used as funding channels or partners and were encouraged to set up their own non-profit housing companies where there were gaps. The big cities in particular did this. The result was a very different style and form of social housing organisation on the Continent from Britain and Ireland. Nonetheless, in all countries, local government was the conduit for government housing strategies.

By 1970, most major cities were deeply involved in mass housing. City-based housing companies, publicly sponsored housing associations, ambitious non-profit bodies, building and housing co-operatives and large city governments were active partners in the process. In the three Continental countries, publicly sponsored companies quickly became large and powerful and these legally independent bodies played a semi-public role in spite of their private and autonomous status. The publicly sponsored companies were mainly responsible for mass estates, though private companies and co-operatives also got involved to a lesser extent. But small private landlords, locally based co-operatives, small-scale voluntarist housing associations, and rural local authorities, on the whole steered clear of the movement for mass housing. Figure 3.1 shows the pyramid of responsibility in the creation of the estates. Social landlords were vehicles for much bigger forces.

SCALE OF GOVERNMENT HOUSING PROGRAMMES

Dynamic postwar politicians often cut their teeth on 'mass' housing programmes. Scale, speed and minimal decent standards were the essentials of success. The style of 'mass' housing quickly became part and parcel of the programmes – large estates, high- and medium-rise blocks, industrialised construction, uniform layout, replicated units, compact flat-building and high technology. A self-fuelling cycle of political ambition, political credibility and political targets fed the boom in building (Quilliot and Guerrand, 1989; Dunleavy, 1981).

Once the initial investment, both in capital and in political credibility, had been made, in order to allow this programme to roll forward, it gathered its own momentum and became difficult to stop. A ten-year time-scale for a large development was common; large contracts could not easily be cancelled; the industrial investment in construction had major implications for employment, supplies and wider economic growth; the numbers of people involved and the size of landlords grew rapidly; and as a result, the forward momentum was sustained at least in part by its own weight.

Massive popular opposition is probably the only thing that might have halted the programme earlier. But in spite of early challenges to Le Corbusier, the architect who most of all articulated the concept of mass, high-rise housing, there were few vocal objections to the estates until after they were built (Power, 1987a). This was partly because programmes and developments were spread across huge areas, with each landlord

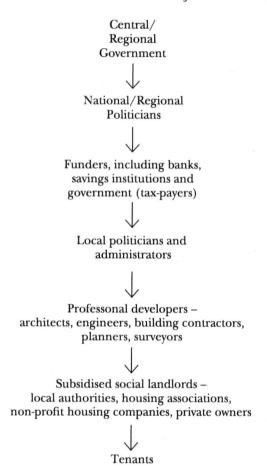

Central/
Regional
Government

↓

National/Regional
Politicians

↓

Funders, including banks,
savings institutions and
government (tax-payers)

↓

Local politicians and
administrators

↓

Professonal developers –
architects, engineers, building contractors,
planners, surveyors

↓

Subsidised social landlords –
local authorities, housing associations,
non-profit housing companies, private owners

↓

Tenants

Source: Author's visits and research.

Figure 3.1   Pyramid of responsibility for mass housing estates

running a separate programme. Therefore the impact and
consequences were temporarily disguised. Also, in spite of
their obvious and immediate problems, the estates helped
house very large numbers in incomparably better conditions,
at least superficially and for the short-term (Donnison and
Ungerson, 1982).

Mass housing was not exclusively high-rise, but the same basic concepts and techniques applied to medium- and low-rise, industrially built blocks, with similar results. Most 'mass' estates comprised a mix of blocks, often including some high-rise, but high-rise dominated the popular image of mass social housing. The terms 'high-rise', 'modern' and 'mass housing' to describe blocks over five storeys are often used interchangeably.

The bulk of the very large and difficult estates appeared over a relatively short time-scale, approximately 15 years, virtually simultaneously in all countries. It was a movement akin to a forest fire. Feedback therefore was too late to stop most of them from being built. A decisive influence on the failure to halt the building of high-rise and mass estates was the separation of development from management. Those responsible for the design, financing and building of estates had little experience of managing rented housing on a large scale. Managers were generally not asked (Power, 1987b).

The real spurt in estate building lasted from 1960 to 1975. By the mid-1970s – earlier in Britain and France – problems were becoming obvious and there was a sharp trend away from 'mass' building towards renovation of older inner-city stock and more individual and small-scale solutions. Governments were finding it impossible to go on funding social housing on such a large scale.

In all countries, the programmes dropped significantly, although far from drying up, social housing output continued into the late 1980s and early 1990s, apart from Ireland where it all but stopped for a few years. The style by then had changed radically.

TYPES OF LANDLORD

Private landlords own two units for every one that is socially owned in both France and Germany and nearly one for one in Denmark. The Continental governments provide special subsidies and incentives to private landlords to help them stay in business. This limits the role of social landlords. The dominance of private landlords and of non-profit rather than public social housing on the Continent creates a very diverse pattern, with many small landlords and few very large ones (see background tables, Chapter 2).

Local authorities in Britain and Ireland dwarf the non-profit sectors in both countries and are much larger than the private-rented sector. There are 2.5 social housing units in Britain for each private rented unit. This ratio has a major effect on the rehousing role of social landlords. Social housing has to meet the lion's share of demand for rented housing and, large as the supply is, the gate-keeping role is often slow and unwieldy, due to the sheer scale and the near monopoly role. In both Britain and Ireland, attempts at making local authorities more business-like have had only limited success because of the public-sector ethos, long-standing practice, complex organisational structures and the requirements of democratic public accountability.

By contrast, Continental non-profit organisations are forced to operate within a semi-private structure that creates a more independent ethos and practice. Their social role and estate conditions are directly affected by this. The independent status of non-profit housing associations is limited by government funding, which in turn is driven by the commitment to house vulnerable groups. Across Europe therefore, Government funding ensures either direct access for the needy under council ownership or more limited access through nominations and lettings agreements under the Continental system. Local authorities are pivotal in the nomination system but autonomous landlords have much greater control over access.

In an attempt to rectify the funding and management problems of council housing, central governments have increasingly intervened in the 1980s, in both Britain and Ireland, in the troubled council sector. This has often led to even greater difficulty, because of conflict over political control. Central government is little better at introducing management discipline than local government.

On the Continent, whenever government has become involved in direct housing provision, usually on an emergency basis only, it has strictly limited this role and passed it on as quickly as possible to autonomous and independent bodies. This has happened in France, Germany and Denmark. The following quotations give a flavour of some of these differences:

There must be a complete separation of the social landlord from the State because of possible corruption. (UNFOHLM, 1989)

Housing needs to be organised in very small units. It doesn't work on a large scale because it involves individual households and individual decisions on all the minutiae that make it work. When we went in for big city companies, we got it wrong. (Ulli Pfeiffer, Germany, 1992)

The [political] Member ethos of council housing is unpopular with the government. (Association of District Councils, England, 1992)

If housing management is healthy, social issues can be more easily sorted out. (AKB Chair, Copenhagen, 1991)

We are low on personal input into estates. (Housing Manager, Dublin Corporation, 1991)

Figure 3.2 illustrates the different control structures of different social landlords, including private landlords subsidised and regulated by government.

The delivery of services to tenants and the approach to estate management vary in different types of housing organisation. The strongest front-line presence lies with non-profit bodies. Priority is given to satisfying tenants and maintaining the value of the property (Salicath, 1987; OECD, 1987). The direct link with tenants through intensive custodial, caretaking and maintenance services is central to the financial viability of Continental landlords.

The role of estate management under the council system is less clearly defined. Services, such as caretaking, repairs and maintenance, generally operate at a low level. Tenants have little leverage and local staff have weak control. Many estates have no caretaking or custodial services and no front-line base at all. Estate managers have an office-based job, chasing arrears and reporting repairs (in some cases). The absence of effective caretaking makes for poor conditions and weak links with tenants. Table 3.1 outlines the advantages and disadvantages of both types of landlord.

I. *Non-profit housing association*

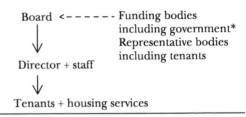

II. *Local authorities*

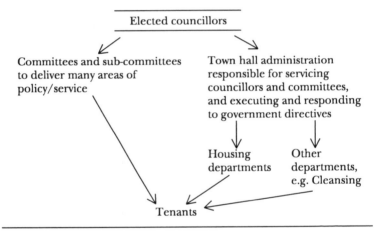

III. *Private landlords*

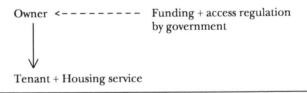

*In British and Irish housing associations, there is direct government supervision, but no representation on the board or committee.

Source: Author's visits and research.

Figure 3.2   Social landlord structures

Table 3.1   Comparison of local authority landlords with non-profit
housing associations or companies

	Advantages	*Disadvantages*
Council landlords	Strong welfare role Rehousing of homeless	Weak management
		Strong bureaucracy

	Electoral pressures to:
	  Build houses
	  Stop high-rise
		Inadequate front-line services

		Very large scale urban landlords
	Participation	Early stigmatisation and strong polarisation
	Inner city rebuilding	
	Racial mixture	Political conflict
	Planning role	Vote-catching policies and short-term investment strategies
	Early shift to renovation	
		Diffuse landlord functions
Non-profit landlords	Single-purpose functions	Weak political participation
	Legal autonomy	Weak welfare commitment
	Balanced budgets	Stronger attempts at exclusion
	Strong front-line services	Conflicts with local authorities where local authority fails to deliver services, for example, street cleaning, social amenities
	Business-like approach	
	Efficiency goals	Nomination system can concentrate disadvantaged in difficult estates
	Aim of broad social mix	
	Strong national bodies	

Source: Author's visits and research.

Non-profit bodies offer much stronger and more viable management structures but less direct public answerability. Many would argue that the lack of answerability and public control of non-profit housing is too high a price to pay for greater efficiency. That judgement depends on whether political control of social housing is considered more important – the British and Irish model – or whether the service to tenants, the repair and maintenance of the social housing stock is more important. Public housing systems have been prone to acute funding crises, low standards of repair and poor management because the nature of politics is vastly different from the nature of housing management.

Strong support for public housing in Britain and Ireland has constrained the potential of non-profit and private landlords. They played no role in mass housing in Britain and Ireland. At the same time, no government, even in former communist countries, has managed to provide sufficient, affordable, and acceptable public housing as an alternative to private provision. Private and non-profit landlords have remained important suppliers of low-cost housing, often resulting directly from their arms-length relationship to government. They satisfy housing objectives – higher quality – as well as government objectives – bigger, more affordable supply – without embroiling government in the nitty-gritty of housing management.

Tenants in the Continental housing structure relate to government, local or central, as citizens rather than as tenants of government landlords. The fact that British council tenants are government tenants has been the nub of much political polarisation in Britain (Cooper, 1981). In Britain and in Ireland, social polarisation is increasingly identified with tenure and is certainly more acute in council housing than in Continental social housing (Bourgeat, 1994; Wassenberg, 1993; Hills, 1993).

SOCIAL HOUSING AND COMMUNITIES

Whatever the form of social landlord, the government drive to expand the number of social units rapidly transformed the size and scale of operation of urban social housing and led to a style of organisation that was often out of keeping with the needs of tenants. Social landlords were driven by units of production and the need for accommodation rather than by social and community needs of a more intangible character. The importance of community networks in housing areas was barely understood or it was largely ignored (Young and Willmott, 1962; Pétonnet, 1973).

A majority of local authority landlords and social housing companies stayed small enough to manage reasonably effectively. They neither built nor own today very large 'mass' estates. But many major urban local authorities and companies became gigantic landlords. In Britain, France and Germany, some of these landlords ended up with over 150 000 properties. Table 3.2 shows the largest of these.

Before its spectacular collapse, the German trade union landlord, Neue Heimat, owned and ran 400 000 properties (see Power, 1993, for a fuller account). Even in Ireland and Denmark, large landlords reached over 30 000. The scale of the major urban, publicly driven social landlords played a significant part in their growing difficulties. It was often the very large landlords that encountered the biggest problems. Mass estates played a big part in this.

While it was true that Continental landlords were on the whole smaller and more contained bodies, reflected in generally simpler management structures, there was none the less a strong tendency for them, under the government-driven housing programmes they executed, to grow rapidly once they had embraced mass housing. Table 3.3 shows the massive additions to the social housing stock in the postwar era. Ireland appeared to be the only exception to the overall explosion in social housing ownership because of its vigorous sales. It had built more than twice the stock which it still owned in 1992.

Table 3.2   Largest social landlords in 1993

Country	Largest social landlord	Number of units
Denmark	Arbejder Bo	33 000
England	Birmingham City Council	80 000
France	La SCIC	150 000
Germany	Neue Heimat	400 000[a]
Ireland	Dublin Corporation	30 000
Scotland	Glasgow District Council	130 000[b]
Wales	Cardiff City Council	33 000

Notes: [a]Collapsed in bankruptcy in 1981; replaced by several large regional companies.
[b]Formerly 200 000 units (pre-1980).

Source: Landlords (1994).

Table 3.3   Social housing stock

Country	1945	1991
France	270 000	4 250 000
Germany[a]	400 000[b]	6 030 000[c]
Britain	1 253 500	6 237 000[d]
Denmark	68 000	426 000
Ireland	84 000	112 000[e]
Total	2 075 500	17 055 000

Notes: [a]Germany does not distinguish between social housing provided by non-profit or by private landlords using government subsidies. The number is dropping rapidly as subsidies end.

[b]Estimate only, allowing for bomb damage and other losses due to the war.

[c]Including former East German public stock and including private social landlords.

[d]Includes both local authority and housing association stock.

[e]Plus 159 674 sold to tenants – total built by 1991, 272 000.

Source: Power (1993).

But the sales policy, more than any other, highlighted the gross unpopularity of mass housing estates, as strong incentives to purchase failed to work in the poorest and often largest modern estates.

Sales policies were popular in Britain where well over 1 600 000 public housing units were sold between 1979 and 1991, mainly under the successful 'Right to Buy' policy. On the whole, dwellings on the large-scale estates built during the boom of the 1960s and 1970s were not sold and remain in public ownership (Power and Tunstall, 1995). Local authorities were still by far the largest landlords by the 1990s and owned over 5 000 000 units in the whole country, over 70 per cent of all rented housing (EU, 1993).

By 1990, Germany was reducing its social housing stock at a rapid rate, as social landlords paid off their publicly subsidised loans. When once the 'social' units no longer carried a public debt, they became part of the private rented market, even though they usually remained in the ownership of non-profit companies. There were attempts at sales of individual units on large estates to residents, but these were generally unsuccessful. Following the extraordinary pressures of reunification, the mass outer estates became more and more valuable for renting to homeless and emergency cases (BRBS, 1994).

Denmark did not adopt sales policies though they were debated. France has supported 'social owner-occupation' since the beginning of the century. Germany also encouraged building for a mix of tenures in the 1970s. Therefore there are often privately-owned units and blocks on both French and German estates.

In spite of the fact that governments were looking at ways of reducing their social housing commitments, the postwar boom in social housing left publicly subsidised landlords in the five countries with a vast stock of over 17 000 000 rented dwellings, around one third of which were on large mass estates.

INCREASING SIGNS OF COMMON SOCIAL PROBLEMS

Ownership and management patterns – the housing aspects of estates – came to be greatly affected by social patterns. For while the council system produced larger, more bureaucratic, more political, more welfare-oriented and more contentious social landlords, Continental social housing showed increasing signs of serious problems too. Common problems across Europe in mass housing estates were often linked to the common role of government in driving forward the mass housing programmes after the Second World War.

The emergence in Britain of the term 'difficult-to-let', or in France of the term *îlots sensibles* (sensitive areas) and *quartiers en détresse* (distressed neighbourhoods), reflected the growing problems in the massive stock. Table 3.4 shows the scale of industrialised or 'mass' building and the proportion of the social housing stock that became classed as 'difficult-to-let', a simplified designation for estates that are hard to manage and increasingly occupied by tenants with few other choices, (Burbidge *et al.*, 1981).

The governments each have rudimentary definitions of their problem stock and we have followed individual govern-

Table 3.4   Difficult -to-manage social housing estates

	France	Germany Old Länder	Germany New Länder	Britain	Denmark	Ireland
Estimated number of industrially built mass units	3 000 000	700 000	2 000 000	1 500 000	250 000	50 000
Estimated percentage of social stock difficult to manage	25%	15%	65%	20%	20%	30%
Number of targeted difficult estates[a]	400	128[b]	240[b]	500	80	80
Estimated number of units on targeted difficult[c] estates	1 000 000	600 000	1 600 000	1 000 000	30 000	20 000
Total targeted estates	1 300					
Total targeted units[d]	3 655 000					

Notes: [a]Government estimates differ but these figures represent the estates identified in government rescue initiatives. There are other estates presenting serious problems.
[b]Most estates have more than 2500 units (**BRBS** 1994).
[c]Degrees of difficulty vary significantly between estates and between countries.
[d]The total of units on difficult-to-manage estates is estimated at 5 500 500. Not all are targeted by governments.

Source: Government research in five countries (see pp. 31–3).

ment designations. Governments have assessed the scale of problems facing particular estates and classed some as out of the ordinary and requiring special help. In all cases, the designation covers not only physical decay but also management problems, including difficulty in lettings, rent collection and repair, as well as additional social and economic problems.

According to researchers in Denmark, there were likely to be more estates that were vulnerable to decline than the official numbers suggested (Vestergaard, 1992). Governments had a strong interest in limiting the diagnosis of problems because of the cost of tackling such estates. With a serious shortage of resources for renovating relatively modern social housing, they were keen to help only the estates with major problems. Therefore, 3 655 000 units on 1300 estates in difficulty represented a carefully targeted group of estates that governments could not escape tackling.

It was possible, and was argued by some, that wider and deeper causes lay behind the malaise in council housing, beyond the confines of ownership and management (Donnison, 1980). The Continental experience of decline suggested that the causes reached beyond the immediate organisational issues. Mass social housing was built as a solution to urban social problems, yet within a short decade of the major boom in building, it had become a problem so deep-set as to permeate the whole urban structure (Castro, 1994).

GOALS AND OUTCOMES

No sooner had the earliest estates been occupied than problems became clear. The building form, the management input and the social support were not strong enough to counter the problems. The failure of mass housing occurred virtually simultaneously with its creation – a bizarre outcome for an expensively ambitious social programme. It happened through the goals, political targets and production style mesmerising the politicians, with little regard for the dynamics of community and social relations until it was too late. Governments were deeply implicated in the mass housing programme. Their costly short-sightedness was to haunt politicians into the 1990s. Table 3.5 shows how diverse mass social housing programmes produced common problems.

While the building programme was still at full pelt, problems were emerging into the public eye. In 1968, a tower block in East London, called Ronan Point, exploded. Five people were killed as one section collapsed like a pack of cards; tower block tenants and landlords all over Britain panicked. The government quickly cancelled all subsidies for high-rise and from that date, no new tower blocks were planned, although several hundred thousand units already in the planning pipeline went ahead. Cities like Birmingham and London were still completing tower blocks in the late 1970s.

In France, as early as 1971, the government convened a special meeting to discuss problems on large, new, outer *grands ensembles* (large, mass estates). Shortly afterwards, planning laws which had created the fast-track, giant, peripheral *Zones à Urbanisation Prioritaire* or ZUPs – urban priority zones – were changed and the size of estates was restricted by law to 2000 units. By then, giant estates like Les Minguettes with 9000 flats in 63 tower blocks, and Maintes-la-Jolie with 8500 units, were largely built and the final stages were in the pipeline. In all, 140 ZUPs, averaging 5000 units each, were completed between 1960 and 1975. Some of these massive *grands ensembles* were to become a focus of unrest and disorder in the 1980s and 1990s.

In Germany in the 1970s, a Social Democratic government was driving housing production as fast as it could in the direction of giant outer estates. Yet because of decentralised funding and planning, the government did not know precisely how many estates were being built, or where, or on what scale. Nor did they know precisely who was building them. Companies often owned partly or wholly by local and regional government, built about 250 of these estates. The German estate programme became strongly linked with the collapse of the giant trade union-sponsored housing company, Neue Heimat, because Neue Heimat was involved in so many of the largest and most difficult outer estates. By 1980 it became clear that the mass approach was failing. In Eastern Germany, the Communist government built 2 000 000 industrially produced units with at least 240 estates of over 2500 units (BRBS, 1994).

Table 3.5 Common and variable features of social housing affecting mass estates

Common features applying to all social landlords	Variable features with different impacts under autonomous social landlords and public landlords		Common problems in mass estates affecting all landlords
	Autonomous	Public	
Government funding	Independent ownership	State and council ownership	State-driven programmes
Little flexibility because regulated and nationally driven	Average size is less than 6000 units	Average size (in Britain) is over 10 000 units	Reliance on 'mass' industrialised systems
	Separate from direct political control	Part of national and local political system	
Large scale – numbers of units is driving motor	Social mix		Scale problems
Housing targeted groups	Access through arm's length nominations by local authorities and state	Welfare rehousing	Location problems
Cost-saving to maximise scale, therefore quality problems		Access directly controlled	Building problems
Minimal standards because of funding problems, rent levels, affordability	Rent levels to meet costs after subsidy	Low rents to ensure popularity	Serious management difficulties due to complex building form
	Private finance plays major role	100% state-financed though rents play increasing role	Social problems – unpopularity, uprooting, instability
Estate-building because of scale and bureaucratic planning	Business-style and balanced budgets	Public welfare style and public accountability	High costs
		Bureaucratic administration	Unadaptable, inflexible approach
Intensive ground-level services – strong caretaking	Intensive ground-level services – strong caretaking	Weak ground-level services – poor caretaking	

Source: Author's visits and research.

In Denmark, by the mid-1970s, the government was encouraging small-scale, low-rise alternatives to mass industrialised estates. Such was the unpopularity of large, concrete estates that many schemes were cut before completion. Large, new-town style estates had been planned, but very few of these ever reached their full complement. The resulting outer estates were often seriously marginalised.

In Ireland, by 1971 the only tower block estate to be built was proving difficult to manage only two years after occupation. High-rise was abandoned. But cheap industrial methods were used to build low-rise houses and flats, mainly in Dublin and Cork, which later proved just as difficult. The 'low-cost' schemes of the 1970s, hurriedly built to house Ireland's growing population, were a disaster. Tallacht, with over 8000 units outside Dublin, became an 'impoverished municipal ghetto' because of its isolation, its stigma and the consequent low level of sales. The Irish experience underlines that houses can be just as unpopular as flats.

Thus the problem emerged under different pressures in each country, but there was a swift and common realisation that large, outlying estates heralded trouble. It became clear that they were often harder to fill, to sell or to manage than more traditional inner-city, albeit more run-down, stock (Copenhagen, 1989). Table 3.6 shows how the government goals created outcomes with unforeseen problems.

LOW DEMAND

The critical factor that ended mass housing was falling demand in the mid- to late-1970s. In Britain, government officials were shocked to see letting advertisements in property pages for government-funded tower blocks after 1968, in spite of allegedly long queues of slum clearance families waiting to be rehoused. The whole idea of government housing was that it would meet almost infinite demand from otherwise excluded groups. There were shock waves among British decision-makers when it became clear that some slum clearance

Table 3.6   Government role in mass housing

Goals	Outcomes
Ambitious programmes	Massive stock of industrial units
Highly visible housing solutions	High-rise, complex design, inhuman scale
Modernism	Streets in the sky, unconventional layout, 'worker' housing, cellular approach
Technocratic solutions	Industrialised, machine-driven scientific systems
High housing standards	Attractive internal dwellings, high internal amenities, reasonable space standards – but little attention to externals, attempt at savings on materials due to high costs
Easily replicated programmes	Monotonous, inhuman scale and style
Fast production	Mistakes built in and replicated, little care with finishes
Greatest possible outputt for lowest cost	Corner-cutting, over-mechanisation, reliance on unskilled labour, over-reliance on concrete, over-dense, over-scaled developments
National, all-embracing solutions	'Identikit' estates all over Europe with similar problems
Prestige and political popularity	Short-term enthusiasm, long-term political liability
Urban redesign	City landscapes and fringes transformed – old slums reduced and replaced by ugly modern estates
Social engineering	Instability, marginalisation

Source: Author's visits and research.

areas were wrongly designated and that people preferred them to a brand new flat. The case of Barnsbury in inner London was the most celebrated (Ferris, 1972). There, slum clearance plans dating from the 1930s were abandoned in 1969 in favour of area improvement, as long-standing tenants refused to be moved. Many people, even in fairly dire conditions, simply would not accept rehousing in tower blocks after Ronan Point. There was talk of it being an 'unnatural habitat' for families; there were reports of 'high-rise blues'; there were suggestions of coercion in the rehousing process (Lambert, Paris and Blackaby, 1978).

In Britain, the problem was made more acute by the general dislike of flats and the fact that most needy households were moving from slum clearance areas comprising houses. Already a sense of nostalgia was growing in communities that were being broken up by the process. There were even reports of old people dying when uprooted (Konttinen, 1983). In Ireland, too, the government was shocked by the clear lack of demand for high-rise flats and Dublin Corporation resorted to priority access for lone parents to try and fill the empty units. Special help was instituted for high-rise families.

In France, housing pressures were enormous up to the mid-1970s. But as certain regions of France lost their traditional manufacturing base, the need for massive housing developments adjacent to factories – such as Renault at Mantes-la-Jolie – declined. Several very conspicuously large estates went into crisis as their funding structure proved unviable in the hard times after the oil crisis, when rents could not cover costs, arrears mounted and rehousing demand shifted away from the securely employed to the more marginal. In the 1970s the population of some vulnerable estates plummeted (Power, 1993).

In Germany, the huge postwar building programme began to reach saturation in the early 1970s. But inner cities, rebuilt on very minimal plans and standards after the war, had become densely filled with immigrant workers. The outer estates programme – a diluted form of new town development – aimed to relieve inner-city pressures in a path-breaking way (Pfeiffer, 1992). However, high-cost rents made it difficult for the working poor to pay their way. Therefore arrears, low demand, high turnover and empty property became inevitable (Gibbins, 1988). Matters were made worse by the government's belated encouragement of low-cost home ownership. Cheap mass units were built for sale in the 1970s by Neue Heimat and other non-profit landlords on some of the largest outer estates, for which there were far too few takers. The property market collapsed and Neue Heimat was bankrupted by a whole string of serious mismanagement errors and deeply entrenched corruption. These failures symbolised the problems of the whole mass housing philosophy.

In Denmark, as in Germany, a very low birth-rate and rapid postwar building created a balance of supply and demand by the mid- to late-1970s. Inner-city renewal pushed families from older tenements into new outer estates, as the popularity of the outer estates declined. Many of the rehoused families were of poor immigrant origin, most often Yugoslavs or Turks (Danish Urban Renewal Unit, 1989). Some estates developed extremely high turnovers and numbers of empty units.

LETTINGS' PROBLEMS AND SOCIAL STIGMA

Thus in every country, the high-rise boom hit demand problems within ten years. This created a lettings crisis for landlords in a system where only eligible households were allowed to be rehoused. Newcomers were frequently debarred from access for a number of years (Parker and Dugmore, 1976). Keeping up a large supply of eligible applicants, willing and able to uproot and move to a completely new and untried area, was difficult. The lettings' problem, resulting partly from the sheer scale and speed of the operation, got the mass estates off to a bad start. It was virtually impossible to personalise the process or help tenants to settle in. Most landlords did not recognise this until much later and therefore did not take special steps to smooth the process of settling. The concentration of strangers had its own unnerving effect, from scale to unneighbourliness.

Lettings' problems were made worse by design. The flats were built as minimal boxes and dormitories for returning workers. They were not designed to allow children to 'let off steam'. This had to happen outside the flat. As children became large teenagers, the imperative to be outside the flat became overwhelming. Conflict over supervision, damage, nuisance, was inevitable. Individual parents did not – could not – control the outside spaces due to the enforced communality. Adult residents lost track of who belonged where.

Natural barriers and limits were absent. Aggressive attempts at control made life for mothers and children miserable. 'No games' and 'Not allowed here' became passwords in the open spaces of mass estates.

Poor housing areas have traditionally experienced deep stigma. The stigma that quickly attached to mass housing estates may have simply been transferred from the original source of rehousing. For example, in Denmark and Germany, the growing concentrations of Turkish and other minorities in certain key outer estates, as a result of inner area upgrading and gentrification, caused a deep stigma to attach to those areas.

In France, the 1 per cent employers' tax carrying nomination rights to estates like Mantes-la-Jolie led to harsh accusations of 'dumping' and of 'ghetto-isation', as immigrant workers who had greater difficulty finding other housing often ended up in the employers' quotas to large estates. It was in the large *grands ensembles* that the supply became readily available in the 1970s, just as immigrant workers were being sucked in and then forced out of their *bidonvilles* (shanties) and other emergency housing. In some cases, the need for immigrant workers was fuelled by the vast building programme which the immigrant workers then came to occupy.

In Britain, the stigma arose from before the war with the whole idea of slum clearance estates. The poorest people in the worst old housing areas saw their homes bulldozed away as 'unfit for human habitation', so they took with them to new estates the image of slum dwellers. That stigma has proved so long-lasting that even potentially attractive interwar estates of houses and gardens have had to be demolished because the slum stigma was so strong (Burbidge *et al.*, 1981; CDP, 1976). It was the stigma attaching to interwar slum clearance estates that led to resistance in many suburban areas after the war to estate-building. Inner-city local authorities were often 'landlocked' and had to rebuild within. For this reason, England built a lower proportion of outer estates than any other country. France now faces similar resistance in the wealthier communes with few HLMs (Conrad, 1992; Conrad-Eybesfield, 1994).

In Ireland, the stigma is most acute because buying is made so attractive and so easy that only complete economic failure would preclude that option. Therefore the stigma attaches most strongly to estates where tenant purchase is out of the question, the estates where those with choice do not move.

Through these processes, each country ended up housing the poor on the large, unpopular modern estates. The isolation of the estates and the concentrations of poverty were an integral part of their stigmatisation, a process of social layering and social segregation or discrimination that has long been observed (Parker and Dugmore, 1976).

THE COSTS AND BENEFITS OF UNPOPULAR FORMS

One of the most powerful arguments in favour of mass housing estates was that they would save money, whereas in fact the long-term costs became a major factor in governments staying involved. No other body had resources on sufficient scale to carry the burden. These costs were almost entirely unforeseen and the hoped-for savings almost entirely fictitious. The arguments in favour of economies of scale were well rehearsed in every country.

- Green-field sites were cheap and easy to develop, as they were free of many urban restrictions. For this reason, a majority of large modern estates were built on the outside of large towns.
- Industrialised building in large blocks and often high-rise towers would be cheap when replicated over many blocks and many developments. Although the initial investment in machinery was high, it enabled large-scale repetition, with unit costs falling as each block was added, thereby providing a powerful justification for super-size estates.
- Uniform, standardised parts would enhance savings. Replicated elements, such as toilet fittings, heating installations, doors and handles, windows and drainpipes, tiles and floor surfaces, identically fitted in thousands of dwellings, would become cheaper, particularly where several thousand deliveries to a single site were possible.

But under this system any mistake was disastrously replicated and required large sums to eradicate later. The whole mass high-rise housing phenomenon was in part a product of that problem – a replicated form, identical in concept if not in exact detail, in order to facilitate endless repetition resulting in tumbling costs and built-in defects.

There were many hidden costs to mass housing that were rarely counted at the outset. For example, green-field sites required expensive infrastructure, new facilities, institutions, and transport links. The wider subsidies required were enormous and never properly forecast. In many cases the infrastructure, facilities and transport were added too late or not at all, causing or intensifying problems. Lack of transport could prove as expensive as providing it, because of difficulty in finding or getting to work.

The problems loomed large, but many of the harshest critics of mass housing did not experience homelessness, overcrowding, harassment or temporary homes. The big gain of mass housing, which was only possible because of its giant scale and the relative speed with which it was executed, was the transformation of urban living conditions. For many households, only overcrowded inner slums – for some, only a shanty or other *ad hoc* dwelling – had been possible. Mass housing offered mass populations unprecedented improvements in conditions. It was this above all that fuelled the programme and in the end validated its rescue. The lack of early protest among the poorly housed reflected their acceptance of mass housing as an exit route from slums. Therefore, while the faults and failures are now clear, it is easy to overlook the hidden gains. Those gains became elusive when once the estates showed early signs of collapse but they should not be forgotten.

THE IMPACT OF CONCRETE

The spread of industrialised building and high-rise development, coupled with design concepts that now appear lunatic – streets in the sky, oversized blocks, unguarded but anonymous communal areas, green fields, inaccessible locations – meant that mass estates both dominated social housing and overturned its popularity at a stroke.

Concrete became the main building medium, partly because it was vaunted as being long-lasting, if not indestructible. But all over Europe, concrete showed signs of early decay and 'spalling', cracking as steel reinforcements corroded through unexpected chemical reactions. Concrete could be poured on site and was therefore supposed to be infinitely flexible, but the concrete building blocks were large and heavy. They were often less flexible than traditional bricks or wood. These characteristics intensified the uniformity, large scale and clumsy design of estates. Many concrete panels relied on bolts which, if not properly installed or missing, led to dangerous structural gaps. Concrete also proved unserviceable in appearance. It quickly turned grey from its early gleaming white. Rain and air pollution caused staining and streaking.

Other problems emerged from the untried but widely replicated techniques. Repainting, repair and servicing were all difficult due to the height and internal layout of blocks. Lack of roof overhangs, of traditional window sills and of guttering, caused serious water damage to the concrete. In driving rain, sealers proved ineffectual at keeping the water out (Glasgow City Council, 1985). Installations were of lower quality than necessary for the wear and tear resulting from dense, enforced communality.

These problems converged, as other forms of new or renovated housing arose – purpose-built single-family, owner-occupier housing and upgraded old inner-city housing. Both were light years away from the mass estates; and households whose economic circumstances were improving voted with their feet. They had come into mass housing, grateful and excited at the break it offered from previous poor conditions. But over time, they could afford more and better, so they moved on. Mass housing therefore became characterised by transience. The distance between estate communities and the wider society was enhanced by these developments. The unexpected decline took each country by surprise but, as social needs grew, there was little question about the role mass estates could play.

SUMMARY: SOCIAL HOUSING ORGANISATIONS

All governments have supported social housing: in Britain and Ireland mainly through direct local authority ownership; on the Continent mainly through autonomous non-profit companies, associations or co-operatives.

Most publicly sponsored landlords joined the 'mass housing' drive and some landlords in all countries became very big under its influence. Governments stopped the 'mass estate' programmes in the 1970s but by then, millions of units were produced or in the pipeline. When populations and housing supply reached rough equilibrium in the 1970s, many estates all over Europe became difficult to let.

Early on, demand fell and empty units grew. Poorer people were rehoused and estates gained a low-status reputation that deterred people with more choice. High rents to cover costs, and targeted allowances to help the poor made the polarisation worse, driving out many lower-paid workers.

The estates were difficult and expensive to run, were harsh environments for families and broke sharply with the traditional landscape. This made them quickly decline.

4 Pressure on Governments

By the mid-1970s, governments were under severe economic pressures, accentuated by the international oil crisis and other far-reaching trends, such as new technology, rapid globalisation of production and competition from newly emerging economies. Those changes played an important if indirect part in the growing crisis on estates. Governments in all five countries witnessed a similar chain of events: growing access by disadvantaged groups to less-favoured social housing; growing poverty and polarisation in unpopular mass estates; crime, disorder and police clashes in certain strategic estates. The events on estates mirrored wider societal anxieties over rapid social change. Many of the wider trends and developments suggested a loss of control, a rapid decline in security, cohesion and social stability. In the public mind, the two processes became linked as parallel decline set in. The area concentration of wider problems was an unforeseen but logical consequence of the mass housing philosophy.

GOVERNMENT SAFETY-NET

Governments had not expected to become re-engaged in estates, particularly as the governments of Britain, Germany, Denmark and Ireland by the 1980s were all in different ways exploring privatisation and a reduction in public spending. Fear of unrest, loss of political credibility and a need to protect limited resources led to renewed government involvement. Underlying the decision to rescue mass estates was the 'safety net' role of European governments for fear of the social consequences of not intervening.

Such was the scale of mass housing that wholesale abolition or replacement was out of the question. Such was its poverty and poor quality that privatisation was costly and generally impractical. Such was its value in housing the vulnerable, for whom governments felt obliged to take responsibility, that action was widely supported. It was this public sense of respon-

61

sibility for marginal social conditions, often only partially developed, that divided European governments from America, even though Americans were increasingly concerned about social breakdown (Jencks and Peterson, 1991).

Urban Europe was more dense, more closely woven and less segregated than American cities. European cities had long traditions of local government, citizenship and participation, albeit often mingled with violence or disorder. The threat of a drift towards American urban outcomes was real but there was a belief that Europe could respond differently. Only governments could provide a broad enough framework. Governments were held responsible for encouraging the creation of estates. If governments did not take responsibility, who else would?

The notions of social cohesion, social responsibility and integration, however weakly interpreted, were unifying themes (Jacquier, 1991). They dated from historic figures like Cromwell, Napoleon and Bismarck, or Irish patriots such as Parnell and O'Connell, and Danish founding co-operators. History had been built, cultures forged, wars and revolutions fought, around the ideas of social advance and state responsibility for the 'commonweal'. In the emerging social crisis, short-term political action became inevitable. If marginal, unpopular social housing estates epitomised the extremes of the threat of breakdown, then governments which had driven the massive programmes, had to respond.

Governments, however despotic, had built their popular base on a response to acute social tensions. The need for overarching intervention was clear, as no purely local solutions appeared feasible. Governments of very different political complexions arrived at this conclusion, from socialist France to conservative Germany and Britain. The surveys and case studies in Parts II–IV describe the process of involvement directly. The detailed steps taken by governments are outlined country by country at the end of this chapter.

UNEQUAL PARTNERS – GOVERNMENTS OR PEOPLE?

Consultation with potential occupiers and involvement with residents over the style of development had been completely off the agenda throughout the entire period of postwar housing estate development. The future occupiers were part of the 'fodder' of development. They certainly voted for mass housing indirectly because they wanted rehousing. They endorsed the political numbers game and were wooed by the technical brilliance which new solutions offered. But their views were never sought on the actual product or its environment.

Nor were their future needs as tenants and occupiers seriously considered. The assumption all over Europe was that the development and rehousing process was a solution of itself. Further action was not expected to be necessary for many years to come. Even in Denmark, with its strong cooperative structures, the development of estates was government-driven, not tenant-driven. This was possible – and maybe inevitable – because tenants were unequal partners in the targeting of government resources. It is unlikely that as many mistakes would be possible today because the failures of mass housing have strengthened the belief in customer feedback. Management concerns have moved to the fore and social problems have underlined the need for resident involvement before, not after, government intervention (Page, 1993, 1994).

Social landlords not housing applicants were close partners with governments in the scramble to build. The development focus meant that the social problems of estates were ignored for several years. The forward momentum of growth and new output of estates distracted attention by providing the safety valve of mass rehousing. Most political pressure during the building of mass estates came from the crude lack of housing, diverting attention away from the consequences.

The 1970s proved a watershed. Simultaneous with the drop in demand for mass estates was the property collapse of the mid-1970s. Programmes were curtailed or redirected because of escalating costs fuelled by steep inflation. This refocused attention on the management of estates, as the development drive began to tail off. Need had fuelled the building programme. But in a curious way, urban renewal and mass building had themselves helped create the pressure for conservation among the population at large.

CRISIS MANAGEMENT

The organisational problems of estates were decisive. The unforeseen faults, the multiple arrangements for cleaning, repair, security, rubbish disposal, required for so many households and units of accommodation, the interaction of age groups, ethnic groups and income groups as poverty became more widespread, all made the management task many times more difficult than previous social housing experience had suggested. The 'management gap' on unpopular estates widened.

Repairs were costly and difficult because of the complex and interlocking style of construction. Many problems were resistant to cure and beset some estates in this study for two or more decades. The management of large structural problems was far beyond the available expertise. The impact on tenants' lives was catastrophic. It turned the short-term gains in housing conditions into a long-term battle over viability. As the faults became more common and more prominent over time, they required bigger resources than even the most efficiently controlled repairs budget could provide. Failure to remedy major defects in industrial system-building would eventually render buildings uninhabitable.

Continental cities, dominated by flats, were controlled by concierges, door porters and security staff. Modern social landlords attempted to preserve this style of front-line management on the new estates. The complexity of the estates multiplied many of the direct costs of this service. Recruitment, co-ordination and supervision were far more difficult. Equipment was more costly and caretaking became a major budget item. By contrast in Britain, as the costs of running the mass housing programme mounted and the difficulties facing caretakers increased, the service was often cut or withdrawn (Parker, 1983). In both Britain and Ireland, most estates had few or even no caretakers at all.

On the Continent, a cycle of high running costs, high rents, high turnover and rent losses provoked serious financial crises, requiring government intervention. In Britain and Ireland, lower rents meant that there was less money for repairs and caretaking and therefore worse conditions (OECD, 1987). Social landlords reacted by 'turning on the fire-hoses'. They attempted to tackle building faults through emergency repairs.

They attempted to tackle social problems by giving caretakers a semi-policing role, making caretakers more exposed and more vulnerable. They reacted to financial crises by further pushing up rents. They responded to lettings problems by letting indiscriminately. The problem was imperfectly understood and the limited resources for management and maintenance were simply not enough to stave off the crisis (Avery, 1987). Estates became like '*une marmite avec le couvercle qui saute*' – a saucepan with the lid jumping (D'Inguimbert, 1989).

LINKS WITH GOVERNMENT

The reaction of governments in the five countries followed a clear pattern. Country by country, studies were mounted and programmes announced. Government inquiries in all five countries showed a complex range of interconnected problems. In outline, they identified four main aspects of estate decline:

- *physical* including design and layout, structural problems, repair problems;
- *management* including lettings problems, empty units and high turnover, arrears, difficulties with caretaking, security and other estate services, staffing problems, weak tenant liaison;
- *financial* including higher costs than income, unrealistically high rents, escalating rent collection problems and repairs costs, inadequate resources to rectify building defects, and rent losses through voids, turnover and vandal damage;
- *social* including poor facilities, concentrated need and a breakdown of controls.

It was obvious that many factors were at work beyond the physical nature of the estates. The problems in the worst areas, those targeted by governments and therefore included in this survey, were many-sided, interlocking and mutually reinforcing. This made them difficult to reverse.

Governments targeted the estates with multiple problems. But in spite of evidence that the estates were affected by more than simply physical conditions, governments directed most of their support towards the physical aspects of the problem, leaving social, financial and management problems largely to the landlords. While they expressed support for management change and social underpinning, they put few direct resources into bringing it about. This was virtually a repeat of the original mass housing programme.

There were several reasons for homing in on physical conditions. They were the most visible aspect of decline, a clear and unifying target that had a measurable output in numbers of improved units and a direct focus for housing staff and residents. They were simpler to organise than social or management rescue. Changes would be immediately noticeable, therefore guaranteeing a short-term political return on the investment. They would ensure the survival of the buildings as a prerequisite of social and management viability. However, government resources for physical rescue were invariably tied to other reforms. For example, the Irish government required local authorities to involve tenants and provide estate-based services. The French government required local mayors to become actively involved and the communes to provide social facilities. The Danish government required social landlords to give tenants on each estate a controlling say in the priorities. The German government helped social landlords to reduce uneconomically high rents on outer estates in order to facilitate lettings, reduce turnover and restore management stability. The British government insisted on local management and tenant consultation in each estate programme.

Once-and-for-all physical solutions were dreamt of in the pattern of traditional government solutions but all governments recognised that the problems lay beyond the buildings. It was hoped, however, that when the estates' dominant physical problems were rectified, they would become more manageable, socially and financially viable again.

NEED FOR WIDER CHANGES

It is easy to illustrate why physical measures alone would not solve estate problems. For example, door security required more than strong doors. It also required supervision and constant maintenance. Large block buildings had onerous maintenance problems, after their roofs and other defects had been remedied. Lifts, heating, rubbish disposal and lighting, are just a few examples of items that must be attended to on a day to day basis. Estate viability required a whole system of integrated, hands-on management, involving a local presence to maintain building services. Therefore just on these counts alone, physical remedies could not work without a much greater input of management and maintenance. Many of the physical problems had grown out of neglect of maintenance and the lack of local management. Management changes were therefore a *sine qua non* of successful physical remedies (Hillebrand, 1988; Elie *et al.*, 1989).

All countries made their restoration programmes conditional on resident consultation of some kind. Basic courtesy and respect dictated that contractors could not simply arrive outside people's homes and start working on a major building project affecting their lives without informing them. More importantly, it was not possible to devise remedies without tapping the knowledge of residents. Although basic faults like roof defects and damp were easily identified and solutions, though sometimes elusive, were dictated by the problem, the 'softening of estates', security measures and environmental improvements were heavily dependent on resident usage, priorities and co-operation.

Therefore, while the main thrust of government spending was the physical upgrading of the buildings, the limited resources available and the character of the estates determined that the improvements would be dependent on other measures, notably management back-up and resident involvement. The money that became available for reinvestment and improvement drew landlords into tackling other fundamental problems. It changed the way they were organised, how they managed their finances, and how they communicated with tenants on whom their success as landlords depended.

The logic for a social dimension to estate rescue came about because estate renewal depended on the motivation and organisational strength of social landlords. Therefore, as social landlords became responsible for some of the most serious concentrations of social problems, they could no longer ignore the wider social issues. Estate communities required more sensitive treatment. Each estate existed as a physical entity, set in concrete, but it was more like a living organism inside a shell or case. The physical conditions – the case – and the physical changes – reshaping or adapting the case – were only part of the task. Working with a living organism is far more delicate than working with concrete.

All the connections within the estates between people, all the usages people made of buildings, facilities and open spaces, and all the problems managers faced in running the estates, formed part of the living inner structure of the estates. The connection between buildings, their use and their management was clear. Virtually every aspect of estate rescue required human management and social responses. Therefore, the rescue programmes did lead to wider organisational changes, although it was unclear whether these changes would be sufficient to make the estates stable and sustainable. Residents did broadly support the rescue initiatives, often out of a desperate desire to solve estates' problems. The rescue programmes therefore, as they evolved, became far more than physical renewal.

GOVERNMENT PRIORITIES

The rescue programmes developed over the late 1970s and early 1980s in fairly similar ways. Each government identified areas or regions of the country with problem estates – most often medium to large cities. They located estates with the biggest problems, normally large modern estates. They focused on regions with the most severe decline or the most intense urban pressures, normally metropolitan centres and major industrial areas. Other areas and types of estate were added in a reactive way, depending on local circumstances (Pinto, 1993).

In all countries, there were more target estates than there was funding available. When programmes began, little was known of the true nature or extent of the problems. Therefore inclusion in the programmes was determined through a series of emerging characteristics:

–   *demand* for the estates – money was usually targeted at estates that were a major urban resource, even if there was slack demand due to unpopularity;

- *notoriety* of estates – estates were selected by politicians, landlords and managers if they brought serious ill-repute to their operations;
- *political activity* – areas and estates attracted resources if they had strong political backers;
- *landlord commitment* – social landlords with the 'ability to spend' and a track record in development very often attracted disproportionate attention and resources;
- *social need* – explosive situations on estates were often a major trigger for reinvestment, because the political price of disorder was high. Estates were targeted where youthful disturbances had occurred;
- *building problems* – estates with the most serious and visible physical problems were targeted.

In Ireland and Denmark, estates only qualified for inclusion in the rescue programme if they had building problems. In France, only *grands ensembles* – large outer estates – were targeted until 1990, though a small number of inner areas were included in renovation strategies. In Britain and Germany, a wide range of types and sizes of estates were targeted but the biggest investment was on the large modern estates.

These criteria were not scientifically devised. They were often generated through political pressure which, in turn, responded to popular perceptions, reflecting the unpopularity and difficulties of large socially rented areas (CNVDSU 1991; Ministère de la Ville, 1993; Danish Programme, 1994; DoE, 1994a, 1994b; KAB, 1994a). But political antennae were less variable than might be expected. The estates across national borders exhibited strikingly similar characteristics. Those that were most conspicuous were at the top of each list. Over time, a process of selection through research, bidding and programming became common.

By the late 1980s, up to one-third of all large, difficult social housing estates were targeted in some way for improvements. In practice, the majority of postwar social housing estates required reinvestment, simply by virtue of their age, their use, and their maintenance requirements. In many ways, the rescue programmes were simply at the extreme end of the need to reinvest. This major reinvestment money could not be found from rents.

All countries had to limit and foreshorten their plans to some extent to match available funds. It was common not to tackle a whole estate but simply to target the worst blocks or areas. Therefore neither the targeting of money nor the focus of improvements was scientific. It was rather an exercise in containing problems (Delarue, 1991; BRBS, 1990; SBI, 1993).

CHANGES IN DEMAND

Estate renewal programmes began as social house-building slowed down. Therefore there was a smaller supply of new units and continuing demand from needy groups. As a result, empty units were a shrinking problem by the end of the 1980s, particularly in estates that were being upgraded through rescue programmes. Generally, estates filled up although areas of severe industrial decline in cities as far apart as Liverpool, Calais and Cork still had empty and unwanted flats on some estates for years. But they gradually filled up with poorer households, less economically active households, more socially marginal households, more ethnic minorities, and more one-parent families. This created complex social demands on management staff and on the tenant community by virtue of the fact that social needs were concentrated. Therefore, as rescue programmes unfolded, a new scale of social problem faced landlords and governments.

Social housing reflected the need for affordable units, a political and social commitment to keep people off the streets. As households formed, or broke up, they had to get their foot on a rung of the housing ladder somehow. If there were not enough 'first rung' spaces, homelessness would result, even where there was a plentiful supply of second and third-rung housing of higher quality. Some social housing estates had increasingly become the first rung, where historically they had been the end goal of families (Willmott and Murie, 1988). This affected the stability of already fragile communities. The result of these trends was a new political commitment in the 1990s to resident-based initiatives to rebuild confidence, generate economic activity, overcome lack of skills, alienation and youth disturbances.

Thus government approaches to estate rescue went through three main phases:

- physical reinvestment;
- resident consultation and management change;
- social and economic priorities

(BRBS, 1990; Boligministeriet, 1993; Delarue, 1991). In order to show how these phases unfolded in the five countries, we outline the chronology of government intervention, country by country. Each country followed a sequence that was closely linked to local conditions but that followed these broader phases. The following is a brief summary:

France

1971–76 – Government meetings about problems in ZUPs, the large outer estates.

1977 – *Habitat et Vie Sociale* is set up by the government to target help at precarious *grands ensembles* that are considered explosive. Les Minguettes is included in the earliest programme.

1981 – Riots at Les Minguettes involving young, second-generation Arabs flash across national press and TV.

1982 – The Prime Minister appoints a special commission to examine the problem of the *grands ensembles*. It reports in *Ensemble, refaire la ville* (Together, rebuild the city) (Dubedout, 1983). The commission is headed by the popular Mayor of Grenobles, M. Dubedout, in recognition of the critical role local authorities must play in any rescue attempt. Financial reforms target improvement grants and more generous housing allowances at the *grands ensembles* in need of renovation.

1983 – The National Commission for the Social Development of Neighbourhoods (CNDSQ or DSQ) is set up to initiate partnership rescue programmes on 23 *îlots sensibles* – very difficult estates – including some of those targeted in 1979. It is quickly expanded to 148 neighbourhoods or estates, covering 1 million units.

1984 – *Comité interministériel à la ville* is set up to co-ordinate government action in peripheral estates.

1985 – The CNDSQ develops contract plans with the *régions*, the *communes*, the HLMs and the *Prefects* to restore the estates over five years. Project leaders are appointed through the *communes*. The projects emphasise social initiatives and local community involvement, alongside physical upgrading.

1986 – Action on Employment is begun as 'most agencies connected with work had deserted the *grands ensembles* by then' (Levy, 1989).

1987 – French DSQ organises an international meeting in Paris to discuss rescue initiatives in 11 countries. Resident involvement becomes a central focus.

1989 – *Délégation interministérielle à La Ville* (DIV) is set up, to link the DSQ and other agencies, such as a special commission to counter delinquency and the educational priority programme, with the aim of pulling together all the ministries (18) concerned with estates, their social, physical and economic problems. Outer estates are now recognised as the critical urban problem. But the *Délégation interministérielle à la Ville* is hamstrung by interdepartmental divisions and strongly centralised state policies.

The *Quartiers en crise* programme is proposed by French DSQ and supported by the European Community – five, then 12 EC member states join in. The French government also creates *Villes et Banlieues de France* to try and link the *maires* of outer communes into action on *grands ensembles* through DSQ, DIV, and so on.

1990 – *Loi du Droit au Logement* is passed, to force HLMs to take greater responsibility for housing needy people. The National Union of HLMs, with support from the *Caîsse des Dépots*, individual HLMs and the government, sets up employment projects on 43 experimental estates – *Insertion Socio-Économique*. Its main purpose is to link young people into work by persuading employers to set up training and recruitment initiatives linked to *grands ensembles*. Within two years, 5000 estate residents have been placed in work, often with contractors working on the estates (Rénaudin, 1991). Serious riots occur at Vaulx-en-Velin and La Réunion.

1991 – Riots at Mantes-la-Jolie and other estates around Paris create big spill-over effects. Political support for the DSQ and DIV declines as the riots are seen to mark the failure of the rescue programmes. President Mitterrand appoints a minister for cities to pull together the strands of a new policy. Four hundred estates are targeted for improvements and additional money is voted. Contracts are agreed with 363 *communes* for estate improvements but the amount of money shrinks.

1992 – the *Loi d'Orientation à la Ville* is passed to encourage the building of HLMs in more affluent communes, avoiding over-concentrations of social housing in communes that already have very large estates. The law proves difficult to enforce. Meanwhile, the Minister for Cities is forced to resign in a corruption scandal – but the DSQ programme continues.

1993 – Support for the estate programme is renewed under the new Prime Minister, Balladur, because of fears of social unrest, racial tensions and acute unemployment. An expanded social housing programme, with 100 000 units a year, is aimed at better-off *communes* without large estates. The social building programme slows down due to cost, affordability, location and demand problems. The richer communes generally do not accept social housing.

1994–5 – Sporadic disorders in estate suburbs boil over. Government announces a Marshall plan for the troubled *grands ensembles* with a heavy emphasis on jobs.

Germany

1975–80 – Difficulties in letting new units on outer estates are reported.

1980 – Failures in Neue Heimat through over-development, international land speculation and financial improbity, come to light – strongly linked to outer estates problems.

1982 – Initial government inquiries into the problems of outer estates result from empty units and financial problems. Immigrant families from inner cities increasingly move to unpopular outer estates.

1982–5 – Neue Heimat scandal dominates the social housing debate and undermines public confidence.

1983 – The government sponsors experimental improvement measures on 18 very large troubled estates to develop remedies for the wider problems of *Grosssiedlungen* – large outer estates.

1983 onwards – Limited dividend companies are allowed to use urban renewal funds to improve outer estates. Special subsidies allow reduction in rents on new, purpose-built mass estates. The ending of special rent levies on higher-income tenants reduces turnover; the income limit for access to outer estates is raised. This leads to a better mix of incomes and lower turnover. Shift from new-build to renovation strategies. **1985** – The Federal Ministry of Housing Research Institute identifies 250 large outer estates of 500 or more units. About one-third of these are in serious difficulty. More detailed studies show the management, financial and social measures that are necessary for the restoration of outer estates (BRBS 1988, 1990, 1991).

1985–9 – Sale and transfer of Neue Heimat property to local and regional government-sponsored social housing companies focuses public attention on 'mass housing' problems.

1987–9 – Great increase in ethnic German immigrants fills up empty property on outer estates – by 1990 no empty units are left.

Great social tensions develop through concentrations of 'social' nominations on unpopular modern estates. Management reforms lead to more resident contact and decentralised services – social initiatives are popular.

1988 – Special government funds become available for building damages and for environmental upgrading.

1988 onwards – A serious drop in the supply of older social housing units occurs, as lettings agreements end. Eligible households can only be nominated as long as there is an outstanding public loan on a 'social' unit. For non-profit landlords, loans usually expire after 30 years. By 1990, most pre-1960 'social' housing units come into the 'free' market and lose their lettings agreements. The loss of nomination rights to older property leads to an increase in 'social' nominations to relatively new outer estates. This helps fill the voids but it enhances polarisation.

There is a new concern to renovate the older inner-city stock, much of which dates from the 1950s. Government urban renewal funds are used for renovation works to inner and outer areas.

1989 – The reunification programme is agreed, creating high social and housing needs.

1989–90 – Findings from the study of 18 experimental estate rescues are published – estates can be made viable and popular with a combination of resident involvement, local management, repair, security, financial reorganisation, more mixed incomes and uses.

1990 – The special tax status of non-profit housing companies is abolished in the wake of Neue Heimat bankruptcy, with the aim of turning non-profit housing companies into private bodies to make them more efficient. The legal change is supposed to encourage investment, create market rents and allow non-profit companies the tax advantages of private landlords. It is hotly debated whether these changes will help or hinder non-profit landlords (GWW, 1991). They allow companies to use rent surpluses from older stock to subsidise repairs and reduce rents on outer estates.

The East German public housing stock of 3 000 000 units is transferred *en masse* into local authority-sponsored housing companies. Conditions on East German estates are calamitous. At least 240 very large estates of over 2500 units need special help.

1991–4 – An expanded social housing programme to meet exploding demand is announced – the target is 120 000 social units per annum. New guidelines are issued on the size of estate developments – they must be smaller, more integrated, with an insistence on social facilities, transport links and more manageable environments.

1994 – New information on the outer estates problem confirms the vast scale of problems in eastern Germany and continuing worries about social tensions on some estates in the western regions.

1995 – The rapid shrinkage of 'social lettings' highlights the change in ethos of many privatised housing companies – less social commitment and a desire to become more profitable.

Britain

1974 – A government postal survey of local authorities identifies serious problems on modern, difficult-to-let council estates.

1976 – The Department of the Environment sets up the Investigation of Difficult-to-Let Housing Estates with a team of government experts. The main finding is that estates of all types and ages can become unpopular. Decline is often extreme; social problems are acute, made worse by the wider management problems of council services. The government and local authorities identify 350 000 difficult to let units.

1977 – Greater London Council tackles 'hard to let' problem by advertising lettings on its difficult estates on a first come, first served basis. This applies mainly to older balcony block estates.

1979–84 – Priority Estates Project is established by government in partnership with local authorities to experiment in rescuing unpopular estates. Money for the repair of estates is made available through the housing investment programme. Other initiatives are funded through the Urban Programme.

1981 – Riots in Brixton and Toxteth cause widespread alarm. A special Merseyside task force is set up, following the riots. The Brixton Enquiry identifies the social, economic and policing problems of run-down housing estates, the lack of work and discrimination, as major causes of disorder.

1984 – Priority Estates Project is extended for a further three years, and again in 1987.

1985 – Estate Action is set up by government to target capital at run-down estates on condition that projects include localisation of management and tenant consultation. Fifty major city authorities are initially targeted. Three hundred and fifty estates are upgraded over five years. The capital money is mainly for environmental improvements, security and rectifying defects.

Violent disorders on Broadwater Farm Estate, Haringey, a well-established Priority Estates Project, shake the country. For a time, it looks like the end of special funding, as Margaret Thatcher calls for demolition. In practice, Estate Action and the Priority Estates Project are extended.

Large-scale voluntary transfers of council housing to specially created housing associations and the delegation of housing management to tenant management organisations are set in train. The local authority stock shrinks and becomes more polarised through Right to Buy, lettings policies and sales.

1988 – Housing Action Trusts and Tenants' Choice are introduced to encourage the break-up of council housing. Housing Action Trusts are specifically targeted at large, unpopular city estates. Tenants, through ballots, decide whether to change the council landlord or not. Many tenants are afraid of transfer and reject both Tenants' Choice and the first Housing Action Trusts. Councils become seriously concerned about housing and other services, as tenants are asked to vote on their future landlord.

1989–93 – Housing associations become the major developers of new social housing. Their programme doubles to 45 000 new units in 1992, using partly private finance, a new idea for social housing in Britain. Estate building by housing associations expands. Need-based lettings are encouraged through government funding and local authority nominations. Therefore polarisation and social problems quickly emerge on new, attractively designed estates.

Tenant-led initiatives on council estates become eligible for government grants to establish Tenant Management Organisations, including Estate Management Boards and Co-operatives – 150 are set up.

1991 – City Challenge is launched by Michael Heseltine to create partnership projects with private sector involvement in 50 major inner-city areas in decline. It includes many big estates and embraces economic and training initiatives, as well as housing. It introduces competition and company structures into housing initiatives. A new-style voluntary Housing Action Trust model is created to take over some very difficult estates, initiated by local authorities.

1991–2 – Thirteen marginal council estates experience serious disorders, with several deaths in police chases and clashes.

1992 – Compulsory Competitive Tendering for housing management is introduced into local authorities, to tighten management performance. There are serious concerns about the impact on unpopular estates, which may be further marginalised under private-sector priorities.

1993 – The Single Regeneration Budget is created by government to pull together many different government social, economic, training and housing programmes. It supplants Estate Action. Many see it as a cut in estate reinvestment.

1993–5 – Several major urban local authorities try to break up large estates through sales, demolition and radical reinvestment.

1994–5 – Proposals to transfer selected urban estates to autonomous local housing companies are developed.

Denmark

1970 – Early lettings' problems on large concrete outer estates create concern in housing companies.

1975–80 – Construction of several large outer estates and new towns is stopped halfway because of low demand and unpopularity.

1980 – Serious building problems emerge on modern, industrially built estates – financial difficulties are reported.

1983-5 – An investigation is set up by government into problems on industrially built estates.

1984 – Housing finance is reorganised so that companies can afford to reinvest in major repair of outer estates. The National Building Fund is reformed to plough back rent surpluses from older estates into remedying building defects. Tenants' representatives are given a controlling role on the boards of housing companies and estate-level boards are created. Estate budgets are ring-fenced.

A special rescue programme is set up, targeting help at 30 000 industrially built units on estates in difficulty – the Danish Building Research Institute estimates the true figure as 80 000 units on unpopular estates.

1985–9 – An evaluation of an experimental programme to restore estates is begun. Tenants' views are documented in detailed surveys. Building emphasis is shifted towards smaller-scale, more mixed, more environmentally sensitive housing developments and inner-city renovation.

1985–90 – Urban renewal programmes push marginal tenants out of inner areas to outer estates. Local authority nominations to new estates are increased, leading in some cases to greater polarisation.

1990 – Political tensions rise over access to social housing by minorities. Reduced support for owner-occupation leads to higher demand for social housing and access problems. Empty units no longer exist.

1992–3 – Findings from the evaluation of rescue programmes are published. Physical and environmental spending is successful; organisational (management) and social problems are still not fully resolved. Programmes are shown to work if well-planned and integrated, with full consultation and thorough (high-cost) improvements.

1993 – A first-ever programme of support for the integration of minorities is created by inter-ministerial government initiative. Some of it is targeted at unpopular estates.

1995 – There are fears of 'ghetto estates' becoming a reality. Local authorities play a bigger social role.

Ireland

1966–9 – National Building Agency puts up 3000 high-rise units outside Dublin.

1971 – Reports of high-rise problems confirm unpopular image – high-rise is abandoned.

1974 – 'Low-cost' low-rise schemes create a boom in social housing for the poor. Tallacht and two other new towns are developed to cope with 'reverse emigration'. Polarisation and management problems grow rapidly.

1980 – Combat Poverty Agency is set up – a main target is poverty on outer estates.

1982–5 – Sales programmes are very successful, encouraging more stable communities and higher standards. But they fail on the worst estates.

1985 – The surrender grant is introduced to encourage economically active tenants on unpopular estates into buying in more popular areas, leaving room for poorer tenants on unpopular estates, causing an avalanche of moves off the worst estates and hastening their social collapse.

1987 – The Ballymun Task Force is established with government and European Community support to pull together key agencies and residents. Proposals are made for a remedial programme on the Ballymun estate, Dublin. The Remedial Works Programme is announced by government to upgrade 80 unpopular estates – about 20 000 units are involved. Money is tied to management reform and tenant involvement.

1988–92 – Government supports initiatives to improve estate management; the Irish Institute of Housing is established; new guidelines are introduced for local authorities on housing management.

1992 – *Plan for Social Housing* is published – marking a shift to small-scale, voluntary-sector programmes. It advocates no more building of social housing estates but the purchase of scattered properties in mixed communities to disperse social housing tenants in the population at large.

1993 – Renewed council building is funded in face of increasing shortages – 3000 starts. Partial demolition of high-rise blocks at Ballymun is proposed.

1993 – *The Lord Mayor's Commission on Housing* (1993) offers a far-reaching analysis of council housing problems, identifying poverty, segregated estates and inefficiency, as central problems. It proposes a radical reorientation of management in favour of tenant involvement. It recommends no more estate building. It also advocates more private involvement, more reliance on voluntary organisations, more infill, inner-city developments and more dynamic, varied solutions to housing problems.

1994 – Tenant participation programmes receive new government support.

In Part I we have outlined the process by which mass estates came to be built, why they declined and how governments became engaged in their rescue. In the next Part, we present an estate-level perspective on government intervention, based on our findings from 20 European estates.

SUMMARY: GOVERNMENT REACTIONS

As societal problems mounted around polarisation, unemployment, family breakdown and racial tensions, so the most unpopular estates experienced growing concentrations of these problems. Governments could not escape responsibility as the threat of disorder grew and as their role in creating the estates was clear.

Although government rescue programmes focused spending on physical renewal, landlords could no longer ignore residents' views or their social needs. It became obvious that estates were living organisms rather than concrete shells, and could only be restored if this was built into their rescue.

The process of intervention and the selection of estates for rescue initiatives were not scientifically determined. Rather governments responded to the threatened collapse of social housing management in the most extreme cases.

Although government funding targeted the buildings, all governments required broad-based action to involve residents and address management and social problems. This emphasis increased in the early 1990s to avert the danger of social breakdown. The chronology of government intervention in each country illustrates these points.

Part II

A Survey of Twenty European Estates

5 Common Problems

INTRODUCTION

The aim of Part II is to document conditions on a range of estates in the five countries, in order to identify the core problems and to record the impact of any changes governments and landlords had introduced.

The 20 estates in the survey shared several features:

- They were among the most conspicuous and most well-known problem estates. Therefore they represented the extreme end of the problem. This made their difficulties highly visible, well documented and important for each country. It made them comparable across borders because of their similar experience of decline. Their common characteristics underlined the wider nature of the problem.
- They were identified by researchers, government bodies and housing specialists within each country, as valid examples of the serious problems facing estate communities.
- They differed, in degree of intensity but not in essential characteristics, from other difficult estates.
- They had a history of government involvement.
- Their variations and their similarities made it possible to uncover a pattern of influences and pressures, leading to a converging experience of social problems in unpopular housing areas.

Many different internal and external influences shaped the specific communities we discuss. The estates were not simply a product of the way they were built, although their most conspicuous characteristic was their appearance. Regardless of country, ownership, size or location, every estate had some problems that related to the way they were managed and their social composition, as well as their physical conditions. It was the combination of problems that made them particularly difficult and that underlined the new and complex role played by social landlords in modern urban communities. The survey presents a brief overview of issues and problems, which are then explored more closely in Parts III and IV.

THE NATURE OF THE ESTATES

First we outline the nature and physical characteristics of the 20 individual estates. Further findings are then presented to show the patterns across estates and across borders. Figure 5.1 shows the location of the 20 estates.

O = 20 Estates

◎ = 5 Case studies

Source: Author's visits.

Figure 5.1   Location of the twenty estates

Location and date of construction

Table 5.1 shows the location and date of the estates. Eighteen of the estates were located on the periphery of the cities to which they were attached. Fifteen of these had poor transport connections and resulting problems with employment and access to services. Two estates were built within the capital cities of London and Dublin, rather than on the edge. Apart from one balcony block estate in Dublin and one outer tenemental estate in Glasgow, all the estates were built between 1961 and 1980, although several were planned in the late 1950s.

Ownership

Table 5.2 shows the ownership of the estates.

All the British and Irish estates were exclusively built and run by local authorities, although there was a small minority of tenant-purchasers and tenants who had exercised the 'right to buy'.

The four French estates were owned, at least in part, by publicly sponsored HLMs. Two of the estates were also partly owned by semi-private or private organisations, called *sociétés d'économie mixte* and *sociétés anonymes*. On two French estates there were blocks of owner-occupier housing, built by HLM companies.

Three of the German estates were primarily owned by publicly sponsored, limited dividend companies. Two of these had

Table 5.1   Location of estates and date of construction

Location	City	Periphery	Transport problems	Total
	2	18	15	20
Date of construction	Prewar 1	1945–60 1	1961–80 18	Total 20

Sources: Author's visits; Windsor Workshop (1991).

Table 5.2   Ownership of estates

	France	Germany	Britain	Denmark	Ireland	Total
Public ownership	—	—	4	—	4	8
Publicly sponsored housing association ownership	4	3	—	—	—	7
Semi-private housing association ownership	2	1	—	3	—	6
Private landlords	—	1	—	—	—	1
Co-operative	—	—	1[1]	1	—	2
Some housing built for owner-occupation	2	3	—	—	1	6
Number of estates with rented units owned by a single landlord	2	1	3	3	4	13
Number of estates with several landlords	2	3	1	1	0	7

Note: [1]As part of the estate renewal programme in Scotland, several parts of the estate have been transferred to tenant ownership co-operatives.

Sources: Author's visits; Windsor Workshop (1991).

some owner-occupier housing, built by the same company as had built much of the social rented housing. One estate among the 14 largest high-rise estates in Germany, was built with over one-third of the units for owners, to ensure a social mix. The fourth estate was privately-owned. This was planned to include a large proportion of owner-occupiers. In practice, they rarely stayed and either rented out or sold their property to other landlords. The privately-owned estate was not classed as a 'social housing estate' but a growing number of its units were subject to local authority nominations of needy households in exchange for subsidies to cover necessary repairs or improvements. This made its social housing role increasingly important, in spite of its still private ownership and management structure (see German case study). This private estate was included both because of its intense physical and social problems and because it reflected the unique German approach to rented housing.

Three Danish estates were owned by privately sponsored, non-profit housing companies, which received public support; one estate was owned by a co-operative. All units were rented and there was no owner-occupation.

The Continental pattern of ownership was varied, whereas the British and Irish patterns were uniform. The varied ownership had advantages and drawbacks. It avoided the straitjacket of public systems and it created pressures for higher standards (Vénissieux, 1989). But it also led to inconsistencies and sometimes tensions (see French and German case studies). The main problem with the unified public ownership of estates was the residual welfare focus and minimal management style.

The differences in ownership did not prevent many aspects from being remarkably similar. All the estates had a large majority of tenants and, except for the private German estate, they were all renting from social landlords. All estates, including the private German estate, had been planned and built under the direct impetus of government subsidies – central, regional or local, direct or indirect.

Size

Table 5.3 shows the size of estates. The size of the estates ranged from 390 to 10 000. The average for all 20 estates was 3319. Only one estate had under 800 homes. All the French and three German estates had 2000 or more units. Seven estates had 5000 units or more but no Danish or Irish estates were that big.

The size of estates tended to reflect the governments' approach to housing problems and the scale of need. The Irish emphasis was not generally on large estates, rather it was on single-family houses. They had the smallest estates. The French approach by contrast was strongly directed towards large-scale estate building and they had the largest estates.

Table 5.3   Size of estates

	France	Germany	Britain	Denmark	Ireland	Total
Under 800	—	—	—	—	1	1
801–1999	—	1	2	4	2	9
2000–4999	1	1	—	—	1	3
5000–10 000	3	2	2	—	—	7
Average size in each country and overall	6125	4011	3750	1347	1360	3319

Sources: Estate owners; government reports.

The 20 unpopular estates tended to be larger than social housing estates in general, although there was little overall national information on the size of estates (BRBS, 1994; Emms, 1990). In the British experience, large, peripheral estates of 5–10 000 units were rare (Power, 1987a). Two such large estates were included in this study because they reflected some of the most significant problems. The same applied to two very large ZUPs in France and two of the West German estates. Their size then made them exceptionally difficult to manage. It affected their lettings among other things, which in turn had a direct impact on social conditions. The size of the estates made them conspicuous. It made their public or social character more dominant and it made stigmatisation easier and more damaging because of the impact on large numbers of people of estate conditions.

Scale made a sense of identification harder and created stronger feelings of alienation and powerlessness. Scale problems provided a recurring theme in national research into estate problems (BRBS, 1986; KAB, 1994a). When once estates reached 200 units or more, they became more complex to manage effectively and required some localised management to maintain conditions (Power, 1987a, 1987b). All the estates bar one, purely by virtue of their size, were difficult to manage.

The biggest estates were intrinsically more complicated. Mistakes, conflicts and unpredictable failures, were more common and problems had a greater ripple effect. Controls were more difficult to impose and therefore abuse and break-down became more likely. This resulted from a combination of size and communality.

The problem of size was not clear-cut. Some of the largest estates enjoyed more and better facilities. Some residents reported finding the large estates 'friendly' places to live (Hillier *et al.*, 1987). Size was not necessarily the overriding problem. The problem of size could be compensated for if landlords took special measures (Plannegruppe GmbH, 1986; Foth, 1986). But the twin problems of size and peripheral locations compounded each other, making almost all the estates intrinsically difficult.

BUILDING STYLE

Industrial construction

Eighteen of the 20 estates were built with industrial methods, using concrete panels, poured concrete or, in one case, brieze blocks. All 18 were built after 1960. The two pre-1960s estates – one British, one Irish – were built with more traditional methods, although they were in large, flatted blocks. All the estates were oppressively uniform with a gloomy, unattractive, dominating aspect.

Flats or houses

Sixteen of the estates, including all the Continental estates, consisted almost exclusively of flats but seven of these had small areas of houses. There were fewer physical problems in the areas of houses than in the flatted blocks.

Four estates in Britain and Ireland were predominantly houses, though even the houses were built in concrete or brieze blocks in the late 1960s and early 1970s, using non-traditional building methods. They therefore shared some of the physical problems of the high-rise blocks.

Table 5.4 shows the type of construction used in building the estates and the mix of flats and houses. Flats were the overwhelming dwelling type.

High-rise

High-rise buildings dominated the popular perception of mass housing of the 1960s and 1970s, and particularly the problem estates. In practice, a majority of social housing, except in France, was not built in high-rise blocks (Boligministeriet, 1987; BRBS, 1986; Blackwell, 1988; Dunleavy, 1981).

High-rise estates were overrepresented among problem estates for several reasons. Many children and young people lived in towers because of the need to house families in social housing; occupation of high-rise by young families led to a high turnover, as families moved on if they could. The living problems for families in high-rise and the high turnover led to lettings' difficulties and pressure to house ever more desperate cases. The consequent social and management problems were difficult to control because of the physical form. The enforced communality and high density of high-rise led to neighbour disturbance and disputes. Lifestyles and child-rearing

Table 5.4   Construction method and type of dwelling

Industrialised construction – concrete	*Traditional building method*	*Uniform style*	*Total estates*
18	2	20	20

Mainly flats	*Mainly houses*		*Total estates*
16[a]	4[b]		20
(with some houses)	(with some flats)		
7	3		

Notes: [a]Includes all 12 continental estates.
[b]Two British, two Irish estates.

Sources: Author's visits; Windsor Workshop (1991).

patterns were often in conflict as very different and often poorly assimilated groups were rehoused in close proximity.

A serious and common problem with high-rise was maintenance. Maintenance problems were invariably difficult to tackle because of the nature of the blocks, the unfamiliar systems and the technical complexity of many of the services. All these factors led to high costs. Inadequate maintenance or uneconomic rents were the frequent results. This compounded other problems.

Table 5.5 shows the mixture of heights on the estates. Fourteen of the estates had long, high- and medium-rise blocks (*barres* in French) which were the most unpopular of all design types. They were often described as high-rise on their sides. Most estates had a mixture of storey heights. The Continental estates had more high and long blocks than the British. The Irish had least.

Table 5.5   Mixture of heights on estates

Predominantly high-rise – 6+ storeys	*Predominantly medium-rise – 3–5 storeys*	*Predominantly low-rise – 1–2 storeys*	*Total estates*
11	5	4	20

Distribution of high-rise and long blocks

	France	*Germany*	*Britain*	*Denmark*	*Ireland*	*Total estates*
Very high blocks – over 12 storeys	3	3	2	0	1	9
High blocks – 6–12 storeys	4	4	3	2	1	14
Long deck and corridor access or balcony blocks	2	4	1	4	3	14

Note: Most estates had several types of block.

Sources: Author's visits; Windsor Workshop (1991).

DESIGN PROBLEMS

Design problems were classed as problems stemming directly from the shape of the buildings, the nature of the construction, and the layout of the estates. All the estates had major design problems. The most common were: the clumsy structure of the estates, the blocks and the environment; the unused open spaces and communal areas; and the lack of security. The internal layout of blocks, with multiple entrances, long internal corridors, external decks, and many units per corridor, per lift shaft or per entrance, made for intense management, social and security problems. Unusual design features, such as stilts, underground garages, podia (wide, open decks above ground), scissor construction (where dwellings overlap each other within a block) and maisonettes, also created physical and social problems in a majority of estates.

The oversize of individual blocks was a special problem on the majority of estates, creating particularly intense social and management problems in those blocks. The enforced sharing, coupled with the overwhelming sense of anonymity, generated by the overlarge blocks, made them generally the most unpopular and difficult on the estates. They dominated the estates and evoked strong criticism in the public at large.

Table 5.6 shows the design problems.

Environment

Environments were difficult to maintain on all estates. The open spaces, one of the supposed benefits of high-rise building (Élie *et al.*, 1989), decayed quickly because they were not designed for specific or functionally clear uses and because they were overexposed and accessible to too many unconnected groups. They were under-used, poorly supervised and unattractive. The poor environments were a major deterrent to applicants, to staff, to visitors, to shops and to other enterprises (Byudvalget, 1993; KAB, 1994a). Residents' negative image of where they lived and their lack of pride very often stemmed from their inability to maintain their estate's environment and the difficulty in controlling the open spaces that belonged to no one.

Table 5.6   The number of estates with design problems

Design problems	France	Germany	Britain	Denmark	Ireland	Total
Layout of environment	4	4	4	4	4	20
Undesignated, unused areas	4	4	4	4	4	20
Security problems related to design	4	4	4	4	4	20
Layout of blocks	4	4	4	4	3	19
Scale of estate	4	4	4	4	2	18
Structural faults	4	3	4	4	3	18
Unusual design features	2	3	3	4	2	14
Oversize of individual blocks	4	2	2	4	2	14
Heating and dwelling problems	2	1	4	2	4	13
Total design problems in each country	32	29	33	34	28	

Sources: Author's visits; Windsor Workshop (1991).

Security

Security problems arose on all estates as a direct consequence of their design and physical construction. Break-ins, vandal damage and fear of attack were common. Control of crime was difficult because of the problems in controlling the blocks and the many escape routes throughout the estates. The large blocks and concealed areas, such as underground garages, lift shafts, internal corridors, enclosed entrances, made the estates frightening and unfriendly to outsiders and newcomers.

Structural faults

Almost all the estates had structural problems and suffered from structural decay, such as leaking roofs and decks, spalling concrete and corrosion of steel supports, faulty panels, fire hazards, damp penetration. These problems were of major concern to governments and landlords, often overriding other physical problems. They were costly to remedy but in no case were they so serious as to warrant total demolition. However, unless these faults were remedied, the buildings could not go on being used. Structural faults were a major element in attracting government resources to estates.

Heating and dwelling problems

High heating costs affected a majority of estates because the insulation requirements of concrete and high-rise were imperfectly understood at the time of construction. Most had estate-wide, centralised heating systems. These systems were particularly common on the Continent. Tenants disliked the lack of individual control over heating levels, and potential savings from central systems were sometimes dissipated through overheating or wastage or both. Obsolete fittings inside dwellings were only a problem in a minority of estates. Generally the internal dwellings were of a high standard and popular with tenants. Only eight estates had defective internal amenities, although the layout and size of flats to suit different sizes of households was a problem on a limited number of estates.

The physical problems we have outlined dominated the public perception of the estates as problem areas. They acted as the biggest barrier to turning the estates around, because the nature of the construction made modification difficult and because it was expensive to rectify physical defects, a prerequisite for other changes.

DESIGN AND LIVING CONDITIONS

There was another equally important aspect to design. The construction of the estates and their physical problems made living conditions difficult for residents in a number of ways:

- the collective structure of the estates made individuals and families feel overwhelmed;
- the clear physical separation of the estates from the surrounding areas by virtue of their location, construction and tenure evoked the notion of a ghetto;
- shared services, such as rubbish disposal, postal delivery boxes, entrance bells, access routes, could be damaged through individual irresponsible behaviour and were difficult to control due to their communal location;
- common entrances to blocks used by many households made it difficult to keep out strangers or to feel secure;
- dark and secluded areas created a sense of fear and anonymity;
- open spaces were too exposed for small groups of residents to control;
- lack of a sense of privacy arose from noise transmission, shared corridors and other internal spaces;
- corridors, decks and landings on many levels led to a strong dilution of numbers of people at ground level and loss of social contact;
- different types of households shared intensely communal buildings;
- family size units created high child densities.

Table 5.7 summarises the social problems affected by design. The interaction of design and behaviour is a contentious subject. Design determinists, such as Alice Coleman, have argued that behaviour is directly affected by design (Coleman, 1985). Here we would argue that design interacts with people's sense of control over their lives in a way that affects the composition of estate populations. We analyse this interaction in the following pages and in Part IV.

Design and welfare

The Continental estates had more high-rise buildings, bigger concentrations of flats, more large blocks, more communal entrances and other heavy concrete structures than the majority of either the British or the Irish estates. The social impact of the estates' design on residents was consequently higher, making the estates unattractive and off-putting. Their distinct-

Table 5.7   Social problems affected by design

Living conditions affected by design	France	Germany	Britain	Denmark	Ireland	Total
Lack of privacy, noise disturbance	4	4	4	4	4	20
Lack of individual control	4	4	3	4	4	19
Communal entrances	4	4	3	4	3	18
Secluded corridors	4	4	3	4	3	18
Difficulties in building social contact	4	4	3	4	1	16
Families with children in high-rise	4	4	1	4	1	14
Overlarge, undesignated areas	3	3	3	2	3	14
Inhuman scale of buildings	3	3	3	3	1	13
Total per country	30	30	23	29	20	

Sources: Author's visits; Windsor Workshop (1991.)

ness and their unpopularity combined to make them stand out in a way that deterred many applicants. As a consequence, these estates housed growing numbers of disadvantaged households in spite of strong and publicly supported efforts to retain a social mix on the estates.

The British and Irish estates, apart from the two case studies, had less intense design problems but they still stood out from their surroundings and incorporated some of the most unpopular and difficult design features, if in less extreme ways. At the same time, the clear welfare orientation of public landlords in Britain and Ireland limited the scope for social diversity resulting from less oppressive design.

The design problems on the one hand and the welfare emphasis on the other were pushing the estates towards a similar outcome across Europe – rejection of the building form, social instability due to the estates' inherent unattractiveness, growing influxes of vulnerable households.

Estate unease

Many social effects of estate design could not be quantified exactly. However, people who lived and worked in the estates in all countries reported these difficulties. There was an imprecise feeling of unease, a sense of latent hostility and often fear, that might be overcome when once someone had moved in, settled down and got to know their neighbours. Its most powerful effect was on would-be residents, acting as a brake on lettings. The link between design, lettings' problems and social problems was strong. Settling difficulties were compounded for isolated and vulnerable households, many of whom found these estates inhospitable environments.

The impact was to instil in residents a strong sense that they could not change external conditions. Concrete was a hard, dominant and inflexible form, making the physical structure of mass estates appear beyond human control. Nevertheless, residents often developed a sense of belonging as they stayed and built ties. Strong ties could evolve over time, as people built their lives and joined together to overcome the problems they encountered on their estates. Estates often combined a rapid turnover in maybe a third of the units; an intermediate group who might not yet have put down roots but might stay, albeit reluctantly, in another third; a significant population of established households in another third.

Figure 5.2 attempts to show how estate populations developed.

Social disadvantage

Official government reports from each country documented the concentrations of social disadvantage on estates (Delarue, 1991; BRBS, 1988; SBI, 1993; DoE (Ireland), 1991). In this section we record the views of the people we interviewed on the estates in the course of the visits, which bore out official findings. All of the estates without exception reported a range of serious social difficulties. Such a high proportion of resi-

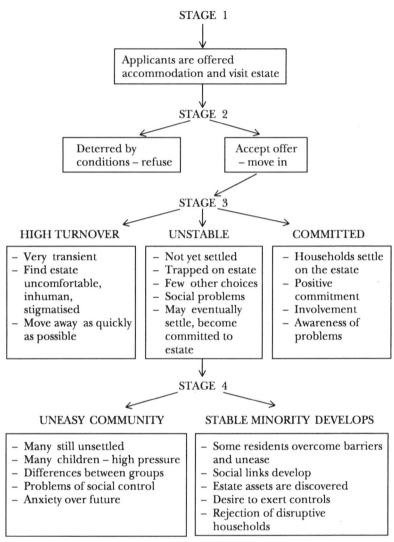

STAGE 1

Applicants are offered
accommodation and visit estate

STAGE 2

Deterred by
conditions – refuse

Accept offer
– move in

STAGE 3

HIGH TURNOVER

- Very transient
- Find estate
  uncomfortable,
  inhuman,
  stigmatised
- Move away as quickly
  as possible

UNSTABLE

- Not yet settled
- Trapped on estate
- Few other choices
- Social problems
- May eventually
  settle, become
  committed to
  estate

COMMITTED

- Households settle
  on the estate
- Positive
  commitment
- Involvement
- Awareness of
  problems

STAGE 4

UNEASY COMMUNITY

- Many still unsettled
- Many children – high pressure
- Differences between groups
- Problems of social control
- Anxiety over future

STABLE MINORITY DEVELOPS

- Some residents overcome barriers
  and unease
- Social links develop
- Estate assets are discovered
- Desire to exert controls
- Rejection of disruptive
  households

Source: Author's visits and research.

Figure 5.2   Settling-in problems and consequent instability

dents were disadvantaged in some way that community resources were severely stretched in attempting to cope.
Housing staff on all estates reported management pressures
resulting from these problems. Table 5.8 outlines the main

social disadvantages that were found to be disproportionately concentrated in the 20 estates.

There were eight characteristics we classed as social disadvantages, commonly found on the estates. So pervasive were these disadvantages that most estates had six or seven.

Table 5.8   Social disadvantages disproportionately concentrated in estate communities

Incidence of social disadvantage higher than average	France	Germany	Britain	Denmark	Ireland	Total
Vandalism	4	4	4	4	4	20
One-parent families	3	4	4	4	4	19
Young people without work	4	3	4	4	4	19
Unemployment and dependence on state benefits	3	3	4	4	4	18
Anti-social behaviour – disturbing households	4	2	4	4	4	18
Police and crime problems	3	3	4	3	4	17
Concentrations of ethnic minorities	4	4	1[a]	3	0	12
Serious incidents of disorder	3	1	2	0	1	7
Total incidence	28	24	27	26	25	

Estates with extreme social conditions	Estates with serious social conditions	Estates with stable social conditions	Total
16	4	0	20

Note: [a]Concentrations of ethnic minorities in council housing are mainly found in London and a small number of other cities. Three estates in this survey were not in areas of high ethnic minority concentrations.

Sources: Author's estate visits; Windsor Workshop (1991).

Sixteen estates had seven or eight disadvantages. Four estates had five or six disadvantages. No estate had fewer than five problems. The pattern of problems was similar across the five countries, although they varied in degree according to national and local trends. The consistency of reports on social problems confirmed the seriousness of the situation. However, the survey findings do not reflect the intensity of any particular problem. Problems occurred to a different degree in different estates. For example, on one British estate, over half of all families with children had a single parent. On a German estate with the same problem, the proportion was one in ten (Plannegruppe GmbH, 1986). The fact that both estates housed disproportionate levels of one-parent families should not disguise differences between estates and countries. At the same time, it underlined the common trend in all countries towards more one-parent families and their greater concentration in unpopular social housing areas. The survey revealed a strong overall pattern but it did not demonstrate the same conditions or the same intensity of problems everywhere.

Race and disorder

There were two problems occurring less frequently than might have been expected:

- the concentration of ethnic minorities (12 estates);
- serious disorder (seven estates).

These findings challenge some of the popular images of the worst estates. Estates could be extremely unpopular without any minorities living there. Minorities usually gained access to unpopular estates because of low general demand for those areas and because of discriminatory barriers to better housing. Their concentration in certain unpopular estates usually reflected their concentration in the worst housing generally and in certain areas of the country, usually the large cities. The absence of minority communities from Ireland and their low representation on three of the British estates confirms that acute decline is not necessarily linked to racial issues, even though in a majority of cases minorities were overrepresented. In Britain, they tend to be heavily concentrated in

London and a few other areas (Power and Tunstall, 1995). Nonetheless, race was a serious extenuating factor, creating additional needs and tensions, reflecting underlying trends towards separation and a pervasive link between poor conditions and ethnic concentrations (Holmans, 1995). Only a small minority of the worst estates witnessed serious eruptions of violence. The threat of disorder or 'rumbling disorder' was real and tensions were visible on most estates. But levels of actual disorder were seriously exaggerated by the media. One major incident was frequently reported as though it was a common, widespread occurrence. The seven estates that did experience disorder were seriously undermined by it and their reputations rarely recovered.

Impact of social problems

It became clear through the visits to the estates that multiple social problems had major consequences for life on the estates. Some problems, such as insecurity, were often caused directly or indirectly by the estates' inherent unpopularity, location and faulty construction, but they then took on a life of their own.

Social problems reduced the status of the estates and this had a serious impact on staff and services, as well as on applicants and employment prospects. Some factors, such as disproportionate concentrations of unemployed young people and one-parent families, magnified the problems of control and insecurity which were inherent in the buildings, as well as intensifying wear and tear. All communal features of the estates became more vulnerable than they intrinsically were because of the social composition of the estates, the instability and the control problems.

In other words, not only did physical conditions fuel social problems, but social problems themselves became compounded as they became more concentrated. This can best be explained by the particular difficulties facing lone parents. A mother with a young child in a high-rise flat on an unpopular estate had great difficulty in creating a secure social environment. If there were gangs of youths congregating in and damaging lifts and doorways or occupying play areas that were designed for younger age-groups, it was difficult for her to give her child freedom to play and explore as the child grew. The mother's insecurity and thus restrictions on the child had an impact on its development. Schooling and general sociability would be affected. The atmosphere of insecurity and the problems of underachievement were reinforced by the alienating environment. The reduced and restricted social contact increased fear and alienation.

If the external environment was poorly maintained and frequently damaged, the mother and child would have little pride of place. Their ability to make things better would be seriously constrained by the wider social climate. They would either withdraw, try to move or give up. When once a number of residents in a block took those defensive positions, the block would tip into disarray because communal conditions were no longer under the residents' control. Conditions could collapse, sometimes completely, and the number of empty units would start to rise steeply. Thus a vicious circle of social breakdown could be set in train.

Figure 5.3 shows the interaction of factors in creating such a vicious circle.

MANAGEMENT AND MAINTENANCE PROBLEMS

The widespread physical and social problems had a major impact on the landlord's task in running the estates. The management problems of these estates emerged within a short period of their being first occupied. Flatted estates were generally harder to manage, but all the estates quickly became problematic.

Most tenants had very high expectations when they moved to the mass estates. Their ultra-modern appearance, the high internal standards of the dwellings, the poor or insecure conditions tenants were invariably leaving behind, all created confidence in social housing. The subsequent disaffection was all the more serious and was a major factor in mounting problems and tenant alienation.

Tenants' attitudes had a knock-on effect on management performance, particularly rent collection. Rent income declined, firstly because of the higher turnover of residents and low take-up of offers among applicants. These problems

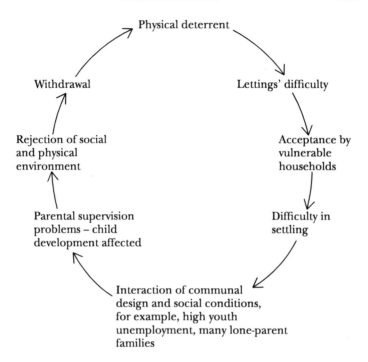

Physical deterrent

Withdrawal

Lettings' difficulty

Rejection of social
and physical
environment

Acceptance by
vulnerable
households

Parental supervision
problems – child
development affected

Difficulty in
settling

Interaction of communal
design and social conditions,
for example, high youth
unemployment, many lone-parent
families

Source: Author's visits and research.

Figure 5.3   Vicious circle of design, lettings and social difficulties

caused rising levels of empty property and loss of rent. Empty property caused greater repair costs and security problems, stretching financial limits further. High costs made the landlord's task even more difficult, leading to cuts in service, neglect of essential repairs and eventually management failure. As a result, the landlord–tenant relationship disintegrated through disappointment and dissatisfaction among tenants, through financial unviability and declining management standards among landlords. In these circumstances, good relations with tenants became progressively more difficult.

Table 5.9 shows the management problems which staff reported during the visits.

Table 5.9   Management and maintenance problems resulting from physical conditions and unpopularity

Problem	France	Germany	Britain	Denmark	Ireland	Total
Large concentration of social renting in distinctly separate area	4	4	4	4	4	20
Caretaking and control	4	4	4	4	4	20
Cleaning and environmental maintenance	4	4	4	4	4	20
Repair, technical	4	4	4	4	4	20
High turnover	4	4	4	4	4	20
Difficulties in letting	3	4	4	4	4	19
High vacancies	3	4	4	4	4	19
Insufficient local staff	4	4	4	3	4	19
Financial problems	3	4	4	4	4	19
Rent losses	3	4	4	4	4	19
High cost of maintenance	4	4	3	4	3	18
Total incidence of management problems per country	40	44	43	43	43	

Note: The degree of intensity of problems varied greatly and was least in Denmark.

Source: Author's visits, 1987–94.

Management spending on estates

Management and maintenance spending on the estates was estimated to range between £0.5 million and £7 000 000 per annum per estate. Spending per unit per year was generally between £1000 and £2000. The figures suggest the scope of the management task, even on the smallest estate with a budget of £500 000 a year. Such a scale of operation required between 10 and 200 staff, depending on the size of estate. Without a thorough-going system of control, estate management on this scale was bound to fail.

The physical separation of the estates from other parts of the social housing stock, the sheer size and organisational complexity of the task, the needs of tenants, the physical problems of the stock, all made essential a localised service with proper control, power to make immediate decisions and discretion to resolve problems. In no case was the local management organisation commensurate with the responsibility it carried or the amount of money involved.

Lack of local controls

During the period of acute decline, insufficient and inadequate local management organisation was possibly the most important element in the eventual loss of management control. Landlords generally recognised the need for front-line services. All the Continental estates had some locally-based management services, particularly caretaking. So did four of the eight British and Irish estates.

The estates, however, were not normally regarded as organisational entities for management purposes. Estates were seen as the equivalent of the 'factory floor' under a good foreman which would tick over without a lot of senior-level attention. Landlords managed with a long arm that touched on areas from time to time, often infrequently. Managers did not expect mass estates to be difficult to manage and therefore did not set up adequate structures to cope. In most cases they did not recognise the need for a senior manager to be permanently involved and on the spot, making sure that every aspect of estate management was attended to and carried out thoroughly and efficiently. As a result, front-line staff were increasingly beleaguered and unable to cope.

On two British and two Irish estates, there was no estate-based service at all at the time when decay became noticed. Virtually nowhere was an estate-based manager fully in charge. Therefore vital decisions were not taken in time, complex problems were not tackled and mounting difficulties went unresolved, until management collapse threatened. This eventually led to a loss of management control in half the estates.

Disrepair and management decline

Technical problems made management services far more difficult. Repairs were the most common source of complaint. Physical problems became steadily more serious and repair problems were often allowed to mount. The poor management of repairs and the inadequate spending on major repairs led to physical problems dominating the management task, making tenants' and staff attitudes far more negative.

Lettings' problems

Governments and landlords could not justify the cost of empty social housing while needy households remained unhoused. Sacrificing a social mix was possibly an inevitable consequence of the problems of mass estates. Letting the estates to ever more vulnerable households invariably took place when once an estate had become conspicuously unpopular. This so enhanced the management problems that it was almost always self-defeating. The primary concern was not for the social viability of the estates, but for the short-term goal of keeping property occupied. It was an inescapable effect of low demand.

The management of social problems

Difficult households were kept out of better areas by social pressures and by landlords wanting to avoid management problems. These families often ended up in the worst estates. Antisocial but extremely needy households, often with several children, were nominated by local authorities on the Continent or rehoused as a direct responsibility by councils in Britain and Ireland. Intense social need created complex management problems in different ways:

- the behaviour of some households disturbed neighbours in a way that was magnified by the communal structure of mass estates;

- some individuals did not conform to generally acceptable standards of household cleanliness or general hygiene;
- control over children was sometimes weak and children often caused nuisance and damage, as well as conflict among families;
- some had serious financial problems and were often poor managers;
- some did not accept or abide by tenancy conditions;
- individuals carried out disturbing activities, e.g. car-breaking, rubbish dumping, fires, break-ins, fights;
- anti-social activities often involved disruptive noise.

Only a small minority of tenants, even on very unpopular estates, displayed these problems. One French estimate was 10 per cent (d'Inguimbert, 1989). But their impact was magnified many times by the communal design.

The normal sanction against tenants causing nuisance and contravening tenancy agreements was eviction. But these families were conspicuously unable to cope and normal sanctions had little impact on their behaviour. Often they had been rehoused because of problems they caused elsewhere or because of homelessness resulting from evictions. Social landlords found it hard to evict, partly because they had an obligation to house these cases as part of their contract with government in exchange for subsidy. This applied under Continental nominations as much as under British or Irish rehousing. Such families were so hard to contain that alternative rehousing options were rare. A further factor deterring landlords from eviction was the difficulty in reletting. These families invariably had their rents guaranteed.

As the least popular estates came to occupy the bottom rung of the housing ladder, so more and more of the most disturbing households ended up there. These households could make life unworkable for other more coping households. The most vulnerable and unstable communities could not shoulder a burden the wider society failed to carry. Landlords lost the ability to control the problem and this became one of the major factors in the collapse of management. The case studies illustrate this problem graphically.

Arrears

Serious arrears were endemic on unpopular estates. Landlords did not generally record the underlying causes of arrears. However, the reported response of many tenants on difficult estates to falling standards and rising problems was reluctance to pay. Steep rent rises to meet growing budgetary problems linked to poor conditions were a major cause of arrears and a deterrent to reliable rent-payers, leading to ever greater dependence on social assistance.

Serious rent losses also arose from the type of tenants moving in. Growing numbers had serious financial problems, as well as other social problems. Young, single adults found particular difficulty in paying rent. They were neither used to budgeting nor paying rent. They found costs hard to control and their incomes were often erratic and inadequate. Lone parents, often the poorest families, with the highest costs, also had great difficulty in staying out of debt. Landlords in all countries found rent collection increasingly precarious, as the incoming population changed. The more stigmatised the estate, the more serious the rent problem. Increasingly routinised, bureaucratic rent collection methods worked badly among families living from hand to mouth.

Social difficulties, negative tenant attitudes, a poor service and poor conditions, made it difficult for managers to adopt a tough arrears policy. As a result, in some areas they ran completely out of control. On one British estate they rose to nearly £1000 per household. Arrears were more widespread in Britain and Ireland because of the looser system of budgeting. But they were a problem in all countries (Power, 1993).

Environmental neglect and insecurity

Open spaces, that were shared by all residents, were a direct management responsibility. The management problems meant that these spaces were not properly cared for, controlled or used. As they decayed, so usage declined further. The decay and abandonment of public and social spaces created vacuums of control that became filled by fringe activities. Reports of crime, vandalism, youth disturbance, drug abuse, were common to the estates in the survey. Occasionally there was serious violence and terrorisation (Élie *et al.*, 1989).

The degree of insecurity and disintegration was very different in the five countries. Denmark had little environmental decay compared with Britain or Ireland, which had pervasive problems (Power, 1993). The common element across all 20 estates was the extent to which the estate environments appeared ugly and insecure in the eyes of residents and staff (SBI, 1993). The environmental conditions epitomised the linkage between management failure, poor design and social disintegration.

LOSS OF MANAGEMENT CONTROL

If landlords could not stop vacancies, disrepair, arrears, breaches of tenancy conditions and environmental decay, they lost management control. The failure to increase management input in the face of rising problems led to disintegrating services that affected most of British and Irish estates and one third of Continental estates. Figure 5.4 illustrates the process while Table 5.10 shows the number of estates at different stages in the process, highlighting the greater loss of control under the public system than under the Continental system. Estates were on a continuum which ended in conditions approaching chaos. Beyond a certain point, viability was threatened. Landlords were unable to hold the line in the face of extreme physical and social problems which took the management task beyond their capacity to respond. The inability of landlords everywhere to resolve the problems of modern mass estates, underlined the urgency of the situation and eventually drew government attention to the estates.

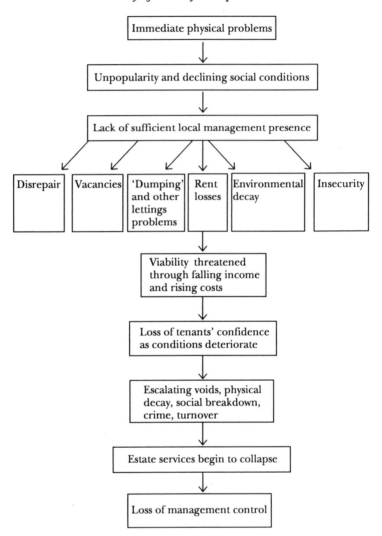

Source: Author's visits and research.

Figure 5.4   Illustration of loss of management control

Table 5.10   Stages in management collapse

	Continent	Britain and Ireland	Number of estates
Increase in landlord problems	12	8	20
Insufficient local management presence leading to declining conditions	11	8	19
Loss of management control and disintegrating services	4	7	11
Total	12	8	20

Sources: Author's visits; Windsor Workshop (1991).

SUMMARY: PROBLEMS ON THE ESTATES

The 20 estates in the survey were large, with on average, over 3500 units per estate; they were almost all on the periphery of major cities; they were mainly built between 1960 and 1975; they were owned by a wide variety of landlords. The estates not only had serious building problems but also intense social pressures and increasing management problems. This combination created such serious conditions that intervention became inevitable.

Inside, the dwellings were generally attractive and popular but the buildings had many technical and structural problems relating to the industrialised method of concrete construction and the scale of the design, with large, complex blocks and an open communal environment. A majority of estates had high-rise towers but medium-rise long blocks were even more difficult. There was advanced environmental decay and neglected, damaged common areas. Security was a serious problem.

Social decline became self-fuelling as more and more disadvantaged people with difficulties became concentrated in a hostile, poorly maintained, insecure environment. Landlords were unable to hold the line on repairs, lettings, rents or environmental maintenance. Therefore conditions deteriorated to a point where they began to run out of control.

6 New Directions

The decline and renewal of estates was different in several ways from the more standard urban renewal projects in older inner-city areas and this affected the course of change. Firstly, very large areas of almost exclusively rented housing were concentrated in the hands of few owners, except in the case of the privately-owned estate. This meant that large amounts of money needed to be channelled through large social landlords to restore conditions. It discouraged incremental improvements, individual or shared community responsibility. Secondly, the government's role in organising, promoting and subsidising the construction of estates made politicians extrasensitive to their decline. Politicians pressed for renewal programmes as a result and felt personally implicated in their outcome. Thirdly, the strong drift to polarisation emphasised the conspicuous character of the estates. Fourthly, the process of decline was not gradual in most cases. Over a short decade, most of the estates went from being gleaming new models of urban social progress to being ugly, damaged, fragmented areas of intense decay and decline. These factors made governments feel responsible for their fate.

SLUM PATTERNS

The settlement patterns of large, unpopular estates drove away many of the more economically active households, creating a powerful social barrier, which less needy applicants became resistant to crossing. Financially, it put the estates in jeopardy. The only estate in the survey that was privately owned collapsed financially, illustrating the risks for private investors of marginal social housing (see German case study). On socially owned estates, the financial problems were disguised for a time by welfare support and public subsidies, but in the end costs overran to a point of near-collapse.

The result of financial difficulties across many types of landlord was to force governments to intervene. Left to themselves, landlords could not do it, as they lost too much money to attract private investment and housed too poor people to offer scope for profit. The estates were too expensive to run properly for poor people without major help and too unpopular to succeed with better-off people without major improvements. Either way, substantial injections of money were necessary.

The estates underlined the new fractures in societies, as well as reaffirming the stubbornness of recurring slum problems (Stedman-Jones, 1976). Old slums were gradually being replaced and their endemic problems of bad living conditions, poverty, disorderly behaviour, crime, unemployment and so on, were expected to go with them (Power, 1987a). The reoccurrence of deep social problems in relatively new social housing areas was unforeseen and alarming.

Estates were fractured communities from the outset because they broke out of dense urban networks into spacious, disconnected areas that almost entirely lacked interchange with the wider society. So few initial supports were in place that 'settling in' was long delayed. Once unstable communities of such size were in place, it became hard to undo the damage. The estates could not be removed, replaced or radically reshaped, except at massive cost. Yet something had to be done. The risk of large urban areas running out of control could not be contemplated, even though they were normally on the edge of cities. The estates smacked of ungovernability and they reminded politicians of their fragile hold on constituents and voters.

For these reasons, governments in all five countries set up rescue programmes for postwar social housing estates during the 1980s, although modest initiatives in Britain and France dated from the mid-1970s. The 20 estates in the survey illustrate these national programmes, their organisation and focus, their impact and the lessons that can be drawn for the future. The case study analysis (Parts III and IV) provides more detailed evidence of the workings of the rescue programmes.

FOCUS ON ESTATES

The governments responded to the crisis on estates with an early recognition of estates as separate organisational entities. Failure to do this by landlords when the estates were first occu-

pied had led to a breakdown in conditions. All government
thinking, planning and action in the rescue programmes were
geared to identifying, locating, visiting and targeting estates,
while documenting the experience of each one. The programmes only existed as estate programmes.

Governments were greatly influenced by other actors in
their approach to the problem of estates. The press played a
major role in identifying the most notorious estates. Once on
the track of dramatic decay or lurid crime stories, serious disorder or breakdown, journalists would herd into the estates
and pick up the most extreme versions of events they could
find. The link between threatened social breakdown and the
estates was constantly made.

The press were fascinated by problem estates because they
contained every kind of human, social and physical problem.
They could chastise politicians and ridicule professionals.
They could blame rejected groups or they could blame society
and show the victims to be cruelly exploited and mistreated.
Sensational headlines pointed to cities on the brink of collapse. The media focus had an overpowering effect on politicians, as they were questionned on their record. Maybe more
than any other factor, press fascination with problem estates
galvanised the political will to act (CNVDSU, 1991).

In all but one example, central and regional governments
were the main funders of the rescue. But inevitably, the key
politicians were local. They were the ones who knew about the
estates and had to live with the consequences of their decline.
As part of the Continental rescue programmes, both landlords
and central government were active in encouraging local political involvement. In Britain and Ireland, local politicians
were the landlords. Residents had often complained about
problems on the estates to their local political representatives.
When conditions became extreme, local politicians were
forced to respond.

Rescue initiatives brought councils or other landlords into
dialogue with central government. Although social landlords
under all systems managed their rented estates with almost
complete autonomy, they became main partners with governments in the rescue attempts. But to succeed, they knew they
had to involve tenants within the beleaguered communities
(SBI, 1993).

Therefore four main actors each had a key role to play in estate renewal:

- *Governments* developed an overall policy towards estate rescue and reinvested in the estates.
- *Local politicians* represented local interests including re-housing concerns. When once a national programme was in place, they invariably fought hard to get a share of the action.
- *Landlords* adopted progressive management and consultation measures, in order to maximise the potential to upgrade conditions.
- *Residents'* needs and their responses either directly or indirectly proved pivotal to the thinking behind the rescue. They became more involved in localised initiatives.

Figure 6.1 shows the interaction of the main actors in the regeneration process.

ANCHORING UNSTABLE COMMUNITIES

Governments decided everywhere to improve the estates for existing residents, in spite of problems of polarisation, because those were the very people who needed housing. It was not contemplated anywhere that people should move out to allow for upgrading. This focus on population stabilisation was important, as it was radically different from the strategy adopted in building the estates, with the focus on population movement, to eradicate slum problems and house new arrivals. Politicians in the 1980s were forced to accept rescuing rather than replacing estates, due to the cost and unmanageability of large replacement programmes. Therefore estate communities had to be anchored and involved.

More positively, there was a belief that improving conditions with the existing communities' co-operation offered some hope of success. Increasingly, renewal was built around this objective, as it harnessed local energy to the renewal process. Preserving communities had become the hallmark of successful regeneration. It seemed an obvious way of creating greater commitment to vulnerable areas, focussing on the people as

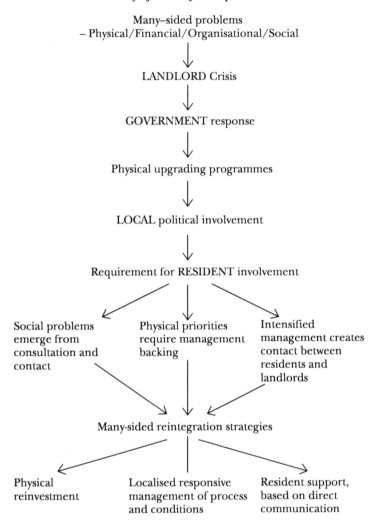

Source: Author's visits and research.

Figure 6.1   Interaction of main actors in rescue process

well as the property. This shift was noticeable in all five countries.

Rehousing large communities was a long, painful and disruptive process. Simply removing tracts of poor urban housing might only serve to displace the problem, whereas careful management might make most housing viable.

Publicly funded housing for poor people was often of poorer quality than the average but it could be upgraded for far less than its replacement cost. The quality of dwellings on estates was generally good and the most acute problems were in public and social spaces. But renewal could transform unacceptable areas, as the gentrification of inner-city slums proved in cities as far apart as Dublin and Copenhagen, London and Berlin, Paris and Glasgow.

The approach adopted in all five countries therefore focused on improvements within the estates, such as repair, security, environmental care, localised services and resident contact, because the programmes were about rescue and restoration, not demolition and replacement.

SHAPE OF PROGRAMMES

All five countries launched rescue programmes before problems or solutions were universally agreed. The programmes evolved in a generally reactive and incremental way, with only a few clear goals and strictly limited cash. While the programmes were being developed, governments began to establish the scale of the problem in numbers and size of estates, the extent of bad conditions, the causes of the problems, the costs of improving the estates, and the responsibility for taking the rescue forward. The government research in each country revealed a strong cross-national pattern of problems in the modern mass estates. Table 6.1 shows the common pattern of problems and responses to estate rescue.

Governments did not wait to reach irrefutable conclusions before taking action. There was political momentum driving the programmes. The critical situation on estates, made public by the media, provoked intervention. Eruptions were relatively rare but uneasy estates could boil over at any time and 'infect' other areas. The French likened it to 'a plague' (Élie *et al.*, 1989). No government could live with inaction because problems threatened the wider society as decay accelerated and they feared they would be held politically responsible. The period of rescue on the 20 estates was fairly close between all the countries spanning the 1980s. Table 6.2 shows the main features of the programmes.

Table 6.1   Common elements of estate problems influencing
government approach to renewal

Problem conditions	Number of countries
Physical problems:	
Scale	5
High-rise	5
Concrete	5
Location	5
Design	5
Extra large blocks	5
Low quality	3
Social problems:	
Concentrations of disadvantage	5
Management problems:	
Remote landlords	4
Bureaucratic systems	5
High costs	5
Underlying causes of problems:	
Polarisation	5
Isolation	5
Monolithic structures	5
Incentives to move/own	4
Costs:	
Rent loss	5
Voids and turnover	5
Repair problems	5
Loss of higher-income tenants	5
Combined, estate-focused response to problems	5

Source: Government research in five countries.

PHYSICAL OR SOCIAL FOCUS?

The primary criteria for spending ranged broadly from physical to social goals: to rectify intrinsic building and technical faults; to improve and humanise estate appearance; to enhance security; to tame, enclose and utilise outdoor spaces;

to create colour; to upgrade the overall image; to rectify any faults in the dwellings; to make residents feel more secure and more positive about the estates; to make the estates more manageable. The physical changes implied more than construction and building activity. They were often to do with image and appearance, popular taste, links with surroundings, family needs and the needs of children and young people. They were strongly linked to behaviour patterns – against crime, vandalism, noise; in favour of families, security, neighbour links, social meeting points. These objectives had ready support from local politicians. For them, spending government money visibly was a core objective. If it restored the estates' fortunes, then a large chunk of their constituency gained. Indirectly they won credit and therefore votes.

Landlords had very different responsibilities from politicians. Spending money on improvements was relatively easy. But maximising the impact of limited resources so that the estates became manageable required care and close attention to detail. Selecting the right priorities, implementing the programmes with least disruption, and putting in place the consultation and management structures that would create a more stable environment and make the improvements last was complicated. Consultation and management competence were the vital landlord roles that had eluded most social housing organisations on their large postwar estates. They would become the litmus paper of viability over the years of rescue.

The task of implementing improvements had not only to be tailored to each estate but to each group of residents in each block. Landlords could only get to grips with the minutiae of the problems by tackling each component part. In all cases, the changes required project teams on the ground to draw up and carry out the programme. Landlords changed the way they operated by force of circumstances.

PIECEMEAL APPROACH

The main characteristic of the programmes was their piecemeal, incremental nature. There was never enough money to

Table 6.2   Summary of approaches to estate rescue programmes country by country

France	Germany	Britain	Denmark	Ireland
Early social initiatives on estates to combat polarisation	Diffuse, local responsibility for estates obscures and limits problems	Government study of difficult-to-let estates	Tenant democracy ensures representation and involvement	Discount sales policies help many estates but *not* the poorest
Government reacts to disturbances with national programme	Abolition of non-profit status limits social housing provision	Experimental partnership projects, estate-based	Estate budgets and estate accountability localise decisions	Surrender grant creates instability on worst estates
Strong social focus involves communes and residents	Growing nominations to outer estates	Focus on local housing management and tenant involvement creates estate turnaround	Focus on building damages restores conditions	Remedial works programme requires resident involvement and localised management
Partnership rescue plans between State, Regions, Communes, HLMs	Financial reforms make housing companies more viable	Local authorities play leading role but strong tensions with central government continue	Ethnic and social tensions arise over urban renewal	Serious management difficulties due to low management presence and overwhelming social instability

Table 6.2 Continued

France	Germany	Britain	Denmark	Ireland
HLMs reform their management towards more localised services	Use of urban renewal funds for estate renewal allows upgrading	Development of tenant management creates bold experiments	Strong resident involvement shapes improvements	Tenant involvement and localised response changes approach to estate problems
Racial problems in estates dominate political debate	Landlords recognise social and management dimension	Underlying pressure of privatisation extends polarisation	Financial problems arise due to high rents and high costs	Growing government support for voluntary social housing
New attempts to co-ordinate different government ministries	Government emphasises income mix and social stability	Shift to economic focus results from economic dependence	Rescheduling of debts creates improvement funds	
HLMs introduce economic initiatives	Massive estates in East Germany pose intense problems	New competitive bidding encourages large 'flagship' partnerships – reduction in estate renewal	Towns initiative focusses funds on racial/ethnic problems	

Source: Government research (see Part I, Chapter 4).

do everything required. The programmes were often based on trial and error, as they were pathfinding and, by definition, predated any clear findings about estate renewal.

Each programme on each estate evolved somewhat jerkily and individually. Programmes were pieced together from many fragments of activity and ideas within each estate. The estate focus of the programmes allowed for the variations and special features of each estate. Renewal of funding over the phases of an estate programme was never certain. Some elements were favoured in some phases, not in others, as time affected political priorities. Some areas moved far ahead of others, based on resident leadership, phasing, or luck (see Irish case study).

The patchwork of changes took on shape and colour, made up of many small elements, turning reactive and *ad hoc* estate rescue into a new pattern of urban renewal. When the problems of estates were so dominating and many-sided but the estates themselves so monolithic, a patchwork approach was possibly the only workable way forward. Table 6.3 summarises the main characteristics of the estate programmes.

Physical measures

Table 6.4 shows the design features that were most commonly tackled. Each physical improvement could be made up of many components only some of which would be applied to each estate or part of the estate. A series of phased but limited changes were introduced. Some estates with a comprehensive renewal plan could only partially execute them due to cash shortages and limited time scales.

The combination of upgrading the buildings, security measures, environmental improvements, decoration and additional facilities greatly enhanced the appearance and atmosphere of the estates, making them look brighter, more cared for and more attractive. Most importantly, they indicated concern to ensure the estates' future.

Physical impact

On all estates, physical improvements created better conditions, better repairs and an eradication of major faults.

Environments also on a majority of estates became more attractive. On most estates, entrances and common areas were made more secure, better lit and maintained, although they were still vulnerable and in one or two cases had quickly been damaged again.

On half the estates, radical physical changes had been introduced and these had been popular. However, they were expensive and could not normally be implemented throughout the estates due to cost. Therefore their impact was limited and tenants were disappointed if their part of the estate missed out. Most estates were so large that at the end of the programmes or at the time of the survey, some areas remained untackled or were not planned for improvements for several years.

The estates in all cases were still physically awesome and a fundamental break-up of the contours of buildings proved elusive. The environments were expensive, extensive and complex, and repair needs were intensive. The estates required continuing renewal rather than one-off improvements, a fact that was not acknowledged by all governments in their renewal programmes, except through the Danish and German financial reforms.

MANAGEMENT MEASURES

The physical measures were of no use on their own. They required careful management if they were to work. Table 6.5 summarises the main management measures.

The most significant management change was a change in approach. Estates were difficult to run but if the right people with the right level of authority were attracted to the demanding task of managing a politically and socially sensitive but valuable asset, the problems shrank.

Breaking problems down into manageable components was the most important change brought about by the estate focus. It offered a key to human and social organisation, often forgotten in the study of society. Most systems operate in complex chains of interaction, with a multitude of interlocking parts. When systems break down, not only do many perfectly satisfactory parts seize up, but the ripple effect is constantly

Table 6.3   Characteristics of programmes

Partners	Government approach	Landlord response	Renewal pattern
Government	Target estates directly	Establish project teams at estate level	PHYSICAL Rectify intrinsic faults
Local politicians	Focus spending on physical conditions	Prioritise changes	Modernise dwellings Improve appearance Increase security
Landlords	Advocate management change	Consult tenants	Improve environment Change image
Residents	Require resident participation	Push management down to estate level	MANAGEMENT Increased attention
Government-sponsored agencies, e.g. welfare, schools		Attempt to minimise costs and stabilise finance	Special estate initiatives More tenant contact
Local organisations	Limit funding – programme uncertainties		

Table 6.3 Continued

Partners	Government approach	Landlord response	Renewal pattern
	Exploit estates' value as housing resource	Focus on filling empties	SOCIAL Consultation Representation Ethnic initiatives Resident support Facilities
	Reorganise subsidies, incentives and financial support so that social housing estates are financially more viable	Piece together physical, management and social targets into estate programmes	
		Take responsibility for programme development	FINANCIAL Restructuring of finances Reinvestment funds More generous allowances Greater rent income Limiting rent increases
	Encourage mixed uses	Work with politicians	
	Discourage demolition, encourage stabilisation	Contain costs and rents	

Source: Author's visits and research.

Table 6.4 Physical improvements showing range of elements and pattern across countries

Physical improvement	Number of estates with physical improvement					
	Total	France	Germany	Britain	Denmark	Ireland
Building upgrading Roofs, insulation, lifts, concrete repair, heating and pipe work, window replacement, balcony repair, common areas, underground areas, removing walkways, installing pitched roofs	20	4	4	4	4	4
Security Upgrading and securing entrances, better lighting, more guarding, lift enhancement	20	4	4	4	4	4
Environment Enclosing areas around blocks, providing play and sitting areas, planting, breaking up open spaces into smaller areas, delineating and separating uses, making environment more green and more easily cared for	20	4	4	4	4	4
Decoration and enhancement External painting, including concrete surface painting, doorways, windows, balconies, fencing, beautifying entrances and stairwells	20	4	4	4	4	4

Table 6.4 Continued

Physical improvement	Number of estates with physical improvement					
	Total	France	Germany	Britain	Denmark	Ireland
Empty units Special programme to restore empty flats	19	3	4	4	4	4
Facilities New facilities built or restored including shops, cafes, community centres, nurseries	17	4	4	4	4	2
Dwellings Changes to dwellings, for example, making some flats larger, making ground floor flats for large families, installing new fittings, bathrooms, heating, etc.	14	4	2	2	2	4
Limited demolition	6	2	0	2	1	1
Total incidence of physical changes		29	26	28	27	27

Sources: Author's visits and national studies, 1987–94.

Table 6.5   Management changes

Management change	Total	France	Germany	Britain	Denmark	Ireland
Special estate initiative to implement the rescue	20	4	4	4	4	4
Focus on repair and maintenance	19	4	4	4	4	3
Special management measures with more staff, higher status and more local decisions	19	4	4	4	4	3
Local office and local team on estate	18	4	4	4	4	2
Lettings aimed at improving social mix and stability	17	4	4	3	4	2
More intensive caretaking, cleaning and supervision	15	4	4	2	4	1
Total incidence of management change		24	24	21	24	15

Sources: Author's visits; Windsor Workshop (1991).

magnified by the interconnections. The originating problem can be quite small but the ramifications can be immense. The only way to tackle such complex problems is to trace the parts that do not work back to the root and untangle the problem at source.

Localising and isolating the causes to specific areas then makes it easier to locate the point of breakdown and to manage the remedy that is appropriate. Each part is slightly different and therefore requires somewhat special treatment. The management role then becomes that of applying the corrective treatment and sustaining the impact of the remedy, keeping vulnerable parts in working order to prevent new seizures, and sending the right message into the wider over-arching system to inform the working of that wider system. The three essential management elements of the rescue were:

- establishing or reinforcing a local management focus;
- creating a special rescue team;
- maintaining a bridge to the wider system (Élie *et al.*, 1989).

It was the yawning gap, the breakdown in communication and the inability to control spiralling conditions from afar that had made estates so difficult and unworkable. Proximity to the problems made them more manageable.

Front line

When once managers moved to the front line, the whole idea of management changed. Management was now about dia-logue, about delivery, about care for the property and control over conditions. These elements had a humanising effect since they made it possible for people to live more normally and with less fear. It enabled landlords to understand their customers' needs and it converted their 'fear of the worst' into a commitment to bettering conditions.

One perhaps surprising finding was that Continental land-lords, with a much stronger caretaking and supervisory tradi-tion and therefore less intense problems on this front than in Britain and Ireland, increased the intensity and quality of care-taking to cope with the greater problems and to respond to the greater pressures on difficult estates. This had a strong effect on environmental conditions and also helped improve security. It was because caretaking was traditionally stronger and better organised on the Continent that it could be en-hanced, reflecting its higher status and service tradition. Caretaking was quickly recognised by managers as a crucial area.

This lesson was not universally applied in Britain and Ireland, even though residents and landlords acknowledged its importance. The caretaking system had been so historically weak and had suffered such decline that in some areas it barely existed. On one estate, it was actually withdrawn! Environmental conditions were generally poorer in consequence in these two countries, even after improvements and this seriously reduced the impact of the improvements.

Caretakers were useful on the Continent in tackling minor repair problems and in liaising with contractors over bigger problems. There was little doubt that attention to immediate conditions prevented spiralling disrepair. Nonetheless, it was unclear whether sufficient resources were yet being targeted at ongoing repair or whether the improvements themselves were sufficiently hardy to stand up to heavy usage. Most landlords believed that more needed to be spent on repairs. The estates were still on a slippery slope because of their intrinsic repair problems.

VIABILITY OF ESTATES

When once spending on upgrading took effect and empty flats were restored, lettings became quicker almost everywhere. The level of empty units fell. On 16 of the 20 estates, special attempts at making the estates more socially mixed were introduced. These had limited success. Rising demand for social housing and rented accommodation generally helped fill the upgraded estates, but often with low-income groups (Power and Tunstall, 1995; BRBS, 1994; SBI, 1991).

At the end of the rescue programmes, most of the estates were still difficult-to-let to better-off tenants and needed special care to retain their viability (*Le Monde*, 1995). The survey estates remained vulnerable to decay. They did not generally become popular with economically stable tenants as a result of improvements and were unlikely to do so because their intrinsic problems of location, scale and oppressive design remained. Management acquired much greater significance in holding conditions, sustaining services, preventing further breakdown, and retaining control of vulnerable parts of the system, due to these wider physical and social pressures.

Management was the essential lubricant for those parts of the system that tended to move easily out of sink, that took more strain than average and that were less clearly understood than more accessible areas. Local management was an essential information-gathering and communication tool, helping landlords, politicians, government and even the press, to understand better what was going on. The social and organisational systems of modern mass estates required constant intervention, supervision and management, precisely because they were artificially imposed and lacked the more 'natural', free-flowing forms of organisation of smaller, more organic, more harmonious communities. In that sense they were a most extreme form of city development (BRBS, 1990). Many of the localised management initiatives were impermanent, incomplete and vulnerable to financial changes. It was difficult for hard-pressed landlords to leave well-functioning, controlled and generally improved systems in place if they were more expensive than generally allowed. When once the necessary improvements were done, levels of service became the target for cuts under budgeting pressures in the 1990s. Management cuts and reductions in local staff reflected a failure to understand deeper estate needs and a short memory of the lessons learnt. The British case study went through two rounds of localisation, cuts, renewed problems and new initiatives in the 1980s. The Danish estate also lost some of the intensified services (see case studies).

Because estate conditions were highly sensitive to reductions in service, landlords were under constant pressure from residents to stay on the estates (Power, 1991). They clamoured everywhere for more local management control. Therefore it was likely that local management initiatives would remain in place, if under modified conditions. But too few resources were being dedicated to core management tasks and to ongoing repair (Vestergaard, 1993).

Management impact

There was no doubt that local intensive management worked better than the previous more centralised system. More local supervision helped reinstate social controls, reinforced caretaking and repair standards and enhanced liaison with residents. Performance generally improved under the impact of closer controls and monitoring.

Lettings were a crucial area where detailed attention paid off. Marketing the estates, vetting applicants, reletting more quickly and with less bureaucracy led to plummeting voids. It gave landlords a much stronger hold on conditions. Security was another major priority and on-the-spot management made a rapid response, links with other services, and general vigilance more possible. It helped a more community-oriented form of policing. Overall management performance rose, relations with tenants improved, and the seeping away of funds through loss of controls ended. But management could not be made easy, only more manageable. For that reason, any relaxation in inputs, controls, staffing or security showed up almost immediately in new problems. Long-term management had to be kept firmly in place with ring-fenced secure funding, as the Danish reforms attempted to ensure.

FUNDING GAP

The rescue programmes involved major government spending and required a big organisational and funding commitment from landlords and social agencies. Therefore, a crucial element that concerned governments was the long-term viability of estates. Two things were obvious – these estates were more expensive to run than other more popular social housing; the occupants could not generally afford rents that would cover costs or, if they could, would not want to pay higher rents for unpopular property and would therefore leave. This funding gap had to be bridged.

The capital costs of the programmes were partly covered by higher rents and by normal housing subsidies, partly by special estate renovation funds. Only in Denmark was capital funding permanently reorganised in order to encourage continuous reinvestment. This seemed an essential reform if the estates were to work in the long run. Otherwise, emergency government programmes would periodically be necessary to fund major repairs. In practice, all countries relied on special government funds for major repairs and therefore special programmes would have to be repeated.

Alongside special funding, housing finance systems changed. Financial reform was a major part of making estates viable in cost and management terms. This implied higher costs for government but organised in a different way, through more individual benefits and lower bricks and mortar subsidies. However, the steadier rent income that flowed from the financial reforms, coupled with better management, restored the financial stability of the landlord accounts and increased the amounts that could be spent on management and maintenance.

The concentrations of dependence and the high cost to governments of higher rents reinforced the reliance of estate communities on the State. The conspicuous subsidies to estate communities had to produce noticeable benefits in order to be justified. The rising cost of the housing allowance systems to support higher rents was under the spotlight in four countries because of steep cost increases. There was a strong desire on the part of all five governments to cut the costs of social housing. Shifting from basic 'bricks and mortar' subsidies to income and rent subsidies had failed to solve the financial problems. This was a major reason for the increasing focus on economic and social initiatives on estates in an attempt to generate economic activity and more income for tenants (HLM, 1993; KAB, 1994b; DoE, 1994a). The deeper problems of unemployment, welfare funding, unaffordable rents were still unresolved, even though financially estate management was more viable. This made the social dimension of estate rescue central to any underlying change.

SOCIAL INITIATIVES

Table 6.6 outlines the main social measures adopted in different countries as part of the rescue programme.

In the *French* programmes, the rescue plans for each large estate included a budget for social initiatives. These ranged from artwork and sculpture, to soundproof music studios for young people, tennis courts and bowling alleys, cafés and local employment companies. The big advantage of targeted money was that it made things happen. It drew the local authorities into the estates, as they were responsible for social facilities.

In *Germany*, city and state governments were responsible for social facilities, while landlords provided meeting rooms for tenants and encouraged social organisations on the estate.

Table 6.6   Main social measures introduced by the rescue
programmes and incidence of all measures
in each country

Social measure	Total	France	Germany	Britain	Denmark	Ireland
Resident consultation	20	4	4	4	4	4
Special projects to help children and young people	19	4	4	4	4	3
Support for tenants with special problems	19	4	4	4	4	3
Provision and upgrading of social facilities	19	4	4	4	4	3
Resident representation in local committees	17	3	3	4	4	3
Employment and training initiatives	14	3	2	4	2	3
Initiatives to help ethnic minority groups	11	3	4	1	3	0
Total incidence of social measures		25	25	25	25	19

Note: Many social initiatives pre-dated the rescue programmes.

Sources: Author's visits; Windsor Workshop (1991).

The German estates were constructed with generous facilities by British standards. The changes introduced through special initiatives were often about upgrading them, about reducing rents so that shops and support services could be made viable and about providing more support for tenant involvement. Voluntary agencies were often active on estates.

In *Britain*, estate improvement money was tied to tenant involvement and sometimes helped fund particular social facilities. This was often achieved by attracting other government programmes, such as Urban Aid, which could be used for employment, play and community services. Voluntary organisations and local authorities were both heavily involved in social initiatives, although many were under funding threats in the 1990s.

In *Denmark*, social facilities were an essential part of all social housing provision, occupying by law at least 2 per cent of the floor space in any housing development. On the unpopular estates, extra resources had to be generated by landlords, tenants and local authorities. European Union funds were actively tapped. In Denmark, generous social facilities and provision were further expanded by the programmes.

In *Ireland*, social facilities were not prioritised in the Remedial Works Scheme. Nevertheless, the estates were so conspicuously poor and their social problems so numerous that community activities and social services were attracted to the estates. The Church and health authorities were active and voluntary self-help organisations flourished. Voluntary activity tended to attract charitable rather than public resources. The European Union, through its poverty programme, was deeply involved in social funding on at least two of the estates for several years.

In all countries some social programmes were prominent and residents became involved. The localisation of management was coupled with resident-focused activity. Employment and training initiatives were a direct response in all countries to the serious polarisation, the disproportionate numbers of out-of-work young people and the gap in skills. Special projects for children and young people were an attempt to compensate for the problems of estate living. They often aimed to occupy idle time, given the dearth of jobs. Special youth projects were designed to overcome the problems of second-generation youth not feeling they belonged to either the host or the originating community. Building confidence, establishing access to jobs, training and housing, were vital for this and therefore attracted resources.

Landlords, governments and churches helped with special projects catering for the needs of ethnic minorities. Special women's projects for North African and Turkish women were set up on several estates, because of their secluded status and their Islamic family structures. Several projects had been set up to help families overcome barriers to integration, whether in health, education, language or general living conditions.

Some centred around churches and mosques, in keeping with particular traditions.

On all estates with minority populations, developing bridges between communities and increasing the social integration of different groups were important goals. Without that, tensions could only be intensified and divisions become exaggerated by prejudice and lack of familiarity. Effort also went into creating social networks, making it possible for people to meet each other and build social links. Support for community centres and facilities was important in making this happen.

Special social services on virtually all estates were developed to help with particularly severe problems. They ranged from family centres to child support agencies. Helping families who could not handle living on these estates was a long-term and elaborate process that did not always work. One answer was to help such families move into more suitable housing where they would be less easily scapegoated and where their behaviour would be less noticeable. Several estates created large family, ground-floor units to do this.

Social problems did not go away and many social problems were deeply intractable. But putting in place better facilities, encouraging residents to have a say, organising support services and adopting special measures for harsh problems, meant that the estates no longer seemed abandoned and hopeless. This view of improved social conditions was borne out by tenant responses to surveys carried out on four of the estates (Nygaard, 1991b; Craig Gardener, 1993; Hope and Foster, 1993; Gifford, 1986).

Social impact

Many facilities faced serious revenue problems in the short and long run, particularly if they were local, voluntary activities. Often local facilities, even schools and health services, needed more support from the city or wider professional community.

Estates continued to suffer from poverty, racial discrimination, low levels of skills, polarisation. Social needs were mounting at the end of the study. Tenant leadership was undermined by this process. The Danes referred to it as a loss of 'psychological reserves'. Activists tended to become over-dominant through lack of competition for key positions. This could lead to burn-out, a bullying style of leadership and cycles of collapse in locally based initiatives.

By a process of attrition, there was inevitably a loss of more stable residents to better housing. Therefore instability had not disappeared on most estates. Only problems had been contained.

OVERALL IMPACT OF THE RESCUE PROGRAMMES

The impact of programmes was assessed, based on local evaluations and views of estate staff (see Chapter 2). Through the study we identified 21 elements that were common to the rescue programmes and that generally contributed to improved conditions. Table 6.7 shows these contributory elements and the number of estates where conditions improved under their impact. Of the 21 contributory elements, 93 per cent helped improve conditions on the Continent; 75 per cent helped in Britain and Ireland. Overall, 86 per cent had some positive impact. It was predictable that the programmes would have positive effects since they were targeting tangible problems with significant resources and back-up. Nowhere had the rescue programmes failed to make a noticeable difference to conditions.

However, the positive effects were limited by negative influences, such as continued low demand, a failure to overcome intrinsic problems in buildings, failure to establish a permanent management structure or get to grips with the more embedded social problems. One or other of these negative influences was present to some extent everywhere but they appeared more problematic in Britain and Ireland, where the outcomes of the programmes were more mixed, more uncertain and more vulnerable to social and political problems. In seven of the eight British and Irish estates, the impact of the programmes was mixed. On the Continent, the programmes on 8 of the 12 estates had a more positive impact. This resulted in part from their less acute social conditions, from their more intensive and more custodial management, and from their greater organisational autonomy and business orientation. In large measure it reflected a more limited social

Table 6.7   Main elements of rescue and number of estates where
conditions improved

Elements of rescue affecting estate conditions	Number of estates where conditions improved	
Physical:		
Building improvement	20	
Facilities	18	
Better environment	16	
Entrances	15	
Management:		
Staff commitment	20	
Functioning offices	18	
Voids reduction	18	
Repairs improvement	18	
Turnover down	16	
Maintenance of common areas	15	
Caretaking improvement	13	
Social:		
More resident involvement	19	
Better landlord–tenant relations	18	
More training	15	
Composition more mixed	6	
General:		
More control over conditions	20	
Better use of space and facilities	20	
Better security	20	
General appearance and environment improved	20	
Better provision of services	20	
Image and confidence improved	16	
	Continent	*Britain and Ireland*
Percentage of all elements bringing about improved conditions	93	75

Sources: Author's visits and evaluation reports.

welfare commitment by the landlords and a greater supply of
private rented housing for needy people.

    The 11 estates with mixed outcomes needed more renova-
tion work, more management control and a stronger hold on
social polarisation. In five cases – one in France, two in

Britain, two in Ireland – the long-term future of at least parts of the estates was in doubt, as demand remained low, social conditions difficult, and management unequal to the task. Table 6.8 sums up the impact of the programmes. The differences in outcomes between the Continent and Britain and Ireland reflected three main features of council housing:

– the greater concentration of council housing in areas of high unemployment and steep decline, reflecting earlier industrial urban patterns and slum clearance;
– the weaker management system, the lower caretaking and repair inputs and the historically lower rent levels, resulting from council ownership;
– the specifically welfare role of social housing under the council system.

Table 6.8   Impact of the rescue programmes

Programme impact	Total estates	France	Germany	Britain	Denmark	Ireland
Some successes	20	4	4	4	4	4
Some outstanding problems	20	4	4	4	4	4
Overall impact positive	9	2	3	1	3	0
Mixed impact – some failures mixed with success	11	2	1	3	1	4
Among estates with mixed impact, future viability in question	5	1	0	2	0	2

Note: Assessments based on reported impacts recorded during visits to estates 1987–94; additional information from local evaluation reports (see Chapter 2).

Source: Author's visits and research.

In Britain and Ireland, any attempts at greater social mixing could only have limited effects because of the tenure divide, the near-monopoly role of local authority landlords and the shortage of private renting alternatives, although there were signs that this might change (DoE, 1995). However, even where the overall impact was mixed, many aspects of estate life had improved and the successful elements of the programmes made the estates far more acceptable. The main limitation was that they did not always go far enough.

Overall, the programmes won general support and *local* enthusiasm. Most of the estates became more viable again under a combination of measures. But local management needed to be made more permanent. The extreme social trends needed a more radical and fundamental approach. And constant attention needed to be paid to physical reinvestment.

These were the limits of the improvement programmes. They did not reverse difficult conditions or make the estates attractive to higher-income groups. The estates, unlike older, inner-city areas that underwent improvements, were not gentrified.

CONCLUSION

Conditions, which had appeared to be slipping out of control, were hauled back into some kind of order. The estates had been through a severe survival test and a majority appeared to have emerged with a new lease of life. Only in areas of general economic collapse, were the estates potentially unviable. Their place in the hierarchy of housing areas was not generally different, but their treatment had changed radically. They were in fact closer to the mainstream of city neighbourhoods than they had been. They became more normal neighbourhoods as they lost their rejected status, received more positive attention and generated more local activity. Cities thrive on action and interchange. That was the key to the overall impact of the programmes.

SUMMARY: RESCUE PROGRAMMES

Governments took action on the 20 estates because the slide was so rapid and extreme. They needed the estates for increasingly marginal groups. They aimed to stabilise existing populations. The programmes were varied, localised and evolutionary in character. Most money went on physical improvements. These upgraded the appearance of buildings, restored common areas and environments, tackled some of the major defects and made the estates look more attractive and cared for. None of this worked without management support on the ground to run the buildings properly, attract more tenants and retain them, reduce arrears and enforce better conditions. The estates continued to house poor households. Local support, high quality caretaking and lettings control were central. Residents had to be consulted, unlike the original mass building programmes, because they were *in situ*. Many different initiatives were encouraged to help community networks grow.

The impact of the programmes was positive in 9 estates and mixed in 11. Conditions had improved more on the Continent than in Britain or Ireland but even programmes with mixed impacts had made estates far more viable.

Part III
Five Symbolic Estates,
Their Decline and Rescue

Introduction to Part III

THE FIVE ESTATES

The spectacular failure of certain 'symbolic' housing estates brought crumbling down the public faith in postwar expansionism, scientific breakthrough and social cohesion, while re-engaging governments in their problems. Problems in social housing estates were built into their very nature since they housed people with economic and housing problems; they provided buildings with problems, due to shortages of resources and minimal standards; market rents were unaffordable whereas low rents made adequate management unaffordable (BRBS, 1990, *Teil B*; Dublin Corporation, 1993). Slums had always been the consequence of those three factors – poor people, poor buildings and poor management. Poor and unpopular social housing proved to be no exception.

The evidence from five extreme estates reveals an unusual story of decline and rescue. It conveys the progression of each community from its dramatic and acclaimed birth, to its near demise and then its carefully nurtured return to life. The human problems were so extreme that their experience was documented in many forms. Local sources within each country were used. These authenticated accounts illustrate the painful consequences of decisions made with good intentions but a deep misunderstanding of urban social relations. The impact of those decisions on thousands of lives becomes clear through close study. The exact planning hit up against human variety and conflict, causing confusion, disruption and decay.

The five stories are exceptionally vivid illustrations of the themes of this study. But they are not separate from the wider experience of unpopular estates. They were chosen from the 20 estates because they seemed to illustrate most clearly what the problems were about and what government reactions were based on. They represent in a graphic way problems that we found to be widespread and pervasive. Although their problems were exceptionally severe within each country, the turns in their fortunes at different stages of development were so

145

similar that they almost mirrored each other. The portraits bring to life the human conditions around which the fate of estates gyrates.

WHY FIVE SPECIAL EXAMPLES?

Choosing famous estates like Les Minguettes, Broadwater Farm and Ballymun was not easy. The most extreme examples are by definition untypical. They can therefore often be used to mislead rather than enlighten. They may confirm unreasonable fears. They are too often dragged before the public eye in a glib and sensational fashion, invariably adding to the burden of their notoriety. But on journeys round estates across Europe, everyone came back to these outstanding examples of decline and ill repute. They were marked out among responsible experts not only for their failures, but also for their successes. Each estate had moved from a seemingly hopeless situation at the outset of the 1980s to a model of social housing regeneration in the early 1990s.

The story of each one was compellingly unique. They belied any conventional pattern of urban development. Findings that are surprising and contrary to strongly held popular beliefs are worth examining more closely. They are likely to shed more light than predictable and conventional findings. It was clear that these symbolic estates did indeed offer a totally different experience from their popular image. It was above all the gap in imagery and understanding between popular conceptions about the estates and reality that led me to make them a centrepiece of this study.

7 Portrait of Les Minguettes, France, 1965–95

ABOUT THE ESTATE

Les Minguettes became the archetypal dormitory city ... – a jungle in the town ...

... It was 1981. The large estate (ZUP) was in a bad way. The signs had been visible for a while. Not a day without a letterbox being torn out, lifts wantonly damaged, abusive graffiti, rubbish bins emptied out of windows, complaints about rampant and aggressive delinquency. Bands of disturbed youths stood out against the enclosed sky-line, spasmodically burning large cars, emblems of a civilisation to which they had no key. The police response was tense, then tough. The worst nightmare had become reality – a cycle of violence, repression, violence – which would never resolve anything...'

... Naturally the people who could, left, distancing themselves from the ZUP. Those who remained resented their captivity and were hostile.

... All these neighbourhoods in trouble were very expensive to run. It was without doubt the financial failure of this type of urban development that led to the kick-start for the recovery of the estate. (Élie *et al.*, 1989)

On the estate, the years 1981–82 were a period of acute crisis. The most spectacular manifestations of this crisis became national news and the attention of the media helped bolster the negative image of Les Minguettes, an image which became almost mythical. Those dark years will be remembered for such events as stolen cars and joy-riders, confrontations between young tearaways and the police, and the boarding up of complete tower blocks in the worst affected areas. (Peillon, 1991)

147

EXTRAORDINARY ZUP

In the French version of Trivial Pursuits, there is a question, '*Où sont les Minguettes?*' – Where are Les Minguettes? The communist mayor of the French Commune of Vénissieux, on the outskirts of Lyons, told this story with bitterness, reflecting as it did the fame of one of the biggest and most troubled outer estates in Lyons.

Lyons is France's second city and was ringed in the boom period of the 1960s and early 1970s with five giant peripheral housing schemes (*Zones à Urbanisation Prioritaire* or ZUPs). Les Minguettes was built in the 1960s, 9500 flats in 63 high-rise blocks of 17 storeys. This forest of towers was interspersed with *barres*, eight-storey long blocks. Les Minguettes almost doubled the population of Vénissieux from 35 000 to 65 000.

Lyons, with over a million and a quarter inhabitants, was bursting at the seams. The car and chemical industries were booming and immigrant workers were pouring into the city. Central government imposed Les Minguettes on the Commune of Vénissieux, determining its size, form and density of construction, with the extraordinary central powers then in place. Eleven housing organisations became the landlords when it was finished, two publicly sponsored, seven private, two semi-public (*d'économie mixte de construction*). Each one owned between 60 and 1700 units on the estate. Little prior thought was given to the management implications of the outer giant estate, or ZUP.

Les Minguettes was built in 14 distinct areas, in groups of three towers (see Figure 7.2, p. 166). The ownership pattern roughly followed this design layout. The estate was built using the most modern techniques, with giant cranes moving round the huge site of 220 hectares on specially laid, circular iron rail tracks. The span of the arm of the crane determined the oppressive closeness of the groups of towers, and the rail track for the crane determined the shape of the giant estate. The towers are usually in tight clusters of three, because that was the maximum that the arm of the crane could handle. The long *barres* follow the length of the crane tracks. The estate is ten times the ground size of Monaco, three times the ground size of Gibraltar. Nearly half of its vast area was left unused.

This unused land was the special contribution of the planners. The ZUP itself saw the open spaces as a no-man's land, making the estate even more marginal. (Élie *et al.*, 1989)

Almost all the flats were family size, many for large families. Over half had three to five bedrooms. The population of Les Minguettes was very youthful from the start. Over one-third of the first inhabitants were under 16 and nearly half were under 21. Today those proportions are almost unchanged. (Some of the estate was built for social owner-occupation and these areas of the estate were more anchored than others. They also appeared better cared for.)

RAPID DECLINE

By 1977 Les Minguettes was facing major problems; certain areas of the estate were heavily stigmatised. The estate generated a sense of insecurity, which caused many original inhabitants to leave. The growth in low-cost owner-occupation fuelled the exodus of French families. The rapid turnover and the high volume of empty flats created instability. Often reluctantly, in the mid-1970s HLMs (housing associations) began letting to newcomers from North Africa, with large families, in an attempt to keep the number of empty units down. This had the reverse effect and led to an even faster exodus of more established French families. By 1977, there were 700 empty flats, and little demand for the estate from traditional applicants.

According to Pierre Peillon of Crepa Habitat, a national housing service with offices in Lyons, estates like Les Minguettes went through several stages of social dislocation:

The population shifts benefited immigrant groups, by allowing them access to social housing, while pushing them out of other, older, low-grade urban areas... Second and third generation young households of immigrant origin were marginalised through belonging to neither culture... In addition in the 1980s, a few families with problems, particularly large families with delinquent young members, created problems for neighbours by bringing the estate into further disrepute. (Peillon, 1991)

In reaction to the high turnover and the growing racial concentrations, the commune introduced restrictions on access by immigrant households in the hope of stabilising the estate. The overrepresentation of minority communities in unpopular estates like Les Minguettes caused 'a collective stigmatisation of neighbourhoods' and 'problems of cohabitation between different populations' (Peillon, 1991). Units were kept empty rather than letting them to 'unwanted' applicants. But the ever-rising level of empty flats only served to fuel the exodus, leading to even greater vacancy rates, insecurity and withdrawal of services.

Within ten years, nearly one-third of the population of Les Minguettes would comprise ethnic minority households, mainly of North African origin. The familiar pattern of stigma, exodus, allocation to the most needy households, further stigma, became deeply entrenched. As the level of empty units rose to nearly 2000, the first national experiment in estate rescue, *Habitat et Vie Sociale*, chose Les Minguettes as one of its special projects. Les Minguettes became recognised as a conspicuous failure of heavy-handed urban development.

From 1979, the exodus from the estate quickened, partly because of the reforms in housing subsidy, which favoured single-family owner-occupation in the outer semi-rural areas, partly because the estate itself had become so troubled. Vacant units rose to 2400, fully one third of all the rented flats. The population had almost halved from 35 000 to under 20 000. Unemployment had risen from 5 per cent in 1975 to 13 per cent in 1984, of whom 40 per cent were from North Africa. The problem was particularly acute among second-generation minorities. Over half of all young North Africans were without work. Many believed the problems to be irreversible. Financially, the HLMs involved in Les Minguettes were on the brink of collapse.

In the hot summer of 1981, there were clashes between North African youths and the police, who were often the only representatives of authority regularly on the estate. Stolen cars were set on fire in 'car rodeos' that were cheered on from high-floor windows. Disorders broke out in and around Les

Minguettes both that summer and the following spring. Violent scenes flashed across the headlines of the national press. The local commune and residents deeply resented the notoriety that Les Minguettes gained but the disorders goaded the government, the local authorities, the Commune of Vénissieux, the City of Lyons, and the housing organisations into action. Les Minguettes was believed to represent only the tip of the iceberg.

The huge boom in production throughout the 1970s had led to an oversupply of new rental units in the outer areas of Lyons. Lyons was acutely hit by loss of jobs, but the five giant new ZUPs totalled over 30 000 units. Many argued that the outmoded, ugly, poor-quality, heavy design frightened away applicants. There were other factors. As the incentives to owner-occupy grew stronger, the intense housing needs of the large numbers of very poor, particularly immigrant households, transformed the population composition over a short period. The population turnover generated its own problems by weakening neighbourhood links, threatening the viability of existing businesses, creating problems for the local schools, tensions between new and established households, between French and foreign cultures.

The commune for political reasons pressed for a higher proportion of rented flats to be built at Les Minguettes. It was unable to arrest its decline thereafter because decline was so rapid and so unexpected. The intense political conflict between the old-style Communist Commune of Vénissieux (some would say Stalinist – one area of Les Minguettes was called after Lenin) and the *communauté urbaine de Lyon* (la Courly), of which Vénissieux was only a minor and poor part, made matters worse (Vénissieux, 1989).

PRIME MINISTER'S NATIONAL COMMISSION

The Mayor of Grenobles, M. Dubedout, was appointed in 1981 by the Prime Minister to report on the riots at Les Minguettes and to recommend to the government action that would reverse the problems of ZUPs. One of the most important findings of the Dubedout report was the urgent need to integrate the youthful North African population of estates like Les

Minguettes. Their crisis of identity – between two worlds – was considered a root cause of the breakdown in control. But it was exacerbated by the hostile physical environment of the estates, the isolation from employment and urban social life, and the lack of integrated, focused management, causing a collapse in communication. The solutions were to be many-pronged, with spending on physical upgrading, social facilities and education. 'Insertion' became a key term in the battle to reincorporate estates like Les Minguettes into the city. The report, *Ensemble, refaire la ville* (Together, rebuild the city – Dubedout, 1983), carried enormous weight and Les Minguettes became a leader in a new round of experiments.

The National Commission for the Social Development of Neighbourhoods (CNDSQ) was formed as a direct outcome of the Lyons disorders and of the Dubedout Report under the Prime Minister's office. Les Minguettes was one of 24 specially targeted estates in France to benefit from an ambitious renewal programme.

In 1981, straight after the disorders, the leading HLM companies responsible for Les Minguettes formed an association called AGELM to co-ordinate a totally new approach to the estate. The initiative was led by the three large associations with several of the smaller ones participating. But some associations remained stuck in their old ways. AGELM recognised that things could not go on as they were, that the future of the estate was at risk, that the new population at Les Minguettes was already deeply alienated, that normal estate services through the *gardiens* (caretakers) were totally inadequate, and that a complete break with what had gone before was necessary. The HLMs did three things. They based on the estate, small teams of radical and ambitious young staff, sympathetic to the situation of residents, with the single goal of establishing a dialogue and finding out what was wrong. They recognised the need to transform the estate physically in order to create a new and positive image. To do this, they accepted the inevitability of at least some demolition. The estate was too dense, too oppressive and too big (Vénissieux, 1989).

The association set up a lettings agency to market the estate to new groups of people. With over 2000 empty units and turnover still rising, there was no question that existing lettings policies and approaches could save the estate. The idea of priority lettings was meaningless where no one seemed to want Les Minguettes.

One of the leading housing consultants, who immersed himself in the rescue of Les Minguettes, wrote an account of the rescue entitled *Roman d'une ZUP*. He describes some of the key measures:

> The most courageous or desperate of the HLMs decided that they had to do something radically different, something which didn't exist yet and had to be invented... The more the problems were discussed, the more they seemed insoluble. This ZUP was not the only one. It was like an epidemic... Some said it was inborn in the ZUPs. Others talked of cutting out the evil at the roots... The HLMs couldn't stop the decline...dialogue between the inhabitants and the HLM representatives was strained, where it existed... Two or three HLM *avant gardes* were sent to form a bridgehead into the community... with a *carte blanche* to pioneer social management...
>
> ...Innovation, renovation, imagination, dialogue, reciprocal care became the big words of a totally new approach to Les Minguettes. But there was little doubt about the enormity of the task. (Élie *et al.*, 1989)

The approach to Les Minguettes was a dramatic break with tradition but the threat to French cities appeared real and the incomparably more violent disturbances of American cities within their ghetto areas fuelled the local imagination. American riots were cited as a central reason for action (Élie *et al.*, 1989). The HLM association set the pace and negotiated with the government new measures to tackle the rapid depopulation of Les Minguettes.

RESCUE PROGRAMME

Government money for improvements provided a catalyst, a partnership in seven layers to upgrade the estate. It involved the State, the National Commission for the Social Development of Neighbourhoods, the regional government, city and local government, other public services such as the

Caisse des Allocations Familiales, responsible for family income support, and the HLMs. The National Commission brought together the partners and helped stimulate the new approach. Complicated as this partnership was, the commune became heavily involved as a leading partner. The central aims of the nationally driven rescue of Les Minguettes were declared to be:

- to save Les Minguettes;
- to make it as internationally renowned for its successful rescue as it had been for its decline;
- to stabilise the population;
- to integrate the estate (ZUP) into the urban structure of Lyons;
- to bring together the different races, assimilating the North Africans in particular, in order to outflank the growing racially motivated National Front Party; but also to limit access by minorities and balance the representation of minorities by encouraging French households;
- to prove that a mass housing estate could be made to work by keeping it clean and attractive, in partnership with the HLM companies.

DEMOLITION

Four of the most notorious tower blocks in the area called Monmousseau were almost empty. They blighted a large part of the estate. They were demolished in an attempt to cut the number of empty units, create a more open environment and stem the decay. Young people from the estate were involved in planting 30-foot, mature, ten-year-old trees in the place of the felled blocks. Nothing smaller was believed to stand a chance. There was great excitement as the giant blocks were dynamited and local schoolchildren joined in the salvage and re-planting work with great enthusiasm.

The transformation of Monmousseau through renovating the remaining blocks, landscaping the area, creating grassed and tree-clad mounds out of the rubble of the demolitions, was truly eye-catching. In 1991, those planted areas had matured, were well maintained and undamaged. Many believed that the selective demolition of the very worst towers marked the beginning of the recovery of Les Minguettes.

A second area of Les Minguettes, Démocratie, with ten tower blocks and 600 units, was also half empty. Residents gradually moved from Démocratie to the better areas of Les Minguettes as vacancies occurred, leaving it semi-derelict. By 1985, it was completely empty and bricked up while awaiting a plan for its future. It was owned by the *office public* of Courly, the council for the conurbation of Lyons, and there were many bitter disputes about how it should be tackled. As a legally separate entity, it was not directly controlled by the commune and, according to local officials and politicians, the Lyons city government had very little commitment to Les Minguettes. In practice, there were sharp political differences over how to resolve the blight of Démocratie, which in turn prevented the full-scale rescue of the estate. Démocratie became a symbol of the problems of ZUPs, disputed, neglected, fought over, hated, semi-abandoned. The international press, throughout the 1980s, used Démocratie to illustrate wider urban problems.

The fate accorded to the estate by the press [was] magnified by their drums... Rumours grew apace. (Élie *et al.* 1989)

In 1985, the commune decided that further demolition was the only solution. The HLM company owning it did not agree and the government was undecided. Four years of stalemate followed, generating further doubts about the future of Les Minguettes and threatening the successful renovation work under way in other areas. The boarded-up blocks stood as an unsightly blight on the future of the estate.

In 1989, an international competition was announced, inviting plans for the renewal of Démocratie. The emphasis was on urban economic development. The aim was to generate momentum for an integrated enterprise-based project. Vénissieux Town Hall mounted a polished exhibition of the five best entries, selected by an international jury of architects, government and civic representatives. Fifty-three firms had entered the competition from as far away as the USA and Taiwan. The banner over the entrance to the exhibition read in grandiose French – 'Symbol of a failed and segregating urban vision'. All the entrants proposed demolition and redevelopment but still the future of the blocks was undecided, locked in a wider crisis. The collapse in the Lyons office property market from 1991, the failure to link Les Minguettes to Lyons through any funded transport plan, the gradual disintegration of the economic rationale for the new initiative at Démocratie, created a constant drain on morale. The blocks themselves were abandoned.

After the competition of 1989, conducted with such style, the blocks remained empty and bricked up for a further five years. When other French estates in Lyons erupted into violent disorders in 1990 and 1991, international photographers, always searching for the most notorious high-rise failures, poured over Les Minguettes, photographing the boarded-up towers of Démocratie – although Les Minguettes was not the main focus for the disorders this time. In 1994, all the partners agreed that demolition was the only possible outcome and in October 1994, Démocratie finally came down (see Figure 7.2, p. 166).

RENOVATION

The renovation work progressed steadily from 1983 and was still in progress in 1993 (see Figure 7.3, p. 166). Different parts of the estate received different treatment, depending on the owners. One block was renovated as an experiment in furnished lettings for students at the University of Lyons. The block included a café, was vividly painted and very popular. Another block was handed over to a Lyons-based national college, Bioforce, training young people to work in developing countries. It was turned into a residential training centre that was both popular and successful. Other blocks were renovated and let specifically to young French couples as a way of increasing the social mix on the estate (Vénissieux, 1989).

An important change to all the towers was the restoration of the ground and first floors to normal usage. The ground floors had been access areas in the original design and first floors were storage units for upper floor flats. Both levels were ransacked, frightening and unusable. They were either made into housing units or handed over to community or commercial uses. Street levels became much safer and more attractive.

The Communist-controlled commune had helped build a swimming pool and Catholic church on the estate and encouraged the community activities of the local priest. Accommodation was also found for a mosque and Moslem centre. A family community centre and a sports centre were added. Children's play areas were developed on derelict open spaces. The rescue programme encouraged youth initiatives, ethnic organisations, women's support, anything that made the estate feel more alive, more like a living, lived-in community. Shops, cafés and small enterprises opened in the renovated ground floor areas, making the streets more lively. There was a large market twice a week, selling food and goods for the large international community – serving the 32 nationalities living at Les Minguettes (Vénissieux, 1989).

SOCIAL INITIATIVES

A special social project was set up in one of the blocks, employing educated young North African women to work with first-generation families from the remote mountain areas of Algeria. These families were the hardest to integrate into estate life and had the greatest difficulty adapting to the estate. The project was very popular with the women, as it gave them for the first time a direct link that they recognised, into French society. Muslim husbands had to be persuaded to allow their wives to participate, but did so because the programme worked within acceptable cultural boundaries.

Many social innovations were targeted at children and young people. The French government introduced additional help for educational priority areas in the early 1980s. The primary schools of the estate were brought into this programme. With 21 special teachers and a class by class action plan, standards of reading and writing rose steeply till they reached a level similar to the rest of the city. This helped restore confidence among families on the estate and teachers throughout Lyons recognised the success at Les Minguettes. In spite of the great progress at primary level, only one in three young people got into the Lycée and of them, only one in four passed their *Baccalauréat*. Therefore a lot more work was needed to build on the progress among younger children.

The older children continued to be the major cause of worry (Élie *et al.* 1989).

Since 1982, young residents have been employed each summer in a holiday programme that involves taking groups of children away to summer camps throughout the long hot months. This diffused a main area of tension by taking away lots of the children who might otherwise be in trouble but also giving summer work to teenagers. There were an estimated 2000 unemployed young people aged 16 to 25 on the site. The renovation programme also offered some jobs to local residents. A local maintenance and cleaning service, a *régie de quartier*, was set up, employing local youth on a self-financing basis. Les Minguettes also formed part of a national pilot employment programme, sponsored by the National Union of HLMs. The three main housing associations at Les Minguettes were each able to take on an employment development worker, with the goal of:

● maximising access to work;
● facilitating changes of use in buildings to create more diverse activity, emphasising enterprise;
● supporting the creation of local services.

This project provided an avenue into jobs for local young people.

Meanwhile, the overall employment situation at Les Minguettes deteriorated over the 1980s, particularly among young people, and even more so among young North Africans. One result of this has been a loss of confidence and a hardening of attitudes among young people. Integrationist strategies quickly lost much of their credibility, as minorities were disproportionately affected. Young, white French residents were often influenced by the National Front. This produced a more long-term atmosphere of alienation and racial tension, undermining efforts at improvement and engaging significant groups of minority youth in a growing rejection of authority (Peillon, 1995).

Simultaneously, an alternative economy of drug dealing was growing and some foothold within Les Minguettes was established by drug-dealers, weakening the efforts of public authorities. According to local experts on the situation, the sub-legal drug networks had an interest in destabilising the French authorities in order to secure cover for their activity (Peillon, 1995). In spite of these strong undercurrents, however, the social and physical improvements at Les Minguettes helped the HLM landlords to restore management control, making financial viability and stability possible again.

MANAGEMENT

The most important and far-reaching changes on the estate were in the way the HLMs ran it. The state made funding for renovation work conditional on innovations in management. These took four main forms:

- New-style staff with social skills were placed on the estate to handle management problems, advise tenants and help market the estate.
- Lettings were removed from the rigid traditional allocations committee of the commune, government and the central HLMs. Marketing the estate was at the heart of the new approach.
- Caretakers – *gardiens ouvriers* – were given much wider responsibilities for day-to-day care of buildings;
- HLM landlords consulted residents over improvements, set up social centres to encourage local initiatives, provided money for resident initiatives and worked with other social agencies to support residents on the estate.

Each HLM organisation opened a management office in their area of the estate. The commune defended the diverse ownership of the estate with 11 distinct companies. 'It's too big to run as a single unit. This way if one part goes wrong, it doesn't drag the rest down' (Vénissieux, 1989). Different HLM associations had a different emphasis. One was more 'commercial and diversifying'. Another was more socially focused and stabilising. Overall, the main management efforts were directed at keeping units occupied, stabilising the existing community, improving services and conditions, and increasing the income level, social and racial diversity of the estate.

Applicants were interviewed and, if accepted, were encouraged to choose their own flat from among the empty units. This increased their own commitment to the estate and enthusiasm for protecting their home. Existing residents were allowed to move within the estate if empty units were available. Empty flats were carefully restored before being offered. The whole system became more flexible, more personal and more polished. The idea of marketing the estate appeared strange at first, because of the public funding and also because of the stigma. But by focusing on the estate's assets, the HLM companies found that they could mount a convincing sales pitch. The lettings agency, set up by the main HLMs, played a central role in reducing the number of empty flats.

The experience of Les Minguettes showed that the dense high-rise estate could not accommodate disproportionate numbers of unneighbourly families. The head of one of the successful HLMs explained:

We can't offer flats to all-comers like we did 15 years ago. We paid too dear for that approach. Today we have a relatively stable, multiethnic social balance.... These difficult families shouldn't be rehoused at Les Minguettes, otherwise we risk sinking again. We can rehouse a few. But we have to keep a balance, including financially. We can't house people who can't pay the rent. It's important to find other specially subsidised housing, with lower rents and in less dense buildings. (Rajon, 1991)

Altogether, the equivalent of 100 flats had been converted into commercial offices, local services, training facilities and so on. Another 100 had been made into foyers and student accommodation specially for young people.

Higher standards of caretaking accompanied the wider improvements. The estate was extremely well ordered, clean and tidy by 1989. Each building had its own member of staff – one per tower. They received training in the new style of management, where pleasing residents and responding to their problems were the hallmark of success. Caretakers were backed by local managers and made to feel central to the estate's survival.

The day-to-day management of the estate was gradually brought under control. Blocks were clean and in a reasonable state of repair; grounds and communal facilities were well maintained and rubbish-free. Overall, the estate was remarkably green-looking, a far cry from the bare and uniform spaces so often portrayed in the press. Empty units dropped from 2000 to 200, although in 1993 and 1994 there were renewed problems with lettings and empty units had risen to between 300 and 400. Arrears fell dramatically from over half of all tenants to only 7 per cent by 1991.

DIVERSITY

Not only did the HLMs become far more visible locally. The buildings were occupied by more diverse groups – more new young households; students; single people. The business orientation had paid dividends in restoring financial viability and acceptable conditions. Four elected councillors lived at Les Minguettes in the owner-occupied areas in 1989. No political representative had lived there in 1984, even though the estate comprised half the population of the commune.

Figure 7.1 captures the new management approaches adopted at Les Minguettes by the successful HLMs. It illustrates vividly the elements in the change and reflects a transformation from the remote, large-scale, impersonal, mechanistic style of the 1960s and 1970s to the much more committed, involved and local approach in the 1980s.

The following summary of the main remedies adopted at Les Minguettes underlines both the long-term and multifaceted approach.

Physical
- limited demolition
- insulation of buildings
- security doors
- small dwelling improvements
- reduction in large units, creation of small units
- conversion of ground and first floor storage to shops and other facilities
- environmental upgrading, planting
- lift and heating overhaul

162

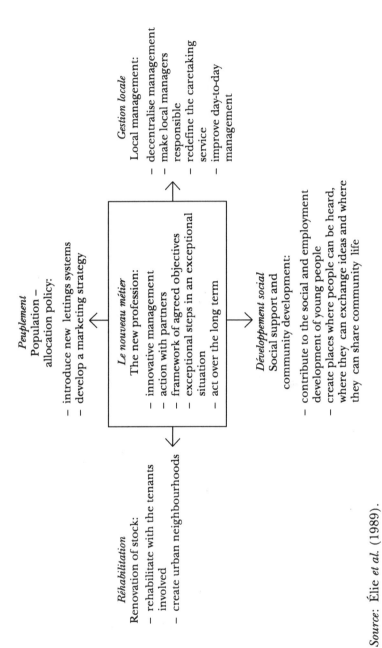

Peuplement
Population –
allocation policy:

– introduce new lettings systems
– develop a marketing strategy

Réhabilitation
Renovation of stock:

– rehabilitate with the tenants involved
– create urban neighbourhoods

Le nouveau métier
The new profession:

– innovative management
– action with partners
– framework of agreed objectives
– exceptional steps in an exceptional situation
– act over the long term

Gestion locale
Local management:

– decentralise management
– make local managers responsible
– redefine the caretaking service
– improve day-to-day management

Développement social
Social support and community development:

– contribute to the social and employment development of young people
– create places where people can be heard, where they can exchange ideas and where they can share community life

Figure 7.1   Model of the new style of management

Source: Élie *et al.* (1989).

Management	– more intensive caretaking with wider range of functions
	– local managers posted and local offices established on the estate
	– combined management agency
	– lettings bureau – advertisements for flats
	– flexible, innovative ideas
	– contact with residents
	– social and financial counselling
	– internal transfers encouraged
Social	– play areas built
	– work with children/schools
	– employment and training opportunities encouraged
	– resident initiatives and involvement supported
	– North African young people contacted
	– school and college initiatives
	– church and Islamic initiatives
	– police contact – better methods
	– youth summer camps
	– special women's and family support initiatives
Economic	– screening tenants for ability to pay
	– upgrading standard of empties to enhance lettings
	– rent arrears control and rent reduction
	– new diverse uses, e.g. Bioforce training centre, student blocks, cafés, shops
	– state support for APL – *Aide personalisée au logement*, higher rents and higher allowances – before renovations complete
	– establishment of *Régie de Quartiers*, economic initiatives and local businesses
	– training initiatives

Les Minguettes was restored through a huge range of different measures, which were strongly driven by the main partners to the rescue. It was only possible to effect change in such a complex development by engaging the commitment of many parties and by attacking the problems from as many angles as possible. The intensive input could only be sustained if the estate was fully occupied. A new rise in empty units – 400 in 1994 – was worrying to landlords, who feared a further management-funding crisis. Their long-term commitment to the estate was being severely tested in 1995 by the wider pressures on marginal outer estates in France (Peillon, 1995). But by the time of writing, most parts of the estate were successfully upgraded. Two-thirds of the blocks had been improved. Residents' organisations had sprung up, cafés and shops were opening. The large, specially planted, semi-mature trees survived, took root and grew. The estate no longer appeared to be ransacked. On the contrary, it looked like a rather proud and well groomed monument to an old-fashioned idea about human needs. The market was full of stalls, purchasers and sellers of all nationalities. The café was full of Turkish and Algerian youth. The climbing frames were full of children of many different backgrounds. The shops were full of goods to satisfy a multiethnic community.

It was unclear whether the attempt to adapt the original 'segregating concept' to a new, varied and more 'integrating' plan would actually achieve the promised integration of Les Minguettes into the city of Lyons. But as long as there were people in need of a home, Les Minguettes looked likely to survive and even prosper.

POSTSCRIPT

Vaulx-en-Velin, Lyons, is a neighbouring outer estate where the renovation process is less advanced. Serious riots broke out at Vaulx-en-Velin in 1990, after a young Spaniard was killed in a police chase. Tensions rose at Les Minguettes. Over the following months, there were incidents of damage and violence on the estate but nothing on the scale of the previous disorders. While riots in other Lyons estates spread across France, Les Minguettes was no longer quite so troubled or so turbulent, even though it did not fully escape the tensions.

The environment at Les Minguettes had changed, the community had stabilised, successful renovations had restored confidence, local managers had regained control of conditions and residents felt more secure. This combination of positive gains prevented Les Minguettes from becoming the new battleground. There was huge relief among those concerned with the future of the estate.

But there were new warning signs. Drug-pushing was becoming a bigger problem. Second-generation Arab households were finding it difficult to get housed, as new groups of French applicants continued to receive priority and as continued attempts were made to limit lettings to minorities. This policy was only partially successful and, in the 1990s, outer estates like Les Minguettes became dominated by youthful minority households. Unemployment was extremely serious in the 1991–3 recession. In practice, the population of Les Minguettes continued to become more polarised.

Nonetheless, Les Minguettes was no longer among the most troubled ZUPs. With a more varied range of customers, an improved estate and a transformed housing and social service, its landlords were committed to its future. They argued that new government funding for difficult areas, through the *Grands Projets Urbains* (major urban initiatives), should be at least partly targeted at continuing the initiatives at Les Minguettes, supporting major repairs, intensive management, settling-in support for new residents, economic initiatives, and other local ongoing measures. Capital spending would 'bring only mediocre social benefits' without these other programmes, in the face of continuing lettings' pressures and strong social tensions (Peillon, 1995).

Race, education, employment, integration, were live and sometimes angering issues for the community. These underlying problems were being approached from a more stable, more orderly, more successful community base. The 'rescue leaders' had gained ground by rebuilding community links and adopting a localised strategy to rebuild social stability. But 'the battle was far from being won'.

Note: Special thanks are due to Pierre Peillon of CREPA Habitat, who contributed valuable information about Les Minguettes and who checked and corrected the detail with meticulous care. Also to Jean Granet of LOGIREL.

Figure 7.2   Les Minguettes – demolition at turnaround

Figure 7.3   Monmousseau – re-planted by children after demolition

KEY DATES AT LES MINGUETTES

1959	Decision to build ZUP
1965–7	1st stage built
1967–70	2nd stage built
1970–3	3rd stage – 35 000 inhabitants
1974–5	Rapid change in population and decline in popularity
1977	Growing signs of troubles and tension
	700 empty units
	Habitat et Vie Sociale was established by government – Les Minguettes included
1981–2	Disorders – 'car rodeos' – riots – national reputation established as a social and housing disaster area
1981	Prime Minister launches National Commission to examine the causes and propose measures to tackle troubled ZUPs
	Association of the HLMs formed to prioritise localised management of Les Minguettes – staff inputs intensified
1982	Major demolition proposals
1983	Formation of state-funded *Développement Sociale des Quartiers* – emphasis on involving residents, meeting social needs, tackling economic issues
	Summer holiday camps organised
	Monmousseau demolished – three towers blown up
1984	2400 empty units
	New management plan
	Establishment of Lettings' Agency on estate between four HLMs – Lyons – Sud Logement
1985	Démocratie is under threat – 5 of 10 towers boarded up – population drops to 20 000
	Demolition of fourth tower at Monmousseau
	Zones à education prioritaire (educational priority areas) set up – Les Minguettes is targeted
1986	*Convention de Plan* with state and DSQ
	Number of empties starts to fall

1986–90	Renovation of buildings, environmental changes, reduction in number of large units, better security, insulation and social facilities
1989	International competition for redesign of Démocratie
1991	Down to 200 empty units – 25 000 inhabitants
	Riots in Vaulx-en-Velin, Lyons suburb, but not in Les Minguettes
1992	Continuing arguments over Démocratie
	Political rift between the Commune of Vénissieux and Courly, agglomeration of Lyons
	Still no transport link
1993	Démocratie comes down
1994	Increase in empty units to 300
	Serious rise in conflict in ZUPs around Lyons
1995	Precarious hold on conditions

Source: Author's visits and research.

8 Portrait of Kölnberg, Germany, 1974–95

ABOUT THE ESTATE

Kölnberg represented the *Zeitgeist* – spirit of the times – growth euphoria...
...The unfortunate building form of Kölnberg hinders social contact and communication between residents...
...The latent feeling of threat throughout Kölnberg makes the task of building trust with residents enormous...
...Prostitution, drugs, street crime, property damage and vandalism stamped the image of the estate on the public mind...
...Second-generation foreign youth is between two worlds, disoriented and without focus...
...The stigmatisation and discrimination against the inhabitants led to higher turnover and rising empty units. This caused rising rents (to cover losses) and falling value of property, which enhanced the stigma and at the same time accelerated the social decline of the estate. (City of Cologne Presentation, Windsor Workshop, 1991)

THE PROBLEM

The Kölnberg estate, 13 kilometres from the ancient cathedral city of Cologne, is set in rich agricultural land, adjacent to the small village of Meschenich. It juts out of the fields, as the cathedral juts out of the city. The tallest block, 90 metres high, has 26 storeys and 540 flats, a truly massive housing structure in heavy panel construction that immediately dwarfs the human spirit. Kölnberg was the highest density, most gigantesque estate in the survey.

Built in 1974, Kölnberg hit a social and financial crisis of such proportions that demolition was mooted for the 1300 flats complex. By 1987, over 50 per cent of its population was

Turkish and 70 per cent foreign. Over half the residents were under 16. Four hundred flats were empty, and many of the 600 scattered owners had defaulted, disappeared or sold up. Their financial investment was in ruins. The management companies responsible for running the estate had lost control and the City of Cologne had refused to help bail out the owners or managers, on the grounds that it was a privately built, profit-making estate.

CONSTRUCTION OF KÖLNBERG

The problems of Kölnberg began before the buildings went up, when the decision was taken to adopt an original method of funding, known in German as the *Bauherrenmodell,* to create a luxury, profit-making, private estate. Six hundred individual investors, often professional people such as dentists and doctors from Cologne, were enticed to part with their capital to a private development company on the promise of quick returns and tax rebates on rapid depreciation. The tax advantages that led to its construction were so great that in effect investors were virtually 'given' the property – at least, that was the original calculation, and that was a major cause of the estate's financial collapse ten years later.

Each investor was expected to buy two flats, borrow at low interest and write off the initial investment over eight years as depreciation. The rents and the value of the property were predicted to rise rapidly giving a quick return. Management costs would be low, as the small luxury one-bedroom flats were designed for higher-income tenants needing a *pied-à-terre* near Cologne. Each owner would have a flat for him or herself (virtually free) and one to rent. The developer was supposed to underwrite the risk with a buy-back guarantee at 130 per cent of the original price, making Kölnberg an attractive and seemingly risk-free investment. The German private rental market thrived on government incentives and tax concessions.

Kölnberg was an ultra-modern estate with high standards of amenity, its own swimming pool and tennis courts, individual car parking for each flat and the most extravagantly *avant-garde* design. Kölnberg was not designed as social housing for low-income families, but as private-rented housing for largely childless, white-collar and professional workers from Cologne. The nine high blocks of Kölnberg were packed together. They totally overshadowed the rural settlement onto which they were grafted and, with 4000 inhabitants, they more than doubled its size.

All the calculations and guarantees that enticed investors in swiftly collapsed, as from the outset demand was slack, far below expected levels. In addition, management costs soared and other charges, such as heating, rose astronomically in the wake of the oil crisis. Income to owners dropped due to slack demand, which in turn created a drop in the rental value of the property. But tenants had to pay higher total rents due to additional charges for services. Owners had to contribute far more to maintenance than had been anticipated. One result was that owners very soon began to shed themselves of the liability. Many investors suffered such high losses that they could no longer contribute to the running costs of the estate. They attempted either to sell their property or to invoke the buy-back guarantee of the company. As a result of this loss of commitment, standards plummeted and only disadvantaged tenants who suffered discrimination in the wider housing market were willing to live there.

The management of Kölnberg had been set up from the outset on the basis that each owner would pay an agreed fee out of rental income to an appointed management company, which would then assume responsibility for all services, all running costs and all tenant liaison. Germany, with its large and active private rental market, has a plethora of such management companies. As the rents fell and owners disappeared, so the income to the management companies dropped. Indeed, the whole system of appointing and controlling the management companies became inoperable. As the finances deteriorated, so the companies raised their charges. More and more costs were passed on to tenants.

The dream of profit and high-class tenants therefore never materialised. Market rent levels were constantly revised downwards due to the initial overpriced value and the intrinsic unpopularity of that style of housing. The depreciation of Kölnberg was so rapid that the tax deductions against depreciation failed to compensate for the investment losses, let alone offer an easy tax break that would be a bonus on an escalating asset. In the long run, this position might have been recovered but in the case of Kölnberg, the crisis was too extreme to allow confidence.

The housing market collapsed in the mid-1970s and Kölnberg entered an accelerating spiral. Most of the owners sold out as quickly as possible to second and third parties, thereby enhancing organisational chaos in the estate. Some owners proved impossible to trace, as the resale value of the property disintegrated and original undertakings to buy back property at 130 per cent of the original price within five years proved unsustainable. The development company failed to honour its commitment. Table 8.1 shows the disastrous string of events.

MANAGEMENT CRISIS

The financial and ownership crisis, under way virtually from the outset, was matched by a management crisis of equal severity. The nature of the estate called for intense and sophisticated management. But the disparate landlords were organised into an ownership body that delegated all direct management responsibility to a chain of companies that failed to integrate their services, and operated under the pressure to make a profit. This might have worked in a buoyant market. But the acute financial problems led to drastic reductions in service. Maintenance was seriously underresourced. Cleaning, heating, rubbish-removal and grounds maintenance proved far more costly than originally expected because of the highly complex building structure, but they could not be properly funded because of owners defaulting on their management fee, tenants' arrears and other costs.

With rising costs, the estate was difficult to market. There was a succession of management companies between 1974 and 1988, which gradually lost control. Facilities were abandoned, entrances, door phones, letter boxes and lifts became neglected, damaged and often unusable. The swimming pool was closed down; there were few nursery school places available for the large population of crowded families. The size of families living in Kölnberg was above average. The estate became very unpopular with residents and notorious among

Table 8.1   The financial collapse of Kölnberg

---

(1)   Original investment package
  – Tax concessions
  – Rising rents, therefore income to investors
  – Right to sell back at 130 per cent of original cost

(2)   Investors – 600 individual owners, each with two+ units

(3)   Payments to management company to run estate – about five different companies involved

(4)   Rises in repair and heating costs, due to oil price hike, inflation and building problems

(5)   Rent levels fall because of unpopular and much poorer conditions than private or social-rented flats – falling income for investors – resale value of property falls

(6)   Buy-back guarantee collapses because the financial package no longer holds water

(7)   Property prices collapse, some landlords disappear

(8)   Costs to tenants and landlords rise, because management and repair problems rise, but income to landlords falls – many landlords fail to pay management fee
  Heating charges rise rapidly after oil crisis

(9)   Management company cannot meet energy and water bills, as owners default on large scale

(10) Exodus of owners and tenants – many owners untraceable

(11) Forced auction of abandoned property – bought by speculative institutions with little commitment to estate

(12) Growing stigma as conditions deteriorate

(13) Lettings to allcomers on whatever terms – Kölnberg advertised to foreigners

(14) Reputation plummets – national press reports create infamous reputation

(15) Finances collapse
  – No repair reserves left
  – Heating bills cannot be paid (even where tenants are paying) because of landlords defaulting
  – Rent losses run to millions

(16) Management firms face bankruptcy

Source: Author's visits and research.

potential applicants. The adjacent village of Meschenich virtually ostracised the inhabitants and reportedly refused to allow them to use facilities in the village, such as shops and bars (Rodenkirchen Adult Education Institute, 1987). They regarded Kölnberg residents as 'ghetto people'. The internal and external tensions in social relations mounted.

LETTINGS SPIRAL

In an attempt to salvage the viability of the estate, the short-term expedient of specifically recruiting Turkish applicants, was set in train. Kölnberg was advertised in Cologne's Turkish community and a large influx of this minority group confirmed the estate's disastrous reputation in the eyes of the surrounding area, and 'accelerated its decline into a ghetto' (Schmidt, 1995). Alongside new Turkish tenants, other immigrants from Eastern Europe, mainly ethnic Germans, German households dependent on social assistance and other disadvantaged minorities moved in. The recruitment of marginalised and unpopular social groups was accompanied by management withdrawal, reduction in basic services, and a rapid exodus of more economically secure households. The small one-bedroom flats were originally let to a single, usually male tenant. But large immigrant families invariably joined the breadwinner and overcrowded the properties very quickly.

The growth in minority households went hand-in-hand with a steep rise in the number of empty units, leading to extremely marginal German households, who were rejected from other more stable areas, moving in. Many flats became squatted, as the level of empty flats rose to a third. Homeless, mainly German households, evicted for arrears, simply moved around the estate, escaping detection in the warren-like corridors and avoiding rent payment as they moved from one management company block to another. The different management companies had no system for tracing tenants through the estate.

In 1980, 30 per cent of the population was of Turkish origin. By 1987, this proportion had risen to over 50 per cent. Between 1985 and 1987, no German tenants at all moved into Kölnberg. German newspapers talked of a ghetto. Alongside the new Turkish occupants, the asylum-seekers, people dependent on social assistance, one-parent families, unemployed and single people, 300 gypsies came to Kölnberg where flats were readily available.

While the luxury estate was transformed into a social refuge, an illegal underworld of crime and prostitution, drug abuse and illegal occupancy also took root. The crime rate in Kölnberg rose to nearly four times the rate for the city of Cologne. Wanted criminals eventually found refuge in the chaotic conditions in Kölnberg (Rodenkirchen Adult Education Institute, 1987). They used empty flats as hiding places. Social conditions had deteriorated so far that the blocks had become virtually unpoliceable. No one knew who was supposed to live where, who the official or unofficial occupants were. The estate became a 'law-free zone where not even fully armed police dared to enter' (Schmidt, 1995). As a result, the conspicuous ethnic minority population became the target of public abuse, as the Turkish community was blamed for the social collapse and spiralling conditions. The estate was severely stigmatised by the fringe behaviour of a small minority of disruptive occupants the estate attracted (City of Cologne, 1991). In fact, managers maintained that 'drop-out' Germans were the cause of most problems, not immigrants.

German newspapers gave banner headlines to the chaotic conditions. The ghettoisation of Kölnberg was among the most extreme in all of West Germany and it had become known by 1987 as the worst estate in the country (Rodenkirchen Adult Education Institute, 1987). Rent arrears rose sharply and evictions increased. This in turn enhanced the void problem and earned an even worse reputation for the estate, as well as increasing the sense of insecurity. It led to even greater financial problems. Meanwhile, *bona fide* residents were marooned with virtually no services and the grounds of the estate were virtually abandoned. In the winter of 1987, heating bills could not be paid by the management company, due to owner defaults and arrears. Rent-paying tenants were literally faced with the total collapse of services.

The estate looked unsaveable. The two biggest blocks were more than half empty and their demolition was seriously countenanced as a way of making the rest of the estate manageable.

There was at this point a rapid turnover of managers, as company after company hit the cycle of bankruptcy.

PUBLIC HEARING ON KÖLNBERG – DEMOLITION?

The finances of Kölnberg proved to be the crux of the problem. The private ownership and tax privileges prevented the city or state from taking responsibility or investing in rehabilitation. At the same time, the lack of direct responsibility or involvement of the city led to a lack of basic social facilities, poor transport links and extreme isolation. But the insolvency of the management companies and the disappearance of the owners led to chaotic social conditions. There was no basis for the rescue of Kölnberg. The private investors had all but abandoned it. As a result, management companies repeatedly gave up and quitted. Meanwhile, the city refused to bail out the estate. The local village, of which it was a part, refused to have anything to do with it.

It was the publicly sponsored social institutions, and in particular the adult education service – *Volkhochschule* – that galvanised change. It was able to identify the true scale of the problem, force the various parties to adopt a changed course of action and play a catalytic role in the new initiative. At the end of 1987, the local adult education institute, which had been increasingly drawn in to the affairs of the estate by the deteriorating social situation and the intense needs of the population, set up a special public hearing on the future of Kölnberg. Local politicians, representatives of Cologne city administration, academics, architects, residents' representatives, Meschenich residents, tenants, the owners, local schools and social institutions, were all invited. National housing experts were asked to come and give their views and advice. The central problems were identified by participants as: 'unfriendly architecture for families'; extreme concentrations of 'problem families'; 'long, dark corridors'; frightening, dark, blind corners; lifts taking 20 minutes per journey; only one kindergarten; 'negative, pessimistic attitudes' and 'a great feeling of hatred' (Rodenkirchen Adult Education Institute, 1987).

Tenant participants highlighted run-down appearance, dirt, noise, lift breakdowns, ransacked letterboxes, lack of repairs, crime and vandalism, poor security, the social composition of the estate, unneighbourly behaviour by other tenants, lack of leisure activities. Tenants wanted a meeting place, more green space, secure entrances and letterboxes. Letterboxes at the foot of the massive towers were an obvious target for thieves and vandals. People could no longer receive money, information or private correspondence because entrances were destroyed and letterboxes became completely smashed and unusable. This had become a symbol of people's loss of the right to privacy, to security and to individual control. The entrance to one of the largest blocks was lined ceiling to floor and wall to wall with 240 individual letterboxes. It was an overwhelming system. Only the most assiduous manager could stay on top. As turnover and empty units increased, so it ran out of control.

The hearing identified the wider organisational and social problems that made Kölnberg virtually unmanageable:

- defaulting owners;
- lack of provision for the large, densely crowded child population;
- conflict between the village of Meschenich and the estate;
- serious tensions among the inhabitants of Kölnberg;
- steeply rising costs and charges, making the flats unaffordable;
- instability and inconsistencies of management companies;
- strong regional decline, reducing demand for housing;
- the oppressive structure and design, unused basements and underground garages, creating an alienating atmosphere.

The hearing invited proposals for the future of Kölnberg and, by bringing together the central actors, made the adoption of those proposals possible.

PROPOSALS

The option of demolition – even partial demolition of the two largest and most difficult blocks – was ruled out by laws governing multiple ownership, which guaranteed the right of

each individual owner to refuse demolition permission. Since
so many owners were untraceable, it was impossible to get
through this legal hurdle. Also lack of alternative suitable
housing in the Cologne region for the 900 tenants made
wholesale demolition impractical, in spite of the number of
empty units. The rehousing problem was magnified by the
reputation of the estate and by the stigmatised population left
in the blocks.

The hearing proposed small, quick measures to improve the
environment immediately. Participants supported the involvement of tenants in self-help and community activities; education and skills training for residents and youth employment
initiatives. The belief in, and heavy reliance on resident-based
solutions was conspicuous but the proposed role for the management company was the linchpin of the rescue plan. It was
clear that the organisation of the estate could only be put on a
sound footing with a reliable, resourceful and determined
manager. But who would take on such a liability? Rent losses
and turnover were out of control; repairs and maintenance
were collapsing; caretakers were swamped. There had been a
rapid succession of failed managers. Conditions were chaotic.

The central tasks for any rescue attempt would be:

- to stabilise the estate and integrate it with the surrounding
  area;
- to help existing residents cope and attract a wider social
  mix;
- to draw residents into the improvement process and overcome their hostility to the estate;
- to sort out a viable financial package and manage the
  process with rigour.

Policies to tackle both the lettings' problem and resident involvement were to be mutually reinforcing. Empty flats had to
be restored as a prerequisite for letting the 400 or more vacant
units. New, more stable tenants would reduce the isolation
and 'ghettoisation', would generate more rent income, which
in turn would attract better facilities and make it possible to
offer support to existing residents.

The hearing produced a complete consensus that crime
and disruptive activities, such as drug-pushing, prostitution,

violence and illegal occupancy, should be stamped out. But there was never a question, once demolition was ruled out, that the *bona fide*, rent-paying tenants should be displaced or replaced, rather that they should receive support and better services. The fact of a majority foreign community at Kölnberg was accepted. It was recognised that they had been badly served by the private owners and managers.

Disaffected, German lawbreakers, rather than foreigners, were identified as the main source of social problems. Some of them were heavily implicated in drug-related crime and, having rejected social norms, accepted few normal constraints on their behaviour. Strong policing was unanimously endorsed as essential to re-establishing control over conditions.

New managers would have to agree to and be able to implement several vital measures:

- tight control over tenancies and over conditions;
- links with the city to allow normal civic services;
- a strong tenant orientation to overcome apathy and alienation and to enhance control and integration;
- an advice and information office to help tenants;
- repairs to entrances, letterboxes and doors to create secure access and to give tenants normal rights of privacy;
- a concerted attack on arrears and empty property;
- the restoration of financial viability;
- more balanced lettings policies to make the community more integrated.

MANAGEMENT TAKEOVER

The most important achievement of the hearing was to open up the possibility of substantial change. It galvanised high-level support for the estate community and it showed up the abysmal failure of the private owner. In 1988, both the City of Cologne and the *Volkshochschule* (adult education institute) opened offices on the estate, in order to help achieve greater integration, better services and support for social involvement. However, these efforts could only take effect if coupled with more radical changes.

The Kölnberg hearing attracted the attention of a major private company, keen to tackle the problems of the estate through a more coherent strategy. The Hillebrand management company took over the general responsibility for Kölnberg's management on 1 January 1988. Herbert Hillebrand, the head of the company, had conducted a management review of the estate after the Kölnberg hearing (Hillebrand, 1988). His report identified the core management problems as: too high inclusive rents; too many owners; too many perverse incentives (for example, owners could claim a special subsidy for unlet flats); too many 'difficult' families; too high a concentration of minorities; lack of support for integration measures; and lack of maintenance investment. Management companies, at owners' insistence, had ended up repaying maintenance funds to owners, to compensate for financial losses.

Conditions were, in Hillebrand's view, at the point of total disintegration. The backlog of repairs ran into millions. Technical services on the estate were collapsing. Owners' debts were increasing rapidly. There were no common or enforceable management rules. Finances were breaking down, as special charges were imposed on the few solvent investors in order to keep anything functioning.

Herbert Hillebrand proposed to Cologne City Council that in exchange for city funds to renovate empty flats, the owners' company would reinvest in the general estate environment in the ratio of five to one. The city agreed to DM 1 500 000 for a rolling programme of empty flats restoration. It would also fund a rent guarantee and 'debt underwriting' for families nominated to the estate by the city. The owners committed themselves to DM 7 000 000 for upgrading the estate by 1995.

The city gained nomination rights to all the flats it funded. One third went to ethnic German newcomers from Eastern Europe (*Aussiedler*). As a result of the agreement between Herr Hillebrand and the City of Cologne, 40 per cent of free units on the estate thereafter became available for 'social' lettings.

By levering in financial support from the City of Cologne and by matching that commitment with significant investment over several years from his own company resources, Hillebrand was able to start the laborious process of regaining control over lettings, repairs, rent income, cleaning and other tenancy matters. When once the rent income started to rise, services could be enhanced. There was a ratchet effect as each newly occupied flat made it possible to expand the service. Hillebrand's improvement strategy was simple, carefully focused and aimed at immediate impact. For the buildings he proposed repainting staircases, landings, corridors and renewing entrances with door controls; renewing letterboxes and putting name plates on doors, bells and boxes; restoring and upgrading lifts; renovating basements and garages, finding alternative uses for some multistorey garages; repairing roofs and roof terraces.

For the environment, he proposed cleaning up surroundings to buildings; restoring the swimming pool and other facilities; improving the general infrastructure of the estate by providing community facilities and local services; introducing traffic management; involving young estate residents in the environmental work; and introducing intensive, continual maintenance services for all common areas.

In order to meet the tenants' social needs and involve them in the rescue efforts, he determined to provide support for tenants' organisations and activities; set up special services to help with social problems; employ young residents to help engage their commitment and offer them training.

Management change would be the pivot of Hillebrand's approach to the estate. His company would introduce tight, intensive, estate-based management; increase caretaking and repair staff; make a social nominations agreement with the City of Cologne; organise lettings from within the estate; get rid of illegal tenants; enforce meticulous basic standards; recover rent arrears, owners' debts, and restore financial organisation.

Hillebrand's approach was to negotiate hard with all parties, including the tenants, and engage in a clear agreement that all sides could accept. He chased every problem through to resolution, working on many fronts simultaneously. He gave high priority to basic problems, such as repair, rubbish, security, resident liaison and support. He invested in core services, adopting a hands-on approach to management. His brother took on the job of managing the estate and, over 18 months, brought the central problems under control.

Hillebrand played the dominant role in sorting out the management of the estate on behalf of the owners, building a new and successful partnership with the City. A smaller company, Stefanac, was responsible for managing a section of the estate and also contributed to some of the changes that worked.

THE ROLE OF THE CITY

Large cities like Cologne increasingly depend on being able to house low-income households in 'social' housing on the edge of cities. The city needed Kölnberg for this reason. The private owners could not fulfil the 'social' role alone. The rescue depended crucially on Cologne City Council becoming directly involved in planning the restoration and in tackling the social problems, as well as supporting a financial rescue package. Under the pressures of reunification and waves of new immigrants, many of German origin, the city became a willing partner in the Kölnberg rescue. The city was so desperate to house needy families that it undertook to underwrite arrears to prevent evictions. The involvement of the city clearly did not lead to greater social integration. In many ways, it enhanced anxieties about the social viability of the community. But it did bring about essential reinvestment, helped fill the empty units, and stabilised conditions. It enabled the management company to reimpose controls, thereby making the estate viable again.

One of the important new initiatives was the city's support for youth training and employment, to help upgrade and maintain the environment, to build children's playgrounds and to generate skills for work. The youth employment scheme, funded through government youth training programmes, got off the ground in 1988 with 20 young, unemployed people working on the estate, with supportive training from two teachers. The management company contributed to this project at a cost of DM 140 000 per year, while the city provided DM 750 000 for materials. The crowded open spaces on the estate were made green, clean, planted, and carefully maintained. A barbecue area was built, the bowling area and football pitch reinstated, and an adventure playground created. The swimming pool was built over and made into a kindergarten.

There were many problems in organising unskilled, disaffected, untrained young people, most of whom had *no* experience of employment, no school-leavers' qualifications at all and no previous access to normal jobs. Recruitment was difficult and the drop-out rate was high (Hofmann, 1989). But over two years from 1988–90, the young trainees painted entrances and corridors, designed and executed murals, restored grounds, and created outdoor recreation areas.

The City of Cologne set up a working group of city employees and staff from different organisations active in the estate initiatives, including schoolteachers, in order to co-ordinate their inputs. A Steering Committee for the estate was made up of representatives of the investors, of the Hillebrand company, of the City of Cologne, and of tenants. Its aim was to oversee the implementation of all the above measures with a united approach.

MANAGEMENT RESCUE

The management company took a firm grip on the estate with surprising speed. Open areas were replanted, protected and maintained; a tenants' meeting room was provided; proper controls were instituted over tenancies and for the first time in years, tenants had their own names inserted in their doorbells and letterboxes. From the moment when the City authorities agreed to the nominations and rent guarantee system, affecting a third of all units, it became possible to implement other changes. Squatters and other illegal occupiers and activities had no room to operate, when once empty units were reinstated and rent income rose sufficiently to expand the services. As more Turks and *Aussiedler* (ethnic Germans) filled the estate, the crime rate fell. This supported the finding from the hearing that crime did not derive mainly from the foreign communities in Kölnberg.

The overall impact of the rescue was startling, even dramatic. There were no empty units by 1989 and any vacancy was relet immediately. There was a waiting list of 100 applicants. Some households that had moved out in the period of most acute decline began to move back. The estate, for all its over-whelming physical scale, was well-run, attractive and clean. Tenants, the vast majority of whom were now either Turkish or East European, supported the change in management style, the strict controls and the rising standards. Two management offices were opened on the estate, as well as a caretaking security centre. In all, including management, caretaking, social support, adult education, there were six offices on the estate. The Hillebrand housing company had 20 employees, including caretakers, based on the estate.

Caretaking and security

By far the most important change in the management of the estate was the introduction of security controls, combined with intensive caretaking. A full-time caretaker was made respons-ible for each block. A glass-fronted control room was built out from the base of the largest block, from which the whole estate could be watched. The superintendent-caretaker con-trolled the estate from this room, playing a role more akin to manager than caretaker. A closed-circuit, high technology se-curity system covered the estate constantly, checked by a watchman working under the superintendent. Video cameras and microphones were placed on every landing and corridor, in every entrance and lift. In that way, from a single vantage point, the supervising caretaker/manager could be in touch with every part of the estate and detect any trouble or break-down. There were 24 computerised video screens around the ceiling of the control room, above the large glass windows, recording all movements of lifts and reporting any problems from all over the estate. All caretakers reported to this central control room.

Security conditions were transformed, making other man-agement measures possible. The crime that had previously been out of control virtually disappeared. There were no longer frequent incidents because detection was instanta-neous. Tenants reported to the control room for keys, for access, for collecting messages, and for any other reason that might arise. It was the nerve centre of estate management. The superintendent caretaker explained that vandalism, damage and disruption had more or less disappeared, simply due to the constant presence of caretaking and repairs staff and close, careful supervision of the blocks. This was confirmed by the police (Dixon, 1995). Tenants were positive about the better conditions, felt more secure and more able to refer problems to the caretakers. The superintendent argued that the consistent management presence had so boosted tenants' confidence and strengthened the community, that previous patterns of abuse had simply disappeared. Standards at Kölnberg had risen to a level comparable to other more popular estates.

Cleaning and refuse

The management company was driven by the core aim of a high-quality service. 'Cleanliness and control' were mottos of Hillebrand. The cleaning of the estate, including the blocks, lifts, internal corridors and parking areas, was carried out under contract to the management company. Refuse was collected and removed several times a day. This unusual level of service was considered essential to cope with the very high density. All areas were cleaned on a daily basis.

Hillebrand believed that if the estate and all its internal areas were clean, it would be lettable. The internal corridors, lifts and entrances, were indeed spotless in true Germanic style. In 1990 it was hard to imagine the decay that had pervaded every corner of the estate only three years previously. This standard was maintained over four years and in 1995 the estate was still meticulously run (Dixon, 1995).

Repairs

Two full-time repairs handymen were permanently employed to go round the estate, carrying out minor repairs. Even the smallest repairs were carried out as quickly as possible. A painter repainted over any graffiti in every entrance daily. There was no graffiti anywhere on the estate at the time of visiting. Each flat was fully renovated and redecorated prior to letting. The owners' management fee was used to pay for the repairs service. The management company took the view that most tenants were too poor to pay for repairs themselves, even small repairs, and that they would not get done unless the management company did them. Speed of repair would prevent decay or damage and ensure the rapid reletting of empty property. It would also ensure the co-operation of tenants in the company's work.

SOCIAL AND COMMERCIAL FACILITIES

The improved management was not sufficient to overcome the social problems of the estate. Cologne City Council, the management companies and the adult education office jointly supported special tenant initiatives and provided or encouraged additional facilities, to try and integrate the disparate ethnic groups and to cater for the intense community needs.

New social facilities were modest in style and scale but appeared to make an important difference to the level of activity. A church-based charity, Caritas, supported a women's centre, offering among other things self-defence courses, sewing classes and German language classes. A children's centre, kindergarten and play areas had been funded by Cologne City Council. A homework centre for children had been set up. There was a special advice centre for refugees. Social science students were working with tenants and with children on the playground. There was a Turkish women's group and a single parents' group. The *Volkshochschule* (Adult Education Institute) maintained its office on the estate and remained involved in community affairs. Cologne City Council and its Social Services Department had also set up an office to work with tenants, offering family support and advice on social problems.

Two major new additions to the estate aimed at helping families and young people. The City of Cologne built a youth centre in the vicinity of Kölnberg, staffed by two social workers. Its task was to initiate activities for youth, both from Kölnberg and from Meschenich. The aim was to foster contact between the two communities. The two management companies, Hillebrand and Stefanac, financed the building of a children's day care centre, which was subsequently rented to Cologne City Council to help fill the gap in childcare provision.

Along the base of one block was a small group of Turkish-run shops, offering Turkish produce. There were two mosques on the estate because of the large Moslem community. Two Turkish coffee houses, a video shop, a chemist and a German bakery were also flourishing on the edge of the estate. But there were no workshops, factories or other employment opportunities and the estate still had only a poor (hourly) bus service linking the estate to Cologne. This was a crippling disadvantage. There was talk of rationalising and improving the transport links but this was slow to materialise. Work opportunities were therefore difficult to come by (Schmidt, 1995).

TENANTS' INVOLVEMENT

The transformation in conditions, in spite of wider unsolved problems, was possible partly because of the continuous efforts to involve the tenants. Tenants participated in joint meetings with the management company. Their support for the changes was crucial. A major disappointment was the collapse in 1991 of the tenants' initiative, set up by the *Volkshochschule* to organise self-help groups and social activities. It lasted for nine months but intergroup hostility caused its early disintegration. Community problems were magnified between the long-standing Turkish community and the more recently arrived ethnic Germans from Poland and elsewhere. The Poles looked down on the Turkish community as plainly foreign, even though the Turks, particularly the younger generation, had lived there for far longer and could speak fluent German, often better than new arrivals from Eastern Europe. Some were born in Germany. Ethnic Germans held them responsible for the low status of Kölnberg and blamed them for its separation from the wider German community. Their central ambition was integration into Germany and emergency measures and funds were introduced to speed this process. But as a result of problems throughout Germany around this issue, some of the special funds have now dried up. The Turks resented the instant citizenship rights of ethnic Germans who could not speak German and the special funds for their integration. Turkish residents, often of 20 or 30 years' standing, were victims of continuous hostility and discrimination, (City of Cologne, 1991). *Aussiedler* accused Turks of clinging to their cultural heritage, claiming that oriental and Islamic practices were responsible for transforming Kölnberg into a 'ghetto'.

Each group had its own networks and both groups related to outside bodies working on the estate better than to each other. For this reason, the emphasis on tenant involvement could only have limited effect, and many hopes of community integration foundered on simmering unease. The tensions underlined the need for long-term community support and measures to counter pressures that otherwise could lead to further conflict (City of Cologne Adult Education Institute, 1994). The 'ghetto reputation' of the estate was reinforced by its continuing separateness, its ethnic rehousing role and residents' difficulty in connecting the estate with the outside world (Schmidt, 1995).

The Adult Education Institute and social services of Cologne City Council were alarmed by the recurring community problems and the difficulty in persuading tenants to work together and accept each other's differences (Schmidt, 1995). This was an aspect of Kölnberg's unusual community that would possibly take a generation to resolve. The social problems of the estate were still intense in 1995. There was still a shortage of school places; relations with Meschenich were still sensitive; ethnic tensions were still strong; Kölnberg was still unattractive to Germans; access to jobs was still difficult; poor transport, language barriers and general discrimination made residents into easy scapegoats for some of the wider problems facing German society. In 1993, in an attempt to prevent further 'ghettoisation', all new lettings at Kölnberg had been reserved for Germans. However, the strategy failed and the goal of blocking lettings to foreigners to increase integration was quickly abandoned (Dixon, 1995). But continued social supports of many different kinds helped the restored Kölnberg community to survive.

The management complexity of Kölnberg and the detailed features of its rescue were of a different order from the other estates. We summarise the main elements of the management rescue below.

Physical rescue measures

- Doors, letterboxes, bells reinstated
- Corridors, lifts, entrances cleaned, painted, secured
- Mirrors installed in lifts to deter vandalism
- Environment reclaimed, restored with youth trainees
- Money from Cologne reinstates empty flats, buildings made viable
- Facilities improved – tenants' flat, nursery, play area.

Financial rescue measures

- Cash from City of Cologne to reinstate empty flats – rent guarantees – nomination guarantees
- Illegal occupants evicted – rents brought under control
- Services funded at lower charge per tenant as income rises
- Owners support new deal in exchange for small return.

Management rescue measures

- Owners agree rescue with management company
- Security controls to stop vandalism
- Constant repairs/painting/graffiti removal
- Caretakers help maintain conditions
- Intensive repair and painting as tenants cannot afford to pay
- Tenants' meetings to canvass views and support
- Eviction of trouble-makers, illegal occupants, non-payers
- Control restored over tenancies
- Rent income rises, more flats reclaimed, staff affordable

Lettings rescue measures

- Lettings agreement with city
- Estate lettings office to control access/market flats
- Access by ethnic Germans – ambitious/upwardly mobile
- High-standard repair/makes flats lettable
- Reinstated doors, bells, letterboxes – give positive signal to applicants
- Waiting list of 100 for estate in 1991

Resident involvement and support for rescue measures

- Tenants' committee
- Tenants' meeting room
- Security office open to tenants
- Intensive staffing to help tenants
- Efforts to integrate Turkish community
- Social initiatives with City of Cologne
- Adult education input to community development
- Ethnic and women's support groups
- Social initiatives to develop intergroup relations/reduce conflict
- Children's and youth programmes
- More play areas
- Church support for women's initiatives

CONCLUSIONS

By 1994, the estate was in a more stable financial situation. The owners had a lettable asset with secure rent income. The management company was investing much higher amounts in core services and, as a result, was able to retain full occupancy and a full rent roll. The investment in repair and management gave the company its financial base, since each additional staff person could be funded from ten more occupied flats. Residents were receiving high-quality services for their rents – in the region of £100 a week including the expensive service charges. A German housing expert commented – 'Housing the poor can be economically feasible in Germany, if well managed' (Kreibich, 1995).

The Kölnberg experience illustrates the dangers of private financial risk-taking, the distortions of public subsidy, the centrality of the local authority's enabling role, the value of intensive estate-based management and the need to work closely with residents, attending to social as well as narrowly defined housing needs. In spite of continuing strains in ethnic relations, the estate in 1994 was incomparably better-run, more stable, more popular and more viable – thanks to a combination of efforts by the City of Cologne and the two management companies, with the co-operation of residents and the advantage of greatly increased demand. The overall impact of the rescue was startling, even dramatic. Any vacancy was relet immediately. There was a waiting list of 100 applicants. The estate, for all its overwhelming physical scale, was well-run, attractive and clean (see Figure 8.1, p. 192). Tenants, the vast majority of whom were now either Turkish or East European, supported the change in management style, the strict controls and the rising standards. The most striking aspect of Kölnberg was the combination of physical gigantism, stark isolation and visible poverty. Within that setting, the highly efficient, tenant-oriented, security-conscious, privately-run management service was curiously impressive. It was all the more strange for its success in restoring such a complex and difficult estate, almost entirely through management initiative, tenant-based activity, intensive repair and custodial services. The secret of success lay in the concerted approach of the Hillebrand company to every aspect of estate management. Neither the population of the estate nor the physical structure had been radically altered. But certain illegal activities had been prohibited. A vulnerable population was now better protected and more likely to survive. The estate itself looked clean, well-run and impressively multiracial. There were large numbers of people milling around the estate when I visited, creating an atmosphere of confidence and friendliness. However, the visible poverty of residents was far greater than on any other German estate in the study. Kölnberg did look very much like another country.

The most spectacular sensation was arriving at the 26th floor of the giant block, looking down the 100-foot long internal corridor, with 20 doors leading off it; looking out onto the tiny play areas and the glass-fronted control room, the massive concrete blocks dwarfing the German countryside. The adjacent village of Meschenich looked like another planet. Kölnberg was the most spectacular monument to gross urban design and financial gambling. But it had been restored to order through sheer crude need and strong management.

Note: Special thanks are due to Stephan Schmidt at Cologne City Council for his advice, careful checking and correcting of details of this account.

Figure 8.1   Kölnberg – general view

KEY DATES AT KÖLNBERG

1972	Decision to build – 600 owners.
	Cologne City Council gives planning permission.
1974–5	Kölnberg is built to luxury standards.
	Oil crisis, high costs, rent values fall, interest rates rise. Therefore repayments become difficult and sale values collapse!
1975–80	Mounting financial and lettings problems.
	Original owners start to pull out.
	Rapid turnover of owners, as management costs soar.
	Charges rise, management and repairs standards fall.
	Flats advertised to foreigners to stave off lettings crisis.
1983–5	Rent losses escalate – properties auctioned – only religious banks willing to buy some flats.
	Management company bankrupt due to defaulting owners.
1984	Twenty arson attacks on estate.
1985	Threat of water and heating cut-offs – DM 3 500 000 owed by owners.
	Crime rate/squatting/arrears soar – nearly four times average.
1985–7	No Germans move to estate *at all.*
1987	400 empty flats.
	70 per cent of population foreigners, 50 per cent under 16.
	Kölnberg hearing in Cologne – convened by City Adult Education Institute under the title 'Should the estate be restored or demolished?'
	Tenants consulted.
1988	New management company takes over (Hillebrand).
	First ever meeting of owners; programme of re-investment drawn up.
	Cologne City Council agrees to help with renovation and reletting – agrees to support social initiatives.
1988–90	Influx of 'ethnic Germans' and asylum seekers, as empty flats are restored. Population rises from

	2500 to 4000. Cologne City nominates emergency cases in return for restoring property.
1989	Tenants' initiative set up, social initiatives. Tensions continue between ethnic groups.
1990	All flats let, management becomes viable.
1991	Short-term support projects come to an end. Estate fully occupied, waiting list grows.
1995	Intensive management still in place. Estate full, environment well maintained, buildings spotless, new nursery, play areas, etc.

Source: Author's visits and research.

9 Portrait of Broadwater Farm Estate, Britain, 1966–95

ABOUT THE ESTATE

Because of the danger of flooding, it was decided to locate the dwellings at first floor level...

...The hasty design and construction of the estate has been repented at leisure... The sheer scale and design of the estate are the fundamental problems and these cannot be modified. The physical improvements... may improve the quality of life on the estate marginally but are unlikely to improve its popularity... The long-term future for the estate seems very bleak, at best the local authority can hope to make it tolerable for the next decade or so, and eventually the possibility of demolition and replacement by a popular housing form may have to be considered. (Burbidge *et al*., 1981)

The estate is so monolithic... It's like Windscale. (Resident, 1977)

The problems of the estate were far bigger than they [the local authority] could cope with. (Power, 1979)

Many tenants live in constant fear of robbery and violence... Relations between black tenants and management is largely one of confrontation. (Pitt, 1982)

The most ferocious, the most vicious [riot] ever seen on the mainland. (Deputy Assistant Police Commissioner M. Richards, 1986)

Their impact [community leaders] in restoring a sense of pride among often bitter and disaffected youths should not be underrated... It is hard to see how dialogue and co-operation could ever be developed without the influence of such leaders... I do not feel I would be honest if I undersold the achievement of what has happened here. (Tricia Zipfel in Gifford, 1986)

Instead of spending £50 000 000 on the place, they should have sent in the bulldozers. (Quoted in *The Guardian*, 20 April 1993)

AN INAUSPICIOUS BEGINNING

The decision to build Broadwater Farm in 1966 was taken by Haringey Council under strong political pressure from central government to develop large-scale housing estates to help the inner-city clearance programme.

Within the borough of Haringey where the estate is located, there was a high proportion of poor quality, private rented accommodation – estimated at over 50 per cent of the housing stock in 1965 – and a large ethnic minority population. Housing need was severe. The council was anxious to act quickly and a 'sketch design with an outline bill of quantities' was the only guidance for big builders when they were invited to bid for the scheme of over 1000 flats. Taylor Woodrow Anglian won the contract for £5 600 000, a very high price at the time given that the land was 'free'. The estate was to be built on publicly owned, poorly drained allotments on the edge of Lordship Park.

From the beginning, the estate was dogged with misfortune. Key design elements, such as enclosing the underground garages and the service pipes to the blocks, were omitted by mistake from the specification but were too expensive to include later. The borough architect proceeded with the scheme, after realising these omissions, because the contract with Taylor Woodrow Anglian was signed and it was 'too late to turn back'. The estate was built on stilts for fear of flooding and included three miles of linked walkways on four levels above ground.

Lettings were difficult from the outset. The flats were designated for Haringey's clearance families, but only half the units could be filled this way as the slum clearance programme itself was running out of steam. The rest went to low priority cases, lone mothers, and young single people. A mixture of young and old in one of the two 18-storey tower blocks proved a disastrous mistake. By 1973, the estate had a reputation for crime, insecurity and poor services. The estate was 20 minutes from a station and not well linked to centres of employment. Many of its residents were poor, often with a background of homelessness; increasingly they were black. Lettings, problems increased its stigma and isolation. By 1976, the refusal rate was 55 per cent and the estate had twice the turnover of the borough as a whole. There were six times the level of referrals to social services (Power, 1987a). As conditions on the estate plummeted, the Housing Committee took strong remedial action, blocking all lettings to homeless families and single parents, unless they specifically asked for Broadwater Farm. The idea was to create positive identification with the estate and a sense of belonging. The new lettings policy produced an almost immediate turnaround and, within two years, the estate had improved to such an extent that the access policies were relaxed again.

INVESTIGATION OF DIFFICULT-TO-LET ESTATES

It was in the middle of this period that the Department of the Environment visited Broadwater Farm, as one of its case studies in the nationwide investigation of difficult-to-let housing estates. There was a mixture of positive and negative findings, the most salient of which were that caretaking and cleaning services were to a high standard and that interracial community contact appeared relaxed and friendly. But roofs and decks leaked, crime and insecurity were big issues, lettings' policies seriously stigmatised the estate, the design and layout of the estate were 'monotonous' and overwhelming in scale. The investigation concluded that demolition within a few years must be a serious possibility because of the generally harsh conditions and inhuman proportions.

In 1979, when the Priority Estates Project was set up, Haringey Council applied to join the experiment, proposing Broadwater Farm as the participant estate. This was rejected mainly on the grounds of the extreme severity of the social, management and security problems. Both staff and residents appeared swamped. The estate was not regularly policed. Most of the 12 shops were empty. The doctor had left the estate. The Tenants' Association was all-white in spite of nearly half the population being of minority origin. The small community hall was bleak and decayed in the extreme. Security doors on the tower blocks were broken. Decks were flooded. The walkways appeared desolate and abandoned:

> There is no feeling of movement about the estate in spite of the number of people. (Power, 1979)

There was little ground for believing that the estate could be made to work as a demonstration project for the national rescue of unpopular estates. Conditions appeared unsalvageable.

Between 1979 and 1982, the estate took a nose-dive into deeper troubles. The police were frequently called in to emergencies on the estate. They used the now disbanded and ill-reputed Special Patrol Group as reinforcement, creating deep resentment among young people, particularly black youth. In 1981 and 1982, there were clashes and disorders on several occasions and relations between the police and the black community became tense and often hostile. This division came to include many older, more established residents, particularly mothers. By 1982, the shopping precinct around the base of the Ziggurat or scissor block, Tangmere, was virtually derelict and the large podium which housed the shops was a windswept, bleak no-man's-land on stilts. There were 75 empty flats on the estate (see Figure 9.1, p. 215).

NEW INITIATIVES INSTIGATED BY RESIDENTS

In 1982, the Labour council lost control of Broadwater Farm ward. It had been considered a safe Labour area and electoral defeat shook the council. The council suddenly started to listen and react. In 1983, in response to pressure from the all-white Tenants' Association, the council agreed to the police setting up a base in one of the abandoned shops in the precinct. This provoked a major outcry from the suspicious and now alienated black community. The police move was stopped in its tracks. Instead, a shop front was given over to the newly formed and predominantly black Youth Association, set up by a long-time resident of Jamaican origin and mother of six.

The forceful and charismatic style of the resident leader immediately won the respect of some of the toughest young people and of the council. With virtually no resources other than the shop front, their own energy and powers of persuasion, the Youth Association operated as a voluntary youth club, cafe, advice centre, estate watchdog and lobby group. But they were operating in a vacuum.

The council then began to decentralise its housing service, placing more staff in the mid-Tottenham area. It found funding for improvements, particularly security; it agreed to open an office on the estate; and it introduced a special lettings' system for Broadwater Farm with local accompanied viewings and more choice for homeless applicants, so that people were no longer forced to move there. It abandoned its block on internal estate transfers to relieve tenant dissatisfaction.

By 1983, the council had set up a full-time neighbourhood office on the estate; had upgraded the caretaking service by appointing a resident estate superintendent, after sending him on a year's training course; allocated twice the ratio of management and administrative staff to the estate, compared with other areas; based a full-time repairs team on the estate; and set up a special panel, with councillors, neighbourhood staff and residents to take control of conditions, directly answerable to the Chief Executive of the council. The Broadwater Farm Panel effectively cut out layers of bureaucracy and left the local staff clearly in control.

At the same time, the council approached the Department of the Environment with the renewed aim of collaborating with the Priority Estates Project (PEP). This time, PEP agreed to help with tenant consultations on capital improvements. Over time PEP became deeply enmeshed in the fortunes of the estate. PEP played the role of honest broker, running block consultations over improvements, supporting key tenants' leaders and the local office, working with the Broadwater Farm Panel, the energetic and go-ahead Director of Housing and other services.

Residents' representatives were given a unique say in staff appointments to the estate under the new local management system. They were represented on all interview panels as a way of ensuring the selection of sympathetic and committed staff. There was a Council decision to offer the maximum number of estate-based jobs to residents and to recruit black staff. Half the new locally based team were residents and half were black. By 1985, there were 40 local staff, including repairs workers and caretakers.

All these changes were little short of revolutionary in council terms. They had a dramatic impact on conditions. The number of empty units dropped from 75 down to 15. The repairs team liaised directly with the local office and responded quickly to all manner of repairs requests, often far outside the normal procedures and guidelines. As a result, tenant feedback was increasingly positive. The new open-plan office within the Tangmere precinct received 700 callers a month. It thrived on contact, on responsiveness and on demand. The staff were trained in working as a team, operating colour-blind, liaising with community representatives, and keeping formal barriers and procedures to an absolute minimum.

The positive changes were underpinned by two other important factors. Firstly, the caretaking and cleaning service was intensified and upgraded. The goals were clear – lift cleaning and checking daily; deck and walkway cleaning and patrolling all day; graffiti removal daily; and staircase cleaning three times a week. These targets were strictly enforced by the outstanding resident estate superintendent, using some of the most advanced and efficient equipment. His one-year training course in cleaning and caretaking supervision had a remarkable effect on confidence and performance. All staff had walkie-talkie radios and kept in constant contact. They could be called on to help with any emergencies and were expected to back each other up. This caretaking system, with nine staff, made Broadwater Farm one of the cleanest and best maintained estates of its kind in the country. Visitors from all over the world came to study its style of service, of community involvement, of youth action and of local control.

The physical upgrading began as soon as the local office was set up. Over two years, more than £1 000 000 was spent on replacing all glass in common areas (mostly broken) with diamond glaze, unbreakable glass – causing a revolution in appearance and condition. Floor surfaces were covered with rubberised material to dull sound and to facilitate cleaning. Corridor walls were brightly painted. Most importantly, flimsy and insecure individual front doors, often on internal corridors where intruders could operate unseen, were replaced with strong steel framed doors and extra security locks. The crime rate on the estate came tumbling down and, by 1984, Broadwater Farm was no longer hard to let. The estate had a far lower crime rate than the surrounding area. Princess Diana came and played pool with the young residents; Sir George Young, then Junior Minister for Inner Cities, helped to secure an Urban Aid grant. Coach loads of German, French, Scandinavian and American housing experts visited. The tenants spoke at conferences; the Youth Association advised other groups. The Priority Estates Project used Broadwater Farm as a model. Bernie Grant, the Chair of Housing, later to become MP for the area, was one of its strongest backers.

The Youth Association began to flourish and expand under the more orderly and responsive council management. With an Urban Aid grant, a co-operative laundry and greengrocer's were set up. Training workshops in photography, dressmaking, design and hairdressing were established. Out of concern for the predominantly white, elderly population, the Youth Association negotiated a meals-on-wheels service and lunch club with Social Services, to be run by the young adults of the Youth Association. An exchange with Jamaica was organised and a summer festival took place to celebrate the fast growing community pride.

FRAGILE PROGRESS

The new local and open-door approach was not without its problems, and Broadwater Farm remained under all circumstances difficult to manage. There was at least one violent confrontation between an angered and difficult tenant and a member of staff, where the staff person ended up in hospital. But the response of staff was to resist putting up screens, to discuss with community leaders the limits of tolerance and then to agree strict enforcement of basic conditions fairly. The staff, though obviously vulnerable to pressure and to problems, believed that their professional approach and their ability to deliver a good local service would prevail over hostility, tension and conflict. The job seemed doable after all.

There were, however, several missing ingredients. Rent arrears for the estate remained absurdly high. The debt was on average £350. Local staff explained this partly by the fact that over 80 per cent of the population was in receipt of benefits. But this did not satisfactorily account for the high debts, given the 100 per cent housing benefit rules at that time. Nor did it augur well for the long-term stability of the local services. Repairs were to a high standard but the input was much more intensive than for other areas. High costs coupled with failure to collect rents made the service vulnerable under less favourable political leadership. Even more problematic was the lack of a local budget for the local office. There were no incentives for local staff to cut costs since they were given no financial discretion or control. No one knew how much anything cost, nor whether the costs were reasonable, and therefore the whole 'overcostly' experiment later became an easy target for cuts.

Broadwater Farm received an excellent service from 1983 because the political will was there to restore its fortunes and because the Chief Executive and Director of Housing were insightful enough to see that concentrating services through an integrated local team stood the best chance of breaking the deadlock that had blighted the estate. But political will and administrative leadership were not enough, as they were likely to change, which they did.

The lack of a local budget was recognised as a major stumbling block to effective decision-making and control. But such was the inertia of the central Council system that no way could be found through the quagmire of central controls to set one up. The Broadwater Farm initiative was recognised as expensive but effective. It was favoured as an exceptional case, rather than pioneering a workable model for the rest of the council stock.

POLICE PROBLEMS

The most serious, missing ingredient was the failure to establish constructive police relations. All local services attended and reported to the Broadwater Farm Panel, except the police. The police did not share the general enthusiasm for some of the Youth Association activities, and they had only poor and infrequent liaison with the young leaders. Staff on the estate were wary of close links with the police for fear of losing the confidence of young black residents. One of the Youth Association's stated goals was to win young people away from crime to more constructive community activities. But this inevitably meant that they communicated with actual or potential 'bad guys'. The police interpreted this as 'harbouring criminals' and 'shielding crime'. It was shown in a survey in 1986 that young black men on the estate were nearly five times as likely as their white counterparts to be stopped and searched by the police on the estate (Gifford, 1986). This was the police response to what they saw as high black crime. The police seemed to see the Youth Association as a potential threat to their control over criminal activity; whereas the Youth Association often saw the police as hostile invaders of their hard-won centre and workshops. Relations were tense.

By 1985, conditions on the estate had improved remarkably. Crime had plummeted, according to police records (Mid-Tottenham Police, 1985). In the summer of 1985, the Youth Association and most of the active leaders went on a Jamaican Youth exchange. It seems that a vacuum arose. Drug dealing appeared openly in the unsupervised and unused underground garages on the estate, mainly carried out from cars driven onto the estate, then off again. The six roads into the estate, and the insecure underground garage areas made coming in and going out easy. Controlling drug pushing from within the estate was difficult, since drug dealers were elusive and menacing.

Tensions mounted as community leaders tried to get the police to act against the drug pushers. The police responsible for patrolling the estate reported a build-up of tension and incidents. The picture was of police and community impotence in the face of serious drug crime. The estate had quite suddenly become a base for underground crime. This time the council and the local leaders called on the police to act (Gifford, 1986). Nothing happened and the drug dealing continued unabated, virtually in the open. When the Youth leaders returned from Jamaica, the situation was virtually out of control.

Meanwhile, riots took place in September 1985 in Handsworth, Birmingham, and in Brixton for a second time within five years, after a black woman was shot in her home by a police officer. Tensions on the estate rose even further and rumours abounded that Tottenham would be the next area to riot.

On 1 October, the local police began a stop and search action on all cars entering and leaving the estate. It was a sudden, blanket action that residents and staff interpreted as provocative and overzealous. They knew which cars needed stopping and searching. The action was called off under pressure, as young black residents showed mounting resentment of the police. Community leaders on the estate were still reporting to the police and were greatly alarmed by the sudden appearance on the estate of well-known troublemakers with serious criminal records (Zipfel, 1985).

THE RIOT

On the weekend of 5 October, 1985 the police raided a house near the estate, looking for a young man, active in the Youth Association, for a minor traffic offence. In the course of the raid, his mother, the occupier, died of a heart attack. News spread like wildfire that the police raid had led to the death of Cynthia Jarrett and, by Sunday afternoon, residents were demonstrating at Tottenham police station. After an angry meeting on the estate, a crowd of young people, mainly male and mainly black, tried to set off again for the local police station to demand a proper explanation for the death. They found exits to the estate blocked by police vans bringing in police reinforcements in riot gear. By then it was dusk.

There erupted an almighty confrontation, with burning cars, petrol bombs, police occupying defensive positions, enclosing the estate and youth moving around the decks and walkways, either attacking the police or trying to escape. Much of the clash was televised and the nation was appalled by the spectacle of sheets of flames leaping up past the concrete blocks and seemingly within inches of an unarmed police force crouching behind protective plastic shields, helmets and visors. Shops were set on fire, a totally chaotic and violent situation raged for seven hours and in the course of it, a community policeman, PC Blakelock, was knifed to death with many stab wounds while trying to protect firemen who went into Tangmere precinct, where an Asian shop had been fire-bombed.

The anger of the police and the nation at the killing of a young policeman who had been well-respected and who left behind a family, was overpowering. The young black men who had been so angered by the death of their friend's mother were sobered by the enormity of the violence and disorder. They were also deeply upset by the loss of so much that they had fought for and gained, particularly respect and support from the wider community. Their violent protest was short-lived and within hours of the disorder subsiding, local leaders were laying even more ambitious plans for the rebuilding of their estate's reputation as a successful multiracial model. Many, including Margaret Thatcher, called for its demolition. Its name became a byword in bad design, yet in many ways, the people 'bounced back'.

The aftermath of the riot was to place further strains on the community – a police siege of Broadwater Farm, patrolled by over 100 officers for several weeks; the arrest of many individuals, several later shown to have been far from the scene on the night of the riot; and the complete breakdown of communication between police and resident representatives, following aggressive police seizures of several clearly innocent young people.

Most detained suspects, including juveniles, were denied access to lawyers and family during long periods of police interrogation... Some detainees were allegedly tricked by police into signing documents waiving their rights and a number claimed they signed statements under pressure, sometimes without even being allowed to read them first. (Gifford, 1986)

The Youth Association became totally preoccupied with the subsequent trials, referring to the riot as a 'rebellion' and an 'uprising', articulating their grievances with passion.

The riot...was not primarily about poverty, unemployment or bad housing... The protest by the youths from the estate was essentially about policing – police activity and police attitudes... there is a deep-seated hostility to the police in many inner city areas... This lack of confidence in the police's fairness, this sense that they can no longer be trusted, is a growing feeling throughout the community, but it affects black people more deeply. (Zipfel, 1985)

An enormous sense of injustice, bitterness and failure, contrasted starkly with the image of successful rescue and turnaround that they had so recently won. It was a community disaster of such magnitude that it appeared to threaten and undermine not only black community initiatives, but also government support for estate rescue. The Priority Estates Project for a while saw its future in jeopardy, as the riot appeared to undo so much of the progress that had been made.

The government rejected the proposal for an independent inquiry. Haringey Council therefore appointed Lord Gifford to head up a full investigation of the situation before, during and after the October riot (Gifford, 1986). Part of this work involved a full-scale, 100 per cent survey of residents, their views on the estate, on crime and on its future. The Residents' Survey (Young, 1986) revealed many positive views about the estate. Broadwater Farm was considered friendly. Race relations were considered good. Estate services were appreciated. The Youth Association and tenants' leaders were respected. Crime was believed to be low, though fear of crime, particularly among women, was high. The estimated low crime rate was in fact borne out by the police's own statistics released later. This survey did much to restore faith in the community. Broadwater Farm witnessed a new wave of activity as people struggled to rebuild its confidence.

STRUGGLE TO REBUILD

The neighbourhood office continued to function and played a strongly supportive role to the many individuals who had suffered as a consequence of the disorders. The Youth Association gained a European Social Fund grant for training and community development. A Community Co-operative was established to win contracts for work on the estate. A row of 21 enterprise workshops were planned at ground floor level to begin the process of transferring human interaction down from the walkways. After years of delay, the council agreed to an ambitious purpose-built Community Centre for the estate.

Government officials showed their continuing support for the estate by providing a further £3 000 000 in Estate Action money between 1986–90 for environmental and landscaping work, for painting the walkways, for vast murals and a mosaic. Much of this work was carried out by the community co-operative set up to help young people from the estate. In all, 60 new jobs were created for residents in 1986. Contractors working on the estate were pressed into hiring local labour.

Money seemed to be gravitating to the estate in support of community initiatives. Slowly, relations were rebuilt with the police, who in 1986 agreed, for the first time, to come and report to the Broadwater Farm Panel. In spite of bitterness among many police and many young black people, enlightened leaders on both sides worked towards calm and improved communication.

In a symbolic gesture of large proportions, the Residents and Youth Associations dedicated a carefully created garden, built on the edge of the estate by the youth co-operative, to the mother and the policeman who both died in that tragic weekend of 5/6 October 1985. They also built a Nations Garden with flags from many countries, representing the many communities of Broadwater Farm. At the opening of the garden, the estate looked brilliant and it won the London Tourist Board Award for its sparkling environment.

NEW MONEY FROM GOVERNMENT

Tangmere Precinct, the scene of the worst rioting and the place where P.C. Blakelock was stabbed to death, had never re-covered. All of the shops had closed. The plan was that the podium and walkways would be removed, the units recon-verted to their original housing use, while shops would reopen on the ground floor in some of the workshop spaces. Concierges would be installed at the base of each block, ensuring full security. Footpaths would develop at ground level. The Department of the Environment and Haringey Council allocated £33 000 000, to be spent over eight years on the walk-way removal and ground-level reinstatement plan.

By the time these works beautifying the estate began to show, much had changed in Haringey Council. Bernie Grant had become an MP and had left the local council. His white successor was far less sympathetic to the estate. Both the Chief Executive and the Director of Housing had left and were replaced by people whose brief was to prioritise other areas. Cuts were in the air, as Haringey Council was forced to set the highest poll tax in the country to try and balance its budget. There was a feeling among the new leaders of Haringey Council that Broadwater Farm had received too many privileges, and was an 'unaffordable extravagance'.

Not only were deep government cuts to London local authorities taking their toll, but Haringey in particular was showing signs of a critical management and financial crisis. Arrears on Broadwater Farm had moved towards £1000 per tenant. Much of this could be traced directly to the breakdown of financial and staff management within parts of the Council. Frozen posts, cuts in repairs, withdrawal of community services, loss of grants to community groups, all meant that tenants and staff became increasingly demoralised and cynical about the Council.

By 1989, the Youth Association had lost some of its funding; the number of empty units had started to climb again; staff turnover accelerated and vacant posts remained unfilled for long periods, affecting caretaking, repairs, housing benefit and virtually all services. The office was moved off the Tangmere precinct into portakabins on the edge of the estate. This change, provoked by fears on the part of women staff over tensions with the Youth Association, represented the symbolic breach in co-operative relations between residents and the council that had been in place since 1983. The council had radically changed its stance towards Broadwater Farm in the light of new political priorities. These new priorities appeared to be: survival through cuts; recentralisation and rationalisation; equalisation of Broadwater Farm with other areas; and resistance to resident control. The local office was now staffed only by housing employees, answerable to the Area, rather than to the local Panel. The senior co-ordinator post disappeared from the estate and the local office no longer had the necessary power to cut through the council hierarchy.

In 1989, the Council reverted, after years of successful local lettings, to its 'homeless only, one offer only policy'. It immediately set in train again the previous scenario of refusals, polarisation and rising voids. By 1991, there were 60 empty flats on the estate, yet the restrictive policy was ostensibly to help house homeless people! This was the third time in its brief history that Broadwater had been pushed into a cycle of polarised and insensitive lettings.

Another casualty of the changes was the huge new Community Centre, built on the edge of the estate, resulting from years of struggle. It cost £2 500 000 to build but, when it was finally ready in 1992, there was no revenue funding to staff it – on a modest estimate it needed 14 workers to function to capacity! It suddenly appeared a white elephant in an area of acute community need. After completion, the centre was used on a limited basis for local activities, but its massive spare capacity and lack of long-term funding were a reminder of past dreams.

The final straw in the new crisis was the abolition of the Broadwater Farm Panel, as the council tried to 'rationalise' its decision-making. Official consultation with residents dropped to almost zero. Leading residents began to talk of breakaway, of 'opting out' of council control and setting up a co-operative to run the estate. They even contacted the Housing Corporation about taking over ownership of the estate. Meanwhile there had been further police drug raids, which heightened community tensions again.

ALTERNATIVE RESIDENT CONTROL

In 1989, as the official Priority Estates Project was coming to an end, the Residents' Association which evolved in the years following the riot, proposed to the council and to PEP a feasibility study into alternative, tenant-led housing management structures for the estate. The DoE agreed to special funding for this work and between July 1991 and November 1992, PEP examined options for resident control.

The option of transferring ownership under the 'Tenants' Choice' provision of the 1988 Housing Act, was too complex and too expensive. Remaining with the council in a climate of political withdrawal and cuts in service was unattractive. Resident leaders favoured a tenant management co-operative, as this gave residents control over staffing and a budget, without lumbering them with the long-term capital and maintenance liability. But there were serious problems in organising an estate-wide tenant structure with sufficient resilience to represent and unite all the different interest groups. The original organisations that had created many of the positive changes still dominated. But many new tenants had moved into the estate, including large African and Turkish groups and some refugees. Some flats were illegally occupied, as the Council's control had weakened. A small group of 'old hands' dominated the decision-making and, while working tirelessly for 'the community', they had come to accept unquestioningly their own dominant position. Tensions were close to the surface particularly between the Afro-Caribbean and African residents. A critical support in these years was the presence on the estate of several church groups, including nuns and a priest. They lived in flats within the community and were welcomed by residents, as they offered background, quiet support and advice.

The new co-operative route was far from obvious to most residents, in an estate with such a complex history and make-up. The PEP feasibility study was inconclusive. It documented the reductions in service leading to tenant frustration but, by and large, it endorsed the performance of the now beleaguered local management office in spite of the cuts. It supported the tenants' initiative and enthusiasm for control but cast doubts on their ability to 'go it alone' in such a difficult climate and situation. It proposed a modified joint management structure for the estate (PEP, 1993).

In October 1992, an estate-wide ballot was held, with an independent ballot organiser agreed by the Council. The question asked tenants whether they were in favour of tenant management of the housing service on this estate. Fifty-eight per cent of resident households voted. This turnout was double the level for local elections. Of them, 88 per cent voted *yes* in answer to the question. Resident support for independent management was impressive, surprising many council staff.

PEP's reservations about tenant control of such a diverse and difficult estate cost it follow-on work. The international accounting and consultancy firm, Price Waterhouse, was then commissioned by the Residents' Association, with DoE and Haringey Council money, to develop an alternative management structure for the estate, putting tenants in the lead. It was an extraordinary development in an extraordinary place.

SHORT-LIVED INTERNATIONAL CONSULTANTS

The consultants soon discovered that their quick-in, quick-out consultancy style was totally unequal to the highly complex and intricate community relations of a dense London estate. Within a year, the residents' representatives were disillusioned with their high-level advisers and were scaling down their views of what was possible.

Haringey Council, having cut back its services and in many ways diluted the Broadwater Farm initiative, began to respond to the pressure of tenant dissatisfaction again. One major new element was the decision to toughen up on rent arrears, leading to the eviction of a number of residents including the founding residents' leader. This action appeared to have the tacit support of residents, unless it simply reflected a community whose back was broken. But it appeared to mark a whole new era on the estate. Arrears were radically reduced and empty property disappeared again. Throughout, the highest standards of caretaking and cleaning were maintained. Empty units were again cut through special lettings and close links between staff and residents. At the time of writing it was unlikely that the tenants would see their ambition of community control realised. A new compromise with Haringey Council appeared, involving the creation of a joint 'company-style board' to run services.

The tasks facing the small and dedicated group of active residents were daunting indeed. Their hard-won community centre threatened to become an expensive liability. The 21 workshops were not all occupied. They were attracting curious and underoccupied young people who made potential businesses nervous. Policing on the estate became calmer and more continuous but at a level that still made the estate feel strained. There were still strong rumours of drug-dealing around the ground level workshops. Police were still suspicious and the recent Appeal acquittal of Winston Silcott, who had been convicted for the murder of PC Blakelock on falsified police evidence, was only reinforcing this problematic situation (*The Guardian*, 1994).

In spite of persistent racial, policing, funding, staffing and building problems, the estate continued to work well, look impressive and involve its residents. Crime levels on the estate remained consistently low and police links with local staff and leaders were more constructive than in the past. By 1994, the first blocks had lost their walkway links and were opened up at ground floor level. The effect was dramatic and positive (see Figure 9.2, p. 215). But the cost (£35 000 per unit) raised questions about continuing the programme. These questions hung over the future.

LESSONS

The lessons of Broadwater Farm are many:

- Political leadership of housing management initiatives is unreliable and short-lived; it is effective in extreme conditions but it needs to be followed by a solid, non-political service that residents have a major role in shaping.
- Police in multiracial areas cannot function without strong community support and without acknowledging the problem of racial discrimination.
- Black young people are greatly disadvantaged in jobs and training; they can quickly become totally marginalised and alienated. They are interested in developing their own organisations and services and need significant help to succeed.
- A budget is an essential tool of decision-making and is necessary in order to prove whether strategies conserve or save resources. Without a locally controlled and dedicated budget, local initiatives will be vulnerable to cuts under wider and changing pressures.

- Caretaking and cleaning services can be run to very high standards in the most difficult concrete complex, multi-storey areas, but it requires training, high-quality equipment, motivated staff and constant effort.
- Estate facilities require careful management by paid staff and long-term funding.
- Improvements are vulnerable to changes and can quickly disappear, particularly in volatile community situations where fundamental conflicts remain unresolved. In this case, the long-standing tensions between young people and the police were almost bound to erupt when an event as significant as a death occurred, apparently caused directly by wrongful police action.
- Central control over the lettings process does not work in areas of low demand; it pushes up the numbers of empty property in unpopular areas because most people hold out for better offers. Rising voids cause spiralling conditions.
- Tenants and community representatives play a vital role in solving local problems but local leadership is volatile. It is hard to ensure the representation of all interest groups in a mixed area. In an unstable situation, there may be insufficient local representatives willing to carry the responsibility for representing the community and determining what should happen.
- Black leadership is very important within a largely black community if ghetto conditions are to be avoided.
- An estate's reputation is hard to live down and, in the case of Broadwater Farm, was only possible when outsiders actually visited and saw for themselves what had been achieved. The press never let up on their consistently negative and sensationalist view.
- Actual crime levels may bear little relation to public perceptions and fear. Since 1984, Broadwater Farm has continuously experienced a crime rate that is lower than the surrounding area. A sense of security is a key determinant of stability.

On Broadwater Farm, articulate spokespeople for the local community fought over many years for better conditions, services, jobs, training and access to opportunity. They were on many fronts successful. This impressed visitors, politicians and service workers, creating a groundswell of support that was almost unique. The mistake would be to ignore the lessons and fail to carry the pattern of community representation and local organisation into the wider field, allowing poor communities some kind of real stake in their future. A young black resident put it vividly:

> Society itself has got to change. It's got to be able to accept black people as black people, because you won't accept us as English people. So now we've been forced apart, we've been categorised and we've got to do it ourselves, and then ask you to accept us the way we are, because you don't want us the same as you. (Quoted in Zipfel, 1986b)

AFTERWORD

By late 1994, the proposals for tenant management had been replaced by the idea of Joint Management with the Council. An Estates Agreement was finally signed between residents and the Council in 1995. Staff were planning to relocate the office again in the heart of the estate. Residents and local staff worked away at improvements, security and survival strategies. Broadwater Farm offers a unique experience of immense complexity. The lessons are hard, but they could not be more significant for the future of difficult estates.

Note: Particular thanks are due to residents, locally based staff and the Priority Estates Project for providing information for this chapter.

Figure 9.1 Broadwater Farm – intimidating design

Figure 9.2 Broadwater Farm after improvements – secure entrances

KEY DATES AT BROADWATER FARM ESTATE

1966	Decision to build
1970	Completed – first lettings
1973	First signs of trouble – High turnover/homeless – ethnic minority community – tensions with police
1976	More polarised and more social problems
	Special lettings proposed
1977	Preliminary Difficult-to-let Report – pessimistic about long-term prospects – acknowledges estate should not have been built
1978–80	Special lettings initiative – improvement in conditions
1979	Rejected as a Priority Estates Project because problems too overwhelming
1980	Special lettings scrapped – Reversion to extreme decay – 'Dumping' of difficult households – High crime rate
1981–2	Disorders – police clashes with black youths
1982	Labour lose control of local council – special initiatives on Broadwater Farm to woo votes
	Voids reach 8 per cent
	All-white tenants' association
	Proposal for police sub-station to curb crime – abandoned after protest by black residents
	Youth association started on estate by local mother
1983	Neighbourhood office opened – 700 visitors a month
	PEP invited in to consult with tenants over improvements
	Special Panel set up to manage the estate
1984	New office ready in shopping precinct
	Urban aid grant to Youth Association – Princess Diana visits
	Co-operative workshops set up
	Physical improvements/security – strong doors

1985	Leadership vacuum during Youth Association trip to Jamaica
	Police tensions mount – drug raids cause friction
	Riot – deaths of local resident and policeman
1986	Estate Action funding – murals, gardens, concrete painting, security doors
	Gifford Inquiry is set up by Haringey Council to explore causes of the riot
	Police report reveals low crime on estate and serious policing tensions
	Police join Broadwater Farm Panel for the first time
1987	Council agrees to build Community Centre
	Renewed drug problems – raids cause new tensions
	Urban Aid grant agreed to build community workshops under the walkways
	New Estate Action capital funds
1988	Many services are cut due to budget crisis
	Empty units start to mount again – reach sixty
1989	Several churches become active on estate
	Arrears are out of control – £800 per tenant
	Office moves to portakabin on edge of estate
	Youth Association is closed through loss of grant
	Tenants discuss forming a co-operative
1990	Many services decline on estate
1991	PEP Feasibility study for Tenant Management
1992	Community Centre, Enterprise Workshops ready
	Ballot – tenants want more control
	Further Estate Action funding – removal of walkways, introduction of ground level secure entrances
	Local management office steps up action on arrears and empty units
1994	Price Waterhouse pull out of the estate
	Local management office reasserts control

1995	Future funding for capital works questionned
	Workshops and Community Centre face viability problems
	Tenant management joint management proposals are replaced by an Estate Agreement.
	Police unit based on estate.
	Health centre opens.

Source: Author's visits and research.

10 Portrait of Taastrupgaard, Denmark, 1989–95

ABOUT THE ESTATE

The vicious circle that plagues Tastrupgard has created many technical, organisational, financial and social problems that interact with each other... The estate appeared to be condemned and notorious in the minds of other Taastrup inhabitants... If there had been no intervention, the Taastrup section [of AKB] would quite simply have gone bankrupt...it would have resulted in an almost irretrievable situation. (Nygaard, 1991b)

When walking the dog, I occasionally would meet another dog and its owner, and talk about dogs, but we never talked about us humans... I felt isolated and I thought this would probably never change... I would never become part of a group. (Retired resident)

Social segregation is more important than the condition or quality of buildings. (Kristensen, 1989a)

The larger the housing area is, the more difficult it is to create the support necessary for community democracy. (Nielsen, 1985)

Some social housing sticks out because of design. It's more socially divided, more stigmatised, poorer quality. (Thomasen, 1989)

Residents must be activated and be brought in and given responsibility for the housing development itself and for the necessary changes in the external physical framework... But changing the colours of the houses doesn't give people a better life. (Nygaard, 1991b)

ORIGINS OF TAASTRUPGAARD

In 1960, the village of Taastrup, 25 kilometres outside Copenhagen, had around 500 inhabitants. By 1989, it had 50 000. The city of Copenhagen bought up land over a 25 kilometre radius from the centre for overspill developments. The aim at Taastrup was to create a new commercial and service centre surrounded by predominantly private housing. A new railway line and new roads linked the area with Copenhagen.

The plan only partially succeeded. Large numbers of houses were built but the jobs did not follow. Taastrup became primarily a commuting area, with many condominium-style developments. One quarter of the housing was to be built by social housing companies. This not only clashed with the suburban character of the area, but it stranded low-income households far away from jobs, services or familiar neighbourhoods. The social housing was built at very high density to save land and to recreate dense inner-city patterns. The plan for the estate included an active commercial centre in the middle to avoid the dangers of 'deadening suburbia'. But Taastrupgaard, with its heavy reinforced concrete blocks, was so unpopular from the outset that it was rarely fully occupied. The major commercial development that was to be part of Taastrup never materialised.

STYLE OF BUILDING

Taastrupgaard contained 981 flats on three floors all above ground in 36 flat-roofed blocks (see Figure 10.1, p. 237). The blocks were interconnected by first floor walkways and access was through garages at ground level. Between blocks and joining the walkways, there were wide concrete podia (industrially built platforms above ground). The decks and open podia were grey and windswept. Running along the end of 35 parallel blocks was one giant linear block of over 300 units, uniting the whole estate into a concrete wilderness. The estate could only be reached through eight internal ground-level entrances, under the concrete decks, each feeding 120 flats.

These entrances led to stairwells up from the huge under-ground parking area that ran under the whole estate. The large, dark garage areas made the approach to the estate and to individual flats intimidating and alienating. The entrances and staircases were cut-off, unfrequented and frightening, 'often with the unmistakable smell of refuse bins' (Nygaard, 1991a). In all, there were 115 internal staircases, each leading to eight or nine flats. It was by far the worst feature of the estate, giving residents and visitors a feeling that their homes were in a dark and ugly bunker, cut off from the world and enclosed in a hard and unwelcoming hole. Of the 981 units, 576 were family size and of these, 251 had three or more bedrooms. Most flats had balconies and high internal space and amenity standards. The population of Taastrupgaard was very youthful, due to the large number of family units. Forty per cent were aged under 20.

THE LANDLORD

Taastrupgaard was developed by a large, long-established but go-ahead, Copenhagen-based co-operative housing company, called Arbejdernes Kooperative Byggeforening (AKB). The company was set up before the First World War and now has 17 000 units. The properties are managed by ten daughter companies, one of which runs AKB Taastrup. Taastrupgaard was one of three AKB estates in the Taastrup area.

Each new social housing development in Denmark is funded in large part out of the rents from that development. There is virtually no cross-subsidisation. The management and maintenance of the development likewise has to be funded from rents. Rents at Taastrupgaard are far higher than average due to the modern complex construction, high maintenance costs and unpopularity. Taastrupgaard was built to rehouse families from Copenhagen's dense urban renewal areas. Because of the lack of jobs and high rents, people with any choice were from the outset reluctant to move there or used it only as a stepping stone to something better.

Difficulties in letting meant that rent losses had to be covered by rent rises. High rents were a major barrier to letting. AKB in 1984 faced a financial crisis due to the threat-ened bankruptcy of the Taastrup area. Taastrupgaard was by far the largest and most difficult estate. As a result of lettings difficulties, the housing company was only too eager to accept local authority nominated families from inner-city areas, to fill the empty flats. These families had their rents guaranteed for five years after moving and paid a special subsidised rent, with the help of local authorities, because of their slum clearance status. Therefore in spite of their invariable poverty, the impact of higher rents was staggered for a period. Local authorities only nominated emergency cases for whom they had to accept direct responsibility, as they wanted to avoid accruing high rent liabilities. If they nominated a family, by law they had to guarantee the rents. The company's reliance on local authority nominations to fill the flats created a strong drift to polarisation.

Gradually, better-off tenants were 'pushed' out through a combination of social stigma and high costs, so people who found it hard to gain access to more popular estates were allowed in, forced to pay high rents through lack of alternatives, and often reliant on the relatively generous social security system. Immigrant families suddenly found that they could get rehoused much more easily. By 1984, 60 per cent of tenants at Taastrupgaard received housing allowances and a quarter were immigrants. This had a landslide effect on existing occupants.

By 1990, the proportion of foreigners had risen to 40 per cent. In Taastrup, the local authority tried to avoid using its nomination rights to house foreigners in social housing areas popular with Danes. One result was a much greater concentration of nominations than average in the very poorest estates like Taastrupgaard, where the stakes were lower and where it was easier to concentrate disadvantaged people through low demand. The housing company, on the other hand, actively tried to disperse minorities across a range of estates to avoid ghettoisation but with only limited success. The turnover in Taastrupgaard by the mid-1980s reached nearly 40 per cent in a single year. The rapid movement away from the estate and the sudden influx of mainly foreigners led to the virtual disintegration of the elected tenant board on the estate. The estate faced bankruptcy as rent arrears, largely caused through vacant units, averaged £160 per flat. With strict ring-fencing of each estate's finances, this made Taastrupgaard insolvent.

SOCIAL PROBLEMS

The estate's social reputation became known throughout Denmark. A five-fold increase in unemployment, the rising proportion of one-parent families, and the sudden arrival of a large minority community, accompanied by a sharp drop in the proportion of working and two-parent families, reduced the 'psychological reserves' of residents, placed new demands on the housing company and greatly increased the estate's unpopularity. Many families with severe social problems were rehoused there in a desperate attempt to keep the estate filled. Nearly half the households were entirely dependent on the state welfare system for their survival.

Ethnic hostilities ran deep, as minorities were considered instrumental in the estate's decline. There were 25 nationalities on the estate, but Turkish families were the dominant minority. On the whole, they had come from remote peasant areas and many wore elaborate, traditional costumes. They usually had large families and mostly had a breadwinner, even if poorly paid. The women spoke little Danish. They were extremely reluctant to participate in the social activities of the estate or the tenant board. In sharp contrast, the Danish families tended to be small, come from inner-city slum areas, with many out of work or in early retirement. They participated in a wide range of activities. The estate had many social and adult education clubs, located in converted underground areas of the estate. But the clubs only involved a minority of tenants. The tenant board, now in serious difficulty, had no ethnic minority representation.

NEED FOR CHANGE

AKB became convinced that something radical had to be done to avert financial and social collapse. The targets for action were many-sided:

-   Taastrupgaard's massive concrete design lacked any humanising features, constructed entirely above ground-level in deadeningly heavy grey concrete.

- Technical defects, leaking roofs, concrete corrosion, wrongly laid sewers, decaying piping threatened the estate's viability.
- Centralised administration gave too little control at estate level, 'uncustomised' delivery and insufficient support services to compensate for the problems.
- The financial deficit resulting from the management and maintenance commitments had to be met from the autonomous estate budget, making Taastrupgaard unviable.
- High turnover due to unpopularity and high rents led to crippling arrears.
- Intense social problems stemmed from the system of nominations, the make-up of the population, and ethnic tensions. The relentless pressures on Taastrupgaard created spiralling social conditions.

A tenant of AKB, resident in one of the other Taastrup estates, became the chairman of the board of the AKB housing company under the Danish law of tenants' democracy. He was immediately forced into a decisive role in Taastrupgaard, arguing from ground level for a major rescue initiative to avert bankruptcy of the estate.

GOVERNMENT RESCUE

Taastrupgaard was not on its own. Around 80 large social housing estates built in the 1960s and 1970s were facing a financial crisis due to low demand, social polarisation and physical defects. The government rescue package for the 'crisis' estates involved rescheduling the existing debt to allow new borrowing, providing index-linked finance for improvements, capital grants to make good the structural problems associated with concrete construction and to upgrade the environment, providing more amenities. Taastrupgaard became a leading experiment in the transformation of concrete estates.

The special approach devised at Taastrupgaard had four main prongs:

● physical, to tackle the buildings and environment;

- organisational, to bring in decentralised management and lettings control;
- economic, to address estate and company financial reform, funding for tenant support and local initiatives;
- social, to increase lettings, resident involvement, training, employment and community activities.

The programme was called The Environmental Project. Tenant involvement, local responsiveness and community development were a central focus of the initiative. Without these, it was believed the project would fail. The goal was to break up the estate, make the buildings and environment more attractive, fill the empty units, enhance the estate's reputation and create a sense of community.

Environmental project

The Taastrupgaard proposals were developed between 1984 and 1986 and were to cost DK200 000 000 – approximately £16 000 per dwelling (Windsor Workshop, 1991). Taastrupgaard received more money than most other projects because of the unusual severity of its problems. It certainly carried out more ambitious structural alterations than other estates in this survey. Even so, the money was insufficient to sort out all aspects of the estate. In spite of the strong commitment to a many-sided approach, it was the physical and environmental improvements that dominated the five-year programme, using up 75 per cent of the available funds. The three main strands of the physical upgrading were: to repair the buildings and transform their appearance; to humanise, brighten and green the environment; to involve tenant volunteers and young trainees in the work of the environmental project. The need to make the estate work socially was a constant preoccupation, in spite of the physical focus of spending. In fact, the physical changes were heavily influenced by this need.

In order to make the improvement programme more manageable, the estate was divided into four areas of about 250 dwellings each; four tenants' sub-committees were set up to propose ideas for their area. Each sub-committee developed its own environmental project. Volunteers were recruited through constant advertising. A 76-year-old activist put it this way:

> I moved from a single family house and did not find it right that tenants were not allowed to make changes. I therefore attended the first meeting of the environment project. I expressed my opinion and that tends to get you elected... Being involved in something keeps me alive. (Nygaard, 1991b)

ORGANISATION OF THE PROGRAMME

A project team was set up by the AKB and based on the estate. The project staff worked from a converted flat within the giant block, painted in an array of bright colours. Altogether, 25 people worked for the project, including the education, training, community development and technical staff. This local base galvanised a remarkable level of resident involvement in the project. Team leaders met fortnightly with tenants' representatives throughout the improvements, to ensure strong links with tenants.

The project worked to break down the large, anonymous areas and to make the estate look more friendly – 'changing and humanising the cold, monotonous concrete'. The plan was to get rid of decks, podia, concrete barriers, walls and underground garages, to put pitch roofs on the buildings and to paint the concrete walls of all the blocks in bright, cheerful colours (see Figure 10.2, p. 237). The four areas covered by the four tenants' committees were painted four different colours – orange, pink, blue and yellow. All the grey surfaces were transformed into pastel-shaded, brightly decorated, pitch-roofed buildings that were far more warm, welcoming and familiar than the previous harsh and hostile environment. The softer, warmer colours combined with the more traditional and weatherproof roofs had an exhilarating, if Noddy-life, effect.

By far the most dramatic proposal was to take the estate down to ground level. In theory, the podia had been designed to provide a break in the monotony of the overhead walkways, a point of social contact and meeting place. But at Taastrupgaard they simply extended the bleak desolation of endless concrete with no obvious function because of severe wind tunnels and the lack of shops, street life or interchange. Residents hated them. The garage areas were partially lit and ventilated by large central air holes that opened up into the podia. This was supposed to expose the garage areas to the outside world. But in practice it created even more concrete on the deck levels because of the high walls around the giant holes above the dark concrete caverns below.

The ambitious new plans proposed removing the concrete upper walkways and podia covering the garages, opening the underground areas to the sky. Garages would be filled with the surplus concrete rubble raising the ground level between blocks by one metre. Topsoil would be laid on the new surface, turning the old underground parking areas into gardens between the blocks. Short steps would go down from the first floor flats to raised private gardens. Communal garden areas down the middle of the blocks would belong to residents from the upper floors who had no individual gardens. This radical surgery was so expensive that it could only be funded for four of the eight parking cellars.

The four remaining deck areas between the blocks had to be treated differently. The holes in the podia were covered over, allowing the removal of the high protective concrete walls. The central decks were then divided into individual patio areas for each first floor flat, with grassed areas down the middle, creating green open spaces between the blocks. In this way, throughout the estate, about one quarter of residents gained a private garden or patio, while the central areas were kept as communal gardens or play areas for everyone.

Each open space between the blocks was developed slightly differently, reflecting the choices made by the different environmental groups. Some communal gardens provided a barbecue and picnic area; some, a children's play area. Within the allocated budget, tenants decided. All the garden work was done by tenants. On some blocks, 40 or 50 people joined in. The Turkish families, many of whom were of recent peasant origin, knew a lot more about gardening than the Danish households, who usually came from inner Copenhagen. Turkish residents were particularly active in this area. They often showed the Danes how to build the gardens and barbecues. The environmental work between the blocks involved many people and created tremendous enthusiasm; it also gave scope for an imaginative carpentry training programme and youth employment project. The outside stairs, fencing, picnic furniture, sitting areas and flowerboxes were built in the carpentry workshop on the estate, using railway sleepers and other sturdy, old wood. Skilled trainers helped young residents. The impact was striking – soft, natural wood structures, blending with the green of the gardens.

By contrast, the insides of the blocks were barely changed, apart from the access to the garages. Previously, tenants and visitors could only reach the estate through the dark garage areas under the podia. Now those internal underground staircases were made partially redundant, as access to the estate had been opened up by the 'concrete surgery'. But the four surviving underground parking areas were gloomier than ever, thanks to the patio-gardens above, closing off the previous light holes. Money ran out before they could be tackled.

Each staircase was allocated a decoration budget, reflecting the cost of contractors carrying out the painting work. Tenants could choose to do the work themselves, saving money and using any surplus for a social event. This innovation galvanised tenants, staircase by staircase, in a way that had not happened before. Most staircase groups had outdoor parties in the new garden areas, paid for from the money saved on the staircase improvements. The approach worked less well in the staircases where there were a lot of elderly or foreign tenants. Even after repainting, most stairwells still felt bare, bleak and enclosed, in spite of being brighter. Overall, the internal access to the flats proved very hard to soften or humanise, with the warren of concrete steps, the lack of natural light, the cut-off and enclosed feeling on stairs and landings, with only locked doors to face you as you climbed. When the tenants were surveyed about their views at the end of the project, their two main complaints were the failure to change the internal staircases and the closing over of half the garage areas, making them darker than before. They still found the approach to most flats inhospitable (Nygaard, 1991b).

In spite of the limitations of the work, the estate looked totally different at the end of the project in 1990. The blocks stood out gaily from the drab, flat landscape. The pitched roofs made the blocks feel more homely and attractive – some would say 'dinky'. The wooden garden fences, steps, sitting and play areas, were cleverly designed and made with Scandinavian flair. The environmental project was a conspicuous success, if only partially done.

COMMUNITY DEVELOPMENT

The housing company gave special resources to develop resident involvement in the Environmental Project. A community worker was employed full-time over the five years of the project to run consultations, to develop the staircase groups, to establish and support resident committees, to try and involve the immigrant communities, to co-ordinate activities and provide information. Throughout the project, a monthly newsletter kept residents in touch with the work. Tenants were trained so that they could be involved in production.

A major ambition of the project team was to create a 'community house' for the whole estate. This was to be the focus of new activities and was to bring together all the different interest groups in an integrated community. It was to be run by residents for residents. However, experience in its development showed the need for outside support in brokering the interests of different groups and in servicing a facility to cover such a big and difficult area. This lesson was parallelled on other estates where community facilities run by groups of residents became fractionalised and occasionally eventually folded. In Taastrupgaard, the community house provided outstanding facilities and popular local events. But the community within the estate was not sufficiently cohesive to sustain it unaided. The same was true of many aspects of tenant involvement on the estate.

EDUCATION PROJECTS

By law, Danish social housing must dedicate 2 per cent of its floor area to community activities, organised by residents.

Danish education authorities must provide a teacher for any activity requested by at least 12 *bona fide* participants. In order to build up the tenants' confidence in restoring the estate, the project applied for grants from the European Union, the local authority and the Adult Education Service to develop a wide range of ambitious training and education projects.

The European Union provided DKr 7 000 000 for the estate (around £630 000), to match the local contribution to education and training. This helped to pay for daily Danish classes for immigrants, mainly Turkish women. It also funded intensive training for the gardening volunteers, special training in community organisation, in making decisions, in resolving conflicts, in presenting information and in speaking in public. The education drive also supported literacy projects, a homework centre and special activities for young people.

The Danish language classes were hard to establish at first and required the agreement of the Turkish men, so that women would be allowed to come. After intensive community development and visiting, 35 women attended daily. Each class was backed by an afternoon of activity, using Danish, to do sewing and gardening. Childcare was provided. Turkish women who had already learnt to read, write and speak Danish helped newcomers.

The most elaborate training programme was the development of a closed-circuit television station for the estate. Residents produced the programmes with the help of local trainers. This television station gave news of events and meetings on the estate, and provided a network for residents, advertising services and events on the estate. It brought some glamour and prestige to the residents who ran their own programmes on it. It was particularly appealing to young people. The cost of the equipment was about DKr 1 000 000 (£90 000). Programmes included local cookery, ethnic programmes, local music and children's shows.

Special training was also organised for tenant board representatives to help them handle the very difficult problems within the estate. The stress on education and training was unusually intense and reinforcing for tenants. Denmark was the only country where it was such a prominent element, deriving partly from the strong co-operative tradition.

MINORITIES

A major problem for the Taastrupgaard project was the difficulty in involving minorities. Language and culture were two serious barriers. The Turkish families were conspicuously different in almost every tradition from their Danish counterparts. The most important barrier was the tension in the Danish community which arose from the presence of foreigners. Immigration is a recent phenomenon of the last two decades and is not based on historic links with particular countries. Local politics, particularly in cities, were becoming increasingly dominated by ethnic issues.

Informal contact between Danish and Turkish residents appeared friendly enough during visits. Children played together without appearing to notice nationality but the large concentrations of minority children created strains in the local schools. Although minorities were only 40 per cent of the estate population, the proportion of children was much higher due to the large foreign families. The Turkish community generally kept to itself and formed its own social groupings, including a friendship club in premises provided by the housing company.

Considerable efforts by project staff to include Turkish representatives produced short-term attendance at boards or consultation meetings, often quickly followed by drop-out. In 1991, two Turkish representatives were elected to the tenant board, but there was a lot of friction over Turkish programmes on the TV station. This issue made the Turkish representatives feel marginal and unwelcome, while making the Danes feel threatened and swamped. Formal relations continued to be strained between ethnic communities at the end of the project but by 1993, two further Turkish community representatives had joined the board. As the Turkish community was less than a generation old, it was too early to say how it might settle and integrate.

In 1994, new government funding was made available to help integrate foreigners in Denmark. Some of it was targeted at areas like Taastrupgaard. This was the first time in Denmark that a special national programme was directed specifically towards the minority community. It was too early to know what effect this first ever integration programme might have by the end of the study.

CARETAKING AND MAINTENANCE

AKB wanted to link their excellent estate-based cleaning and maintenance service more closely with the tenants and involve the caretaking staff directly in the environmental project. The caretaking and maintenance of the estate was broken down into the same four areas as the environmental projects. Each team had a local mini-office and its own budget. Each office was staffed with a head caretaker/manager and a heating maintenance technician. Three caretakers worked in each area. They made sure the blocks and surroundings were spotlessly maintained. They reported faults, carried out minor repairs, liaised with tenants and supervised their blocks. They commissioned repairs contracts, kept heating systems and other services in order. The caretaking teams were given special training in tenant relations. They liaised closely with the main estate office as well as their local committees.

Each local caretaking office had a sub-committee of residents controlling its own 'sub-budget'. The team spirit and resident liaison made the caretaking initiative exciting and rewarding for staff. The highly localised, high quality service resulted in estate conditions that far surpassed estates in other countries. Not for nothing was cleaning the largest day-to-day spending item in the estate budget. This exceptionally intensive management at a more local level than the estate was expensive. The company cut the 'sub-structure', once the improvements had been completed, on the grounds that such intensive management would no longer be needed. This change, which directors argued was inevitable, was greatly regretted by local leaders.

ESTATE OFFICE AND LETTINGS

A large, attractive and airy office on the estate, fitted with pine furniture and trailing plants, was responsible for co-ordinating the management of the estate. The four staff did not directly run the day-to-day cleaning and repair, as each mini-caretaking office was responsible for its own area. The office supervised and co-ordinated everything that had to be done on the estate and worked with the tenant board, providing a vital outward and inward link for the community.

A special lettings' officer was appointed to run the waiting list, offers, viewings and actual lettings and transfers from the estate. The central system alone had proved too cumbersome, inflexible and insensitive. The waiting list for the estate in 1991 was over 500. Although this showed a healthy revival of demand, the vast majority were single people, many of whom would be short-term tenants and for whom the flats were too big. Allocations, except for emergencies, were done in date order, with the six top applicants being told of the first vacancy. If number one did not accept, it went to number two, then three, and so on. In that way, turnaround times were cut to a week. The pressure was on applicants 'to take it or leave it'. Tenants on the estate and in other parts of AKB got priority for internal estate and company transfers. This built up a sense of choice, stability and satisfaction. The children of tenants were encouraged to become tenants themselves in order to build community stability and a unifying sense about the estate. There was a conscious attempt to stop the discriminatory concentration of Turkish families at Taastrupgaard, still the least popular estate in the area, by trying to secure a wider choice of offers. The local authority was pivotal to changing the 'ghetto trend' that was already far advanced and AKB worked hard to involve officials and politicians.

By the end of the project in 1990, the estate management service matched standards the company expected on all its estates:

- the budget was balanced and there was a rolling 16-year planned maintenance programme;
- arrears had dropped back to less than 1 per cent;
- empty units had disappeared;
- the caretaking service was outstanding;
- the estate was physically transformed;

The most radical management change was the new style of service that came with localisation. The estate community was now at the very top of managers' priorities, whereas in the central service, the administrative system was most important.

Employees in a decentralised organisation will not only undertake traditional operational tasks, but will also have to be communicators, helpers and mediators. (Nygaard, 1991b)

OUTCOMES

The most important outcome of the upgrading, the intensive management and the resident initiatives was the rising popularity of the estate. The estate was full for the first time in two decades and the turnover had dropped from 40 per cent at the beginning of the 1980s to nearer 10 per cent at the end. One effect of this was that by 1990 Turkish households were no longer gaining access in such significant numbers. Pressures on the housing market in general, cuts in support to owner-occupation, and the resultant higher demand for social housing from better-off groups, even for relatively unpopular estates, worked in favour of filling the estate. Higher demand, above all else, determined the rescue project's success (Villadsen, 1989).

In 1990, when the special funding ceased, a comprehensive residents' survey was carried out to evaluate the project (Nygaard, 1991b). This showed that the vast majority approved of and supported the improvements. However, 85 per cent of those interviewed believed that some fundamental problems remained, such as the staircases, the approach to the estate and the remaining fully enclosed underground areas. Many people still wanted to move off the estate, particularly those in work, and many felt that the shortage of money to remove all the decks and take the whole estate down to ground level was a major shortcoming of the environmental project.

Nevertheless, the several hundred tenants that had become involved in the project were more committed than before and wanted to stay. Those not working – mainly unemployed, elderly and people taking early retirement – were the most satisfied with their homes and the most pleased with the improvements.

The project had achieved its four core objectives:

- transforming the appearance of the estate and remedying the building defects;

- upgrading the environment;
- involving residents in building a new sense of community;
- making the estate solvent by reducing empty units to zero.

But the estate was still not integrated with the surrounding community. By 1995, there were signs that the underlying polarising drift was reinforcing the separation of the Turkish community into what was sometimes called 'Denmark's first ghetto'.

The issues for the future of Taastrupgaard appeared to be:

- how to keep employed people on the estate and engage them in its future;
- how to generate more economic activity within the estate;
- how to limit the number of social casualties so that the estate retained its fragile stability;
- how to involve minority representatives more readily to reduce prejudice and discrimination;
- how to sustain community involvement and care for the new environments now that the project, with its excitement and glamour, was over;
- how to sustain and fund the very intensive management of the estate, after special help was withdrawn;
- how to make the surrounding community take more seriously the social 'ghettoisation' that seemed an inevitable consequence of much wider urban pressures in Copenhagen.

The project was incomplete, but the foundations of viability were laid. In 1993, the special government committee on towns, convened by Parliament to consider social and ethnic problems, proposed a new support programme for integrating minorities in difficult areas. This was almost certain to generate a new phase in the Taastrupgaard project; it also marked a completely new departure for Denmark, highlighting the difficulties of integrating areas like Taastrupgaard. The attractive Danish model of co-operation, social responsibility and tenant democracy, was to be promoted in the new, diverse communities where ethnic tensions could otherwise overshadow remarkable achievements. In 1995, the social problems of Taastrupgaard and other similar communities were in the minds of politicians and housing professionals as they grappled with the deeper economic and social tensions that lay behind the spotless estate with its brightly painted concrete walls.

Note: Special thanks are due to Jesper Nygaard and the AKB association for generous help with information and checking the text for accuracy.

Figure 10.1   Taastrupgaard – too much concrete

KEY DATES AT TAASTRUPGAARD

1960s	Copenhagen City Council acquired land for social housing in the outer ring, including Taastrup
1970–2	Taastrupgaard is built, lacks basic infrastructure Commercial centre does *not* happen Lettings problems – estate extremely unpopular
1972–8	Attempts to resolve serious financial problems
1974	Problems set in, high turnover Rents too high for viability
1980–2	Immigrant families move in – large Turkish community
1984	AKB Company reports problems to government – building 'damages', maintenance, social problems, financial crisis AKB Taastrup is among first areas to elect tenant majorities on boards
1985	Parliament launches rescue programme for difficult to let estates

238

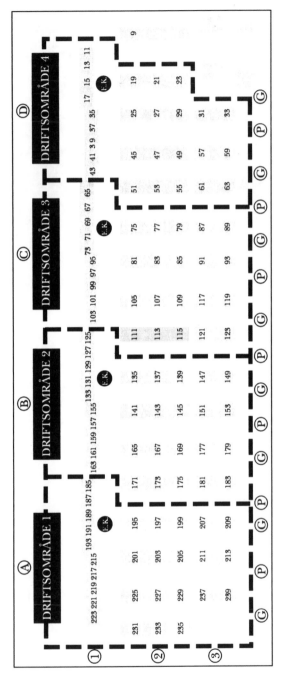

Figure 10.2   Taastrupgaard – making the estate more friendly

Key: Areas A, B, C, D – orange, blue, pink, yellow, concrete painting. *A – D* environmental groups. *G* and *P* –
garden and patio areas alternately
Driftsområde 1, 2, 3, 4 – 4 areas of estate. *EK* – 4 caretaking offices. – (*1*) Long block – 300 units. (*2*) Middle
blocks – 27 units. (*3*) Small blocks – 16 units. *Source. AKB*, 1988.

1986	Estate faces bankruptcy – AKB sets up local office and project team
1986–90	Environmental project – concrete decks removed, gardens built, pitch roofs added
	Estate board revitalised
	Estate subdivided into four areas with mini-boards and offices
	Special caretaking initiative and local lettings
1988	EC training funds
	Local offices set up on estate
	Estate TV company developed
	Turkish language classes
	Carpentry and gardening projects
1989	Community house built
	Taastrupgaard becomes an international model, presented at major conferences around Europe
1990	Rescue project ends
	Turkish representatives on Board – but quickly leave
	Intensive caretaking 'normalised'
1992	New representatives taken onto Board
1993	Evaluation shows success of project but work incomplete
	Town Committee reports to parliament on social integration and special measures to help minority communities
1994	New round of government spending on estate rescue initiatives, particularly targeted at helping minority communities
1995	Taastrupgaard still conspicuously disadvantaged – underlying social problems – new attempts at community involvement and integration

Source: Author's visits and research

11 Portrait of Ballymun, Ireland, 1966–95

ABOUT THE ESTATE

Ballymun was the most ambitious high-rise housing estate in the history of the country. In the early days, Ballymun was the place to be...
... Hundreds of vacant and wrecked flats, vandalism and decay, drug problems, all combine to give the impression of a community falling apart at the seams... a purgatory unfortunate souls had to pass through before moving on to greener pastures. (Ballymun Task Force, 1987)

There are too many cuckoos and not enough house-builders in Ballymun... (SUSS Centre, 1987)

Ballymun needs all inclusive strategies which try to tackle all the factors causing decay and deprivation simultaneously. (Ballymun Task Force, 1988)

Refuse collection will be isolated from the entrance foyers, and storage methods will be improved to reduce smell and general nuisance...
... The success of the renewal programme will hinge crucially on the commitment of people who live in the community, appreciating and protecting what it puts in place. There was widespread local involvement in its conception and design. (Dublin Corporation, 1991)

The Ballymun Job Centre exists because people living in an area of high unemployment are determined to do all in their power to build a future with work... business start-ups as well as job placements... (Ballymun Job Centre, 1991)

Overall, the results of the survey support the view that the pilot refurbishment has been a success. (Dublin Corporation, 1994)

It is clear that the government will not entertain the idea of housing construction on a large scale in the foreseeable future – probably never again. (Dublin Corporation, 1991)

Public housing caters for that section of the population unable to provide adequate housing from its own resources... those unable to exercise this responsibility depend upon local authorities to meet their housing needs... (DoE (Ireland), 1991)

PROBLEMS FROM THE START

In the 1960s and 1970s, Ireland was undergoing rapid economic growth and urbanisation. The outward flow of Ireland's population slowed and in the 1970s, for the first time since records were kept, returning migrants were to outnumber emigrants. Housing demand was running high and a new large-scale estate like Ballymun seemed a godsend. Although opposed by local councillors from the outset, high-rise excited the imagination of government interventionists, in spite of a strongly held national love of single-family houses.

Ballymun was built between 1966 and 1969 as a major symbol of modern Irish government. The National Building Agency, set up specially to execute the project on behalf of the Department of the Environment and Dublin Corporation, imported French technical design – the Balancey industrialised system – to create Ireland's one-off 'high-rise folly'. The estate comprised seven 15-storey towers; 19 8-storey spine or deck access blocks; ten walk-up 4-storey blocks; and 400 single-family houses. Over half of the 2814 flats had three bedrooms and the eventual population of Ballymun was between 15 000 and 20 000. In 1966, when the first tenants moved in, often from slum clearance areas or poor inner-city terraced housing, the estate was pristine, with its gleaming white towers and 'spine' blocks, 73 lifts, ultra-modern district heating system, wide open grass areas – nearly 500 acres – and its proud new inhabitants. It had good transport links, located close to Dublin airport and on fast bus routes to the city centre. A brand new shopping centre was put up by a private developer, as the estate was completed. A golf course and swimming pool followed. But low-rise Dublin and rural Ireland did not take to the experiment with modernity. Quickly the flats experienced above average turnover, as the big incentives to become an owner-occupier enticed away anyone with even modest means. Over the 1970s, 1400 houses were added to Ballymun. The houses were far less difficult and more popular than the flats. Many tenants transferred from flats to houses, many of which were bought by sitting tenants under the tenant purchase scheme (Power, 1993).

From the outset, the management of Ballymun was a problem. Although there was a rent collection office and repairs depot on the estate, both offices answered up to seniors in the City hall and covered a much wider area. While Dublin Corporation employed one repairs worker and one administrator for every 30 dwellings on average, there was less than one staff to a hundred dwellings on Ballymun. Tower blocks and spine blocks had caretakers – there were 30 in all – but they had no ability to maintain lifts or carry out communal repairs. Co-ordination and supervision on the ground was almost non-existent. Intensive estate management for such a large estate was 'very limited' and, in the words of a senior housing official, the Corporation 'was low on personal input into the estate' (Dublin Corporation, 1991).

FIRST SPECIAL PROJECT

The Area Health Board, responsible for social work and community support in the Dublin area, was quickly persuaded to set up a special Ballymun project in 1968 to try and develop the embryonic community by helping people to settle and form support groups. Eventually, towards the end of the 1970s, there were encouraging signs that the estate might take root, as turnover began to drop (SUSS Centre, 1987). But Ballymun had earned a reputation in the wider community for poor services, insecurity, transience and poverty. Dublin Corporation gave additional points for transfer applicants if they lived in flats, which led to a high turnover in Ballymun. The generous tenant purchase schemes also encouraged the outward flow of economically active tenants from Ballymun flats. No one wanted to buy them and the government recently decided 'not to proceed with the sale of any local authority flats' (Dublin Corporation, 1995). As Dublin Corporation sold off a majority of its houses to sitting tenants, so areas of high flats like Ballymun, where there were major obstacles to purchase, became 'welfare enclaves', with a large majority of the population dependent on State support. People who aspired to buy would not accept an allocation at Ballymun if they could help it. Letting Ballymun became a serious problem.

Many of Ballymun's problems stemmed from its size, from the deep unpopularity of flats in Ireland, from the lack of local management, and from the fact that tenants could not realistically exercise their right to buy in such an expensive and unpopular multistorey complex. These features led to ever greater social problems, as its unpopularity determined who moved in. A deep cynicism prevailed over its condition and decline. By 1977, there were serious worries over Ballymun's future.

In 1980, the Ballymun Community Project was set up with a grant from the Corporation to help train tenants' associations on the estate and encourage their development. The Corporation itself set up an office at Ballymun, staffed by members of the Community Development Section, which generated considerable support for local tenants' associations. Many new groups emerged. Between 1980 and 1984, the turnover rate at Ballymun began to drop – from 19 per cent to 14 per cent – though this was still very high. It is probable that some of the drop in turnover, measured by new lettings as a proportion of the total number of tenants, was accounted for by a rise in empty units. Many flats were simply not relet.

ONSET OF THE CRISIS

In 1985, the turnover shot up. There were 1171 new lettings to flats in that year, nearly half of all the flats. There were a number of reasons, linked to government and city policy far beyond the bounds of Ballymun. Firstly, lettings to newcomers were changing dramatically, as the composition of the city's waiting list changed. By 1985, over half of those registered for council housing were 'non-conventional' – that is, non-married – households. If they were lone parents with one child, they were frequently allocated flats. At Ballymun, married couples with children had comprised four-fifths of new tenants in 1980 but by 1986, 68 per cent of new tenants were single people and unmarried or lone parents. Between 1980 and 1986, 68 per cent of all council lettings were to people dependent on state benefits. The composition of applicants generally for Dublin council housing was changing radically away from two-parent families (see Figure 11.1 and Table 11.1).

Another change confirmed the rapid decline in Ballymun's fortunes. As the housing supply expanded in the building boom of the early 1980s, the size of Dublin's housing list shrank from 6071 in 1980 to 4484 in 1985. Because flats were intrinsically unpopular among tenants, the City Council reserved 50 per cent of lettings of new houses to transfer cases, many of whom were from flats. An even higher proportion of lettings to new inner-city dwellings (60 per cent) were allo-

Single men   1984 – 7%;   1985 – 25%;   1986 – 33%;
Married couples   1980 – 78%;   1986 – 22%;

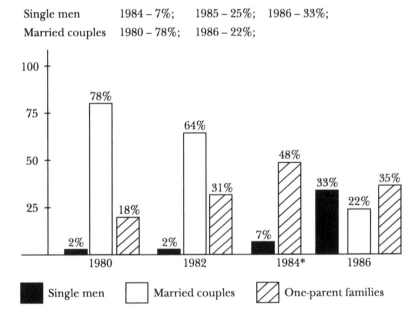

Note: *Married couples missing for 1984.
Source: SUSS Centre (1987, pp. 10–11).

Figure 11.1   Changes in lettings on Ballymun, Ireland, 1980–6

Table 11.1   Turnover on Ballymun, Ireland, 1980–6

	1980	1985	1986
Total new lettings in year	887	1171*	1474 (based on figures January–June)

Note: *Dublin Corporation's figure for 1985.
Source: SUSS Centre (1987).

cated to transfer cases. This reinforced the desire to move among flat dwellers and prevented people from putting down roots. As soon as people could, they transferred to houses. Inevitably the priority for the houses went to more established, more stable tenants. As people moved out, empty flats became harder and harder to let. The people left behind in this process were poorer and less favoured economically and socially.

> Relationships between neighbours on any housing estate develop slowly as trust is established and they learn to do small things for each other...key [people] are among those who leave...transience strikes right at the foundations of community. (SUSS Centre, 1987, p. 5)

SURRENDER GRANT

From the perspective of Ballymun, the government made matters very much worse by offering a £5000 surrender grant to any tenant willing to move out of council housing into the private sector to buy. An important goal was to enable more council tenants to become home-owners. The new policy expanded access to council housing for very disadvantaged and homeless people, the 'non-conventional' single parents and single, otherwise homeless men – who appeared to be in-creasing in numbers. The surrender grant of £5000 had little appeal to tenants in good council housing, who had the right to purchase their home at very large discounts worth much more than £5000. But to tenants in Ballymun, it offered a powerful incentive and the chance of a lifetime; if they wanted to escape from a high-rise flat and from being a tenant on this estate. It facilitated many moves from the estate, where low-income people often aspired to purchase but could not achieve it without moving. By 1987, 10 per cent of Ballymun tenants joined the surrender grant scheme. Demand for Ballymun evaporated, fuelled by the exodus and by the general drop in demand. Even opening up lettings to previously excluded single people did not create enough demand to fill the empties. The number of boarded up flats shot up from 150 in 1980 to 300 in 1986. By 1989, it had reached 450.

The rapid change in the composition of the population, the dramatic rise in the number of empty dwellings, the loss of confidence generated by the surrender grant take-up, and the rapid rehousing of single, homeless people, many of whom could not cope with flat-living in Ballymun, all created an atmosphere of mayhem on the estate. Standards of service plummeted, as the city increasingly used Ballymun to take the weight of mounting social problems. Although Ballymun was less than 10 per cent of the city's council stock, it housed 45 per cent of the city's single parents, 29 per cent of the homeless and 59 per cent of the single male applicants. Many of these were discharged from institutions, had a long history of instability and stayed only a short while on Ballymun (Kelleher *et al.*, 1988). Instability was maybe the biggest problem.

Other aspects of the estate's structure were beginning to cause serious concern. The 73 lifts and 147 open entrances to the blocks were a constant target of abuse and a harbour for threatening activity. The youthful population compounded the estate's problems, generating inevitable wear and tear, vandalism, graffiti and noise problems. Repair costs at Ballymun were three times the city average. To make matters worse, arrears were double the city average with over half of all rents unpaid. The shopping centre, once popular and successful became a dark and decayed drug-dealing centre. Up to 20 random shop vans were set up on the grass as substitutes and steel containers became the new secure trading centres (see Figure 11.2, p. 263). One in six flats were empty and Ballymun's future seemed precarious.

RESIDENT ACTION AND LOCAL RESPONSE

In 1984, there was a major trigger for resident action. The Bank of Ireland closed its Ballymun branch, the sole bank on the estate – only a limited part-time service survived. Residents' groups, up in arms, formed the Ballymun Community Coalition to fight for the estate. One of their first decisions was to organise a credit union to replace the bank. The Coalition over the following years was to change the tide of events in Ballymun.

In the same year, Dublin Corporation set up a committee for the estate which for the first time recognised Ballymun as a special case, although it did not win the confidence of tenants or local activists, who were not allowed to attend Corporation committee meetings. The Special Committee to monitor and implement proposals for the betterment of Ballymun:

> ... is made up of local councillors and members of Dublin Corporation.... Tenants' groups have for a long time requested positions on the committee but to no avail. They still cannot sit in the gallery though members of the press are welcomed. (SUSS Centre, 1987, p. 32)

Corporation officials visited estates in Britain to see how chronic decline could be tackled. One of the estates they visited was Broadwater Farm, Haringey, where local management and tenant involvement were having a dramatic impact. This encouraged the belief that Ballymun could be saved, but only with the residents, not in spite of them (Whelan, 1991). Dublin Corporation adopted a radical new management approach to Ballymun.

FIRST LOCAL OFFICE

In 1985, the Corporation set up its first local office on Ballymun, working directly with the tenants. It chose the Shangan area where there were several tenants' associations, strongly organised into a Community Council. They were extremely vociferous over conditions, particularly the chaotic lettings situation. Shangan comprised 781 units, mostly flats, including two towers. An estate officer with an assistant and a community development worker were based full-time in an office in Shangan. There were daily meetings with the local repairs team to organise a blitz on empty units and to clear the backlog of repairs. There were frequent meetings with tenants over problems of rubbish, crime, noise, damage, empty units, and other disturbances. The tenants' associations were given an adjacent office in the flats. The Community Council played a major role in recommending tenants for empty flats, advising the office of new empties, reporting damage and generally acting as guards, custodians and information links. Eighty per cent of all new lettings were on tenants' recommendations, made possible by generally low demand and the commitment to rebuild community links. Within a few months, the backlog of repairs had disappeared and, under the impact of the intensive effort, around 100 empty units were restored and let. The cost per repair dropped, due to the localised system (Whelan, 1991). The tenants' enthusiasm for the initiative was enormous. The Corporation installed a secure door with entry phones on one of the entrances as an experiment. This was such a success that tenants collected among themselves to instal seven other doors. These, however, quickly broke under constant use. Nevertheless, the overall impact of the local office and the tenants' involvement was remarkable. Shangan was full, and a model of resident involvement.

SCREENING LETTINGS

The role of the tenants in screening applicants was most extra-ordinary. The Corporation had moved from a position of excluding residents from the meetings of the Ballymun Special Committee to allowing them direct input into lettings, albeit on a consultative basis. The Corporation retained the final control. The threat of total collapse of management, fol-lowing from the previous lettings policy, led to a dramatic change in approach. The generally favourable supply and demand situation had made Ballymun's viability precarious. The surrender grant, the oversupply of unpopular dwellings, the instability of many single, previously homeless households, the unsuitability of Ballymun for ever bigger concentrations of disturbed and fragile people, all created a quest for new solutions. The most prominent and useful actors became the residents who were organised into associations or pressure groups. Tenants were successful in stopping the policy of indiscriminate rehousing of single and homeless people. Local studies had shown that 40 per cent of these applicants, even after accepting a flat, did not take up residence at Ballymun and the majority left within a year (Kelleher *et al.*, 1988). Homeless support and campaign groups argued against indiscriminate rehousing of vulnerable single people on Ballymun and backed the tenants in their attempt to restore controls. Families with children were favoured. Adult children of residents were often rehoused and over 50 per cent of lettings on Ballymun were to new households forming on Ballymun itself. The youthful population, high density and overcrowding in flats as children grew up, favoured this approach. Single people had to be over 21. Unmarried mothers could be rehoused at 18. Tenants tried to identify households who either were too transient to stay for more than a short while or who needed special care and who could not cope with unsupported living in high-rise flats. They also tried to screen out tenants with disruptive behaviour to help the estate regain some stability. Ballymun already had disproportionate numbers of residents with psychiatric problems: a special project was created to support them called LINX. There was general agreement that no more such cases should be housed at Ballymun, since it made things worse for them and for other residents. But Ballymun continued to house ever higher proportions of welfare recipients. On the whole, only very low-income and relatively vulnerable people aspired to Ballymun. Therefore, there was no question of excluding the poor and favouring an 'elite'.

The success of the tenants' associations and the local office in Shangan won the admiration and envy of people all over the estate. Empty units were still climbing elsewhere on the estate but Shangan was full and, for the first time in Ballymun's checkered history, responsible and committed tenants were working in close concert with the council to try and save their homes. The Corporation had committed itself irreversibly to tenant involvement and was willing to consider a large measure of tenant control. By 1986, a survey of nearly 500 tenants across Ballymun conducted by SUSS (SUSS Centre, 1987) showed that over half of interviewed residents wanted to stay on Ballymun, admittedly in some cases because of lack of realistic alternatives. The strongest criticism of Ballymun in the survey findings was the repairs service. Forty-three per cent said they wanted to stay on Ballymun permanently. A majority of respondents had lived on the estate for over five years and represented a strong and stable core. The large-scale rapid turnover had happened alongside this more permanent group (see Chapter 5, Figure 5.3). Tenants' associations burgeoned, found new life, formed coalitions, sometimes clashed or collapsed and re-formed. Ballymun had generated over 90 active groups and associations by 1987. There were 32 officially recognised tenants' associations.

1987 was a watershed for Ballymun. The surrender grant was scrapped by the government and a Remedial Works Programme was announced to restore run-down estates. Ballymun was not included in the first round of estates designated for special funding. Padraig Flynn, then Minister of State in the Dail responsible for the Remedial Works Programme, now European Commissioner for Social Affairs, stated:

Money alone will not solve the problems. New policies will not work unless the people want them to work... (Flynn, 1987)

The Ballymun Community Coalition decided to run a community candidate for the national elections in order to create pressure on government and force priority to be given to Ballymun. Eight hundred votes were cast in favour of the local community candidate, threatening the political status quo and creating powerful momentum for local action.

BALLYMUN TASK FORCE

The Coalition decided to set up a special Task Force to develop a housing plan for Ballymun, representing the local community, and inviting the Area Health Board, the local TDs (elected members of the national government), and other organisations working on Ballymun to join in. There were eight community delegates, forming a majority of the Task Force but there was an outside Chair to ensure independence and to lever in outside support. The three main goals were to upgrade the physical environment, increase security and establish social stability. Comprehensive local estate management and resident involvement were taken as essential prerequisites. The Task Force aimed to combine the different interests of the estate and the outside bodies concerned. It developed proposals for physical renovation, localised lettings and housing management, community development and social support. It won the backing of the council, the government and the European Community; it expanded the role of residents and pressed for resources. It argued that economic stability was impossible as long as people moved immediately they found work. It concluded:

> Stark, unrelieved poverty is the main factor underlying the crisis…a poorly planned housing and physical environment aggravates poverty…[but] poverty on a wide scale leads to a deterioration of housing and of the physical environment, no matter how well planned it is. (Ballymun Task Force, 1988)

The Task Force became a conspicuous unifying structure on the estate. It helped to keep all parties in the ring and working together in a single forum. It operated by consensus and it fought continually for Ballymun's tenants. The Task Force helped with the design of the remedial works, argued for the extension of local management offices across the estate, supported local tenants' representation, and argued for high standards, both among residents' groups and statutory bodies. Important progress resulted from a number of elements together: European Community funding for a worker and local office through the Combat Poverty Agency; Dublin Corporation's willingness to listen and respond within its changing management style; the opening of local housing offices; the support of the government, both among politicians and civil servants; intensive community development;

the co-operation of different interest groups around Ballymun's renewal. When European funding for the Task Force ended, Dublin Corporation provided support.

REMEDIAL WORKS PROGRAMME

A major remedial works programme for Ballymun was announced in 1988, based on the success of local management, the dynamism of the tenants' organisations and the stated desire of the majority of residents to stay put. By the time remedial works were agreed, 17 per cent of the estate was empty – 450 units. Physical problems fuelled the social unease. The Ballymun Task Force concluded that:

> The present physical layout of the flats and their environs make it very difficult for tenants to exercise personal and collective control over the area in which they live… Security is undermined by an inability to identify who has or has not legitimate business in their area, lack of opportunities to monitor comings and goings, many and easy escape routes for wrong-doers. (Ballymun Task Force, 1988)

The problems at Ballymun were so immense and required such high reinvestment that the improvement plan proposed 11 phases over ten years. The area to be covered by the first phase was selected by active tenants' representatives in an estate-wide consultation, with the sensitive help of a community architect from the 'Corpo'. Selection was based on the severity of problems and the energy, organisation and commitment of tenants. Allowing tenants to prioritise the phases was an extraordinary gesture in favour of resident involvement by the Corporation. It demonstrated the ability of both residents and the council to break the mould. It required unanticipated generosity, foresight and tolerance among tenants to reach agreement on prioritising the work in favour of a single area, when all were so needy.

The works proposed for Phase 1 were ambitious and expensive, costing £20 000 a unit, covering 280 units. The final cost of Phase 1 was nearly £6 000 000. It included:

- restoring the concrete panels;
- waterproofing and colour-coating the blocks;
- upgrading the balconies with the addition of window boxes;
- enclosing areas around the blocks as private gardens for residents;
- securing all entrances with steel doors;
- closing off all surplus entrances and creating a single, secure main entrance to each block with concierge door staff;
- overhauling lifts and changing the layout of the landings including the closure of open decks and installation of secure doors at each landing;
- creating an enclosed play area for small children for each individual block;
- planting a neighbourhood park.

The most important aims were to create an atmosphere of security; to make it possible for individual tenants to control their homes; and to transform the visible appearance and the environment of the blocks (see Figure 11.3, p. 263). Each block would be secured with a perimeter fence and gardens, so that tenants would take on responsibility for maintaining their block. The Corporation's community architect, in laborious and sometimes daily consultation with residents, adapted the plans until everyone was satisfied. For example, he made the railings enclosing the grounds around each block higher, to create a stronger sense of security, at the request of tenants. He described his work with tenants in this way:

> Dealing with these associations can be difficult and time-consuming but this is a small price to pay for the involvement of interested and committed people... They disagree, fragment, regroup and undergo the effects of personality clashes, etc. They are, however, composed of interested, active and involved people, whose interest and motivation is impressive. (Dublin Corporation, 1991)

Phase 1 of the remedial works was delayed by two years of haggling between Dublin and the government over costs and over the organisation of the contract. Eventually, the improvements were carried out between 1991 and 1993.

BALLYMUN CREDIT UNION

Alongside the physical and management renewal, other developments were changing Ballymun. Ballymun was the poorest estate in the study. Its poverty was a major cause of the bank closure in 1984. After two years of training with the Irish League of Credit Unions, a group of 20 residents in 1987 formed a much-needed, member-based savings and loans society. By 1990, 2188 residents had bought membership shares in the co-operatively organised union. By 1994, there were over 5000 members. Savings in the year to December 1990 totalled just over £500 000 and loans for that year £413 000, an average of £190 per member (Ballymun Credit Union, 1990). By far the biggest single category of loans was for home improvements. The next biggest categories were holidays and Christmas. By 1994, there were £1 000 000 in reserves and an annual turnover of £1 000 000.

With a walk-in 'bank' in the shopping centre, the Union was run on an entirely voluntary basis, until 1994 when a manager was appointed. Defaults and bad debts amounted to £11 000, just over 1 per cent of turnover. The Credit Union was a strongly reinforcing product of both the poverty and the community resources of Ballymun. It helped a very large number of people, both through the involvement it inspired, the training in budgeting, accounting and organising it offered, the confidence and co-operation it developed, and the direct assistance it gave in times of need. The Credit Union was launched with a start-up grant of only £7500 from the Corporation and after this, operated on the basis of self-sufficiency. The board remained committed to the voluntary principle, involving over 20 regular tellers, and board members meeting weekly to transact business and recruit new members. Junior members, of whom there were 200, were particularly welcomed. Its progress was impressive:

> We are pleased to report that the membership continues to grow at a good rate...reflecting the continued importance

of the credit union to the community. (Ballymun Credit Union, 1990)

The Ballymun Credit Union was one of the most practically useful, lively and dedicated initiatives in any of the estates. Most of its leading members were women and all the trained volunteers around during the visits were women too. Mutual aid was particularly important, where outside support was so remote and so hard-won. Council officials and politicians could not disguise their admiration for the tenant leaders who made it happen – 'outstanding self-help' were the words of the senior housing manager. The homogenous culture of the estate, with a strong religious backcloth, appeared to help this member-based co-operative development.

THE BALLYMUN JOB CENTRE

The official unemployment rate at Ballymun was 60 per cent in the late 1980s, of whom 80 per cent had been unemployed for more than two years. The Job Centre, which also opened in 1987, was a further example of local initiative and resident involvement. It was set up as a community-based co-operative with a board comprising residents and funders; two-thirds of the management committee were residents; it had the support of private employers, including IBM which was represented on the Board, and senior politicians, including Garrett Fitzgerald, the ex-Prime Minister. It was registered with the Department of Employment as an official job centre; it employed seven full-time staff, all local residents. By 1991, 3420 local people seeking work had joined its register; 647 had been placed in full-time work; 386 had gained short-term jobs; and 119 had joined training courses. One hundred and three had found jobs for themselves. Five local businesses had been set up. Overall one-third of those registered had been helped in some way.

When the work on installing security fences, gates and doors was agreed in Phase 1 of the improvements, the Job Centre successfully negotiated for a resident-based concierge company to be set up as a co-operative, employing five local people. This worked well in controlling access to the improved blocks and establishing a close relationship between residents and concierge company. Security in the improved blocks was transformed (Ballymun visit, 1994).

The obstacles to work for residents and particularly young residents were enormous – loss of contact with work opportunities, cost of travel and phone calls, loss of confidence and self-esteem, all created huge barriers. The Job Centre broke down those barriers and put people directly on track for work. One of the biggest barriers facing residents seeking work was the hostility of employers to Ballymun. In overcoming this, the Job Centre was particularly valuable. The intermediary role of the Job Centre, on behalf of both tenants and employers, led to changed expectations, greater opportunities and work contact. The Job Centre also provided special support services to residents with severe social problems, trying to find placements for them in tailor-made projects.

FURTHER LOCALISATION

The creation of the Task Force, the Credit Union and the Job Centre, the beginning of the Remedial Works Programme for Ballymun, and the success of the first local management initiative, all made the future of Ballymun seem more promising.

In 1989, the council extended its estate-based housing management experiment from Shangan to a second area in Coultry Road, because of its active tenants' associations and community council, the success of the first office and pressure from tenants to extend the local service. The council used the same staff to service the second office, with similar success. The 70 empty units were 'blitzed' by the now established 'voids squad' and by 1990, there were no empty units in Ballymun East. As Phase 1 of the renovation work began in 1991, the third local management office was opened in Balcurris Road. As each area was opened up, residents played a major role in advising the council and in trying to sort out community problems. The local area offices became more stretched, as the same staff from the first office were expected to cover more areas of the estate on a more part-time basis. They became more and more thinly spread, as in total only three part-time additional estate officers were deployed to the estate. Nevertheless, they did continue to achieve their primary target of cutting voids, clearing the backlog of repairs and involving residents.

In 1990, the Corporation appointed a chief technical officer for Ballymun to take responsibility for all repairs and maintenance, lifts, district heating, drains, lights and other technical services. The complex nature of the high-rise construction and the interlinked main services required a specialist input and close supervision. There were 30 tradesmen in the Ballymun team; they had only been completing on average one repair a week before the improvements began. The Chief Technical Officer set up the special voids squad, which greatly accelerated repairs and reduced costs. The number of repairs per tradesman was nearly ten a week by 1991, ten times higher than previously (Whelan, 1991).

Since then, an office covering the fourth area of Ballymun has opened and the estate developed a waiting list of people wanting to move in for the first time since its opening. Empty units were no longer a problem. For the moment, Ballymun is likely to continue to be in high demand because of the much improved conditions, the shortage of social housing in the Dublin area, the growth in female-headed, lone-parent households, and lower emigration rates due to unemployment elsewhere in Europe, particularly Britain. The tightening of controls on illegal immigrants to the US was a further dampener to the long-running exodus. All these factors created renewed demand for low-cost social housing in Ireland and for Ballymun in particular.

THE THREAT OF DEMOLITION

There were delays in starting Phase 2 of the works while an independent evaluation assessed the improvements to date and the cost of further upgrading. The evaluation showed the overwhelming popularity of the improvements among residents, their success in enhancing security but their more limited impact on structural and design deficiencies. The consultants recommended selective demolition in later phases of the work and higher investment in remedial works to repair roofs, clad the buildings, replace defective piping and do more comprehensive internal works. While the cost of Phase 1 was £20 000 per unit, the estimated cost of later phases was £34 000 (Craig Gardener, 1993). The failure to reroof the blocks, insulate outer walls or remedy internal plumbing problems had left the improved blocks with unresolved defects. The most serious visual oversight was the failure to upgrade the stairwells and improve or replace the lifts. These common areas were startlingly bleak and uninviting, even in the improved blocks, but the cost of all-in improvements was considered prohibitively high.

The very complex, disruptive and costly nature of the work – £84 000 000 for the whole estate – led the government to question the rationale for such elaborate work to an intrinsically difficult and unpopular area. However, the popularity of the new works, the success of the local offices in getting rid of voids and encouraging tenant involvement made Ballymun more attractive and more resilient. As building of social housing virtually stopped at the end of the 1980s and demand rose, so the high cost of replacing 2800 flats reinforced the logic for saving Ballymun and continuing the renewal. Even the higher costs of complete renewal represented considerably less than the replacement cost (see Part IV). The real gap would almost certainly be higher because of rehousing problems and other costs involved in redevelopment (Power, 1993). The blighting effects of a partial demolition plan might also set back the progress, now that all the units had been filled. In November 1994, the Corporation released its long-awaited response to the evaluation, proposing to demolish 560 units in six unimproved tower blocks and their replacement with houses. The main arguments were the balance of costs, the quality of the final product, and the long-term problems foreseen in retaining all the towers. Camera crews and press reporters crowded through the concierge and Task Force offices, looking for dramatic evidence of the justification for demolition. The declared public image of Ballymun became solidly negative again, as sensational headlines announced the demolition plan (Dublin Corporation, 1994).

A VIABLE ESTATE?

Ballymun in 1995, in spite of the radical improvements, was in a far from rosy position. As the only large high-rise, flatted estate in the country, it was not the first choice for families with children and its 2800 flats remain intrinsically difficult to manage. Even the improved blocks still had the problems of roof leaks and damp penetration. The estate was still dominated by poverty and high unemployment. Its place in the hierarchy of estates is still low, although it was no longer the worst estate in Dublin. But Ireland's high overall levels of unemployment meant that estates like Ballymun continued to house high proportions of very needy households.

Ballymun's future viability depends on three elements: integrating the large open spaces with the blocks in the improvement programme, so that they can be used, cleaned and protected; a steady continuation of the remedial works programme, providing security for the many large blocks; consolidating the local management initiative, with adequate staff and a full-time senior manager, a budget and management authority, so that the whole area is covered with an integrated and high-quality service. Dublin Corporation recently set up a new base, run by a high calibre 'supremo' in the newly upgraded shopping centre to attempt this integrated management approach (Dublin Corporation, 1994).

Total upgrading across the whole estate is essential and urgent because most of the entrances and lifts are still unguarded, subject to vandalism, and highly insecure. Most of the 450 acres of open space on the estate are still unplanted and undesignated. Most of the still unimproved blocks are streaked with rain and pollution, grey, almost permanently damp and covered in graffiti up the stairwells, balconies and lifts. Ballymun is still a long way from being saved and only a tenth of its total area has been upgraded. The improvements in Phase 1 have been carried out very much in isolation, and decay may quickly set in unless the whole estate continues to experience an upward momentum at a fairly rapid pace. Selective demolition will almost inevitably lead to the blighting of individual blocks pending demolition. If the towers are to be demolished, it should be done speedily and the site rapidly rebuilt. Ballymun is unusually bleak, partly because the demand on maintenance and custodial services is so intense, and partly because it is so poor. The one area that has so far been upgraded is a great success with the tenants, with its attractive play areas, neat gardens, secure, sturdy and well-designed railings and gates. That new local environment, covering one small area, could be copied.

YOUTHFUL POPULATION

The sheer volume of young people on Ballymun – 4200 under 18 (Irish National Census, 1991) – makes it quite unlike any other estate. It makes for noise, energy, vitality and sometimes conflict. Children and young people are everywhere. Each balcony and entrance is full of them. The school playgrounds and football pitches are alive with them. The 1400 3-bedroom flats exaggerate the tendency to concentrate large families in a poor area.

Young people have time on their hands, so there is a lot of hanging around. This makes the Corporation concerned about protecting the upgrading works in the blocks. When the planting of the enclosed gardens and play areas in Phase 1 was complete, children from the blocks promptly dug up some of the delicate new plants and sold them outside the church after Mass! In spite of this, the Phase 1 improvements, play areas, secure doors, have stood up well to enormous wear and tear and look good two years after completion. The door controls greatly reduced trouble within the improved blocks and the enclosed play areas are well used. The sheer numbers of children, about 300 in the first improvement area, make control difficult in an environment that was ransacked from its inception and that is now being upgraded in slow, small, expensive stages. Will the high fencing surrounding Phase 1 be enough in the face of so many other social and economic pressures? It depends probably more than anything else on keeping local management in place and continuing to work closely with residents' representatives; on creating new opportunities for young people; and continuing to stabilise the estate.

THE ROLE OF THE CHURCH

The Catholic Church plays an active role in the Ballymun Community, both formally and informally. There are at least two independent priests living as tenants in the estate, running community support and community development projects from their flats. One of them is responsible for a tenant training programme. They are valued members of the community. Their purpose is practical rather than religious but they are known as priests and they are often used as go-betweens, both by residents and by the authorities. The actual church and Catholic school on Ballymun have a major presence in the estate, influencing events and activities. Many of the voluntary groups, play-schemes and self-help co-operatives are linked to the Church – including a first communion, dressmaking co-operative. No matter how strongly families are urged not to buy elaborate white 'bridal' dresses, shoes, bags, gloves, veils and jewellery for their girls, smart suits, shirts, waistcoats, ties for their boys, joining in this traditional ritual is a sign of membership and acceptance.

One ironic side effect of the Church's hold on the population is the huge increase in young unmarried mothers (as opposed to divorced, separated or widowed mothers). Young people are adopting a much freer attitude to sex, but in the absence of readily available family planning advice or services, girls are more likely to become pregnant. Abortion is outlawed (as was divorce, before the 1995 referendum) and it is difficult for girls from poor families to do anything but carry through their pregnancy.

As Ireland moves further towards other European countries on these matters, so the values of the younger generation are changing. There is far less stigma attached to being an unmarried mother than previously, and on Ballymun nearly one-third of all households are in this category. Many single parents are under 21. Stable marriage often seems unattainable, with long-term unemployment and emigration problems. Childbearing offers young women a clearly recognised step into adulthood, bringing some status and independence. In a strange way, the role of the offical Church, the breakdown of traditional families and the youthful population go hand-in-hand.

CONCLUSION

In 1994, Ballymun was blazoned across British and Irish television screens in a play by the prizewinning Irish author,

Roddy Doyle (BBC 1 RTE, 1994). Like so many, he was intrigued by Ballymun's problems and portrayed its often disadvantaged residents vividly. Residents, politicians, managers, community activists, were enraged by this new blow to their reputation. In the battle for continued improvements in Phase 2 of the remedial works, confidence was all-important. Making Ballymun's struggles into light evening entertainment, however serious the underlying purpose, was a below-the-belt assault on public confidence in the improvements. A poetry reading for residents by Roddy Doyle did not compensate (Ballymun Task Force, October 1994). But in spite of many remaining problems, in October 1994 all the empty units had gone. There was a waiting list for the estate. The shopping mall was glass covered, attractively lit and paved. Dublin Corporation was pushing new-style progressive management. The estate, with all its volatility and vulnerability, would surely survive, as long as the battle for the improvements was won.

Note: Special thanks are due to Frank Fallon and his colleagues in Dublin Corporation, Sean O'Cuinn and staff at the Department of the Environment and members of the Ballymun Task Force, for their many helpful ideas, comments and corrections to this portrait of Ballymun.

Figure 11.2 Ballymun – unimproved with steel-clad shop van

Figure 11.3 Ballymun – improved block with secure entrances and
play area

KEY DATES AT BALLYMUN

1966	National Building Agency set up by Irish government to speed production of local authority housing French Ballancey high-rise design and production method imported to build Ballymun
	Some local politicians oppose construction of Ballymun
1966–9	Ballymun is built with 2800 flats and 400 houses
1966	First tenants move in
1969	Shopping Centre is built by private developer; swimming pool, golf course added
1970	Health Board sets up special community support initiative to help the unique high-rise estate 'settle down'
	1400 houses added over next few years. Turnover of tenants on Ballymun prevents stability
1977	Serious physical decay sets in
1980	Ballymun Community Project is set up with a grant from the Council to support and help train tenants' associations
1980–4	Dublin Corporation begins to rehouse lone mothers on flatted estates. Ballymun rehouses predominantly lone parents, single men and previously homeless people
1982–5	Dublin's waiting list drops from 6071 to 4484
1984	Dublin Corporation sets up a special housing committee for Ballymun – without tenants' representatives
	The only bank on Ballymun is closed – part-time service
	Ballymun Community Coalition is set up by groups working within Ballymun
1985	The government introduces Surrender Grants. Ballymun experiences a massive exodus
	50 per cent turnover
	Dublin sets up its first local management initiative. Within a few months, the empty units and repairs backlog are cleared

1987   Community Coalition runs a community candidate for Ballymun in the General Election
        Ballymun Job Centre is set up
        Ballymun Credit Union is set up after two years' training, to replace the Bank of Ireland! It now has over 5000 members
        The surrender grant is scrapped
        The Remedial Works Programme is announced
        Ballymun Task Force is set up to draw up a housing plan.

1988   450 empty flats on Ballymun
        Strong resident action against drug abuse
        11-phase programme of remedial works is announced

1989   Second local management office is set up

1990   Works start at Balbutcher after 2-year delay
        Chief Technical Officer is appointed, to be based at Ballymun

1991   Local management is extended to third area
        Empty units fall to 150 after voids squad is set up

1992   Local management is extended to fourth area

1993   Phase 1 work is completed
        There are no longer any empty units on Ballymun and the estate has a waiting list
        Funding for the Task Force ends
        Independent evaluation shows the remedial works are popular but incomplete. It proposes demolition of selected blocks and phased replacement of the whole estate in the long-term

1994   Television series on Ballymun, exposes its social problems and reaffirms its stigma
        Dublin Corporation announces plan for demolition of six towers and continued improvements of rest

1995   New doubts over future

Source: Author's visits and research.

Part IV
Chaos or Community?

12 Extreme Decline in Five Symbolic Estates

INTRODUCTION

The story of the five symbolic estates, whose histories we described in Part III, revealed a very strong pattern. Not only were the essential characteristics of the five estates similar; so was their experience of decline, their position at the extreme end of a spectrum of problem areas, their role in the social housing market, their cumulative slide towards chaos, ending in the loss of viability of their landlord services. In Part IV we draw together the threads from the five case studies in an attempt to understand the complex processes at work. First we present the dominant characteristics of the five estates. Then we examine the nature of their communities and the racial question. Lastly we analyse the local interplay of buildings and people with the resulting pressures on management structures and community relations. Part IV uncovers the deep-seated social consequences of polarisation in mass estates. Table 12.1 presents basic information about the five case study estates.

TENURE AND OWNERSHIP

Table 12.2 shows the different landlords on the five estates. Only the Danish estate was exclusively rented. In France, some areas of the estate were dominated by attractive, low-rise, privately-owned homes, making up 20 per cent of the total stock. The German estate was set up to include many resident landlords. Fifteen per cent of the property, about 200 units, was still directly owned by private individuals who retained a direct interest in the property, ran their flats themselves, and in a few cases actually used them for family members. But almost the whole estate was rented out. In Britain and Ireland, there were virtually no owners in the flatted areas. The small number of 'right-to-buy' owners in London was concentrated

Table 12.1 Location and physical characteristics of five estates

	France	Germany	Britain	Denmark	Ireland
Main city to which linked	Lyons	Cologne	London	Copenhagen	Dublin
Distance from centre city	13 km	13 km	7 km	15 km	8 km
Location	Peripheral	Peripheral	Outer, within city	Peripheral	Peripheral
Number of units	7171 social rented 2100 owner-occupied	1322	1063	981	2814 rented 400 owner-occupied
Date of construction	1965–73	1974–75	1967–70	1970–2	1965–9
Flats	95%	100%	97%	100%	85%
Houses	5%	–	3%	–	15%
Type of construction	Concrete; high-rise and medium-rise	Concrete; high-rise	Concrete; high-rise and medium-rise	Concrete; medium-rise	Concrete; high-rise and 'spine' blocks

Sources: Author's visits; Windsor Workshop (1991).

Table 12.2   Ownership and tenure on five case studies

Country	Ownership	Tenure
France	Variety of housing associations 11 HLM societies 2 *offices publics* 7 *sociétés anonymes* 2 *sociétés d'économie mixte*	80% social renting; 20% owner-occupiers (social co-owners)
Germany	Private investors Originally 600 individual private investors – now mainly owned by investment companies and 200 individual companies	99% private renting; of which 15% rented out directly by owners (200 units); about one-third social lettings nominated by Cologne City
Britain	Local authority Haringey Council, outer London	99% council tenants; a few houses sold
Denmark	Non-profit housing company Arbejdernes Kooperative Byggeforening	100% social housing tenants
Ireland	Local authority Dublin Corporation	85% council tenants; some tenant purchasers (houses only)

Sources: Author's visits; Windsor Workshop (1991).

among the few houses, while in Dublin 400 houses had been acquired by tenant purchasers. In no case did the ownership structure protect the estates from cataclysmic decline.

TYPES OF ESTATES

The estates were difficult for poor households, particularly the young, the elderly, lone parents and minorities with large families, the very groups that were concentrated there.

There was a very big difference in size between the Danish, German and British estates with 1000 to 1500 units, the Irish estate of over 3000, and the French estate of over 9000 units. A thousand social rented units in a single discrete area stood out rather than blended into the urban patchwork. Although the estates were too distinctive to form part of the surrounding area, they were too poor and had been built in too uniform and too mono-functional a way to support the wide range of services necessary for self-sufficiency. This gave them the worst of both worlds – poor services and dependence. However, the larger estates supported more services, due to their greater size, than the smaller ones, and therefore were in some ways at least potentially more attractive.

The combination of their size, with their tenure and the low incomes of their inhabitants made these five estates notably more difficult than smaller estates with similar characteristics. Smaller estates were, according to all landlord organisations, more easily integrated with their surroundings.

JUTTING OUT OF THE LANDSCAPE

One of the greatest distinctions of the five estates was how clearly they all stood out from their surroundings. They had been designed to do this, by their creators – architects, developers and politicians – confident of the prestige that would follow. In later years, when they proved unpopular and hard to let, this distinctiveness became a major liability. It became easy for popular fantasies to evolve around the estates' unique appearance. The fact that physically they failed to blend into either town or country, while juxtaposed between both, made it easier to attach social 'myths' to them. The British estate, for example, was likened to 'Windscale', a nuclear plant; the German estate to an alternative Cologne Cathedral and to Kolditz. The distinctiveness fed the imagination of journalists and made them compelling to media prophets looking for extreme images to illustrate doom-laden visions.

CONCRETE COMPLEX STRUCTURES

The estates represented some of the most elaborate examples of technically complex, often untried, modern factory building systems producing dense, medium and high-rise, flatted estates. The concrete panel construction, the complex service systems – refuse, lifts, heating – the communalised structures were all fault-prone and antisocial in character. The vast bulk of units were in large blocks of four or more storeys, although three of the estates had a small number of houses. In all cases, these were popular and were used to try and keep stable residents and local staff within the area. Four of the five estates had extremely high towers of over 17 storeys and a predominance of flats in high-rise blocks of six or more storeys. Problems of damp, cold, and wind tunnels, of mechanical failure in heating and lifts, of insecurity and lack of personal identification, of disrepair and refuse disposal problems, stemmed in large measure from the type and style of construction.

In addition to oversized towers, large slab blocks were common on all the estates. These shared many of the problem characteristics of towers, while being almost as conspicuous. Slab or deck-access blocks had some additional problems. In particular, the long balconies, decks and internal corridors, the numerous entrances and the greater number of people with access to the block, made for even bigger problems of insecurity, loss of identification and alienation than the towers created. The problems of slab blocks in Denmark and England were compounded by the fact that blocks were linked together by bridges and decks. The long walkways at many levels were often deserted and therefore frightening. The slab blocks often had greater noise problems because people could only reach their flats through overhead decks or internal corridors. These invariably created vibrations in dwellings below. They were called 'streets in the sky' but they were built as ceilings. All the estates had either internal corridors or external decks, or both.

While most of the blocks on the estates were large and warren-like, dwarfing the inhabitants and compounding disturbance, each estate had some extraordinarily large blocks. In France, Ireland, and England, the tower blocks had around

100 units within each. In Germany, the largest tower, with massive internal corridors, had 540 units in it. In Denmark, the giant slab block running the length of the estate contained over 300 units. The ziggurat or scissor block in England had 160 units.

The huge scale of individual blocks, particularly in the German and Danish cases, was a major deterrent to human contact. The internal routes through these blocks were overwhelming in their sheer scale and repetitiveness. The sense of being lost in a maze, the loneliness and sense of abandonment in the often empty and dark corridors, was undermining and tension-creating. Within each estate, there was a hierarchy of buildings that usually placed the largest and most complex blocks at the bottom. Table 12.3 summarises the scale of the individual blocks.

Table 12.3   Scale of blocks

Country	Estate scale
France	63 towers, 17 storeys high, 100 units each; some lower blocks, 8 storeys high.
Germany	5 blocks, 2 highest have 26 storeys and 540 units each.
Britain	2 high-rise blocks, 18 storeys, 102 units each; 10 blocks of 4–6 storeys; 1 ziggurat; 27 houses.
Denmark	1 very long slab block with 400 units; 33 other long blocks.
Ireland	36 blocks: 7 15-storeys high, 100 units each; 19 8-storeys (long blocks); 10 4-storeys. 400 houses.

Sources: Author's visits; Windsor Workshop (1991).

FACILITIES

Facilities varied greatly between estates. They depended on national systems of funding and also on the size of estate. On all the estates, facilities were numerous, modern and publicly provided. In Denmark, provision was most elaborate, Ireland had the most self-help groups and least purpose-built facilities. Table 12.4 shows the facilities at the time of the Windsor Workshop. Contrary to popular images of poor areas, it was not true that the estates lacked facilities. During their early years, the estate facilities had been inadequately provided but gradually, often in later building or improvement phases, facilities were added. Then, as populations plummeted, facilities that had eventually been built declined, or even closed down. Only in the more recent period of rescue attempts, did social and community facilities regain necessary support. The phasing of facilities and adjusting or adapting them to changing needs was a major problem. Facilities had been provided in three main stages: during the initial building period; during the period of decline and crisis; and during the rescue period. But there were some serious gaps in provision. For example, the German estate, which had been built as luxury housing for small adult households, experienced a serious shortage of

Table 12.4   Facilities on five estates

Facilities	*Number of estates with facilities*
Shops	5
Community flats	5
Outdoor recreation areas	5
Play areas	4
Schools	4
Training centre	4
Café(s)	4
Family support centre	4
Nursery	4
Church	3
Mosque	3
Youth centres	3
Community centre	3
Swimming pool	2

Sources: Author's visits; Windsor Workshop (1991).

school and nursery places for young children. In Denmark, in Germany, in Ireland and in Britain, the estates had no proper community centre for the first 15 or 20 years of their existence. This gap was keenly felt by residents and social support agencies.

Shopping areas were provided on all estates. Their main problem was their viability and their quality in poor communities. Shops had closed in London and Germany. The three smaller estates fared worse for shops than the large Irish and French estates, though in Dublin, the shopping centre became seriously decayed.

Revenue problems

Community and social facilities faced virtually continual revenue funding problems. The poverty of the estates made dependence on external funding almost total. Facilities provided as part of a national public service such as schools were the most stable and most durable. Facilities that relied on resident initiative and voluntary funding or short-term grants often flourished for a short time, then hit a difficult period in sustaining voluntary input or in renewing the commitment from the local authority to provide grants. Facilities that relied on private sector money, mainly shops, banks and cafés, operated with difficulty and were reported to charge higher than average prices, on the grounds of transport, security and insurance costs. Given the low income of these communities, it was hard to see how services could avoid either public subsidy or charitable support. The alternative was a low-level operation, often at above average cost. Many facilities and services fell into poor condition during the time of acute decline.

POPULATION AND SOCIAL NEED

Table 12.5 shows the population of each estate, including total numbers and changes over time, proportions of young people, of minorities, and estimated levels of unemployment. All estates suffered major population losses by the beginning of the 1980s, which had serious consequences for services. All the estates had been built for a far larger population than they

Table 12.5   Population characteristics of the five estates

Country	France	Germany	Britain	Denmark	Ireland
Size of units	Large units, large families; slack demand for these units	Many 1-bedroom units; therefore overcrowding	Nearly half 1-bed; therefore lots of young singles; rest 2- and 3-beds	251 with 3-beds or more; 576 with 2 or more beds	Mostly family- sized units
Number of inhabitants	35 000 (1975) 20 000 (1981) 25 000 (1991)	2400 (1987) 4000 (1991)	3000 (1970) 2000 (1983) 3000 (1991)	2200 (1985 estimate) 2800 (1991)	15 000 (1970) 11 000 (1987 estimate) 13 000 (1991)
Young people	35% under 16	32% under 16 (in 1987 1340 under 18 – 55%)	20% under 16 (1991 census)	40% under 20 (estimate 30% under 16)	30% under 18
Unemployment (1987)	13% but 37% for foreigners (4.5% in 1975)	30%	40% 60% among youth	15% officially (increased 5-fold 1970–85 – 45% of all adult house-holds with no earner)	60% (of whom 80% long-term, that is over 2 years)
Proportion of ethnic minority households	30% (of whom ⅔ North African)	70% (1755 Turkish, 1022 other foreign – ⅔ Turkish – ⅓ ethnic Germans, Poles and so on	60% (primarily Afro-Caribbean – 42%)	25% of units / households (40% of population, of whom vast majority are Turkish)	Virtually none

Sources: Windsor Workshop (1991); some follow-up information from author's estate visits and from Census.

ended up with. This meant that many projected services never materialised, for example, transport in Lyons, where the population dropped by 16 000 in the five years following its completion. The population loss meant that school intakes dropped dramatically and some schools were cut or closed down.

The isolation of the estates created a need for their own local services – particularly doctors, schools, shops, and transport – but there were real problems of sustainability, due to the distance from the city, the changing structure of the populations, the poverty of many residents and the fluctuation in number of households. Demand for all the estates rose in the mid- to late-1980s. As populations went up, services for families and children in particular were put under great strain. The needs of young residents changed within a restricted period – a bulge in kindergarten-age children would become a bulge in primary school-age children and then teenagers over a ten-year period. The estates were not self-contained or balanced in terms of their demands on services. For example, in France in 1991, there were disproportionate numbers of newly-forming, young adult households of North African origin, as a result of their families having moved in in the late 1970s with young children. In Germany, there was a chronic shortage of infant places, while in Ireland, there had been a surplus of school places which later vanished.

The estates housed far above the national averages of children and young people, of unemployed and low-income households. The British estate had many young adult households. The youthful populations had an impact on levels of unemployment, as each year the proportion of school-leavers from the estates looking for work was far above the average in the population as a whole. This made the provision of services both more urgent and more difficult.

Racial factors

In Ireland, there was virtually no immigrant or ethnic minority population. Therefore this discussion concentrates on the other four estates. There were large concentrations of ethnic minority populations on these estates, far above their representation in the countries as a whole, in the cities in which they were located, or in social housing. Such concentrations were not common to all of the difficult estates in this survey (see Part II), although they usually occurred where the estate was linked to a city with a large ethnic population. The process of letting to ethnic minorities began early in the history of the estates when they first proved unpopular and difficult-to-let. The point at which these estates were built coincided with a crude balance of new dwellings within the countries. This resulted in vacant and unlet units early on in the life of the estates.

Landlords in France, Germany, Denmark and Britain faced government and local authority pressure to house minority groups who had previously been largely excluded from social housing in all countries. This happened simultaneously with serious lettings difficulties on some estates. Such was the rapid turnover of population, that large numbers of immigrants were able to gain access over a fairly short period. For many minority households, previously excluded, the estates offered a significant improvement in conditions. Thus by 1980, when the estates were approaching their lowest ebb, between 30 and 70 per cent of the populations were of minority origin – at least two to three times the general level for the cities to which the estates were linked.

Large concentrations of racially distinct minorities were highly conspicuous in unpopular areas. But the estates did not become unpopular as a result of the new communities that occupied them. These estates at the bottom of a hierarchy of housing choices had disproportionate turnover and a major problem of empty units before newcomers moved in, making their rehousing possible. The growing minority communities were a consequence, not a cause, of unpopularity. The arrival of minorities followed on from the rapid decline in conditions resulting from rising turnover and vacancy levels. Therefore they were directly associated with deteriorating conditions, and blamed for them, as the case studies showed. The public perception of the estates deteriorated significantly, partly through racial stereotyping – but also through discrimination. The standard of services dropped because of the image of a 'black' or ethnic minority area as a bad area. These pressures meant that white native-born households avoided moving to those estates if they could and many moved off as quickly as possible, if already there. The arrival of minority families accelerated an already advanced process of rapid turnover and low demand. This increased management problems resulting from social discontinuity, high volumes of vacated properties, and an influx of culturally distinct and socially excluded households. The accompanying financial and repair burdens stretched management resources, compounding the problems of decline. Initially, landlords, including social landlords, were unused to dealing with large communities of distinct minorities. It was several years before they accepted responsibility for poor conditions or became proactive in race relations, rather than simply assuming that decline was an inevitable result of the expanding immigrant population. The racial factor became self-perpetuating, as housing need among minorities continued unmet. This reached its most extreme in the case of Germany, where for 2 years (1985–7) no native Germans at all were rehoused in the estate, in spite of one third of the estate being empty.

Minority households were on average much poorer because they more often did low-skilled jobs. The second generation were more often unemployed, and therefore even more disadvantaged. They had on average larger and younger families. They were more likely therefore, to be overcrowded. Added to this, they had difficulties in assimilating, partly through rejection by the host community. Figure 12.1 attempts to illustrate the process of exclusion that led to large groups of racial minorities being concentrated in the least favoured estates. The ensuing barriers created community and racial problems that sometimes led to a breakdown in normal social relations. There were fears among local political leaders and within the estates that the ethnic composition of the estates would create 'social ghettos' (City of Cologne, 1994).

Minority youth

There were wider effects from the concentration of racial minorities. Schools were affected by the disproportionate numbers of minority children. Difficulties included language, culture, religion, low teacher expectations, intergroup conflict and underachievement. In addition, teenagers and young adults who were disproportionately of minority origin faced

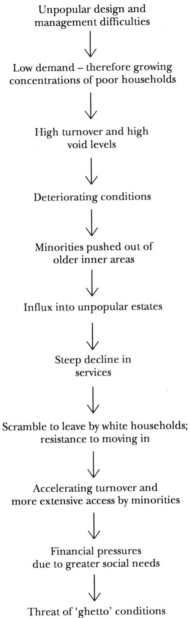

Unpopular design and
management difficulties

↓

Low demand – therefore growing
concentrations of poor households

↓

High turnover and high
void levels

↓

Deteriorating conditions

↓

Minorities pushed out of
older inner areas

↓

Influx into unpopular estates

↓

Steep decline in
services

↓

Scramble to leave by white households;
resistance to moving in

↓

Accelerating turnover and
more extensive access by minorities

↓

Financial pressures
due to greater social needs

↓

Threat of 'ghetto' conditions

Source: Author's visits and research.

Figure 12.1   Decline of estates and minority access

special difficulties over their identity. They no longer fully identified with their parents' culture of origin. But nor in most cases had they been assimilated into the culture of the host community. In fact they felt strongly rejected by it and they found this rejection deeply confusing. This 'confused identity' among minority youth was reported in all four estates with large minority populations (Dubedout, 1983; City of Cologne, 1989; Boligministeriet, 1993; Gifford, 1986). It may be best summed up by a young black witness at the inquiry into the disorders on the London estate in 1985, whose feelings were echoed in the French and German examples:

> If you're cut off from a society, then maybe you know, you don't mind seeing that society crumble, and it may be that you don't even mind being part of what makes that society crumble. That's how the youth see it. They see it that they are deeply alienated from society. They're not allowed to take part and to show they're capable, and that they have a positive, constructive contribution to make towards this society. (Quoted in Zipfel, 1986b)

The concentrations of minority households on the four estates raised much bigger questions about the future of cities, to do with the prospects for integration when once separate areas or communities housed a majority of racially distinct households. Two of the four estates had experienced serious disorders with strong racial overtones. All four estates had community divisions that could not easily be bridged (City of Cologne, 1995). By combining poor conditions with conspicuous minorities, barriers became higher and racial acceptance or tolerance more difficult. Residents within such areas experienced heightened pressures resulting from racial stereotyping. Job access became more difficult, expectations were lowered and failure or low achievement became almost inevitable. This process was particularly well documented on the French estate (Élie *et al.*, 1989). It was recognised by social agencies and it was increasingly recognised by governments (KAB, 1994a; Pfeiffer *et al.*, 1996; Ministère de la Ville, 1993).

On all four estates, the development of large minority communities had created special demands on services and special problems of communication. Minority households, over and above any other disadvantages they might experience, suffered from not being immediately accepted as equal citizens with the dominant population. Where 'minority' households were in a majority on an estate – in the British and German cases – this led to bitterness, tension and insecurity. Young people were particularly conscious of the problem and the sense of rejection could be overwhelming. There were many areas of friction – over language, music, food, children, family patterns, religion and so on. Community tensions and mistrust appeared particularly high in Germany and Denmark – in the German case, between ethnic German immigrants and the large Turkish community; in the Danish case, between Danes and Turkish immigrants. In the London estate, tension was rising in the early 1990s between the more established West Indian community and the more recent West African community. In France, there were tensions between young North Africans and their parents, as well as between racial minorities and whites. In spite of this, a visitor walking round the estates would be struck more often by a sense of familiarity and coexistence between groups, particularly among children and young people, than by an atmosphere of hostility or tension between residents.

It was the coupling of racial disadvantage with estate unpopularity and high concentrations of minorities within restricted, unpopular areas, that led to the growing use of the term 'ghetto' to describe conditions (Salicath, 1987; Tapie, 1993; City of Cologne, 1994; Nygaard, 1995). The problems associated with this population shift were not yet fully iterated.

IRISH EXPERIENCE OF MARGINALISATION

Because the Irish estate housed almost exclusively Irish people, with a common religious, cultural and ethnic background, it helped us to identify causes of extreme stigmatisation that did not relate to race. The decline in popularity was similar in Dublin to the other estates: the rise in empty property and problems with letting; the exodus of economically active households, and the influx of marginal people; the rapid turnover and consequent community instability; the conflict between those more established residents who resented the estate's decline and the newcomers with poor prospects who realised they were being 'dumped' on the estate; the concentration of youthful households, young single mothers and transient, previously homeless men. The resultant growing social conflict, loss of control, rising crime and negative media publicity was as disastrous in Ireland as in the other countries. The outcome was the extreme polarisation of the estate and an intense malaise within it.

It became clear that the European pattern of decline was not caused by the racial identity of newcomers (Jacquier, 1991). Rather it related to the inherent unpopularity of the estates, the failure to establish a stable and secure community, the incrementally lower status of newer inhabitants and the consequent loss of public confidence. The people at the losing end of the social pecking order became conspicuous because of the nature of the estates, their separation from mainstream urban society, and the growing concentration of mainly disadvantaged groups within each area. This process appeared as extreme in an all-white community as in a multiracial or predominantly minority community (Campbell, 1993). It created a similar sense of ghetto-like separation with high social barriers and a desire to avoid the area by those that could. But where the estate housed conspicuous racial minorities, it was race that became the most noticeable social characteristic.

INTERACTION OF STRUCTURE AND POPULATION

The structure of the estates interacted powerfully with the populations they housed. In three of the estates – France, Denmark and Ireland – the majority of the units were family-sized. The majority of family units were in large deck access blocks or in high towers. The serious shortage of suitable and affordable family housing for the most vulnerable households, coupled with the commitment to house families with children as the highest priority, led to a demand for space in unpopular estates to house the least favoured households. Their rehousing in the least popular social housing rather than face homelessness, made concentrations of vulnerable families with children in large blocks on unpopular estates inevitable. The German and British estates had particularly acute problems.

In London, the high-rise towers which contained only one-bedroom units were originally used for young lone mothers, mixed up with elderly people. This had proved very difficult both for the mothers with their children and for the elderly. In Germany, where the estate had a predominance of one-bedroom units, large foreign families with children crowded into the small flats originally let to a single tenant. The overcrowding was acute. Small units, unsuitable for families with children, became over-occupied and quickly run-down, leading to social isolation and a self-reinforcing sense of failure among families.

Children in towers and large blocks almost inevitably created disturbance. They were out of sight almost as soon as they were outside the door. As the children got older, they very often could not be contained. The communal stairwells and entrances of blocks then became difficult to police, protect or maintain. Teenagers created even more disturbance because of the noise and damage resulting from their often unrestrained exuberance. These problems made for great difficulties in letting the largest blocks, as respectable and ambitious families tried to avoid exposing their children to conditions they could not control. In all cases, the lack of general demand for unpopular estates and the need to house certain vulnerable groups, for example young single mothers, often meant that the people congested together in a tower block or long slab block were intrinsically unsuited to the type of accommodation.

For the landlord this problem had many knock-on effects, not only in maintenance, but in applications for transfers and in deterring new applicants. It meant that the families with children who moved in or who stayed were generally the families with limited choice and often greater problems. In sum, high-rise blocks were found everywhere to make family living difficult and to have a negative effect on the overall viability of the estates. The general wear and tear and large numbers of children had a dampening effect on demand and created social pressures on landlords.

Difficult families

Whether blocks had many family-sized units or not, they tended to be used to house children under pressure. The biggest problem was with large family units of three or more bedrooms. Demand for these had fallen drastically in Denmark and France, as larger families with someone in work had more often than not moved into an owner-occupied house. Large flatted units on these estates were the most difficult-to-let and could often only be let to very disadvantaged, poor families. Even then there were too many large flats. The enforced communality of large blocks compounded the serious social difficulties of the families. When once a block or area of an estate became associated with difficult families, problems accelerated, sometimes in an extreme way, as these families had an impact that went far beyond their actual numbers. Their own problems often made them impervious to external social pressures, unable to adapt to the needs of neighbours, and unresponsive to attempts at control or enforcement, at least as long as the estates were in their phase of decline. Social workers often earned a bad reputation through their inability to solve deep-set family problems. Large, unneighbourly or antisocial families became simultaneously both cause and victim of accelerated decline.

INTERACTION OF PROBLEMS

The pressures on estate communities fell into three main categories – the buildings, the people and the services. These problems compounded each other, leading eventually to the near-breakdown of the communities. The building problems did not fit simple categories, since each estate had particular physical characteristics that made it unpopular with occupants and applicants, as well as difficult to manage for landlords. A strong pattern nonetheless prevailed – of heavy, dominating, inhuman, ugly, neglected physical structures. Table 12.6 shows the incidence of physical problems across all the estates, revealing the common core of difficult design, unmanageable upkeep and negative impact on social relations. Table 12.7 shows the particular problems of individual estates.

Public rejection of the buildings

The physical problems of the estates were so visually overwhelming that, within a short period of their construction, the

Table 12.6   Common pattern of physical problems on five estates

Physical problem	Number of estates with problem
Unconventional design	5
Very large blocks (over 100 units)	5
Expensive heating	5
Bleak or unmanageable spaces around blocks	5
Ugly or frightening approaches to buildings	5
Security problems resulting from design features	5
Hard-to-protect common areas	5
Problems in concrete structure and surfaces	5
Expensive maintenance of buildings and installations	5
Other physical maintenance problems	5
Underused and insecure underground garages, basements and ground floor storage areas	5
Internal corridors and access to flats	5
Above ground access routes throughout the estate	2

Sources: Author's visits; Windsor Workshop (1991).

estates were condemned in the eyes of the public in general and of policy-makers in particular. The rejection of the building form had serious consequences. It guaranteed that they would stand out for ever, since they would not be copied. They were a total break with tradition and in no case was it planned within the five countries that estates would be built in this form again. There was unanimity that the estates were, in physical terms, a disaster. This made the problems appear insurmountable. Alternatives were much easier to conceive than proper remedies. The non-traditional building forms threw up unexpected problems, over and above the obvious difficulties of high-rise, high-density estates. For example, postal deliveries became impossible and strangers invaded empty spaces because of the size of blocks and the difficulties

Table 12.7 Specific problems on individual estates

France	Germany	Britain	Denmark	Ireland
High tower blocks very close together	Extremely dense construction	Leaking roofs	One extremely large linear block	Very large estate
Very large estate	Very little open space	Insecure fire doors	Underground access	73 lifts
Ground and first floors unused	Stark contrast to surrounds	Cockroach infestations along heating ducts	Heavy concrete decks and podia	Wide open areas with no obvious use
	Long internal corridors	Underground garages	115 internal staircases	Defective lifts
		Above ground shopping precinct		Open unguarded entrances
		'Scissor' maisonettes		Some areas semi-derelict
		3 miles of overhead walkways and internal corridors		Long balconies

Sources: Author's visits; Windsor Workshop (1991).

in securing entrances. Letterboxes, doorbells and locks acquired a totally new meaning for people living in these conditions. The continuous cockroach infestations, breeding in the heating ducts and invading flats periodically, was another example. The appearance of the estates was far more important than might be supposed. Many residents expressed a sense of shame over physical conditions and felt they lost contact with the outside because friends and relatives were reluctant to visit, put off by the sense of insecurity (Nygaard 1991a, 1991b; Peillon, 1995).

Inadequate attempts at physical remedies began early, but partial cures were quickly undone again. Roof leaks, for example, were persistent. The cockroaches proved impervious to all known treatments for many years. Damage to letterboxes, doors, security systems and lifts were often repeated almost immediately following repair or reinstatement. Two estates were built entirely above ground. This appeared to be a particularly off-putting physical feature, though it is not clear whether, with so many other problems, it made the crucial difference. But the freezing of ground floor areas had a specially powerful impact on human contact and on security. It meant that community links had to be forged, familiarity and a sense of being on home ground had to be created without there being any traditional or conventional space within which these feelings of belonging and ownership could grow. On the estates built above ground, the spaces at ground level were so rarely used for day-to-day activities that they acted as a positive deterrent to communication and contact. In no way were decks, lift shafts, corridors or landings a substitute for street-level activity.

The building problems were too serious to be remedied through a better repair service. They required a level of reinvestment that was simply not available in the short run. The possibility of reinvestment was not even considered for a decade or more because of the newness of the estates and the strong political resistance to accepting the scale of the problems. Admitting responsibility for their physical failure was difficult. Therefore, there was a tendency to blame the people who lived there and to ascribe the strong build-up of social problems to the concentration of disadvantaged people, rather than to building or management difficulties.

SOCIAL PROBLEMS

Social problems were difficult to quantify or even to define
clearly. But they often appeared to swamp people on all five
estates. The occupants brought with them special needs.
The people with choice, with money, with advantages, with
confidence, generally did not move to these areas. Moving to a
large, unpopular outer estate held many deterrents and few
gains compared with waiting, if you could wait. This created a
skewed rehousing and social pattern on the estates.

The modernity of the estates, which was initially an asset
and an attraction, was rapidly turned into a liability because
the internal modernity of the flats was undermined by major
external physical barriers, which soon became a symbol of a
hated form of modernism. These barriers generated a strong
sense of alienation and prevented many people from settling
or coping. Table 12.8 shows the most significant social problems that tended to occur on most or all of the five estates at
the time of the most serious decline. Table 12.9 shows the
problems estate by estate.

Selection of tenants

The sifting out of those groups with choice is well described
and documented in British and Danish research into unpopular estates (Burbidge *et al.*, 1981; Hope and Foster, 1992; SBI,
1986). It was not a precise process. It often happened without
specific groups or individuals being necessarily singled out or
targeted. It was much more a matter of subtle and often
unspoken pressures working in favour of better options for the
better-off and the least favoured outcomes for the most
marginal.

Within the social housing context, this was quite a finely
graded process, since the vast majority of all incoming tenants
were on low incomes. Yet most social housing estates did not
attract the stigma of these extreme examples. It was common
on these estates for many households, even a majority, to have
many of the socially disadvantaged characteristics. The build-
up of social problems was linked to the concentration of
households with many different problems, rather than simply
to the fact that some people had some problems. The concen-

Table 12.8   Social problems common to estates at time of
climax of decline

Social problems[a] identified by housing officers and social agencies	Number of estates
Poverty	5
High proportion of one-parent families	5
High proportions of young people congregating in communal areas	5
Tensions between the police and young people and between different groups within the community	5
Vandal damage, graffiti, crime and abuse of common areas	5
Frequent incidence of unneighbourly behaviour	5
High proportion of families dependent on welfare	5
High unemployment, particularly among young people	5
Concentration of difficult, antisocial or unneighbourly households	5
Drug-related problems	4
Lack of a settling in process[b]	4
Ethnic minority communities, requiring special help to overcome discrimination and other disadvantages[c]	4
Community tensions and problems with participation	4

Notes: [a]The social problems listed were identified as more
concentrated in these estates than in other low-income
rented estates.
[b]Only in Ireland was any special provision made for helping
the community to settle down and get used to high-rise
living (see case study).
[c]Asylum seekers, refugees, distinct language groups, etc.

Sources: Windsor Workshop (1991); local managers; government
reports; social agencies; case studies.

tration of difficulty had knock-on effects on services, staff,
applicants and community relations.

There was an even more imprecise line between those in
need who managed to overcome problems and those in need

Table 12.9 Social difficulties on five estates

Country:	France	Germany	Britain	Denmark	Ireland
Social difficulties reported by managers and social agencies during visits[a]	Problem families (les familles lourdes)	Sharp division with nearby village	Poor police relations	Large numbers of children	Acute stigma
	Little participation	Very bad image	Poor image	Language and cultural problems	Crime and vandalism
	Vandalism	High dependence on 'social help'	Sharp division with surrounding area	Tenant apathy	Drug problems
	Disorders/police tension	Apathy and suspicion	Lack of community centre and other facilities	Difficulty in getting minorities involved	Single ex-homeless men
	Insecurity and crime	Crime/drugs	Very heavy call on social services	Difficult families	Very large numbers of children
	Drug and alcohol abuse	Too little child support	Strong community tensions	Tensions between Turkish community and Danish community	Transience
	Underused, poorly placed facilities	Lack of nurseries	Drug dealing	Poor support for community activities	Very poor facilities
	Racial tensions	Facilities too expensive to maintain, e.g. swimming pool	Large groups of young men 'hanging about'	Few 'psychological' reserves	Many difficult households
	Large numbers of young second-generation Arabs	Intergroup hostility	Very high unemployment		Very unstable community
		Serious overcrowding			Many lone parents
		Breakdown of tenants' group			Family poverty

Note: [a]Confirmed by government studies.

Sources: Author's visits; Windsor Workshop (1991).

who did not. In the estate populations, many ethnic minority households were in work; many one-parent families coped with parenting. Nonetheless the pressures of poverty, discrimination and social vulnerability bore more heavily on people with extreme disadvantages, making some failures inevitable (Power, 1994). Failure was more common in areas where many disadvantaged people were housed together because of indirect effects, for example on schools or other services, creating a compound effect, a strong collective 'atmosphere of failure' that consequently influenced people's view of their neighbours and indirectly, of themselves. The combination of circumstances that created failure pushed those least able to the most marginal areas, leading to a concentration and reinforcement of social problems in those very areas where help was most needed. Failure became a pattern of life and supports were insufficient to redress the balance. Failure demotivated not just its victims but its helpers too. These communities had become truly marginal by the early 1980s due to repeated failures.

The decline did not mean that no one wanted to live on the estates. In fact, people in desperate need, people in very poor or insecure conditions, people without much chance in the wider housing market were often grateful to move to these estates. Once rehoused and settled, people could become strongly attached to their flats and, even when conditions outside were very poor, they showed a remarkable sense of identity with their home. As a result, people who lived on the estates frequently had a far less negative image of the estates than the outside world (Gifford, 1986; Ballymun Task Force, 1987). This fact provided a positive thread in the life of all the estates, which could be unravelled and built upon when a rescue was attempted. Leading residents often reacted against the pervasive common sense of failure and spearheaded local action to re-establish social controls and create more normal conditions.

Families, children and antisocial behaviour

The numbers of children imposed many extra demands on estates – the need for play spaces, after-school facilities, holiday activities, youth clubs, as well as schools and nurseries.

Poor provision of these extra facilities, required at a much higher level than in more typical areas simply to cope with the higher numbers of children and young people, was a major cause of damage to buildings, entrances, lifts, grass areas, sheds, garages and anywhere else that children could play or make mischief. Much damage, that was commonly described as vandalism, reflected the insufficiently child-proof fittings and constant wear and tear.

Vandalism itself occurred in almost direct relation to the presence of children and young people. Lifts, letter-boxes, doors, refuse chambers, lights, railings, plants and vehicles were targets of youthful damage. Because communal entrances were so numerous – over 200 in Ireland, over 100 in Denmark and France – and because there were so many lifts – 75 in Dublin, 100 in Lyons – it was virtually impossible to control them all or to stop the 'hard' young person, bent on destruction. Graffiti was similarly difficult to control. Only with an intensive presence of supervisory staff and specially adapted facilities to cope with large numbers of young people, were the estates viable. The unusually high levels of youth unemployment, resulting from high concentrations of young people as well as from poor educational standards, added to the potential for vandalism, crime, conflict with authority, and with older residents. Figure 12.2 outlines this process.

Young adult households and estate instability

The estate populations were disproportionately youthful, not only because of the large numbers of children, but also because the adult population tended to be young too. The unpopularity and high turnover of the estates meant that more households than average moved out and younger than average households moved in. Special lettings directed at young, single people were often introduced to help fill vacancies. These incoming households needed somewhere desperately and had few footholds in the housing market. Such young households tended to have or be about to start young families, so high concentrations of young children went with high concentrations of young adults.

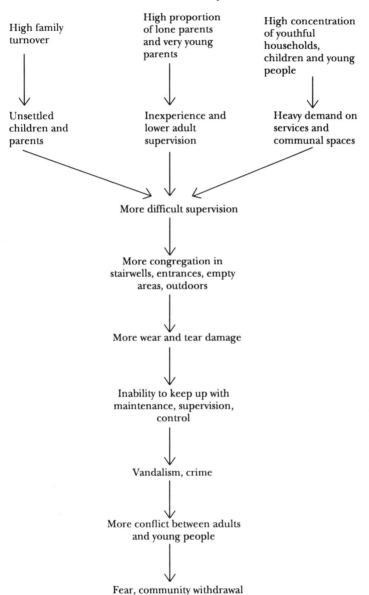

Source: Author's visits and research.

Figure 12.2   Interaction of estate problems with the disproportionate concentrations of young people

Young adult households made particular demands on services. This was because they were often poorly educated with little work experience and few job skills. Unemployment over time created negative attitudes towards society and towards work, leading to antisocial behaviour and instability. This could affect young men into their mid- or late-20s (Pitts, 1995). Groups of young adult males tended to congregate around shopping areas, garages or other social facilities – frustrated, bored and unoccupied. Their energy and desire to be in groups was often regarded by older residents as threatening and disruptive. On at least four of the estates, drug abuse, drug dealing and drug-related crime had occurred, mainly among groups of young men. The effects were serious, leading to police–youth clashes, adult–youth alienation, disruptive behaviour, and fear of crime, particularly among women. Drug abuse and drug-related crime were considered a major threat to any progress made on the estates (Peillon, 1995). It tended to affect the estates in waves, being driven underground by police action, to re-emerge when conditions relaxed a little.

The presence of young, single adult male households without work had a major knock-on effect on the young female population, leading to many unstable relationships. On all estates, there was a high proportion of young, single mothers, some of them teenagers. Many of them had difficulties with the full responsibilities of parenting and housekeeping. They sometimes attracted young men in a series of unstable relationships. Violent domestic scenes and rivalries were reported on the estates, leading to disturbance for other residents and a feeling that the estates were going down and were rough places to live (Ballymun Task Force, 1987; City of Cologne, 1989, 1991).

It is difficult to say that youthfulness was directly to 'blame' for many of the estates' troubles. It is more accurate to suggest that young people who, by definition, were often just building their adult independence, developing new family relations, and trying to secure work, could not form a stable community. Many elements of their lives were still very unpredictable. Their own moods were volatile. Their levels of aggression and energy were much higher than in more mature adults. Their concentration in disproportionate numbers, therefore, inevitably created instability. The support structures were either not available, not accessible, or not adapted to cope with youth problems.

SOCIAL FRAGMENTATION AND BEHAVIOURAL BREAKDOWN

The biggest social problems lay in the lack of conventions about neighbour relations, where very disparate groups, each with their own problems, failed to identify with each other. This was not only a racial divide, which certainly existed either explicitly or implicitly on four estates. It was also a divide between generations and between household types. The British left-wing notion of a 'rainbow coalition' of interests at the bottom of society was never more belied than by the social fragmentation on estates. For example, many policing tensions in France and Britain resulted from older residents calling the police against younger residents, particularly of minority origin. Another common divide was between 'respectable' and disarrayed households. On French estates, there was frequent negative reference to '*les familles lourdes*', literally 'heavy families'.

Social stress led to a surge in demands on social support services, which had often not been foreseen. In fact, because of the belief that the estates *per se* would solve many social problems, the very opposite was the case and too little provision was made. Not only were settling-in supports lacking, but also social service and family support teams, in spite of the concentration of families with severe social problems. In Ireland and France, special social work teams were placed on the estates but even they were totally inadequate for the level of need. Eventually the other estates had special social workers too.

Loss of controls

Young people understood less and less clearly the boundaries of behaviour as estates declined. Adult supervision was weakened and young people often rebelled. The following are some of the reasons:

– weakened adult control, linked with a high proportion of one-parent families;

- conflict within families resulting from step-relationships and the appearance of new and unstable partners;
- the concentration of young adults within existing and often crowded families;
- the failure of many estate schools and the loss of educational motivation, particularly among young men;
- intergenerational conflict in immigrant households;
- racial tensions resulting from divergent family patterns;
- the sense of failure and rejection.

It was inevitable that young people would feel frustrated, angry and hemmed in by so many family, ethnic and social problems. Many young adults enjoyed little status through lack of jobs, money or skills. They therefore sought other 'fringe' ways of gaining recognition. Crime was one; graffiti another; gang formation another; anti-police and anti-authority attitudes another (Élie *et al.*, 1989). The growth in problems of control increased employment difficulties as negative stereotypes filtered out from these areas. Reputation was all-important and there were many reports of employers refusing to consider job applicants or referrals from a particular estate because it had become so notorious (Élie *et al.*, 1989; Ballymun Job Centre, 1989). As a result, the process of youthful disarray became self-fuelling like so many other aspects of the problem.

The fact that young people were so numerous enhanced the strength of youthful groupings and diluted the power of adult controls. Of itself, the large number of young people could be regarded as an asset. But in the context of unpopular estates, with their building difficulties and social need, it was a tremendous burden. The vast majority of young people were in some way dependent on their families or on state support, or on both. Much of their strident behaviour was an attempt at asserting independence in a situation of dependence where there was little prospect of real independence and autonomy. The problems young adult households faced on the estates were in large measure common to all young people. The salient difference was the concentration of that age group in one area, the racial divide that separated many of them from older and more stable sections of the community, the combined effects of unstable, unemployed young adult males and the concentration of vulnerable, young female, lone parents.

It is hard to pin-point precisely the damaging impact of such concentrated instability. But local people talked freely about the problem. In France people referred to 'these wild settlements', 'cursed areas' and 'the misery and rot' (Élie *et al.*, 1989). In Germany, the serious increase in youth crime was causing grave consternation (Pfeiffer *et al.*, 1996).

Police relations

The police had great difficulty policing the estates for many not always closely connected reasons – their design, their isolation, their communal areas and entrances, their lack of informal social controls, their population instability, their racial composition, the disproportionate numbers of young people, their management difficulties, their level of empty property. The police were called on to intervene in the estates many more times than normal because of all these problems. Frequently they encountered young residents around the common areas of the estates. Clashes were almost inevitable, and became in fact extremely serious in the British and French cases (see Part III). On both estates, these confrontations led to outbreaks of violence in the 1980s. The disorders and police clashes generated even more prejudice and hostility, particularly in the police, making the youths deeply uneasy and the police susceptible to deep prejudices (Gifford, 1986). These attitudes were not peculiar to the police, although clashes with the police were probably the most damaging and most publicised of estate conflicts.

There was not a simple cause and effect relationship between design and social disarray. Rather the old slum patterns were recreated through a pecking order in the hierarchy of neighbourhoods, linking people at the bottom with places rejected by the successful in a symbiotic relationship. The role of social landlords thus became far more difficult than ever envisaged.

MANAGEMENT SERVICES

The estates at the point of their most acute decline became almost impossible to manage. There were two clear measures of management failure – the volume of empty units and the level of arrears. Without keeping property occupied and maintaining the flow of rent income, it was not possible for landlords to continue providing a reasonable service. Lettings and turnover problems led to a high level of rent arrears. On all estates these two functions interacted till they reached a point of threatened unviability. Table 12.10 shows how serious the lettings and arrears problem were at their height.

The problems stemmed from the earliest days of the estates, as the following difficulties show:

– the inconvenient locations, coupled with the non-traditional pattern of urban settlement;
– the lack of local ties or any neighbourhood structure at the outset because people were rehoused from all over the city;
– the lack of any marketing to ensure takers for the sudden boost in supply;
– the inability of landlords to process the volume of lettings required at the outset, as large blocks were handed over, causing delays in filling brand-new units;
– the lack of any welcome service for new tenants on the estates, underlining the strangeness of the environment;
– the failure to provide facilities in tandem with the first residents moving in;
– the lack of accessible mechanisms to sort out teething troubles, to ease the flow of lettings and to pressurise higher up the system for a response to problems;
– the lack of direct feedback mechanisms from residents due to remote management structures and the lack of a cohesive community or opportunity for building one;
– the bureaucratic systems created in the mass housing era making those responsible for ensuring the viability of the estates remote from the problems.

The service gaps meant that the inevitable hiccups in making a major new enterprise work either became stuck in a slow-moving system or were not noticed, since there was no route by which staff with any power made contact with ordinary residents or *vice versa*. It was particularly striking that this com-

Table 12.10   Management of the five estates

Country	France	Germany	Britain	Denmark	Ireland
Percentage of empty units	30%	38%	7%	15%	15%
Date	1984	1985	1982	1984	1986
Number of empty units[a]	2400	500	75	150	285
Date	1984	1985	1982 15 1985 60 1992	1984	1986 450 1989
Turnover	15%	Around 25%	16%	35%	31%
Date	1981	1985	1983	1981	1985
Arrears level[b] i.e. percentage tenants in arrears	50%	10% but only 55% of flats occupied	90% – £800 per tenant	5%	16%
Date	1981	1987	1989	1985	1987[c]

Notes: [a]The average level of empty units in social housing was between 2–4%.

[b]Records of arrears were not kept in a comparable way in different countries. Nonetheless, all landlords documented serious mounting problems. The sources of information were local management bodies in the five countries. Arrears were reported as far worse on these estates than other estates.

[c]A majority of tenants paid almost no rent under the differential rents policy.

Sources: Author's visits; Windsor Workshop (1991).

bination of problems emerged everywhere on all estates, although the intensity varied with time and location.

In the absence of positive marketing, potential tenants would either not know about the possibility or be put off by the strange ultra-modernity and the rumours of problems that had quickly gone into circulation. This was coupled with

inexperience in managing that type of housing and the consequent failure to understand the need for marketing or for
providing the front line back-up that might have made them
viable. For these reasons, the management gap widened very
quickly. When once this happened, it was difficult to recover
conditions or regain control within the existing housing
management systems.

Impact of empty units

The lowest proportion of empty units was in London, probably because the estate was within the city of London, where
overall demand for low-rent housing consistently and
significantly outstripped supply. But the level of empty property and turnover even on this estate was far above average
and too high for management to control readily. All the other
estates were located much further out and therefore were
much harder to fill with city residents. The empty units in
France and Germany – one third of all flats – caused the
virtual collapse of management on the estates. But even at 15
per cent in Ireland and Denmark, the estates became unviable. The empty units gave a visible signal to political support-
ers that the estates were not wanted. This diluted their
commitment and made them reluctant to commit further
funds to their viability. They invited theft and damage to
empty units, leading to insecurity, high repair costs and delays
in reletting. They also encouraged squatting and the use of
empty space for illicit purposes. Groups of young people were
reported to move from empty flat to empty flat, creating un-
controlled hide-outs or drug-taking circles on at least three
estates.

A high turnover had an impact on the volume of empty
units but was a rather different problem. It created chronic
instability and neighbour problems. At its worst, in Denmark
(1981) and Ireland (1985), nearly one-third of the units
changed hands in a single year (Windsor Workshop, 1991). It
was impossible for caretakers, managers or fellow-residents to
keep on top of any aspect of management with that scale of
turnover within a single, large housing area. It meant that rent
accounts were constantly out of date, arrears pursuit was in
many cases impossible; benefit calculations and payments were

continuously changing; repairs costs were higher due to movements in and out, and damage was caused by transient and unstable households. It was difficult to control children's behaviour in common areas if many adults were strangers. Children and teenagers were themselves disturbed by the high level of movement, whether they were in stable or moving families. Even indirect effects, such as problems in school discipline resulting from high turnover, had an effect on estate life. For example, caretakers found children's behaviour more difficult to control if they did not know the children, or if the children were unsettled. If the children were doing badly at school, they might adopt more negative attitudes generally and *vice versa*.

Unbalanced communities

The most significant knock-on effect from empty property and high turnover was the abandonment of attempts at 'balancing the community'. Lettings followed a downward spiral, chasing poorer and poorer applicants. Sheer poverty was rarely unaccompanied. Personal problems were often linked with extreme poverty. Many problems compounded each other and had a drastic impact on lettings, on turnover, on neighbour relations, on ghettoisation, and eventually on economic viability. In the French case, efforts at letting were all but abandoned by two of the landlords. In the British case, lets were concentrated on homeless families, lone parents and ethnic minorities. Few precautions were taken over new applicants. No special measures at integration or support were adopted before acute problems surfaced. The signal to the wider community was that the estates were rejected by more successful groups. Therefore their troubled reputations were enhanced. Unless strong compensatory measures were taken, it seemed axiomatic that the status of the area mirrored the problems of the occupants. As lower status occupants moved in, the voids grew, further lowering the area's image. The economic weakness of poor households, their dependence on state benefits, their marginalisation from wider society, made them unable to protest effectively over conditions. Landlords, with a sense of defeat over declining conditions, gradually withdrew management effort.

Rent losses

The acute decline, the difficulties of managing such large estates through a remote system, the high turnover, all made arrears difficult to control. The serious loss of income resulting from empty units crippled the management and repair services. In France and Germany, where there were many landlords within the single estate, evicted households sometimes simply escaped to a different landlord. Arrears were difficult to reduce when once they reached a certain level because staff, already demoralised by the unpopularity of the estate and the difficult management task, simply could not counter enough of the downward pressures to make a real impact. In that sense, arrears were a product of many factors that rent collectors and arrears chasers did not control. Figure 12.3 attempts to illustrate this.

Unmanaged

Whether landlords were public or private, they failed in all five cases to apply basic management principles to these estates until they faced threatened collapse. Either the landlords were too dispersed (Germany and France), too bureaucratic (Ireland and Britain), or too detached and structured in their application of management principles (Denmark). The estates formed part of wider management organisations. The problem estates were therefore invariably a lower priority than more successful areas. The basic failure was the failure to manage the problem at first hand. The insufficiently responsive structure, the absence of a dedicated manager, the failure to address the housing market and to adapt management methods to the unexpected circumstances led to management failure. Table 12.11 summarises the most important management problems at the point of most acute decline, showing how pervasive the problems were.

COLLAPSE OF THE FRONT LINE

The caretaking service was one aspect of management that survived even the most extreme crises in conditions.

Physical and environmental problems

Decayed and insecure common areas

High turnover

Downward lettings spiral

Stigma

Increase in empty units

Illegal occupancy

Difficulty in reletting empty property

Loss of rent income

Reduced management service

Higher rents to cover costs

Rent rises compound arrears

Rent losses threaten landlords with bankruptcy

Source. Author's visits and research.

Figure 12.3   Problem of containing arrears on five estates

Table 12.11　Management problems on the five estates

Management problem reported by managers during visits	Number of estates
High[a] level of empty units and turnover	5
Low demand relative to other estates, and by economically active tenants	5
Serious disrepair	5
Weak management control system	5
Lack of tenant confidence and poor communication with the landlord	5
High[a] arrears	5
Environmental maintenance problems	5
Difficulty in enforcing tenancy agreements	5
Inadequate local management staff above the level of caretakers or maintenance staff	5
Caretaking and cleaning problems	4

Note:　[a]'High' indicates that the problems were more severe than in other social housing estates, including other unpopular estates, according to local managers.

Sources: Author's visits; Windsor Workshop (1991).

Caretakers were the front line in reporting on problems and controlling conditions on behalf of the landlord. In Ireland, it was of a non-specialist kind. On all the other estates, including the London estate, it included some responsibility for technical as well as custodial services. In France in addition, caretakers carried responsibility for rent collection. Caretakers provided a visible and valued service. But for caretaking to work there needed to be a level of local organisation above the caretakers in order to give them back-up, support and direct supervision. Its absence left caretakers coping with complex problems almost unaided at the front line. Even where the caretaking service itself was relatively good, it was often directly undermined by other service problems, such as rubbish disposal, repair and maintenance. One of the most difficult jobs was control of the extensive communal areas and the prevention of vandalism. Caretakers inevitably got caught up in social problems, particularly with young people and children. Yet they lacked the authority to enforce standards. Only at the most rudimentary level could they actually control things or make things work. Yet there was no one with direct management control at the estate level to take up their problems or back up their efforts.

As building problems mounted and as social controls failed, caretakers faced an undoable task. They could carry on at a rudimentary level, trying to push back problems. But without a senior manager, their role was unequal to the task. Worsening conditions led to demoralisation and high turnover; recruitment of replacements proved difficult; and residents attacked caretakers with increasing ferocity, as the only representatives of the landlord they could reach. Caretakers often became authoritarian in an attempt to retain control and meet tenants' demands for action. This almost always backfired.

Gradually, caretaking hit problems on the estates through failure to hold the line on conditions, so their status dropped, their authority diminished and their jobs became ever more difficult. This further undermined the respect of young people, difficult to control under the best of circumstances. Caretakers were forced into a semi-policing role in an attempt to stem the damage. Their failure exacerbated the tensions with residents, who were often ambiguous about what they wanted caretakers to do. They might advocate a 'good clip round the ear' for other people's children, but not accept it for their own. When once caretakers could no longer cope, the estates spiralled. But caretakers were not withdrawn. They were left on the estates to hold the line against chaos. Caretakers found themselves personally exposed, sandwiched between an unresponsive management system and an unsettled, disarrayed community.

THE SLIDE TOWARDS CHAOS

The slide began long before its severity was recognised. The estates progressed towards acute decline during a period when mass estates were still being built as a solution and while the estates were still relatively new. By the time intervention and rescue were mooted in each country, the situation on the five estates was becoming chaotic. Living conditions were intolerable and resident flight was threatening the survival of the estates (City of Cologne, 1994). The vacuum in management, alongside the much greater than average management and maintenance requirements, was a recipe for disaster. The clustering of extremely needy people in much greater concentrations than originally contemplated, without local support, reinforced the slide to management chaos. When once these problems took root, they fed each other.

Over a period of several years, the process of decline accelerated in a vicious circle. If the problems had had a single recognisable cause, then action might have come faster. As it was, the multiple problems of very difficult mass estates of the 1960s and 1970s ensured that no single solution ever worked, such as the attempt to keep flats filled or to keep caretakers on the ground. The result was near chaotic conditions. Table 12.12 shows the chronology of decline and Figure 12.10 shows how the slide occurred on each estate.

Urban disintegration

The five estates reached their nadir at slightly different points, but they all experienced a similar fate. Conditions reached

Table 12.12   The chronology of decline

Country	France	Germany	Britain	Denmark	Ireland
Onset of decline	Early 1970s	From 1976	From outset: 1970	From outset: 1972	From 1970
Physical, social management problems recognised	1976	1980	1975	1981	1980
Date of most extreme decline	1981	1987	1983	1984	1985

Source: Windsor Workshop (1991).

Table 12.13   The slide towards chaos on the five estates

Country	France	Germany	Britain	Denmark	Ireland
Stages in slide	Populaion drop	Building and financial problems	Difficult to fill at outset	Very unpopular form	Unique building form, therefore alienation
	Letting problems	Owners lose commitment	High turnover and concentratin of needy plus minorities	Area very isolated	Unsettled and poor community
	Lettings to North Africans	Management and letting problems	Police problems	Hard to let and manage	More children than adults
	Exodus accelerates	Neglect of facilities	Difficult-to-let	Pressure of urban renewal	Low take-up of tenant purchase
	Empty unlettable units	Plummeting demand	Investigation predicts demolition	Rehousing of poor households	Surrender Grant
	Whole towers virtually abandoned	Empty units	Building problems	Growth in minorities	Mass exodus
	Building problems	Financial collapse – owners defect	Lettings ever more polarised	Exodus of better-off	Some areas semiderelict
	Facilities decay	Immigrant influx	Police/youth clashes	Building problems	Demolition talked about
	Joyriding and riots	Very disarrayed – crime, and so on	Media coverage stigma	Security problem	Very high turnover and empties
	Press notoriety	Owners sell out	Cuts in service	Minority tensions	Lettings to single homeless and one-parent families
	Demolitions	Demolition considered	Access to homeless only	Demand plummets	Abandonment of open spaces
	Financial crisis			Demolition of walkways and podia proposed	

Source: Case studies.

such a low ebb that the estates became almost household bywords for urban disintegration. Journalists picked the most sensational aspects. Crime, damage to buildings, clashes with the police, racial tensions, youth gangs, violence, crude poverty, 'sponging' on the system, hatred or rejection of authority, destructive behaviour, family breakdown, were all labels of condemnation that attached to these areas.

The problems of society were underlined by the reports from the estates. Fears of breakdown spread. Residents suffered under the added burden of infamy. No efforts by 'respectable' residents appeared equal to the problems. At least partial demolition of the estates was muted in all cases. Collapse appeared inevitable. The estates were written off by the wider society as 'horrific hell-holes'. Housing staff became extremely reluctant to work in them. Their fate seemed sealed. They looked unlikely to survive. Figure 12.4 attempts to summarise this process on the estates.

SUMMARY

The five case studies show in detail how the decline of estates came about. They stood out in such sharp contrast to typical urban landscapes that they became symbols of grotesque modernism. They were overwhelmingly inhuman, harsh and forbidding in appearance. They had giant, flatted concrete blocks and bare, unusable open spaces. On the other hand, they had many facilities, some of which had been abandoned, neglected, or poorly funded. Four of the five estates had high ethnic minority concentrations. This enhanced their needs and their stigma but it did not directly cause decline, as the all-white Irish estate showed. The extreme estate environments affected residents and *vice versa*. All the estates had many young people and young families who were not well adapted to such insecure and communalised environments. The estates were socially fraught, turbulent and very difficult to manage.

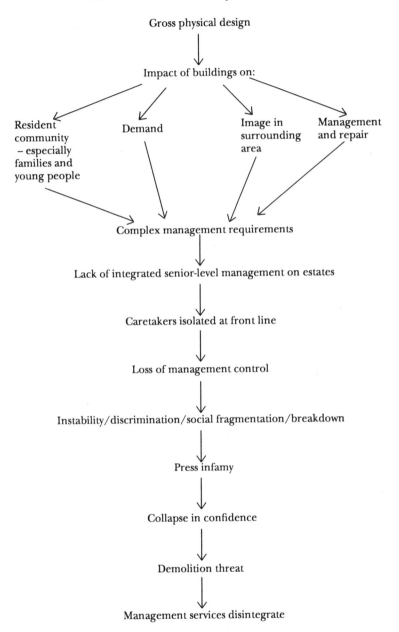

Source: Author's visits and research.

Figure 12.4   Pressures on the estates

13 A Change in Estate Fortunes

TURNAROUND

The five symbolic estates gained such notoriety in each country that they seemed likely to be destroyed by their very reputations. Neither landlords nor politicians could see a way out. Conditions were desperate. The conflict over their future, whether in Lyons, Cologne, London, Dublin or Copenhagen, provided a catalyst for action. It involved the police, schoolteachers, librarians, youth workers, employers, community organisations, churches and other voluntary bodies, as well as housing specialists and governments. The turnaround was as dramatic as it was unforeseen.

As the 1980s advanced, these most famous or notorious social housing estates attracted a new kind of attention. Politicians, housing experts and media representatives were taken to see the success stories of government rescue programmes. The most dramatic and conspicuous successes were the same estates that had been condemned by researchers, policy-makers, the courts and journalists in the late 1970s and early 1980s. Their appearance and condition at close quarters, as they underwent renewal, bore little relation to the graphic horror stories that continued to appear in newspapers. They displayed a form of 'internal combustion' which created the momentum for change. The engine that drove the problems also seemed to drive the solutions. Each estate began to claw back a desperate situation from the brink of collapse through highly responsive and localised programmes. Different communities, landlords and governments reacted to the particular problems of their 'symbolic' social housing estates in particular ways. Yet the very individual histories of the estates revealed many similar patterns of renewal, just as they had in the emerging crisis.

The rescue initiatives on the five estates had many *ad hoc* ingredients. Some of the action was resident-led and this evoked constant interest and engagement. Many of the changes were landlord-led, including the improvements to the physical appearance of blocks and environments. The most visible changes were inspired by government cash incentives. Estates that had declined rapidly through mass provision and remote bureaucratic management became pioneering experiments in an alternative, hands-on style of management. Solutions were bound to be variable and responsive, since a central cause of failure had been the over-rigid, pre-cast planning and remote management. There was general agreement that mass estates would never be built again today but for those that had to live in them, they must be made to work. Attempting to reverse the problems from one angle only would not work. Managers had tried; social workers had tried; money had previously been spent on the buildings in isolation from the other problems. The question was whether combining the varied elements of change in a mosaic-like pattern would have a different kind of impact.

ROLE OF GOVERNMENTS

Each estate became part of a major central or local government rescue initiative. Only the German estate was primarily a local programme because of its private ownership structure. The London and Dublin estates were both local authority initiatives in the first instance but central government became quickly involved. In Denmark and France, the framework for tackling problem estates was laid down by central government. The Danish programme emphasised resident involvement, while France stressed the involvement of elected local mayors. Social landlords, backed by the local authorities and regional or central government, ran the programmes. Table 13.1 shows the organisation of the estate rescue initiatives. The role of government was central in restoring physical conditions and in no case was upgrading attempted without major central or local government backing. Governments at central and local level contributed funds not only to restoring physical building conditions, but to upgrading estate environments, providing social facilities, funding additional training programmes. Table 13.2 illustrates the dominant role of government. Of the

Table 13.1   Organisation of estate rescue initiatives

	France	Germany	Britain	Denmark	Ireland
Date of first intervention	1979	1987	1983	1984	1983
Original initiative	State-sponsored rescue programme	City-sponsored adult education initiative	Local authority response to police and residents' demands	National government-supported rescue programme	Local authority and resident initiative
Level of government involved	Central first, then local involvement	Local, within federal financial framework	Local and central	Central but involving local government	Local and central
Local authority as key actor	√	√	√	√	√
Central government as main funder	√	–	√	√	√

Sources: Author's visits; Windsor Workshop (1991).

Table 13.2   Ingredients of government intervention

Ingredient funded by government	Number of 5 countries where government funded ingredient
Physical repair	5
Physical upgrading, e.g. security	5
Improved appearance of blocks	5
Environment	5
Additional social facilities	5
Estate/youth training programmes	5
Employment initiatives	5
Government funding for resident initiatives	5
Changes in housing finance to improve management viability	4
EC anti-poverty and training funds with national support	3

Sources: Author's visits; Windsor Workshop (1991); government reports.

ten main government-funded ingredients, on average nine attracted public support on each estate.

Rescue programmes passed through many different layers of intervention – national, local, physical, social, organisational, resident-focused. Intervention on all the estates happened over a number of years, often with programmes running simultaneously. Government policy evolved in the process of attempting the rescue, while new initiatives and funding programmes evolved in each estate as the rescue took hold. Landlord experience and resident involvement, as they grew, actively helped to shape later stages of the rescue. The case studies in Part III clearly illustrate this.

In all estates there was a co-ordinating and decision-making forum, a local landlord organisation, and a resident involvement structure. Local politicians were important in all countries, whether or not the property was council-owned. Other representatives included residents, social agencies, minority organisations, funders such as banks, schools and police. Table 13.3 shows the stages of intervention and Table 13.4 shows the different rescue structures.

GOOD MONEY AFTER BAD

Demolition was the most difficult issue that faced decision-makers at the outset. On all the estates, demolition had been proposed either for certain blocks or for some design features, such as decks or walkways, or for the whole estate. It was ruled out as an unrealistic option for the whole estate in every country, because the replacement cost was prohibitive and because the rehousing process would have been too difficult for such large numbers of people. The five estates housed nearly 50 000 people and would have cost around £1 billion to replace (1995 estimate). Partial demolition was proposed for Ireland in 1993–4, and was carried out in France in 1983, 1985 and 1994. But where the renovation costs were high, they were nowhere near the cost of new-build houses in four of the five estates. However, estate improvements were unlikely to wipe out the enormous disadvantages and stigma of the estates. Nor would they resolve the physical problems of mass concrete construction, root and branch. There was a nagging consensus that the cities would be better off without these estates. So although wholesale demolition was ruled out in every case, it never completely vanished from the agenda, even though total demolition was an unrealistic option for the foreseeable future. At their lowest ebb, the estates still housed many poor families. The smallest estate housed over 800 households; the largest, 7000. Landlords and governments would share the responsibility for rehousing them if their homes were removed through demolition. Finding enough available units to re-house such large and difficult populations, in spite of high levels of empty units, was impossible in the short-term.

The prospect of years of delay, the unacceptable cost, the relatively recent construction of the estates, the upheaval and social problems of dispersing yet again such large, poor communities created a rationale for saving the estates. People had to live somewhere; that somewhere had to be cheap; and at least the estates were there. Rescuing the estates, therefore, superseded demolition as an option. Table 13.5 summarises the decisions producing this outcome in each country.

STEPS TO RECOVERY

We have ordered the steps taken in the process of renewal under three main headings–physical renewal; organisational and management changes; social relations. They each depended on the other, as we showed in Part II and they came about broadly together. They matched the process of decline we have already discussed and were a direct response to that process.

Physical renewal

Physical changes were a prerequisite of other improvements and were directly linked to them through their impact on tenants, on the lettability of empty units and on management more generally. They were attractive to governments because of the immediate results. They gave landlords a direct rationale for becoming estate-based and resident-focused. Many measures were common to all the estates, as Table 13.6 shows. Table 13.7 summarises the main actions on each estate to restore physical conditions. We were able to uncover the estimated costs of upgrading physical conditions. On no estate were major programme budgets devolved to a single, locally-based organisation which could make transparent the full volume of spending. Nor were all of the programmes in any country fully co-ordinated. The programmes were spread over 6 to 15 years and covered a wide range of different public, private and voluntary bodies, as well as a range of local, central and international government funding agencies. Our figures therefore only cover the costs of building and environmental upgrading which were directly controlled by landlords. The capital cost of the renovation to the five estates is shown in Table 13.8.

Cost of renovation and rebuild

The average amount spent to date per unit on the renovation of the estates was significantly less than the cost of a new-build

Table 13.3 Stages of intervention on each estate

Country:	France	Germany	Britain	Denmark	Ireland
Special programmes, dates	1979 – State-sponsored Habitat et Vie Social 1983 – Special management initiative by HLMs 1983 – Développement Social des Quartiers under Prime Minister's Office 1985 – State-sponsored Educational Priority Area initiative	1987 – Co-ordinated initiative by Adult Education Institute of City of Cologne 1988 – City of Cologne social and tenants' initiative 1989 – City of Cologne funds remedial works to empty units in partnership with private owners	1976 – Local authority early lettings initiative 1983–9 Government-sponsored Priority Estates Project 1983 onwards – ESF and local authority training initiatives, with government support 1985,1992 – Government-funded estate action	1983–90 – Special support from housing company for tenant training and for management initiative. Local authority involved in social provision 1984–9 – Government renovation programme 1985–9 – EU-AKB special training project 1985–90 Environmental project	1969 – Authority-supported community project 1983 – Dublin Corporation management initiative 1983–9–EC-sponsored Combat Poverty Programme with government support 1987–EC-funded funded Task Force

Table 13.3 Continued

Country:	France	Germany	Britain	Denmark	Ireland
	1989 – International architectural competition for renewal of La Démocratie	1989 – Youth employment initiative sponsored by City and landlord	1985, 1986 – Government and local authority-funded Urban Aid	1993 – New government programme targeted at minorities	1988 – Government remedial works
	1989 – Experimental employment initiatives	1989 – Hillebrand management company pulls together rescue structure on behalf of private landlords but involving City government, Adult Education and residents	1989 – Tenants opt for independent study on estate's future		1992–3 – Phase 1 evaluation – demolition proposed
	1991 – National HLM economic development initiative		1991 – Tenant management		

Sources: Author's visits; Windsor Workshop (1991).

Table 13.4   Rescue structures

Country	France	Germany	Britain	Denmark	Ireland
Co-ordinating body for Rescue	DSQ Commission combining central and local government, landlords, financiers and resident organisations	Public hearing involving all parties sponsored by city adult education department	Local council panel involving local residents and politicians, sponsored by local authority	Project committee representing all parties including local authority, landlord, residents	Taskforce representing all parties with government and local authority funds and local authority representatives
Landlord organisation	Association of owners	Owners' management committee with representatives from estate and city	Neighbourhood office	Estate management office and project office	Local design team set up by local authority
	Local offices		Design team office		Estate offices
	Lettings and marketing agency set up by local HLM companies	Co-ordinating management company office	Repairs team	Caretaking sub-offices	Housing office
Resident organisations	Régie de Quartiers and other local voluntary groups	Tenants' committee supported by adult education institute	Youth Association (residents)	Estate board under jurisdiction of housing company and local authority	Community companies running activities with government funds
		Other voluntary groups	Community association	Many voluntary groups and initiatives	Tenants' associations, voluntary organisations
			Resident co-operative company		Church-based groups
			Resident steering group to sponsor changes		

Sources: Author's visits; Windsor Workshop (1991).

Table 13.5   Demolition decisions on estates

France	Germany	Britain	Denmark	Ireland
600 units in 4 towers demolished in 1983–5	Demolition of largest blocks proposed in 1987	Demolition first mooted in 1977 by DoE in difficult-to-let investigation	Half of concrete deck areas demolished in 1986 – no dwellings lost	Demolition discussed but rehousing problems plus prominent resident action rule it out
Rescue of other areas launched	Legal problems plus cost led to abandonment of demolition proposals	Later proposed after riots in 1985	No proposals to demolish estate	Proposed in 1994 for 600 units – likely to go ahead
Another 640 boarded up and demolished in 1994	Full occupancy, high demand and restored management remove need for demolition	In 1991 walkways began to be taken down	Long-term viability and acceptability questioned	
Plummeting numbers of empty units removes demolition threat short-term	Questions remain over long term	Demolition ruled out through community opposition		
New demand problems raise prospect of further demolition		Occasionally still mooted		

Sources: Author's visits; Windsor Workshop (1991).

Table 13.6   Physical measures to improve conditions on five estates

	Number of estates
Security, e.g. doors, fences, lighting	5
Remedy to spawling concrete	5
Painting of external concrete	5
Upgrading of entrances	5
Upgrading of environment	5
Planting and gardens	5
Play areas	5
New facilities (sometimes through changing existing structures)	4
Removal of decks	2
Providing enclosed play areas attached to blocks	2
Demolition of blocks (as yet only implemented in one)	2
Providing planting boxes and plants for balconies	1

Sources: Author's visits; Windsor Workshop (1991).

house (SBI, 1991, 1993). However, in Ireland a review of the improvements to date suggested that work had been inadequate and the full renovation cost of £33 000 would be coming dangerously close to the replacement cost of £45 000 for a new two-storey house (Craig Gardener, 1993; Dublin Corporation, 1994). Given that the estate renovation left relatively unpopular tower blocks in place, the Dublin government was seriously considering other strategies, including some demolition. In both London and Dublin, costs of later phases of renovation were predicted to be far higher than earlier works.

In London, the predicted cost for future work was £35 000 per unit to remove walkways and establish ground-level, secure access to all the blocks. The impact on the one block completed was impressive. But a thorough evaluation of the completed block was yet to be carried out. Thirty five thousand pounds represented over half the replacement cost. This was considered questionably high and later phases of the work could be at risk (London Borough of Haringey, 1994).

Table 13.7 Steps to restore physical conditions on each estate

Country	France	Germany	Britain	Denmark	Ireland
Main action to restore conditions	Restore abandoned ground and first-floor storage and access areas through alternative usage	Repair all blocks	Secure doors to individual flats	Repair building damage	Fence in open areas around blocks
	Paint external concrete of towers	Build over closed swimming pool to create nursery	Control entrances to high-rise	Put on pitch roofs over flat roofs of blocks	Repair concrete and paint blocks
	Convert some blocks for alternative uses, e.g. students	Provide bowling pitch	Paint walkways and external blocks	Demolish half major decks and turn into ground floor gardens	Repair and paint balconies and plant window boxes
	Demolish 4 blocks and plant mature trees, with local schoolchildren	Secure entrances, instal individual doorbells and restore letter-boxes	Build community centre and workshops	Halve number of underground garages	Secure entrances and introduce concierge system
	Convert units to move large families to ground floor and produce more small units	Upgrade lifts and all common parts	Repair roofs	Improve small flats and turn some bigger flats into smaller ones	Provide enclosed play areas and small parks
	Improve environment	Restore empty units on a rolling programme	Begin removal of walkways and introduce ground floor entrances with concierge controls	Upgrade environment and stairwells	Repair heating and lifts
		Upgrade environment	Bring down shops and other communal facilities to ground floor	Build community house	Upgrade environment
		Provide more community facilities	Create gardens	Create small communal gardens for blocks and provide private ground floor gardens and patios on remaining decks	Improve internal dwellings
		Build security control centre with video sound links to every lift, entrance, landing			Upgrade shopping centre

Sources: Author's visits; Windsor Workshop (1991).

Table 13.8   Capital cost[a] of renovation to the five estates

	France	Germany	Britain	Denmark	Ireland
Estimated capital spend to 1991	£26m[b]	£8.5m	£6m[c]	£20.7m	£5.5m
Estimated per unit cost of renovation work to date	£13 500	£11 000	£6000[c] (pre-1993)	£16 000	£19 500[d]
Predicted cost of planned programme[e]	—	—	£35m (£35 000 per unit)	—	£90m (£33 000 per unit)
Estimated cost of new-build 2-storey house	£70 000	£120 000	£60 000	£70 000	£45 000

Notes: [a]National currencies have been converted to sterling at rates applicable in October 1993. They give a basic idea of the scale of investment and costs incurred.
[b]This figure covers environmental and general upgrading with more intensive work to some blocks.
[c]Programmes up to 1991 were relatively limited. One block has been fully renovated with a unit cost of £35 000.
[d]Only one part of the estate, involving 200 units, has so far been modernised.
[e]Ambitious future programmes could be modified later.

Sources: Author's estate visits; Windsor Workshop (1991); official reports.

In Denmark, a government-sponsored evaluation of estate programmes showed that higher spending on renovation was justified by the much greater impact and success of the improvements. The most expensive renovation was less than half the full cost of new-building (SBI, 1993). In spite of this, beyond a certain point spending on the estates would appear too high to be acceptable. Based on the case studies, maybe half the replacement cost was near the acceptable limit.

The central question in all countries was how permanent and complete the renovation works would prove to be. The careful evaluations carried out on the Danish and Irish estates of the improvement works already completed showed that due to pressure on funds, several important elements in the renovation programmes had been omitted or modified downwards. The evaluation conclusion in both countries was that more money would need to be spent on these estates in order to justify the expense already incurred and to secure the future of the estates. In spite of these limitations, improvements were popular with residents and in the short run restored the viability of those areas tackled.

Expensive surgery

On all estates, elaborate and radical improvements were identified as requirements for a full rescue. But this treatment was either limited to specific units and blocks; or circumscribed due to lack of funds; or as yet incomplete. Only Germany adopted a different overall approach that was limited and incremental. In no case could the full scale of proposed works be contemplated. The estates had all been built in such a way as to make total redesign prohibitively expensive. But the areas that were radically redesigned were in fact the most successful.

Spending on the estates was justified by the argument that it extended their useful life by long enough to 'pay back' the investment; it met real housing need, at a significantly lower cost than the cost of replacement, even in the more expensive and contested Irish and British cases. But to meet this argument, spending was never high enough to overcome the estates' inherent physical problems. On less extreme estates, the scope would be greater as it would be less costly.

In no case was it clear that the rescue would remove the need for further reinvestment within ten years. Nor was it clear that it would ultimately restore the popularity of the estates or do away with their intrinsic design problems. The estates were still too different and too physically inhuman to rise in popularity with the general public. The main impact of the spending was on the morale of residents themselves, on staff who worked there, and on needy applicants.

Impact

On all the estates, the physical reinvestment had a major visual
impact. The blocks looked bright and clean through external
repainting. Entrances, lifts and stairwells looked cared for as a
result of refurbishment, although these improvements had to
be policed through increased and improved custodial caretaking, resident involvement and more intensive management.
The estate surroundings were maintained, green and re-
ordered to encourage resident activity. Extensive planting,
play and amenity areas, new pathways and private gardens
were created through intensive consultation with residents
and the involvement of estate schools and youth in some of
the work.

The creation of activity centres – more shops, more social
facilities, more recreation areas, more large family units at
ground floor level, more gardens around blocks – made the
estates look more typically urban, less abandoned and less
futuristic. It became easier to foster a sense of belonging, of
ownership and commitment. Measures to address particular
problems on particular estates – lighting, fencing, benches,
resident gardens, balconies, carpeting of landings and corridors, mirrors in lifts, murals, sculptures and so on – provided a
composite set of relatively small physical improvements that
made the estates more looked after, softer in contours, more
secure and more inviting to people, more human.

ORGANISATIONAL AND MANAGEMENT CHANGES

Humanising the estates required above all else contact, dialogue, and visible management. Establishing control over
estate conditions was fundamental to the rescue programmes
in every country. In all five countries, landlords based more
local staff within the new local management offices on estates,
enhancing caretaking responsibilities and standards, expanding repairs and cleaning, adopting a proactive marketing role
in lettings. These changes needed the support of residents in
order to overcome the wider social problems that had
swamped front-line staff. Creating a local management office
provided the key to establishing tenant links and reasserting

control over conditions. It was impossible to separate the way landlords changed their management from the way they dealt with tenants. Table 13.9 summarises the main management initiatives on each estate. The new management patterns on the five estates are shown in Table 13.10.

The local offices proved to landlords that most tenants were not irresponsible and hostile. They were desperate for things to work; they were trapped by bad conditions and they needed help. What is more, tenants wanted landlords to re-assert controls that would prevent alienated and disturbed residents from breaking the law. It was therefore far more possible than imagined to claw back control. It required dynamic personalities, strong leadership, a grip on problems, authority and quick results, to start building landlord–tenant relations again. Clear, direct and constant communication through the local offices made the two-way process of up-grading conditions and winning resident support possible. This underlined strongly the interaction of buildings and people. Localised management became an obvious and in-evitable solution as its impact was immediate and direct. Yet during the years of disintegration, landlords had not heard or heeded the residents' clamour for local action, for contact, for supervision, for a stronger landlord presence. The estates had experienced a collapse through lack of local management. But ironically, it took the collapse of distant management to persuade landlords that an alternative might work! Therefore the impact of the local management initiatives on the five estates was particularly important and significant. The degree of change was dramatic (Élie *et al.*, 1989).

Impact

The main impact of management measures in all five estates was to provide a more intensive service which affected core conditions; to raise the morale of front-line staff, enhancing their status and performance; to tailor the physical changes to management and social needs; to reassert control over a situation of near-anarchy; and to relate changes to the needs of residents. Figure 13.1 shows how these changes created upward momentum. Table 13.11 shows the dramatic reduction in

Table 13.9 Main management initiatives on the five estates

France	Germany	Britain	Denmark	Ireland
Local management offices opened by HLM	Integrated management office, 1 firm to co-ordinate services	Local management office opened	Local lettings and management office with more senior staff	Set up local management offices in 4 areas of estate
'Worker-caretakers' carrying out repairs	2 repairs handymen continually checking blocks – instantly repainting over graffiti	Special intensive caretaking backed training	Divide estate into 4 by areas, each with caretaking office and own sub-budget	Involve tenants in selection and screening
Social and employment initiatives linked to management	11 caretakers – strong control over estate conditions	Open plan local office	Intensive resident involvement measures	'Voids squad'
Social counsellors to advise tenants in difficulty	Nominations from City of Cologne to empty units	Local panel to control local decisions	Reduce concentrations of specially difficult families	Maintenance co-ordination
Business approach to marketing the empty units		Hiring residents for local jobs	Attempt to get minority representation on estate board	Locally based upgrading team
More intensive cleaning		Local co-operative enterprises		Support for local groups – provision of community flats

Table 13.9 Continued

France	Germany	Britain	Denmark	Ireland
Screening out of difficult tenants	Social support for families in difficulties	Residents employed in repairs contracts	More intensive local management, care-taking, cleaning, and repairs	Resident consultation and involvement
Collaborative structure between HLMs	Job creation to upgrade environment	High input on management	Long-term planned maintenances	Appointment of estate co-ordinator and technical chief to local base
Flats provided for community use	Entrances – daily repainted and clean-up	Local repairs team		
Special youth focus to avoid vandalism and conflict	Cleaning standards raised radically	Attempts at limiting concentrations of very needy families		
Special training for new management and caretaking approach	Reduce rents/costs so tenants can afford to pay	Constant lift checks		
Blocks converted from rented housing to educational use	Control centre – visible link to residents and caretakers	Special anti-graffiti measure – instant clean-up		
	Eviction of 'criminal' households	Multi-racial staff team		
		Eventual links with local police		

Sources: Author's visits; Windsor Workshop (1991).

Table 13.10   New management pattern on the five estates

Management change	Number of estates
New local management offices	5
Special lettings initiatives to limit concentrations of disadvantaged tenants	5
Increased levels of contact with tenants	5
Special mechanisms for involving residents in estate decisions	5
Increased numbers of local housing staff	5
Greater input into repairs service	5
Several sub-offices on each estate	4
More intensive caretaking and cleaning	4

Sources: Author's visits; Windsor Workshop (1991).

empty units on every estate by the early 1990s resulting from more intensive, localised management.

ROLE OF TENANTS

Management change could not work on its own. One of the strongest benefits of the intensive localised management was that it forced landlords into dialogue with residents and highlighted social needs that had to be addressed if the estates were to be viable.

Social wellbeing and management control were closely related – for example, stamping out vandalism was essential to improvements in maintenance; vandal control was both a management and a social issue; training young people for work and involving them in activity was essential to improving security and controlling vandalism; security was partly a matter for the police, partly for managers, particularly caretakers, partly for residents. Reducing rubbish nuisance was essential to improving standards of cleanliness but it required both efficient systems, co-operation of residents and, where

More secure/more stable conditions

↑

Resident involvement and support

↑

Stronger local presence

↑

Improved lettability

↑

Higher morale/performance

↑

Upgraded conditions

↑

Priorities for reinvestment

↑

Immediate management action

↑

Link with residents

↑

Estate base

↑

Rescue project

↑

Crisis

Source: Author's visits and research.

Figure 13.1 Positive impact of management initiatives with resident involvement and support

Table 13.11   Change in numbers of empty units

	France	Germany	Britain	Denmark	Ireland
Greatest number of empty units	2400 (1984)	400 (1987)	75 (1982)	150 (1984)	450 (1989)
Empty units at turning point in rescue process	200 (1991)	0 (1991)	30 (1994)	0 (1991)	0 (1994)

Sources: Author's visits; Windsor Workshop (1991).

necessary, enforcement. Residents had become 'part of the problem' as controls broke down. In a management vacuum, many individuals felt unable to exercise any form of responsibility or control beyond their own front door. Many people's behaviour as a result had become collectively more irresponsible and socially either more disruptive or more withdrawn.

Because the social problems were so extreme, landlords had no confidence that conditions could be tackled without first winning the support of residents. This was considered the key to reversing spiralling conditions on all five estates. Addressing social needs was therefore as important as attacking physical and management problems. Landlords had too little control, but they could only expand control in partnership with residents. Therefore landlords needed to identify strong residents, willing to play a leadership role to help rebuild social controls alongside management control. Each estate developed different mechanisms for involving residents. On all estates, tenants' representatives had a recognised say in decisions about their estates. This included the organisation of physical improvements, the social facilities, management initiatives, particularly security, cleaning, repair and empty property. Table 13.12 indicates the most important mechanisms that were devised. Landlords proved willing to deal with

Table 13.12 Mechanisms for involving residents in each country

	France	Germany	Britain	Denmark	Ireland
Role of tenants	Consultation over improvements	Tenants' committee to provide link with manager	Dominant tenant leadership	Tenant board	Detailed consultation
	Régie de Quartiers (resident-led employment project)	Tenants' representatives on management committee	Community initiatives organised by tenants	Detailed consultation	Strong tenant voice in management and improvements
	Special social support project for individual families	Training employment programme	Tenant representation on council panel to manage the estate	Employment initiative	Representation of residents in all local groups
	Ethnic initiatives to help integration	Special support for needy families	Tenant bid to take over the estate, but not viable	Many clubs, etc.	Involvement in policy, e.g. allocations
	Special youth leadership programmes	Ethnic initiative	Tenant training	4 Area residents' committees	Many local activities including job centre
	Training programmes	Special efforts to harmonise different ethnic groups	Tenant involvement in contract work	Special support for tenant training	Voluntary groups
	Summer play programmes involving local youth	Children's play programme involving local youth	Involvement of young people in social and work programmes	Incentives for participation, such as cash for social events	Community representation in Task Force
				Special efforts to involve minority representatives	Focus on tenant management but not a realisable option
				Involvement of young people in environmental upgrading	

Sources: Author's visits; Windsor Workshop (1991).

residents' representatives. They not only encouraged involvement; they tried to organise and support it where it did not already exist.

In the British and Irish estates, government encouragement of tenant responsibility for management led to efforts by some tenants' leaders to organise a tenant management organisation. However, these initiatives were too ambitious, given the complex, large-scale structure of the estates, the landlord problems and the serious social pressures (see case studies). Landlords did not support full tenant control, nor were tenants' leaders ever in a strong enough position to achieve it.

Creating social networks

Landlords, as they came closer to the ground, were able to see that the estates were often deeply alienating environments, militating directly against social contact. The vacuum caused by resident withdrawal was invariably filled with hostile and damaging activity. To overcome these problems, a conscious attempt was made to establish public activity in communal spaces, to instate guards and security devices, and to privatise areas that were part of or adjacent to individual blocks or dwellings.

Governments also came to recognise the need to provide more than simply housing. They saw the economic and social gains from a variety of services and activities. As the renovation programmes got under way, resources were put into upgrading and expanding facilities. Each estate had a whole series of *ad hoc* clubs, tenants' groups and voluntary initiatives. These were located in empty flats, garages, storage areas, shops, and other unused spaces. There appeared no shortage of local groups demanding space, even though they often went through short life cycles. The surplus spaces found in underground areas, under walkways, in flats unsuitable for occupation were provided by landlords, usually responding readily to requests due to the large surplus of unused areas. In Ireland, Denmark and France about 60 flats or basement areas per estate were provided for clubs and other activities.

Important amenities included swimming pools, outdoor recreation areas, churches, shops, cafes, workshops and training centres. Play areas were variable in quality, as they required supervision and maintenance if they were to work. They were most useful if they were close to the buildings where the children lived, within easy reach of mothers, and equipped with strong, modern climbing structures that could withstand teenage use. Play areas were popular but readily abused.

Ethnic and religious centres played a special role on these culturally distinct estates. In France there was a Moslem centre as well as a Catholic church; in Germany and Denmark, Turkish centres; in London, an Afro-Caribbean-led youth association. On the Irish estate, Catholic organisations were conspicuous and active, but churches were also involved in three other estates and appeared to play an important community role.

Church activists

Church activists were working in four of the estates, responding to the inequalities that these estate communities experienced. They were drawn by the problems of homelessness, poverty, child neglect, racial discrimination, unemployment and youth problems to try and support tenants directly. On three estates, priests, nuns and lay religious lived in flats alongside more typical residents, trying to identify with their problems, strengthening community ties and drawing in help. Occasionally they came to occupy leading positions in local organisations. More often they worked behind the scenes, making their religious and social support available without, as far as possible, standing out. Their unusually high level of education, compared with most other residents or staff, their commitment to the residents, and their general desire not to be conspicuous, made them an unusual and unexpected resource for many of the new groups that sprang up.

Youth and training

Youth centres, youth cafés and other facilities for young people, were provided on all five estates. They were difficult to run and to control and did not usually cater for anywhere near all the young people who gathered on estates. They often attracted young people to *outside* the facility, where they 'hung about'. This was almost certainly because young people wanted simply to gather, rather than be organised, particularly older age groups. It seemed difficult to provide adequate social facilities for young people when their training and employment needs could not be met. They had too much time on their hands but a very unclear sense of direction and therefore often made inadequate use of the facilities that were available.

Levels of unemployment were so high and training so urgently needed that on all estates, special job-linked training initiatives were set up. In three cases, youth training projects attracted European funds as well as local funds. Some of the youth training was integrated with the upgrading of the estates. Trainees and unemployed residents helped build gardens, fencing and play equipment in Denmark and Germany; they were involved in environmental contracts in London; they helped with play schemes and maintenance in France; and they helped run the concierge system in Ireland. Training schemes were often short-term and dependent on the improvement works. It was hard to keep them going permanently, when once capital programmes were completed. This severely limited their impact. Special French and Irish organisations, linking young trainees with established employers, seemed more likely to succeed in the long run (Ballymun Job Centre, 1989; UNFOHLM, 1993).

Table 13.13 shows the pattern of social initiatives that accompanied the management changes. Table 13.14 sets out what happened estate by estate, illustrating the development of new facilities and projects. Experience from the estates illustrates not only the scope for a many-sided transformation of social as well as physical conditions, when once the landlord had created an estate focus; it also underlines the continuous nature of demands and needs in difficult-to-manage estates. Managing large, complex, social rented estates, with their many organisational problems, their wide range of social facilities, and their highly disadvantaged populations, was a difficult ongoing process. Therefore mechanisms to provide constant responses, as new problems emerged or old problems recurred, were vital. Consistent, long-term organisational infrastructure was found to be essential, if facilities were to survive for the benefit of the community and if residents' representatives were to be involved and able to influence events.

Table 13.13   Social initiatives on the five estates

Social provision	Number of estates
Additional space for residents' activities	5
Employment and training initiatives	5
Special youth programmes	4
Shops, cafes, banks, etc.	4
Involvement of Church groups	4
New community centre built	3

Sources: Author's visits; Windsor Workshop (1991).

THE PATCHWORK APPROACH

Our analysis of physical, organisational and resident responses has shown the clear patterns of intervention. Yet each estate influenced the way the initiatives developed. National structures and funds played a significant part but, as importantly, the rescue initiatives arose from the actual situation on estates – the very opposite of the way they were built, to stamp out individual and local problems. On all the estates, large government funds were drawn down but the rescue initiatives were varied and changing ground-level experiments, each with many small, localised components. They only worked because landlords decided to move out to the estates, putting real management resources behind the initiatives. The flexibility and energy that flowed from this approach were the characteristics that made estate rescue programmes different from other more standard programmes. The combined effect of small, specially adapted steps tailored to particular situations provided the main explanation we found for the radical reversal in fortunes, in spite of continuing problems on the five estates.

Funding problems and reform

The local patchwork of management and social changes was underwritten by financial reforms, which were aimed at

Table 13.14   New forms of social provision on each estate

France
- New church built with involvement of commune
- Youth cafes
- Tenants' centre
- Youth centre
- Training centre
- Play areas
- Shops/market
- Residents' contract company (Régie de Quartiers)
- College in one block
- Special social project for immigrant families

Germany
- Tenants' meeting room
- Women's project including self-defence training,
- Youth training project
- Children's play area
- Turkish community flat
- Adult education office and programme
- Youth employment initiative
- Nursery initiative organised by church charity
- Church charity involved in supporting estate

Britain
- Large community centre
- Enterprise workshops
- Communal gardens
- Nursery
- Community flat
- Youth organisation
- Café
- Festival
- Old people's lunches and other welfare projects
- Two Church groups on estate
- Training Centre

Denmark
- Community house
- Workshops
- TV studio
- Adult education
- Play areas
- Youth training and employment initiative
- Small garden areas attached to groups of flats
- Language initiative for Turkish residents
- Tenant training programme
- Environmental Projects

Ireland
- Community flats
- Job centre
- Many tenants' associations, each with own base
- Shop fronts in shopping centre for tenant initiatives, e.g. credit union
- Training initiatives
- Special project for vulnerable tenants
- Catholic Church very active in community initiatives
- Priests living on estate
- Children's activities
- Co-operative workshop

Sources: Author's visits; Windsor Workshop (1991).

making the owners of difficult estates more financially stable and therefore more able to respond. In every country, the funding of social housing had in part generated or accentuated the problems facing estates in acute decline. For example, inadequate provision was made for major repair or renewal when the estates were built and inadequate allowances were made for ongoing repair. The subsidies to build provided powerful incentives but the subsidies or incentives to manage were weak or ineffective. The central financial problem was the balance between income and expenditure after the estates were built. If rents were high enough to cover the costs, they were too high for tenants to pay. If rents were low enough, the estates could not be maintained.

Governments changed the financial structures to try and remedy this imbalance between costs, needs and rent levels. Different governments adopted different approaches; there was often more than a single solution. Table 13.15 attempts to summarise the most common problems and solutions. As financial changes were introduced to increase revenue and funds for reinvestment became available, the estates regained some kind of financial stability. Government resources for estate improvements were increased simultaneously with financial controls being tightened. In this way, management incentives were increased and performance improved.

Financial reforms were closely linked with the system of rents and housing allowances. This study did not examine either aspect of the housing finance systems in detail (see Ghekière, 1988). But Table 13.16 shows average rent levels on the estates, average spending on management and maintenance for four of the estates and proportions of tenants receiving housing allowances. They reflect conditions in 1991 on the five estates and do not necessarily reflect the wider situation in each country precisely. The high proportion of tenants receiving rent assistance is the most striking feature.

MEASURES OF VIABILITY

The simplest and most direct indicator of change was the viability of the estates. Levels of empty units were the most direct measure of estate problems and estate viability. This

Table 13.15 Financial problems and solutions attempted in different countries

Problem	Number of countries	Solutions	Number of countries
1. *Rent levels*			
Too low	3	– Push rents up	2
Too high	2	– Special subsidies or financial reorganisation to lower rents or limit rent rises	3
Rising rapidly	3	– Allow special rent support to targeted families	5
		– More generous housing allowances/benefits	3
2. *Management and maintenance allowances*			
Inadequate funds for major repair problems	5	– Increase rent income	4
		– Make special repair funds available	5
		– Increase allowances for management and maintenance spending	5
3. *Rent losses*			
Voids, arrears, turnover and slow relet times, threatening insolvency	5	– Major management effort to cut arrears and voids and to increase income	5
		– Government pressure on local authorities to improve performance	2
		– Rescheduling of debts, tighter financial management	5
4. *Funds for major repair*			
Too limited	5	– Governments (central/local) provide special funds for reinvestment	5
5. *Social problems*			
Affect financial viability	5	– Governments fund estate rescue to keep housing available for targeted needs	5
		– Governments support social initiatives	5

Sources: Author's visits; Windsor Workshop (1991).

Table 13.16   Average rents, average management and maintenance costs, percentage of all tenants dependent on housing allowances in the five estates

	France	Germany	Britain	Denmark	Ireland
Average rent – exclusive of charges – for 2-bedroom flat (in £ sterling)	44	50	40	75	20
Spending on management and maintenance per unit per week (in £ sterling)	–	35	38	46	28
Percentage of tenants receiving housing allowances or paying reduced rent (Ireland)	66	–	80	60	70

Sources: Author's visits; Windsor Workshop (1991).

measure was reasonably reliable since the level of empty units rose, even in areas of high demand like London and Cologne, when conditions became difficult or service levels were cut (PEP, 1993; City of Cologne, 1989). Empty units affected physical conditions through damage, increased spending and unsightly decay. They affected social conditions by attracting ever more disadvantaged and disruptive tenants, as the vacuum in lettings became self-fuelling. They affected management by creating security and financial pressures and by knock-on effects on repairs and further turnover. They had been the signal to everyone that the estates were in trouble. Refilling the empties when the downward pressures were so strong was a positive demonstration that the estates were improving. Closely linked to this was a change in the arrears levels. There is a direct connection between arrears management and general management control (Audit Commission, 1984). As management control was reasserted and as conditions improved, arrears fell. The dramatic reduction in the numbers of empty units, increased demand and increased rent income, meant that the estates could be made to work.

In Continental estates, arrears had dropped significantly. Arrears were still a major problem in Britain and Ireland, indicating insufficient management and financial reform or management control. Nonetheless, they were beginning to fall significantly in London by 1993. In Ireland, the financial system of differential rents and 100 per cent government subsidy for management and maintenance offered little incentive to managers or to tenants. Even so, in both cases better lettings performance meant more rent income.

The measurable changes in lettings and arrears performance illustrated the landlords' improved management control. The improved performance suggested that the estates had become more popular and therefore pressures to provide adequate services were greater. The success in restoring management reflected the greater local control, the enhanced communications with residents and the value of the upgrading. A certain sign that this was really the case lay in the unexpected growth in waiting lists of applicants wanting to move to the estates. For the previous eight to 15 years, landlords had been struggling to find applicants at all. Now people were queuing to move in, as the figures in Table 13.17 show. These changes were matched by changes in the pattern of arrears. Most new applicants were needy households. Many were single people. But their active demand for rehousing, rather than being pushed reluctantly into the estates, in itself made a big difference to the atmosphere of the estates. Figure 13.2 attempts to summarise how the estates became more attractive to live in as all the different changes took effect.

SOCIAL GHETTOS

We need to look beyond the immediate restoration of viability to the wider impact of the programmes on the long-term prospects for the estates. The most important elements in this were the underlying physical distinctness of the estates, the inherent difficulties in managing large, separate, low-income areas, and the underlying trend towards marginalisation. Were the estates becoming social ghettos?

343

Table 13.17 Changes in the proportion of empty dwellings, turnover and arrears on the five estates

Country:	France	Germany	Britain	Denmark	Ireland
Percentage empty at crisis	30% (1984)	38% (1985)	7% (1982)	15% (1984)	15% (1989)
Percentage empty units 1991	2.5%	0%	1.5%[a]	0%	0%
Turnover at lowest point	20% (1981)	25%[b] (1985)	16% (1983)	35% (1981)	31% (1985)
Turnover 1991	15%[b]	Below 10%	10%[b]	15%	15%
Arrears at lowest point – percentage of tenants owing rent	50% of tenants (1981)	10% of tenants[b] (rent was only collected from 55% of property due to voids and illegal occupancy)	90% of tenants[b] (average debt £300 per households in 1983; rose to £800 per household in 1991)	5% of tenants	16% of tenants
Arrears after turnaround – percentage tenants owing rent	7% 1991	5% – all properties (1991)	Arrears began to fall rapidly in 1993 but still average very high	1.4% (1991)	Still double city average
Numbers of applicants on waiting lists, 1991	700	100	Some demand through special lettings	500	500

Notes: [a]When management was withdrawn and lettings policies relaxed in 1990, empty units rose to 6 per cent again but fell back when management controls were reasserted.
[b]Estimates based on local information.
[c]Arrears are estimated differently in different countries. We have attempted to use a simple measure applicable in all countries, that is, percentage of tenants in arrears of over four weeks. This makes it possible to show both the proportion of tenants with historic arrears and the impact of action on arrears.

Sources: Author's visits; Windsor Workshop (1991).

Crisis conditions provoke interventions

↓

Government rescue programmes channel resources
towards estate renovation

↓

Landlords consult with residents
over priorities for change and improvement

↓

Local bases are set up
to establish new approaches to estates

↓

Management initiatives develop,
for example, more intensive caretaking

↓

Social facilities expand or are restored

↓

Estate appearances are softened
and made more secure

↓

Social networks develop
through support for tenant initiatives

↓

Housing subsidies/finance are reformed
to increase landlord income

↓

Greater performance incentives are built in

↓

Empty units and arrears levels drop

↓

Control over conditions is re-established

↓

Demand for estates rises

↓

Waiting lists form

↓

Estate conditions become more normal

Source: Author's visits and research.

Figure 13.2   How estate conditions were restored to manageability
and acceptability

The term, social ghetto, was used in all five countries (Salicath, 1987; Toubon and Renaudin, 1987; Dublin Corporation, 1993; BRBS, 1986; Taylor, 1995). Housing managers, local and central government officials and social organisations used the term to refer to the growing concentration of very poor and socially vulnerable households in these estates. It meant that new lettings tended to go to ever higher proportions of marginal households, such as unemployed, lone parent or minority ethnic households. It meant that the estates remained stigmatised and socially precarious without significant additional support. It was the combination and concentrations of social disadvantages that evoked the notion of a ghetto. All countries were committed to avoiding this outcome as it smacked of segregation, discrimination, and ghettoisation. But even concerted lettings policies directed at diversified occupation seemed unable to achieve it. When German managers attempted such an approach in 1993, it failed and they reverted to rehousing according to demand (Dixon, 1995). In practice, this meant almost exclusively minorities and ethnic Germans. The great sensitivity of this issue made it difficult to arrive at solutions that would ensure some kind of racial or social balance. The British and German estates already housed a large majority of households belonging to ethnic minority groups by 1991, but avoiding racial ghettos and keeping the estates racially mixed involved attracting white applicants, which was an elusive goal. Racial concentrations and social polarisation were still dominant issues on all the estates, even though the extremes of unpopularity had been reversed. This affected political attitudes and prevented the estates from becoming more integrated into the wider urban community, even though their conditions were significantly better (Boligministeriet, 1993). Table 13.18 shows what happened.

Race, poverty and management change

In the previous chapter, we showed that minority communities were clearly not directly responsible for poor conditions; nor, as the findings from this chapter show, did their presence make the rescue of estates in decline particularly intractable. This important fact is underlined by conditions in Ireland. As

Table 13.18 Intervention in lettings affected the drift to ghetto conditions

France	Germany	Britain	Denmark	Ireland
Stopped decline; stable	City nominations filling voids with asylum seekers	Homeless only allocated after 1988	Most new tenants are needy	Continues to house very needy
Trend reversed in some areas through student lets and screening of applicants	Very few West Germans moving in	Voids rose steeply again as a result	More unemployed, etc.	Now long waiting list
Estate is still primarily seen as housing for low-income, unemployed, single parents and North Africans	Ever higher percentage of foreigners or ethnic Germans	Reinstated more local control in 1991; improved	Only generally acceptable to low-income or otherwise excluded households	More selective access – screening out very unstable
	Disturbing households excluded	Still high percentage of homeless, minorities and single parents	Queues building up again, so more selective allocations	But many very poor, large families
	More socially stable	Media image of estate still deters applicants	Rehousing of children of tenants	Continuing negative image
Image of estate still a problem	Generally very poor	Considered by general public as largely 'black community'	Attempt to disperse Turkish community	
	Attempts at blocking rehousing of Turks and East Europeans failed and abandoned	Still unpopular though some groups now queue to get in	Tight control over access	
	Accepted as estate for marginal 'foreigners'		Still considered a difficult estate	

Sources: Author's visits; Windsor Workshop (1991).

in the other four cases, management rescue proved possible and quickly effective. Therefore we can conclude that poverty, marginalisation and racial disadvantage were not of themselves an insuperable obstacle to management reform or estate rescue.

It was possible to distinguish between landlord performance, which affected conditions directly, and social problems, which affected conditions indirectly. These could be partially alleviated by higher landlord inputs. Nonetheless, the social needs, generated by concentrations of poverty and of ethnic minority groups, had to be addressed through special social programmes. Ignored, the problems enhanced the stigmatisation of the people needing help and of the communities where they lived. It was not possible, therefore, to reduce management or social services inputs when conditions improved because the social composition of the estates was fundamentally unchanged. Wider structural and housing changes were needed to change the more fundamental problems of estate segregation.

EXCLUDING DISRUPTIVE HOUSEHOLDS

The rescue initiatives were successful in improving conditions on estates with large minority communities and on the Irish estate with a high concentration of low-income and vulnerable households. These communities had become involved in and were part of the improvement process. They benefited from the special efforts that were made to restore the estates and were therefore important partners in change. Following the improvement programmes, none of the estates significantly changed the type of households they rehoused: the poorly housed; ethnic minorities; lone parents; unemployed people. But they systematically attempted to exclude those with serious behaviour problems, a completely different issue. Disadvantaged households were not, except in rare cases, disruptive to other people's lives. But disruptive households had made the lives of many disadvantaged people miserable. In some cases they had destroyed the fragile social equilibrium.

A common result of the improvement programmes was the much stronger management hold on lettings. Disruptive households causing serious nuisance, damage or crime were forced to contain their behaviour or forced to leave. This was a primary management focus and became accepted as an essential management tool. In the last resort, it involved court action and sometimes the police. Access by families with extreme social problems that impinged on collective conditions was limited; and households with a previous record of serious disruption were, wherever possible, screened out and denied access. This was achieved through a combination of strict management vetting and resident pressure. Landlords now encouraged residents to become involved in exerting community control. It was the only way that difficult social problems could be resolved in such a collectively built environment.

All the estates had gone through periods of accepting all-comers, of rehousing purely on the basis of stated need, and of accepting the wider communities' desire to chase 'undesirable' households into the most marginal areas, resulting in heavy over-concentrations of problems. It was this that had led to the term 'ghettoisation' and that turned out to be one of the most dominant and common characteristics of declining estate communities (Peillon, 1995; City of Cologne, 1994; Kelleher, 1988). The rationale for excluding particularly disruptive households from mass estates lay in the structure of the estates and the poverty and instability of the communities, which could not contain disruptive behaviour effectively. These two factors made absorbing above-average numbers of households with serious behaviour problems virtually impossible. The ultimate justification for exclusion lay in the virtual collapse of social and management cohesion, greatly exacerbated by extreme antisocial behaviour. When once normal social controls disintegrated, as happened on all five estates, imposing new and tighter controls became a prerequisite of successful restoration of conditions (City of Cologne, 1994; Élie *et al.*, 1989; SBI, 1993).

One of the most significant findings of the case studies was that as soon as a small number of the most disruptive households were removed, social and management conditions began to improve. This might involve one in 100 households or even less. The German, British and Irish estates had experienced this dramatic change. The most disruptive households were more likely to be indigenous excluded households than more recently arrived minorities. Where lettings were relaxed again or removed from tight local controls, as happened twice in the London estate, estate conditions rapidly deteriorated again, causing a sharp expansion of empty dwellings. The very laxity of lettings policies directly created the conditions that caused an exodus and a rise in unlettable property (Power, 1987a). Where lettings could be made more socially balanced, the new lettings policies had a strong and positive impact (Rajon, 1991).

Carefully organised lettings and management control are not the same as discrimination, although this has sometimes been suggested. Discrimination usually works in a much more subtle and pervasive way (Parker and Dugmore, 1976). All the case study estates continued to house target groups of people in great need. Because of their physical style, reputation and intrinsic problems, the estates were still heavily disfavoured in any lettings hierarchy and they clearly still housed disproportionately needy people. In this sense their 'ghetto' character had plainly not been reversed. But central finding from the five estates was that only by controlling access in communally designed and highly disadvantaged areas could the breakdown of social controls be prevented. Even where there were severe homelessness problems and high general demand for social housing, as the German, British and Irish case studies showed, high levels of empty property resulted from social breakdown. Only by excluding seriously disruptive households could social breakdown be prevented and the estates remain occupied. In Part V, we discuss some of the wider changes needed to address this problem.

OUTCOMES

Physical, social and management conditions changed radically in the course of the improvement programmes on the five estates. But the programmes did not fundamentally transform these poor communities into integrated and economically self-supporting areas. They did create more and better services and conditions, giving residents more opportunities and reasserting control over a situation that had threatened to run out of hand. The changes were fragile. Far more needed to be done if the still wide gap between these marginal communities and the cities was to be narrowed. Upgrading was a continuing process involving cycles, possibly as short as ten years. Permanent local management, requiring senior backing and strong local powers, could not be diluted once more normal conditions had been instated, otherwise renewed decline followed very quickly. This was because of the intrinsic management needs of the estates. The pressures to rehouse the most needy had to be limited to exclude those who could not cope or contain their behaviour in large, transient, multi-access estates. Such households could not survive and nor could their neighbours under such intense social pressure as the most difficult estates still created.

The rescue programmes on the five estates made communities into exciting experiments in change. Change was visible and attracted significant publicity, just as the crises had done (Timmins, 1995). It was surprising because the physical barriers to the estates, their intrinsic isolation and separation from surroundings were not overcome by the renovations. If anything, the changes made the estates stand out further due to the use of bright colours, better lighting, concrete painting, new facilities, some of which were shared with the wider community. The estates went through fairly rapid up-and-down cycles. Decline could be arrested, as long as landlords responded quickly. But the nature of the estates and their populations made them volatile, difficult to manage and vulnerable. There were serious limits for these reasons to the roles that tenants could play. They were central to all the changes but they were not in sufficient control of wider elements to keep control on their own. The estates were too large, too complex and too major a public resource for small groups of tenants' leaders to take full control. For that reason, landlord control proved to be the central key. On the other hand, landlords could not do it on their own either. They needed co-operation from residents and the pressure they could exert to maintain standards in adverse conditions.

Management was all-important but, necessary as it was for success, it was not sufficient on its own to combat the wider problems facing estates (Glennerster and Turner, 1993; Murie, 1995). Youth problems, ethnic tensions, political and reinvestment problems, all undermined the long-term stability of the estates. Their high profile, resulting from their conspicuous structure and their concentration of problems, had blighted their image in a very public way. To the extent that this was inescapable, it is possible that the estates would remain a refuge for the needy and would never fully enter the mainstream.

SUMMARY: CHANGE IN ESTATE FORTUNES

Each estate went through a major crisis, in two cases with violent disorders, that provoked radical intervention. Demolition was considered in all cases but was ruled out due to rehousing pressures, social needs and the cost of replacement. Measures to restore conditions were implemented in small phases over several years, reinstating empty units, securing entrances, planting and enclosing open spaces, painting and brightening the buildings. Radical physical change was tried but was too expensive to be possible throughout the estates.

The most *avant-garde*, dynamic project leaders were based at the front line to push through the rescue and get control over conditions. Conditions became more orderly but the buildings still looked gigantesque and extraordinary. The populations were stabilised through scores of small programmes and initiatives. New residents were attracted when once the blocks were restored and close, tight management was in place.

The estates in their most acute decline had housed very disproportionate numbers of the most difficult tenants. Preventing this was a prerequisite for management viability. The dense communal estates could not absorb or contain disruptive behaviour. Therefore lettings control became axiomatic. But the estates continued to house extremely needy and disadvantaged communities, which prevented their full integration into the mainstream of surrounding cities.

Part V
Can Mass Housing Estates
be Rescued?

Introduction to Part V

The study of mass estates in Europe set out to expand our understanding of marginal urban communities by explaining how and why mass housing estates came to be built, examining the role of government in their creation, decline and rescue, exploring the interaction of social and physical problems, and assessing the attempted solutions. There are many theories to explain mass housing, government intervention in poor communities and acute area-based social decline. Mass housing itself was the application of a theory of social engineering to address area, housing and social problems. This detailed examination of the international experiment in mass housing demonstrates the failure of that theory. The scale of the failure made it all the more urgent to understand what went wrong with mass estates and what, if any, solutions had been found to their problems. One thing was clear – neither the causes nor the solutions were one-dimensional. Only by piecing together the many-sided experiences of estate communities was it possible to understand the transnational nature of the problem.

The final part of the study examines the social consequences of increasingly polarised and isolated urban communities; the reasons for governments and cities taking increased responsibility for these problems in the context of the continuing need for affordable and readily available homes; and the attempted solutions to the crisis in housing management that the study uncovered. We conclude by synthesising the findings into a model of change.

Part V of the book explores the important themes that have emerged from the close study of 20 difficult and unpopular mass housing estates in five European countries. These themes have run through the whole study and are central to the concluding discussion:

— The physical and social structure of estates interact in an often negative way, causing intense decline and a collapse in control. Therefore any successful solutions we found

involved more care, more control, more social and economic diversification to prevent social disintegration.
— Urban housing areas require careful management in order to succeed. The stronger and more direct the management system, the more likely it is to bring conditions on estates closer to the mainstream.
— Marginal, isolated and socially excluded communities need to be integrated with the wider community, if they are to regain viability, both for the residents and the owners and the city as a whole.
— No amount of individual effort would be equal to the deep urban problems the estates encapsulate because their intense decline results from and reflects much wider societal problems, requiring broad-based, collective solutions.
— Democracy cannot survive deep cleavages that the estates reflect; the majority that is successful will therefore support attempts at integration.

Part V comprises two chapters. Chapter 14 sets the failure of mass estates in the urban context and explains the centrality of the management and landlord role. Chapter 15 discusses the relevance of marginal housing areas to democracies and argues the value of integration and social cohesion to prevent whole communities from splitting off from mainstream society. It then looks at how large, separated housing areas can be made to work in spite of the pressures towards greater social breakdown. We assess the validity of a 'patchwork' interpretation of successful city renewal and we propose a model of estate rescue, based on our findings. In the final sections, we attempt to answer the central questions about why marginal areas matter, why they recur, and whether they are rescuable.

14 Managing Mass Housing

URBAN EXTREMES

The story of troubled housing estates is a small part of a much wider drift towards loss of cohesion and possible social breakdown. Estates underline the failure of postwar attempts to build large-scale collective solutions that unify communities and nations (Glennerster, 1993). They show the harsh impact of increasing polarisation resulting from rapid economic change, some of the long-term implications of mass labour migrations and the geographical concentration of need. They underline the strongly recurring pattern of urban decay.

Many works have been dedicated to examining these deepset urban problems and attempting to explain them. William Julius Wilson, the Chicago sociologist, argues in *The Truly Disadvantaged* (1987) that economic restructuring cut away the employment base of North American inner cities only a generation after the mass migration of black people from the south to northern jobs. This in turn undermined family and marriage structures, leaving women with little incentive to marry and men with few recognised roles. The economic collapse of the North American urban ghettos coincided with the promotion of equal opportunities, thereby denuding the poorest inner areas of their brightest and most successful leaders. These areas lost viable shops, schools, churches and other intermediary organisations or 'social buffers' as Wilson describes such institutions. The result was an undreamt-of level of social and economic disintegration in North American inner cities (Wilson, 1987).

The emotive debate on the underclass has raged on both sides of the Atlantic as Wilson's thesis has been challenged and extended (Murray, 1989; Jencks and Peterson, 1991). Such are the fears of American-style outcomes in Europe that politicians, public and social administrators alike use the term 'ghetto', often inappropriately applied to large, poor and separate housing estates, almost as a way of forcing action before it is too late (EC, 1991).

357

There are obvious parallels between Wilson's analysis and the experience of large and unpopular urban housing estates in Europe, built to serve a booming economy but left devastated by the collapse of major industries and the loss of the local employment base, housing increasing proportions of those left behind in the race for jobs and economic advance. The globalisation of communications and markets is having a profound effect right at the bottom of industrialised societies. Inevitably this affects estates built to meet the needs of a previous era – mass production factories and a large employed work force, much of it imported from ex-colonies and other less developed regions. Estates in this study had far above average concentrations of workless households and increasingly of ethnic minorities.

LARGE-SCALE CHANGE

The American economist, Robert Reich, explains in a penetrating book, *The Work of Nations*, how the unskilled, previously in demand for advanced, large-scale mass production, in a worldwide scramble for jobs, will experience falling wages, declining security, and marginalisation in a sharply divided world (Reich, 1993). At the losing end of this economic shift, the residents of marginal estates are increasingly squeezed. The steeply rising rates of unemployment in some estates, show the consequences of the wider processes. The distance between marginal communities and new job markets is growing. The extreme alienation of unemployed young men on unpopular estates reflects the impact of the Reichian sequence of events on the younger unskilled and undervalued workforce (Campbell, 1993; Ministère de la Ville, 1993). The social landlords we studied were facing the direct consequences of these changes. In the books we have discussed, these ideas were abstract concepts. On the estates they represented social collapse.

The pressures of new economics led to break-up and change within organisations, the creation of smaller, self-driven units, and reliance on front-line problem-solvers. Old-style bureaucracies and hierarchies could not respond fast enough or flexibly enough to the unforeseen problems they faced. According to modern management analysis, new-style organisations had to be more fluid, more organic and more directly involved with customers if they were to survive in a global economy (Peters, 1987; Handy, 1993). Management change was sweeping through social housing organisations as they were forced to respond to a new and far more difficult management task than they originally envisaged. They faced the pressure to move out to ground level in hundreds of different areas, with the tools of hands-on management, or they faced loss of control. Social housing organisations in this study became part of the 'chaotic' front-line management revolution, because traditional 'dinosaur' management had collapsed on mass estates (Quilliot and Guerrand, 1989). The German housing ministry summed it up: 'lack of local management could be a main cause of problematic decline' and 'it was not thinkable to achieve improvements in estate conditions without resident involvement' (BRBS, 1988).

The political importance of social housing meant that politicians often forced the pace of reform, as it was political vision that had created the mass estates. In a climate of financial retrenchment and disenchantment with the consequences of mass house-building, new ways of doing things had to be literally invented. The idea that governments could change their role so radically was driven by sheer necessity, a process that is entertainingly described in *Reinventing Government* (Osborne and Gaebler, 1992). 'Entrepreneurial Bureaucrats' have been identified by Patrick Dunleavy as a new breed of social administrators, seeking alternative ways of creating and transforming services under the changing state of Government by moving out and handling problems directly (Dunleavy, 1990). Unpopular estates encapsulated new needs and bred new, frequently *ad hoc*, alternative experimental responses, along the lines of the small-scale, bottom-up initiatives identified by Michael Harloe in his original analysis of *The People's Home* (Harloe, 1995).

RENEWED INTERVENTION

There was a circular process leading governments to support the renewal of large-scale, dense estates. They were built originally to address a common shortage. Their subsequent rapid decline generated demand for single-family or small-scale housing that was greedy of land and expensive. The limitations of distance and cost in owner-occupier programmes created new pressures on inner areas and on high-rise estates – gentrification of the first and renewed demand for the second. The need for cheap solutions, as new shortages emerged, led to estate renewal. There seemed no escaping dense, low-quality housing for low-income people in cities if needy people were to be housed and city sprawl limited. Figure 14.1 illustrates the inevitability of estate renewal.

The estates conspicuously broke with both urban and rural traditions. But the alternative scenario of endless little boxes or *pavillons*, as the French call them, positively created a climate which favoured high-rise. As high-rise materialised, people with choice rejected mass outer estates. But for the foreseeable future, governments will not be able to replace them because there is a limit to land, to owner-occupation and to subsidies. Very poor people cannot afford high-quality housing and governments can only provide it on a strictly limited basis. We are faced with rising demand for millions of cheap, dense and subsidised units. The estates offer precisely this and therefore in large measure the estates are likely to survive, except in areas of exceptional low demand due to industrial collapse and advanced social breakdown (Provan, 1993).

The German study of outer estates by Olaf Gibbins identified four phases in the process of estate renewal. These phases broadly apply to all countries in the study: the emergence of physical and other problems; rising turnover and instability; declining standards and growing financial problems; intervention and renewal (Gibbins, 1988). Governments instituted rescue programmes in the 1980s when estates were far down the road towards unviability, making their task costly, difficult and slow but central to estate renewal. Our case studies illustrated the survival potential of estates in spite of the obvious failures.

PRECARIOUS PROGRESS

The government interventions underlined the instability of large, peripheral estates as the rescue process failed to 'nor-

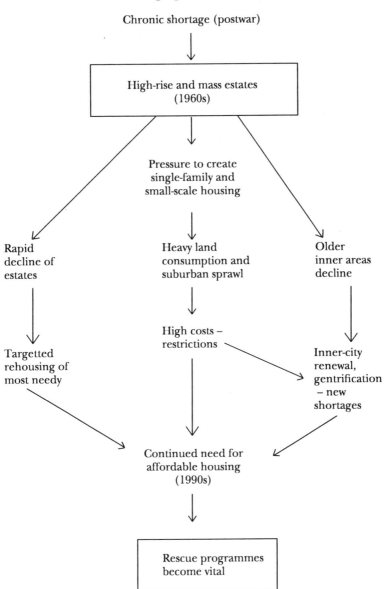

Chronic shortage (postwar)

High-rise and mass estates
(1960s)

Pressure to create
single-family and
small-scale housing

Rapid
decline of
estates

Heavy land
consumption and
suburban sprawl

Older
inner areas
decline

Targetted
rehousing of
most needy

High costs –
restrictions

Inner-city
renewal,
gentrification
– new
shortages

Continued need for
affordable housing
(1990s)

Rescue programmes
become vital

Source: Author's visits and research.

Figure 14.1   Process of estate renewal

malise' the estates. The estates retained their conspicuous and often outlandish appearance. Nor did they lose their low status reputation because the rescue programmes worked around the existing, usually poor populations. The estates required continuous attention and reinvestment. It was an uneasy progress. The danger of very poor slum conditions re-emerging was everywhere apparent.

The deep problems of the estates and their unique, probably unrepeatable style, had led to a questioning of their survival. The pace of at least partial demolition was quickening (Conrad, 1992), although selective partial demolition was not the same issue as total demolition. In practice, demolition was rarely a strong option, as residents would be shunted to whatever was available, experiencing years of blight and upheaval. Many would fail to achieve their rehousing dream and the costs of the process were cripplingly expensive, as Barbara Ward forecast a generation ago (Ward, 1974). Even in the worst cases, restoration was cheaper than rebuilding and it avoided the additional costs that flowed from displacing whole communities.

The size and complexity of the estates led to short-term, limited spending for short-term improvements being favoured over more radical, more expensive, longer-term investment. The cost of wholesale radical 'estate surgery' that would physically transform the estates usually proved too close to replacement cost to be supported, however desirable. The time-span needed to complete a renewal programme in very large estates could be ten years or more, whereas governments were re-elected every four to seven years. Renewal timetables were constantly subjected to government constraints in order to achieve quick, visible results within short time-scales.

With the limited reinvestment that took place, most estates became more viable. The reinvestment worked in large measure because of the combined benefits of physical, social and organisational improvements. They were generally popular with local staff and residents, offering gains in security and appearance that had a disproportionate impact on morale and atmosphere. Smaller-scale reinvestment effected sufficient changes to extend estate life, if accompanied with management reform and resident involvement. Governments favoured this approach because it embraced the wider social and organisational problems that were plainly part of the decline, while avoiding costs so high as to call the whole approach into question. Most estates were restored to precarious viability. However, as population growth slows, the overall housing stock increases and new social housing continues to be built, demand for the worst mass estates may fall again. In France and Britain there were anxieties of this kind as social house-building expanded in the 1990s (Guenod, 1994; LSE Housing, 1994). This could bring into question again the future of some of the estates we have described (Power and Tunstall, 1995).

THE MANAGEMENT PROBLEM

The approach to estate building and estate rescue was dominated by physical conditions. But there was an internal dynamic to estates, which affected both the landlord's organisational approach and the lives of residents. How estates were run, how community needs were met, how conditions were maintained, how occupants survived, largely determined whether estates worked in the long run. Sustainability after improvements related at least as much to how the buildings were used, managed, cared for, and how the people – staff and tenants alike – were treated as to any immediate impact of physical improvements themselves (Rogers, 1995; BRBS, 1988, 1990). Therefore rescuing estates was more like painting the Forth bridge than running a lifeboat service. Extra facilities, where added, needed permanent staff and support if they were to survive. Resident-based structures needed nurturing, as without wider support they almost inevitably foundered. Estates were large and complex structures, requiring intensive ongoing inputs. In this sense they were no different from other large social structures. Estate rescue did not turn unpopular estates into stable, secure, economically viable areas free of ongoing needs,but they became more manageable and therefore more popular.

The new organisational approach that landlords adopted in their effort to regain control over conditions relied not only on housing services but had to draw together the different services involved with estates in an attempt to tackle the multiple social and economic problems in a co-ordinated way. But the inertia of government institutions and the segmented controls of different government departments in all countries made close, ground-level collaboration difficult. Without doubt, many resources were wasted and long-term stability undermined through service divisions and needless invisible armies of administrators answering to diverse Ministers, jealously guarding their programmes. The creation of the Délégation Interministeriélle à la Ville, in France in 1989, was an attempt to resolve such conflicts. The British government in 1994 combined a multitude of regeneration programmes into a Single Regeneration Budget, aimed at rationalising area renewal spending. But the cumbersome interdepartmental structure of the new programmes and the competition and protectionism of government departments meant a serious loss of local control and local funds (Delarue, 1993).

The estates had not evolved sufficient organisational links at ground level to create stable collaborative structures across the huge battery of public and semi-public services that concentrated programmes on marginal estates. This made the changes and improvements more precarious and more costly than necessary. Services to poor areas did not bring as much benefit as they did to more secure areas. Schools and police were two examples that frequently recurred of services that often underperformed in the mass estates.

AN OVERARCHING ROLE FOR GOVERNMENT

Publicly funded programmes and services were vital to the estates because the estates were usually seen as a 'public' responsibility, even when they were independently owned, and because estate communities were unusually dependent on these services. Certainly this was true when they went wrong, even when entirely privately-owned, as the German case study shows (see Chapter 8). This was because only governments could play an overarching role in brokering serious community conflict. Only governments had the authority to intervene in a crisis of threatening proportions. Only governments could soften the impact of economic change or provide essential underpinning for the failures at the margin of society, though it is argued by pure free marketeers that this may simply slow the process of essential economic adjustment. Governments came into being to broker wider interests that could not be served by any one group or by more limited organisations. The role of governments evolved in periods of economic development and transition because the interests of the successful could only in the end be adequately protected by some sort of consensual and representative structure. Cromwell's argument for democratic government on this basis holds good today. Governments therefore have a unique brokering role that on the right, as well as the left, has been reinforced by social pressures. Governments represent and therefore help create and hold together an essential unity of purpose, a collective acceptance of law-making and law-abiding, an underpinning that reinforces our sense of communal security. Thus while the role of government is changing rapidly and the style and scale of government are under almost constant attack, nonetheless all communities rely on governments to do something about the toughest problems. Governments are needed, particularly in times of flux and uncertainty or crisis (Power, 1992).

European countries have stronger governments, more underpinning, greater cohesion and stability than America. If urban problems are less acute in Europe than the United States, it may partly be a result of better government. If government is stronger, with more public support for government intervention, then governments are correspondingly more heavily relied on to maintain cohesion and prevent or reverse decline in times and places of upheaval. For these reasons, European governments played a more active role in the cities where the estates were found (Power, 1992). For these reasons they responded to the crisis on mass estates.

BOTTOM-UP PRESSURES

Governments often shun the need for action in chaotically difficult conditions, unless forced to intervene through bottom-up pressures. This survey showed how bottom-up pressures galvanised top-down reactions and created radical new approaches after, not before, the crisis on estates emerged. It was the reaching down by government into relatively small neighbourhoods or estates that marked out the rescue programmes.

The survey highlighted a combination of the most effective, localised strategies across all five countries, involving immense attention to detail and significant flows of support from governments to the furthest extremities of the urban communities. This 'arterial' system, flowing into many small and fragmented areas, had brought estates back from the brink of collapse in almost every case. The rescue of unstable communities illustrated what was possible when government effort was focused, when communication was direct and when action was sharp but incremental, responsive and adaptable.

Estate renewal preserved existing populations as far as possible and aimed to build on their strengths, responding to bottom-up signals. This made estate rescue above all a stabilising process, indubitably one of the reasons for its positive impact, even though it left in place populations with above average needs, a physical and social environment that was expensive, difficult to run, easily disrupted and damaged. Because problems were highly localised, even though they were linked with bigger problems, governments could only work through landlords and with local communities, combining a top-down with a bottom-up approach.

THE ROLE OF SOCIAL LANDLORDS

Managing the problems, the resources, the staff, the contracts, the consultation process, the decision-making, the co-ordination of services and programmes was vital to the rescue of the estates. Stability was only achieved through careful management. Governments provided the resources for restoration, the political will to help marginal communities and the sense of direction but landlords on the estates were the axis of the management process. There were clear reasons for this:

• The initiative to tackle many-sided problems lay primarily with the landlords as the main property owners. To survive as landlords, they had to make the estates work. Because the estates were organisational entities, the owners had to bear the primary responsibility for conditions. Therefore the landlords had to manage the changes.

● The only way to provide adequate physical conditions, reasonable repair and maintenance services was through full rent collection, close supervision, swift, prompt action on arrears, controlled lettings, rapid reletting of empty property, strong action on nuisance. Therefore the local landlord service was vital to the establishment of viable estates. Local management became central.

● Many wider services were needed to make estates viable – lighting, rubbish removal, security, open space maintenance. Many local services, such as schools, health and social services, also relied on landlords for basic conditions. Only landlords were in a position to provide the cross-links and co-ordination. Other services had to work if landlords were to manage effectively. This need confirmed their role as the axis of estate co-ordination.

● Problems that affected tenants also affected their housing. Social problems had long been intricately bound up with social rented housing (Hill, 1883; Daunton, 1984; Quilliot and Guerrand, 1989). Landlords of difficult estates had discovered that they could not solve most estate problems without understanding residents' problems, knowing the residents' views and responding to residents' needs. Many solutions depended on residents' support and involvement. To achieve this, landlords had to become more proactive. They had to develop new and more effective ways of communicating with residents. The new communication revealed the extent of social need and its impact on estate conditions. Landlords therefore became a main link to residents.

● Estates were different from more traditional urban residential areas. Their concentrated social ownership, their uniformity, their separation, their lack of more normal urban diversity, made them more clearly a major responsibility for the owners. As they were usually unsettled areas, they relied more heavily on the landlord than more established areas would. The failure of local social networks had created a 'deadening' environment. Landlords had to generate local social activity to revive the estates. Landlords as owners of estates were also the axis of social initiatives, pro-

viding the infrastructure for social development, though
they could only do this as an aid to the main social
providers.

● Landlord control over conditions was particularly important because residents came from many different and
sometimes conflicting backgrounds. Landlords had responsibility for enforcing common rules. To ensure the
survival of the estates, landlords became the brokers of
conditions and standards. Residents expected and needed
them to play this role. Local leadership required wider
support and, though the landlords were not the sole actors
in changing conditions, the landlords' role in rented areas
was pivotal.

Landlord management was not the only controlling
element. For example, policing and social provision were as
fundamental. The support of a majority of residents was a
further precondition of change. They went hand-in-hand and
were mutually dependent. But landlord management was a
prerequisite of other forms of control (Power, 1984, 1991).
For these reasons, the change in landlord approaches to
estates largely determined the outcomes of the programmes.
To the extent that landlords adopted a strong and concerted
approach to management on the estates by recognising social
as well as organisational and physical needs, the estates
became potentially rescuable.

Sustaining the new intensive approach was burdensome and
uncertain. It was reported in Denmark and Britain to be more
expensive, at least in the short run (Vestergaard, 1985; Capita
Ltd, 1993). There were signs at the end of the estate rescue
programmes that local management and resident influence
were being diluted in favour of more 'normal', that is less intensive services. As estate conditions were brought under
control, so landlords often reduced their inputs (SBI, 1993).
This suggests that the new management approach to estates
was insufficiently rooted in social housing organisations. On
the other hand, the experience of these estates affected social
landlords more generally, as social housing itself acquired
greater social needs (Provan, 1993). There was a wider push,
far beyond these limited experiments, towards a more
localised, more socially focused management (Delarue, 1991;

Dublin Corporation, 1993; Vestergaard, 1993). Whether the management shift would go far enough or be strong enough to cope with new social pressures was an open question at the end of the study.

STRONG AND WEAK MANAGEMENT

British and Irish landlords did not create as much impact on estates as the more autonomous Continental landlords. They were more vulnerable to budget cuts and political changes than the more stable, independent non-profit associations (see British case study). They had greater difficulty in devolving management control due to their complex administrative procedures and the requirements of political accountability. They were more weakly organised as a result of political ownership of the estates. They were less free to break out of the hierarchical straitjacket and less entrepreneurial or business-oriented, almost by definition, than the Continental managers. The British and Irish estates were jeopardised by weak landlord organisations (Power, 1993).

The study confirmed the view, elaborated in the OECD study of European housing finance (OECD, 1987), that arm's length social landlord structures were stronger, more service-oriented, more responsive, more efficiency-driven and more focused on the direct landlord role than state landlords. Governments that tried to deliver services themselves were weak managers, becoming encrusted with regulations, procedures and top-heavy central administration, even where there was a commitment to decentralisation. This proved particularly true of mass social housing as the study of *The Eclipse of Council Housing* showed (Cole and Furbey, 1994). Table 14.1 attempts to reflect the dichotomy between strong and weak management as opposed to strong and weak ownership patterns.

The shift in British government support in the 1980s towards semi-autonomous housing associations undermined council housing, reaffirming its residual role and limiting its scope for reform. The development of arm's-length social housing organisations, now strongly supported by all major British parties, represents a move towards more independent

Table 14.1   Contrasts between strong and weak management
and ownership patterns

	Management	Ownership
British and Irish pattern	– Weak management – Minimum autonomy	– Strong political ownership – Dependent
Continental pattern	– Strong management – Maximum autonomy	– Weak political ownership – Independent

Source: Author's visits and research.

forms of organisation and a less direct role for government
(Wilcox and Bramley, 1993). It reinforces one of the assumptions underlying this study – that independent ownership and
management structures provide a mechanism for introducing
greater flexibility, autonomy, business efficiency and investment into the complex management tasks of social landlords
(Windsor Workshop, 1991). However, the change away from
strong political ownership would not prove to be a solution
per se, based on the findings from the Continental examples in
this study. Bigger social and economic trends appear to have
at least as strong an influence as ownership on social housing,
even though the stronger management and weaker political
ownership structures of the Continent provided a better
framework for the success of rescue programmes. In the next
chapter we look at how marginal estates were affected by that
wider picture.

SUMMARY: MANAGING MASS HOUSING

Urban societies create severe pressure on individuals, leading
to marginalisation and intense poverty at the bottom. Mass
estates replicate these problems because they are caught up in
very wide changes in the economy and in the pattern of work;
in the racial and social composition of European cities; and in

the way organisations operate. These changes intensify divisions. But governments inevitably attempt to restore, rather than remove, problematic estates because they provide a cheap and available alternative to homelessness. Low-income estates are generally in demand, whatever their intrinsic problems, as long as they are properly managed and located in areas of housing need.

No level of spending converted large, complex, separate, concrete estates into popular and integrated areas, as long as they continued to house existing populations of very poor people. Most government programmes were extremely limited and incremental, rather than radical, due partly to cost, partly to the impracticability of displacing large, poor populations. Such large and distinct areas of acute social need required many different services. Continuing, incremental, localised effort, focussing on social needs as well as buildings, made the estates more stable, more viable and more manageable. The stronger management structures of independent landlords proved more successful than the weaker management structures of politically dependent landlords.

15 On the Edge of Democracy

We concluded the last chapter with the argument that strong management patterns had more chance of succeeding in the mass estates than weak ones. But the underlying economic pressures may be so great as to swamp that success. The very mass housing solution itself, based on economic growth and success, became a serious problem, based on economic decline and crisis. The social consequences of the many wider and more underlying pressures were nowhere more visible than in the peripheral estates of this study. Estates became marginal, partly through structural, ownership and occupation patterns. But as those problems grew, so they were extended by the economic pressures, pushing workless households and the marginally employed to the most marginal areas. The casualties of economic and social change became concentrated in the failing mass housing areas.

SOCIAL INEQUALITY

While people and areas fail through a combination of complex processes and pressures, few believe that the failure is intentional or the consequences deserved on the part of vulnerable groups or individuals. This study has clearly shown how residents of marginal areas have far less than equal chances, quite apart from any intrinsic or personal problems they may have. This puts some responsibility on the wider society to help make good the deficit suffered by marginal communities. There is the additional factor that the prospects for successful individuals and communities are adversely affected by the marginalisation of less successful individuals and areas. It was on this basis that important social legislation was passed in Britain in the late 1970s, such as the Race Relations Act (1976) and the Homeless Person's Act (1977). It was for these reasons that social exclusion and 'insertion' became such powerful concepts in France in the 1980s (Dubedout, 1983; Ministère de la Ville, 1993). In spite of integrationist and equalising pressures, however, democracy takes care of and listens to the majority and some people fare badly as society evolves. Some therefore will remain excluded, disempowered and alienated unless special steps are taken to include marginal areas. People who struggle to survive at the margin become underrepresented in the wider system. Their ability to participate becomes more and more limited as their societal role narrows. Even where they participate, people without work or with low-skilled work in a job-scarce, skill-driven market, have limited voice and little real power. If they belong to a minority ethnic group, their participation may be even more circumscribed, as they may have limited rights of citizenship and participation anyway and they may find themselves not only disadvantaged in the job and housing markets, concentrated in failing industry and failing areas, but also unable to contribute to the wider society (Pfeiffer *et al.*, 1994). This leads to a strong sense of rejection. The process of exclusion may have become an inevitable outcome of rapid change, but it threatens democratic advance and social peace (Ministère de la Ville, 1993).

The sense of rejection and consequent withdrawal from social involvement created a deep apathy among many residents on the estates in the study. As apathy swamped marginal groups, their ability to conform or to co-operate disintegrated. In the young, the frustration that this generated eventually led to hostility, destruction and occasionally violence. Our study shows that the trend towards 'ghetto conditions increased the likelihood of social explosions' (Levy, 1989). The threat of social breakdown and loss of control was real.

European urban societies were grappling with area decline, intergroup conflict and social breakdown in estates on the edge of their cities in a context of budgetary pressures, a whirlwind of economic change and unclear government directions. 'Social cohesion' was a unifying idea embraced everywhere, but nowhere were marginal communities or separated social housing areas integrated or acceptable to a broad mix of occupants. All the progress found and the impacts identified were circumscribed by these wider, deeper trends. Our survey of five extreme examples showed that social separation, based on area, on economic inactivity and on income, made reintegration elusive. Social segregation and exclusion were strongly linked to housing segregation.

RACIAL DISCRIMINATION

Where concentrations of racial minorities grew rapidly on the estates, community integration became even more difficult, because racial barriers fed stereotyped images, thereby raising the existing barriers still further. They also undermined more mixed rehousing patterns through pervasive racial prejudice among white applicants. In many parts of Europe where large ethnic minority communities gained access to unpopular social housing estates in the 1970s and 1980s, the disproportionate concentrations increased the stigma, separation and discrimination suffered by minority communities. The very fact of concentrated rehousing in unpopular areas confirmed the reality of exclusion. Attempts at reducing racial concentrations generally failed (see Part III).

European governments were articulating emotive fears about 'racial ghettos', but we found few strategies for preventing the concentration of ethnic minority households in the least favoured areas. This was a particularly damaging experience on large, separate estates because they were difficult to leave for those who were discriminated against. Estates then began to take on the true character of a ghetto. The very concept of 'social housing estates' may have made this continuing trend towards ghettoisation inevitable. The drift to polarisation was too strong to prevent intense concentrations of disadvantage, particularly racial disadvantage, as long as the urban housing stock was ordered in a highly stratified and area-based way. In this, we may be closer to the American experience than we want to admit (Le Roy, 1991).

LOCATION AND ECONOMIC OPPORTUNITY

In many ways the opportunities for estate residents were limited most of all by their location. Apart from one Irish and one British example, this study was about peripheral estates, precisely because location had such a strong negative influence on opportunity. In general, a much larger proportion of British and Irish estates were found within inner-city areas, offering more opportunities for renewal, for mixed housing solutions and mixed uses (Peckham Partnership, 1995). Demand was potentially higher, integration more possible, transport problems less intractable and job opportunities greater. Too often, however, extremely polarised lettings, coupled with weak management, undermined this potential. A new British government objective became to restore inner-city areas by breaking out of estate identities altogether, turning estates into streets that blended into the surrounding urban area, becoming part of much wider regeneration strategies. Location could greatly help this approach but so far only a few estates have been involved (DoE, 1994b; Hulme Regeneration Ltd., 1991).

Continental associations, with many more large outer estates than Britain, have openly tried to stabilise these communities by actively rehousing more varied social groups. Central to the success of the approach was the creation of the economic and social activities of a normal small town, a precondition for more mixed communities. The very large-scale, high density developments on the Continent encouraged more interchange, more activity and more facilities. This 'new town' approach offered some promise. Germany had possibly gone furthest in this direction, aided by the 'even playing field' approach to tenures. Denmark and France had also diversified their estates to some extent (SBI, 1993). This made varied ownership, incomes and integration more feasible. However, most city authorities and landlords paid too little attention to how to link estates to the surrounding or adjacent cities. Most estates had slow, inefficient and costly transport and poor employment links.

The concept of 'strategic renewal of estates', developed in the Netherlands to tackle large, difficult estates embraced a more explicit approach to integration. It involved some demolition and new-building of higher quality units through private investment; some sale of existing units to up-market owners to create higher quality renting for higher income households; and economic investment through varied uses of buildings and land that were previously for housing only (Wassenberg,

1993). Investment would be attracted by the more viable social mix. These ideas became a core goal of the British Single Regeneration Budget and were broadly endorsed by all the countries in our study. By attracting and retaining different incomes, different qualities of housing, different ownership and tenures, different activities, diversification and integration would become possible. However, they were costly and so far had only been tried in a few flagship experiments. Meanwhile, to avoid a repetition of past mistakes, all the Continental countries had changed their social house-building guidelines to create clusters of more integrated, more varied social housing and to avoid the large 'social ghettos' of the mass housing era (Loi d'orientation, 1992; BRBS, 1988, 1990; Créteil visit, 1995).

YOUTHFUL WORKFORCE

One potentially hopeful factor in the evolution of estate economies was the predicted future need for a younger labour force, as European populations aged. The estates tended to house disproportionate numbers of young adults. The more cut off they were, the less available they were for work. All governments and landlords were giving much higher priority to training and job links, not only to make estate communities more viable by overcoming dependence and welfare costs, but to create attractive investment opportunities to incoming employers and to provide essential workers for the services required by those in employment.

Work was an important way of validating young lives. Work conferred not only an economic but also a social role. In addition, the need for nannies, gardeners, car mechanics, drivers, waiters, security guards, cleaners, not to mention technical and information-based jobs, was hard to satisfy. Yet potential workers were often cut off from potential employers. The French economic opportunity programme (Renaudin, 1991) and the British Single Regeneration Budget illustrated the beginnings of a shift in approach towards economic opportunity, training, proactive job links, local enterprise and private investment. The German government was also deeply concerned about jobs under the impact of rising unemployment, particularly in the rapidly declining Eastern mass housing estates and was contemplating similar initiatives to France and Britain (Pfeiffer *et al.*, 1996). It was possible to see how far the estate programmes had moved from mass failure, through a 'local rescue' focus, towards concern for the integration of vital youthful populations.

SOCIAL EXCLUSION

In spite of economic and social initiatives to diversify activity in the estates and help young people, many of the inhabitants were facing even greater economic difficulty after 15 years of further economic transformations than when the estates' crisis first emerged in the late 1970s. The pressures to keep rehousing economically vulnerable and marginal households were ever stronger. Therefore it seemed unlikely that the polarisation, already advanced, would be easily reversed (Provan, 1993). The twin destabilising factors of high mobility among young, more economically active residents and intense needs among more marginal households stranded outside the work economy, would create negative pressure on marginal communities far into the future. Figure 15.1 illustrates the continuing negative pressures.

But while wider pressures on estates worked in a negative direction, intervention and action simultaneously worked in a positive direction. Though negative pressures had swamped conditions as they mounted, a counter-cycle of external and internal reinforcement could be put in motion and kept in place. Figure 15.2 illustrates the process of reinforcement that took place.

The countervailing economic and social pressures towards greater marginalisation and exclusion had not prevented rescue programmes from reshaping conditions. Rather the progress resulting from landlord and government interventions at least partially limited the effects of ever greater levels of economic vulnerability. Although this did not apply to all the estates over the period of the study, it applied to a majority as we showed in Part II. The socially reinforcing processes we have discussed limited the negative pressures but one of the most difficult issues was how to sustain the new approaches

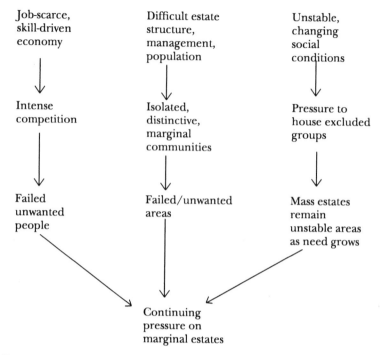

Source: Author's visits and research.

Figure 15.1   Continuing negative pressures on mass estates

and fund on a long-term basis the higher inputs the estates required.

THE COST OF MORE EQUAL CONDITIONS

Each phase of democratic evolution has required a sacrifice of those within the democratic system in order to integrate those that threaten it from without. Those in power make this costly choice in order to preserve the democratic institutions they lead and in order to prevent the collapse of social order (Kerner, 1968; Scarman, 1986). The costs are borne by the majority. Estate renewal was no different, for in European democracies, the majority have contributed to the cost of integration of the minority in order to avoid social fractures

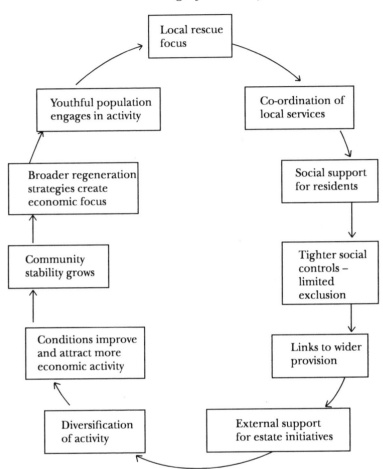

Source: Author's visits and research.

Figure 15.2   The process of social reinforcement creating the potential for renewal

opening into chasms, as the pace of change has quickened (Dahrendorf, 1992). The poor cannot pay enough to secure the standards of the majority. This gap creates tensions, particularly when the effects are visible in large, publicly supported areas, such as housing estates. Low standards create spiralling conditions and social decline. High standards are expensive and often 'unaffordable' for the poor themselves or for taxpayers, whose support is essential. This dilemma evokes the tension between private affluence and public squalor that dominated postwar transatlantic dialogue over the creation of public and social services (Galbraith, 1962). Who pays for what and for whom is at the heart of many European political debates.

The problem was epitomised in the dilemmas facing landlords over rent levels. Government subsidies were restricted. Estates were expensive to manage. Landlords needed enough income to fund intensive management and maintenance. But estates retained their low-income populations. Residents could only afford higher rents either if they were poor and received housing allowances – increasingly the case – or had higher incomes through employment – a declining pattern. Otherwise they could only afford low rents. The higher rents rose in large, difficult estates to cover higher costs, the greater the incentives to leave for those in work, the greater the poverty trap for those out of work and the more reliant people became on benefits. Yet only higher rents made reinvestment possible. The balance between affordability, adequate rent income and intensive management was precarious and inevitably involved either direct or indirect subsidy, if landlords were to maintain reasonable conditions.

The income and spending imbalance underlined the primacy of good management, as the quality of management transformed the use of resources and made limited rent income go further. The case studies illustrated the potential resources unleashed by careful management and the contribution it made to overall standards within a community. But this still did not resolve the basic problem of economic rents being too high for the poor.

The affordability dilemma underlined the centrality of economic integration, the need for access to jobs and incomes, the need for training for new work opportunities and the need for smoother transitions into or out of work. The pincer effect of no work and dependence, high rents and poverty trap, is biting deep into the viability of estates. But work and an adequate income, independence and affordable rents, remained elusive goals at the end of the study for too many of the residents of marginal estates. Levels of public support could not easily be cut, as we have shown, without serious social consequences. Therefore, developing a new economic base for marginal communities remained at the very top of European housing agendas, but the deeper economic processes at work in such areas were still too unclear to allow for easy solutions.

COLLECTIVE PROVISION

Collective local provision was one way of equalising conditions, while creating more localised economic activity. Every additional caretaker or cleaner, for example, was an addition to the local economy while providing a collective local service. Collective provision is part of the very nature of communities. But reasonable housing, a safe environment, play and social facilities, became far more important where household incomes were limited and where neighbourhood relations were strained by high turnover and the rehousing of marginal households. Lower incomes meant people could not provide individually for 'social goods'. Greater social problems meant that overarching local structures had to be created and supported with outside help, if areas were to work.

Unless some services were provided communally, there was little chance that people in poor areas could experience anything like normal conditions. Area decay was inevitable where people were surviving on minimum incomes and had barely enough for direct personal needs, such as heating, food and clothes, let alone repair, gardens, social facilities. Only through some form of collective provision could shared needs be met, if individuals had insufficient income to pay for those social and collective goods or services. The needs could be simple, like a playspace or sophisticated, like a school or health centre. A most vital form of collective provision on estates was the guarding and supervision of communal areas because this both ensured the individual rights of households in an intensely collective environment and limited the negative effects of concentrated social problems. These needs underline the inevitable reliance of individuals in cities on collective systems requiring active local government.

The logic for collective provision and collective investment in poor areas was strong. It raised standards for large numbers certainly more cheaply and easily than trying to achieve the same aim, purely through individual income support. All the experience to date suggests that while income support on its own helped to meet individual needs, such as clothes, food, it did not work so well for more collective needs, such as child-care, education, health, transport, because income support could never be set at high enough levels to ensure even approximate equality of access. The American government has found it impossible to maintain or restore city standards through individual income measures, such as proposed British nursery vouchers for these reasons (Wilson, 1987; Lemann, 1995).

All the integrating potential of a national education system or transport links would be lost if we withdrew collective provision. The significance of collective provision of services in overcoming racial divisions, urban polarisation and social breakdown is highlighted by American studies of precisely those social failures (Lemann, 1991; Jencks and Peterson, 1991). European communities have a sense of social responsibility in relation to already existing, publicly funded services, such as education, policing and health. These have a powerful integrating role, if protected, in the difficult situations we now face in our cities, as the French, British and German case studies showed particularly vividly. The logic of estate regeneration programmes was built around this notion of more integrated, more equalised collective conditions in all the countries of the study.

INDIVIDUALS OR AREAS?

Our evidence showed that by amassing scarce resources and targeting effort at provision for an area rather than for individuals, the impact was magnified. Governments, local authorities, landlords (where distinct), private bodies, publicly funded services, such as schools or police, all in different ways pooled scarce resources on estates. Schools in particular could have a radical impact on the prospects for young people, a fact highlighted by the French case study (Élie *et al.*, 1989). The pooling of small amounts per head created significant resources that then motivated people to contribute more of their own efforts to the common good. For example, spending on environmental improvements for an area had a big visual impact and encouraged individual effort, as long as the improvements were designed to involve residents and break through communication barriers, particularly with younger residents as happened in the Danish, German, British, Irish, and French estates (see Part III). The best and most lasting improvements often had the residents' stamp on them, implementing their ideas and engaging their efforts (SBI, 1993). These efforts were essentially collective while they relied on many individual contributions.

Therefore the idea that collective provision militates against individual responsibility was not borne out by the experience of estates in this study. As long as the provision was sufficiently localised and sensitive to local needs, it gave people the chance to become involved and take responsibility (Etzioni, 1993). This made the notion of local communities, informal networks and community responsibility attractive to politicians and managers alike across very different systems (Ministère de la Ville, 1993; BRBS, 1994; SBI, 1993; DoE, 1994a).

COMMUNITY AND DIRECT DEMOCRACY

An essential feature of localisation of organisational responsibility was the focus on building community links. Isolation was often a cause of great social difficulty. It was only when residents pooled their ideas and priorities that they gained sufficient control and status to make things work. Pooling energy and knowledge helped compensate for their shortage of cash when their energies were harnessed to make changes effective. The credit union on the Irish estate and other local enterprises such as the *Régies de Quartiers* in France, illustrate this (Behar, 1987). Pooling the interests of different racial groups within single estates was also a key to involvement, youth progress and integration. Where community links developed, it became possible to build a *modus vivendi* between contrasting generations and cultures (Élie *et al.*, 1989). The Youth Association meal service for the elderly was an illustration of this in the British case study.

The idea of atomised, individualised existence is new and it does not apply where people are not able to survive independently. It may not apply to most of us. The notion of self-help communities is a step away from overdependence on government but in the direction of community support rather than strong individualism (Etzioni, 1993). It is not surprising therefore, given the needs of the estate communities, that ideas of self-help and mutual support abounded. In spite of centuries of debate, there is no consensus on whether we are primarily self-centred individualists or social animals (Giddens, 1994). The truth almost certainly lies between the two. Citizenship, family, education are built around ideas of combining and sharing, just as freedom and democracy are built around individual responsibility, alongside individual rights. One outcome of the tensions between rights and responsibility, dependence and independence, individual and collective needs is the emergence of new forms of direct democracy (Stewart *et al.*, 1994). This encourages the type of small area focus and organisational autonomy that our research found to be successful in estate communities. It underlines the need for involvement at a level that individuals recognise.

An important key to the re-invigoration of democracy and participation is to target areas small enough for residents to identify with. People with limited experience, due to low incomes and lack of formal education, have difficulty relating to, and do not feel part of, wider systems. They also have few ways of feeding into, influencing or controlling those systems. Their only hope is to gain leverage over their own local conditions. The separate structure of estates made this local focus essential, as all the survey estates demonstrated. The mission became clearer and there was less waste, when once there was a strong local identity and a manageable scale of operation. Figure 15.3 shows how local and collective provision emerged from bottom-up pressures and top-down interventions.

SOCIAL CONTROL OR SOCIAL BREAKDOWN?

Each local area required and developed its own local organisational structure, yet such structures were extremely fragile in marginal areas. If residents identified with their local area

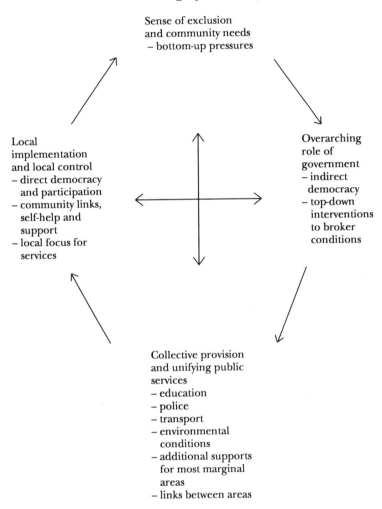

Sense of exclusion
and community needs
– bottom-up pressures

Local
implementation
and local control
– direct democracy
 and participation
– community links,
 self-help and
 support
– local focus for
 services

Overarching
role of
government
– indirect
 democracy
– top-down
 interventions
 to broker
 conditions

Collective provision
and unifying public
services
– education
– police
– transport
– environmental
 conditions
– additional supports
 for most marginal
 areas
– links between areas

Source: Author's visits and research.

Figure 15.3   Interplay of top-down and bottom-up reactions to
localised needs

rather than the wider community and programmes succeeded
primarily on a small area basis because of their responsiveness
to community needs, then the stability and reliability of local
controls became essential to survival. The pressures towards
disintegration of basic rules of conduct on large, unpopular

estates were so intense that strong communal controls were essential to survival and stabilisation. Higher turnover and weaker community links required stronger protection of property and enforcement of standards; concentrations of households with social problems required more intense support; higher crime required more policing; and so on. All of these problems were heightened by the scale and communal layout of mass estates. They implied more intensive inputs and more external help, as well as more local resident involvement, in getting the responses right. This was where direct democracy became particularly important but also problematic.

Resident leaders, as they emerged on estates, called for enforcement of common rules of behaviour and sanctions against law-breakers, for example, against vandalism, property damage, noise and other nuisance, violence. Local managers, caretakers and police supported these demands. But they required the support of the wider community, including the courts; otherwise, poor, marginal areas could echo the chaotic lawlessness of the earliest urban slums. The ungovernability of some American public housing projects had led to the widespread recruitment of armed guards to protect women and children from armed gangs and the mass eviction of drug-pushers to stop widespread intimidation (Lemann, 1991). In Europe, the beginning signs of such troubles were appearing. The limits of social tolerance need to be understood in the context of the basic human need for security in the face of incipient breakdown.

The development of tight social controls, over which, if properly implemented, most resident leaders had few reservations, was an inevitable reaction to a direct threat to survival. People in peaceful neighbourhoods could take control for granted. Without social controls, conditions on the estates we visited disintegrated. Governments could only respond to control problems effectively from small, well-established local bases. This takes our analysis full circle.

FRICTION AND RESISTANCE

More stable areas have in-built resistance, controls and barriers to instability and crime, deriving directly from people being anchored within the community. Community instability and weak controls in marginal estates sometimes led to the loss of normal boundaries of behaviour. The 'dumping' of difficult-to-house law-breakers among vulnerable and economically weak households reduced the stability of some areas to such an extent that resistance to abuse, violence and other crime was lowered. These areas then spiralled into disarray. Case studies from all five countries showed this process at work.

The contrast between more stable communities, with their stronger resistance to breakdown, and unstable communities, with their weak resistance to breakdown, can be illustrated by the physical resistance of still and moving objects. It is more difficult to overcome the inertia of a static object and to start it moving than to accelerate a moving object, which has already built up momentum and has overcome friction resistance. This 'friction' principle should alert us to the dangers of exposing rapidly changing and unanchored communities to further pressures. As they are already in rapid flux, they will simply spiral faster. Their resistance is so low that the outcome may be an accelerating slide out of control. Disorders on estates were often a result of this slide in control. Figure 15.4 illustrates the scientific principle of friction and resistance, as applied to the social principles of stability and breakdown, with which we are concerned.

Residential areas need a core of stable residents in order to develop and sustain local services, conditions, networks, community organisations, in the same way as all organisations do in order to maximise stability and prevent destabilisation. This informal social underpinning grows with time through people's common experience. A school, a hospital, an office, a factory or building site would not operate effectively without a stable core of people being committed to the core purpose of the organisation, with the right skills to carry it forward (Martens, 1996). So it is in communities. Mass estates were artificially created in unstable conditions and have frequently been unnecessarily denuded of stable residents through the overburdening and destabilising pressures they have suffered. That is why special measures were needed to remove those pressures, enhance stability and anchor people in the estates with the skills and commitment

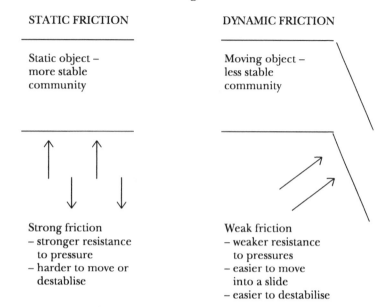

STATIC FRICTION   DYNAMIC FRICTION

Static object –   Moving object –
more stable   less stable
community   community

Strong friction   Weak friction
– stronger resistance   – weaker resistance
  to pressure   to pressures
– harder to move or   – easier to move
  destablise   into a slide
                                   – easier to destabilise

Source: Author's visits and research.

Figure 15.4   The 'friction principle' in relation to community
stability

to make them work. For this to happen, conditions on estates
had to be acceptable and that required intensive management, localised, high-quality services, special supports and
control over conditions.

It was because local communities sensed the instability, the
threat of breakdown, the weak resistance to pressure, that they
constantly returned to the need for control, for anchoring and
for stability. Therefore while localisation offered real hope of
additional resources, better services and more integration, it
could only work in the context of modern democracies being
willing to give higher priority to social order and urban integration. The localisation of initiatives and services had to
engender greater local control if it was to succeed. The local
communities we studied needed to be more anchored within
more stable cities, if they were to resist such negative pressures. The stronger reinforcement of community controls
required linkages with the wider community.

AREA FOCUS AND WIDE STRATEGIES

Can the need for a small-area focus and collective local provision be reconciled with the need for integration within the wider city? Cities only work small area by small area. They are made up of many parts, interacting and constantly moving. The size and shape of urban components are constantly changing (Jacobs, 1987). When cities are run with over-centralised systems, the strong get more, since they have better access to the larger system. That is why poor areas need to be targeted with ring-fenced and localised resources and why small area programmes are central to successful renewal. Crucially, those small, localised, intensively managed, collective programmes must happen across many areas if cities as a whole are to work and the problem is not simply to be moved around (Maclennan, 1992). William Wilson argues, almost ferociously, for forms of support that help richer, as well as poorer, neighbourhoods as a way of ensuring continuing local programmes for the poor (Wilson, 1996). Governments had ordered the lives of many of the poor from the top down through social housing programmes. But the broader aim of mixed and integrated developments should militate against the creation of discrete and separate estates. The mass estates epitomised the problems of special targeted provision on a large scale, whereas their rescue implied an attempted break-up of mass structures, a focus on many different elements and an integrating approach.

Many of the local solutions we found were *ad hoc* because of the overcomplexity of wider strategies, the high cost and long time-scale of all-embracing solutions. A fluid and reactive approach allowed new forms of problem-solving; it encouraged detailed and locally specific solutions. Residents expressed more faith in personal and local than in remote and all-embracing systems (DoE, 1989; BRBS, 1990). But the pieces of the patchwork of solutions needed to fit with all the adjacent pieces and had to be firmly joined to them on all sides, if the patchwork approach itself was to work. The argument for small local units of organisation is part of a bigger urban strategy, implying hundreds of such units, operating together. We are not describing a seamless web, but a complex, variegated, colourful pattern of many contrasting but linked parts.

It is the variety, colour and movement that makes city areas attractive.

LOCALISATION AND LINKAGE – A MODEL OF CHANGE

This dynamic pattern of urban development helps us to define a model of estate change. The model incorporates the three original propositions, laid out in the introduction:

- that estate rescue is possible if enough elements of support and change are put in place;
- that these elements must be locally applied;
- that local rescue implies a major role for residents.

But our findings also reinforce the idea of linkage that proved as critical as localisation to the survival of estates. Where localisation was the base line, linkage became the goal. This was because the wider structural problems relating to work and wealth could not be resolved within individual communities. The approach to estate renewal we uncovered relied on, and was vulnerable to, much bigger changes that no government was able or willing to solve.

Therefore linkage implied two further elements: the first derived from the need for external support; the second underlined the dependence of estates on factors even governments found hard to control. The five elements we ended up with offer a framework within which unpopular, marginal estates can be made to work as part of the wider city:

- estates require *many-sided solutions* because their problems are many-sided;
- *a local focus* is necessary to create a viable, operational base that is linked to the community, expanding the level of local activity and the quality of services;
- *resident involvement and community stabilisation* are essential parts of the improvement process;
- *collective provision and outside support* link estates to the wider community by closing some of the gaps resulting from poverty;

– *the role of government* in mediating economic and social change is vital to anchoring vulnerable communities.

All five elements depend on the wider city as well as on local change. The external and internal processes involved are mutually reinforcing and interdependent.

● By tackling physical, social and organisational problems together, the multiple problems of estates can be contained and the limited resources can create visible impact.

● By operating within a discrete community, residents identify positively with the improvements and co-operate in building stronger social networks. By making projects sufficiently localised, project leaders are able to exercise initiative, discretion and imagination in tackling problems.

● By involving residents, broadly the right priorities are selected and residents become more confident of solutions.

● By targeting resources at general conditions on estates – appearance of blocks, environment, communal entrances, security – and at local services which already operate, often inadequately, everybody gains. The residents of the area all enjoy better conditions and the areas become more acceptable to the wider community, less of a liability and less volatile.

● By bringing government resources down to the local level, areas are linked to the mainstream, as common standards begin to prevail. By managing resources carefully, conditions become controllable and impact is magnified. But only by diversifying activity and incomes, can large estates be integrated into wider urban networks. Only through broader changes in the local and wider economy can the problem of work be tackled.

The model of 'patchwork localisation' that emerged from the estate rescue programmes not only demonstrated that estate conditions could be improved; it also demonstrated the important link between estate improvements and city development. Essentially, the successful workings of cities are about the successful management of neighbourhoods and *vice versa*. The creation of many small linkages between city areas recalls the rich, varied, but well organised patterns of patchwork pieces. Integration has to tolerate variation and diversity if the joins are to hold. The links need strengthening if the polarising tendencies are to be overcome, but the links rely on local structures while needing central institutions to provide essential resources, back-up, direction and support (Le Roy, 1991).

It will remain the case that large peripheral mass estates offer less than ideal conditions and therefore that those who succeed in moving out usually gain in status rather than those who stay (Martens, 1996). Nonetheless, if the combination of localisation and linkage can hold estate conditions and help build estate communities, then in spite of the many remaining uncertainties, the decay and despair of true ghettos may be averted and the visible progress protected.

Maybe in France, where mass estates dominate the edges of cities more than in any other country and where over-rigid state systems have caused serious urban dislocations, the problem is better recognised, if no easier to solve. The late French President Mitterrand, while visiting Lyons after the riots of 1991, identified four government principles or priorities in tackling the acute problems of peripheral urban estates:

● the first ... is to concentrate state efforts on the 400 neighbourhoods in greatest difficulty ... where disorder reigns, where there is a lack of social cohesion. If we ignore the future of these areas, we may find tomorrow, more dramas of the kind that you have witnessed here [Vaulx en Velin] ....

● the second ... is to organise for diversity in the large estates. We wanted to industrialise the city. We developed architectural uniformity. But it seems to create tension, perhaps also often despair and rebellion. Why did we separate housing from shops, work, leisure, sport, culture? ... Then there is this terrible segregation, gathering people with problems into the same neighbourhoods ... children of foreign origin into the same schools. We must unite all our energies to break these mechanisms of exclusion. ..

● the third principle is to get inhabitants [of these areas] to participate, particularly young people. I remember when we visited Les Minguettes, and suburban estates around Paris Nord ...there was visible hostility ... Without the broadest participation, residents will not find identity,

dignity or citizenship ... young people must take posses-
sion of their neighbourhood.
● the fourth principle, very difficult to put into practice, is
that it is essential to find work for the people of these
areas. It will be necessary to provide training ...
Unemployment, particularly long-term unemployment, is
the most brutal form of exclusion. Everyone is affected,
adult and youths.These people are simply abandoned ...
they too often then get used to being out of circulation
and they lose their social identity. It is vital to connect
these areas with the economy. (President Mitterrand in
Ministère de la Ville, 1993)

If we fail to do these things, then area segregation will confirm
the status of dependence and lead to the chaotic outcomes
that have proved all too possible in all countries of this study.
Figure 15.5 summarises the French government analysis of the
problem and policy directions it advocates.

AVERTING CHAOS – A SOCIAL OR HOUSING
QUESTION?

Inequality and social breakdown create unease throughout
society. The fact that established and widely supported institutions of government have failed to solve or adequately contain
social problems leaves citizens feeling exposed and anxious.
Yet the idea of an 'underclass' and the threat of urban disorder are not new problems. Elizabethan cities were forced to
respond to urban destitution and what they saw as the onset of
social breakdown (Briggs, 1987). These problems were as
nothing compared with the horrors of new Victorian cities,
with their 'hordes' of people excluded or 'outcast' (Stedman-
Jones, 1976). Where social housing estates became housing of
last resort for desperate people and the first rung on the
housing ladder to prevent actual homelessness, then acute
pressures were bound to accumulate.
    People at the bottom in periods of fast change and growing
wealth can become totally marginalised or simply break down.
Our whole society is changing to a point of no return – the
composition of our families and our city populations, for

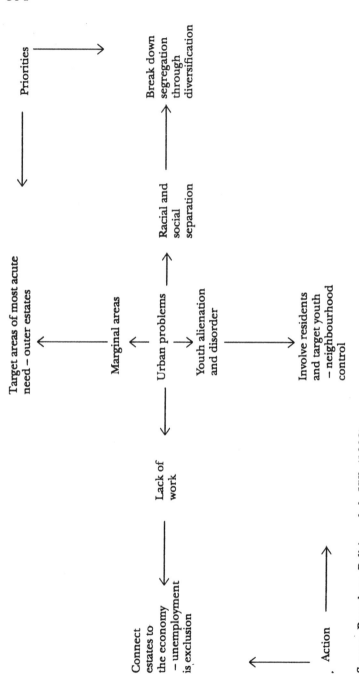

Source: Based on *Politique de la Ville* (1993).

Figure 15.5   French government principles for action on outer estates in response to disorders

example. There is a sense of chaos, because old welfare systems no longer match the problems we face, as Suzanne McGregor so well expressed it (McGregor, 1993). We only imperfectly understand the interaction of social, community and housing problems, but housing has a major effect on the social structure of cities. Housing is socially divisive because it is often built for separate social groups in unequal areas. According to Michael Harloe in his recent study of European social housing, apart from brief unifying phases after major wars, most European governments have regarded social housing as a residual form of provision for needy groups, thereby ensuring the division and decline we encountered (Harloe, 1995). There are many pressures to build large-scale, low-income estates. But the damage to community and the risk of social chaos call into question large-scale housing programmes that concentrate social problems in specific areas that then spill over into wider city areas. There are many more integrative models of housing provision involving small, adaptable approaches, tailored to many different needs and incorporating many different perspectives and directions (Clapham and Kintrea, 1992; Harloe and Martens, 1990). Table 15.1 summarises the changing role of social housing.

It was expedient to push the poor and the marginal into specially built but increasingly undesirable areas but the intensification of problems that this created, invoking images of ghetto-like conditions, underlines the link between *social* and *housing*. Housing solutions have not worked on their own. In particular, concentrating social problems in specific housing areas, however adequate the housing, magnifies those problems out of all proportion. It is a tendency replicated in many countries and unfortunately sometimes in new and well-built areas, as recent British evidence shows (Page, 1993).

Area-based social problems have fed the theory of the underclass, with its damaging negative interpretation of seemingly hopeless lives (Smith, 1992). The greatest flaw in this interpretation of poverty and dependence is that it assumes a point of no return for the people trapped in its grip. The rate of exit from the most marginal areas disproves this view (Jencks and Peterson, 1991). So does the potential for change within those areas across Europe, as this study has shown.

Table 15.1 Changing role of social housing

Continuing role of existing social housing	Changing role of social housing	New forms of social housing	Overarching role of government in social housing areas
– Core role of providing affordable homes to meet need	– Majority better housed	– Smaller scale developments	– Responsibility for law and order
– Large irreplaceable stock	– Ageing stock, distinct from more recent housing	– More mixed developments	– Democratic representation
– Most stock good quality	– Growing gap in conditions unless upgraded	– More community-based initiatives	– Protecting the public good
– Housing lasts 60+ years so stock will stay in use	– More out-of-work households	– More private orientation	– Protecting vulnerable groups
– Standards inside dwellings high	– More polarisation	– Experiments in new forms	– Providing for casualties and emergencies
– Low-income households need cheap housing	– More special needs	– More self-help	– Guaranteeing citizen rights/responsibilities
– Even difficult estates can work with care	– More difficult management task	– More flexible tenures	– Integrating diverse communities
	– Slow and more specialised additions to stock	– Social role more clearly recognised	– Preventing/overcoming injustice/discrimination
	– High demand from single, mobile, young, in work and student households	– Tenant control and tenant involvement	– Creating conditions for greater prosperity
	– Need to preserve stock	– Links to work and training now essential	– Allowing/encouraging community involvement
			– Reinvestment/regeneration/ rescue of estates

Source: Author's visits and research.

The complex social, racial and organisational problems of mass estates, not to mention their awesome physical aspect, require tight urban management. It involves welfare services, education, the police, health and local governments, as well as landlords. By changing the way low-income housing areas are managed, people gain more equal standards and therefore more equal opportunities. For such large, separate areas to become viable in the long run, we need to find a more secure balance in the long-standing urban tensions between social and economic priorities, buildings and people, quantity and quality, chaotic change and community stability.

There are fewer differences across Europe than we imagined. The themes of separated housing areas, social inequality and exclusion are uncannily common. We are part of a larger community. National governments have a diminished role in many senses. But they are more critical than ever in other senses. They can help produce visible, short-term change by reaching down into areas that may explode, thus contributing to the advance of democracy in the longer term. Across Europe governments have been playing this role, to avert the danger of a breakdown in civil order (*Le Monde*, 1995). Figure 15.6 shows the contrary pressures towards order alongside the pressures towards breakdown.

Social administration in the face of rising social pressure is vital to the survival of mass housing estates. Its centrality has been demonstrated, both by the impact of its absence and by its success to date where the management of housing, social and community conditions received high priority. Poverty, racial concentrations and social problems did not of themselves prove insuperable obstacles. But there had been a somewhat naive belief among housing and social policy-makers that housing provision on its own would solve social problems. The social dynamics of housing areas were given insufficient recognition. There was a high cost for this failure, a cost we cannot escape.

This underlines our conclusion: that social housing is as much about social as it is about housing issues. If this is true, the place of social as well as housing solutions in resolving area problems and conflicts must be recognised. To succeed, this requires participation and involvement by residents themselves. For without bottom-up approaches, we are likely to

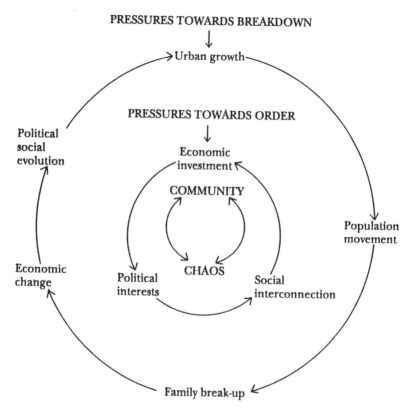

Source: Author's visits and research.

Figure 15.6 Contrapuntal social development

impose wrong solutions again. Social administration in this sense is not about the meddling grip of the state on poor people's lives; but about creating a sense of control at ground level through pushing out our costly social institutions right into the areas where they are needed, thereby averting chaos and creating community.

SUMMARY: ON THE EDGE OF DEMOCRACY

In the final part of the book, we reassess the inevitability of problems in mass housing estates on the edge of cities across Europe. The opening propositions of this study about localisation, resident involvement and many-sided solutions to local problems are revisited.

Democracy

In a democracy, the majority wins and minorities are under-represented. People who fail are pushed towards marginal areas where the barriers to participation become even greater. People then withdraw and area conditions deteriorate rapidly. The wider community, as marginalisation and lack of voice affect services, shares some responsibility for this on the unifying principle of an equal chance for all. Society has an interest in overcoming the segregation and potential conflict that can result. This leads to attempts at reintegration.

Social integration

To work, large, separate estates need mixed uses, mixed ownership and mixed incomes. This can only be achieved through a 'new town' approach, with varied local services, transport links and people in work. Most estate programmes did not achieve social and economic integration. There was a growing emphasis on jobs and training, because estates housed a youthful workforce that could contribute to society, if linked in to the city.

The cost of more equal conditions

Mass estates proved expensive to run properly, not just because of their inbuilt physical problems, but also because of their organisational complexity and social needs. This made a low-rent policy unworkable. High rents were only workable with generous housing allowances, because of the large low-income population; but tenants in work faced steep payments, as benefits were limited and targeted to the very poor. High rents and high costs in the end have to be partly funded by the wider community, if estates are to be made viable.

One major contribution to improved conditions lay in collective services. Poor people could not afford individual solutions to many problems. And estates could only work as communities if communal needs were taken care of. Individual responsibility and self-help were not enough on large, low-income estates.

Community, equality and direct democracy

It is important to operate at the most local level possible, so that residents can identify and participate; and so that localised services maximise community gains. More marginal areas have greater problems of social control and therefore, as residents get involved, they want tighter controls to make the areas viable. The wider society needs to support residents' pleas for stronger enforcement in marginal areas, on the basis that stable areas have higher resistance and unstable areas have lower resistance to chaotic pressures.

Cities as patchwork

Cities only succeed through many small, successful neighbour-hoods. Localised programmes need to be developed across many city areas, so that the whole benefits as well as the parts. The parts need to fit together through loosely co-ordinated, 'patchwork' strategies.

The successful model of local estate regeneration developed through our study requires:

- many-sided solutions
- a local focus
- resident involvement and community stabilisation
- collective provision and outside support
- government support and wider economic links.

Successful cities are built on successful neighbourhoods. Therefore localisation and linkage have to be combined. The late French President Mitterrand summed up the essential features of strategies towards estates:

- targeting effort on the worst areas
- diversifying activities and social groups
- a focus on participation, particularly of the young
- training and work.

Conclusion

Social housing involves social, as well as housing policy. The idea that housing provision of itself would solve deeper social problems has proved wrong. A combined social and organisational focus can improve conditions radically, preventing chaos and helping to build community.

Summary of *Estates on the Edge: The Social Consequences of Mass Housing in Northern Europe*

The survey of 20 unpopular European estates showed that government-sponsored mass social housing was bound to be used to meet the government target of housing the needy. The combination of location, physical structure, weak management and social targeting created catastrophic decline. But intervention worked if it brought landlords and tenants together on the ground, if different services were linked, if people as well as buildings were targeted and if the estates became more integrated with city life.

The estates declined as residents lost any commitment to stigmatised areas, creating a potentially violent, destructive situation, from which all sought to withdraw. As disintegration threatened, governments took action alongside landlords, tenants and other bodies. Local authorities played an important, enabling role but were less adaptable and business-like as direct landlords than the more independent Continental landlords.

There was uneasy progress in most estates. Continuing reinvestment was essential to overcome the constant pressures towards polarisation. The model of successful change requires a varied patchwork of solutions, a local focus, community involvement, collective provision outside support and strong links with the city. This model works in some of the most difficult areas of social housing. Its resilience, under often intense social pressure, makes the combination of localisation and linkage to the city a promising way out of 'ghetto' conditions.

Appendix: Basic Facts about the Twenty Estates

Country and main city	Location: distance from main city (km)	Size: number of units	Style of construction
France			
Paris	30	8 500	Dense, concrete, high-rise
Lyons	15	9 000	Dense, concrete, high-rise
Paris	10	5 000	Dense, concrete, high-rise
Romans	5	2 000	Dense, concrete, high-rise
Germany			
Cologne	10	6 100	Dense, concrete, high-rise
Cologne	15	1 245	Dense, concrete, high-rise
Düsseldorf	8	2 000	Dense, concrete, high-rise
Düsseldorf	10	6 700	Dense, concrete, high-rise
Britain			
London	7	1 100	Dense, concrete, high-rise
Glasgow	10	7 000	Some high-rise, rest rendered tenement blocks
Hull	8	5 950	Industrially built houses, some high-rise
Rhondda	3	950[a]	Industrially built houses, a few flats
Denmark			
Aarhus	4	1 767	Dense, concrete, high-rise
Copenhagen	6	1 740	Medium-rise, industrially built blocks
Aarhus	4	880	Dense, concrete, medium-rise
Copenhagen	10	1 000	Dense, concrete, medium-rise
Ireland			
Dublin	5	3 300	High and medium-rise, concrete, and some houses
Dublin	6	916	Brieze block houses and a few flats
Cork	3	834	Industrially built houses with some blocks of flats
Dublin	0[b]	390	Brick-built, dense balcony flats

Notes: [a]200 maisonettes have been demolished since 1991; now 750 units.
[b]Central location. Only non-industrially built estate in survey. Inclusion reflects Ireland's early postwar building in inner city.

Source: Visits to estates.

References

AKB (1988) *4 Drifts-omraader i Tastrupgaard* (Tastrupgaard, AKB).
AKB (Arbejdernes Kooperative Byggeforening) (1991) in Anderson *et al.* (1991).
AKB Chair (1991) Personal observation (Copenhagen).
Anderson, H., Nygaard, J. and Bisgaard, N. (1991) *AKB Taastrupgaard – An Improvement Project in Danish Non-profit Social Housing – Presentation Documentation of Taastrupgaard*, for the LSE European Social Housing Workshop, Cumberland Lodge, Windsor (London School of Economics).
Association of District Councils (1992), Seminar at London School of Economics on 'Compulsory Competitive Tendering', 21 March.
Audit Commission (1984), *Bringing Council Tenants' Arrears Under Control: A Review* (London: HMSO).
Avery, D. (1987) *Civilisation de Corneuve – images brisées d'une Cité* (Paris: L'Harmatten).
Ballymun Credit Union (1990) *Annual Report* (Dublin: Ballymun Credit Union).
Ballymun Job Centre (1989) *Report on Progress Since 1987 Opening* (Ballymun: Ballymun Job Centre).
—— (1991) *Ballymun Job Centre – The Staff and The Services You're Looking For* (Ballymun: Ballymun Task Force).
Ballymun Task Force (1987) *Ballymun's Future, Report No. 1*, December (Dublin: Ballymun Task Force).
—— (1988) *A Programme of Renewal for Ballymun – An integrated Housing Policy* (Dublin: Ballymun Task Force).
—— (1994) Visit to Phase 1 of Remedial Works Programme, Dublin Corporation, October.
BBC 1/RTE (1994) *The Family*, drama based on the book of the same title by Roddy Doyle.
Beattie, J. (1993) *Social Anthropology* (London: Routledge).
Behar, D. (July 1987) *Les Régies de quartier: suivi – évaluation* (Arcadie Paris: Plan Urbain and CNDSQ).
Blackwell, J. C. (1988) *A Review of Housing Policy – No. 87* (Dublin: National Economic and Social Council).
—— (ed.) (1989), 'Towards an Efficient and Equitable Housing Policy', *Administration* 36(4), special issue.
Boligministeriet (1987) *Den almennyttige boligsektors rolle paa boligmarkedet* (Copenhagen: Ministry of Housing).
—— (1993) in *Den rigsministeren, justitsministeren, kirkeministeren, socialministeren, og undervisningsministeren Furste Rapport fra Byudvalget* (Copenhagen: Indenrigsministeriet).
Bourgeat, Y. (1994) Response at Priority Estates Project National Conference, Manchester, 23 February.

BRBS (Bundesministerium für Raumordnung, Bauwesen und Städtebau) (1986) *Der Wohnungsbestand in Grossiedlungen in der Bundesrepublik Deutschland*, Heft Nr 01/076 (Bonn: BRBS).

—— (1988) *Städtebaulicher Bericht, Neubausiedlungen der 60er und 70er Jahre. Probleme und Lösungswege* (Bonn: BRBS).

—— (1990) *Städtebauliche Lösungen für die Nachbesserung von Grosssiedlungen der 50er bis 70er Jahre, Teil A: Städtbauliche und bauliche Probleme und Massnahmen, Teil B: Wohnungswirtschaftliche und sozial Probleme und Massnahmen* (Bonn: BRBS).

—— (1991) *Vitalisierung von Grosssiedlungen*, June (Bonn–Bad Godesberg: BRBS).

—— (1994) *Grossiedlungen Bericht* (Bonn: BRBS).

Briggs, A. (1987) *A Social History of Britain* (Harmondsworth: Penguin).

Burbidge, M., Wilson, S., Kirby, K. and Curtis A. (1981) *An Investigation of Difficult to Let Housing*, vol. 1: *General Findings*; vol. 2: *Case Studies of Post-War Estates*; vol. 3: *Case Studies of Pre-War Estates* (London: Department of The Environment).

Byudvalget (1993) *Forst rapport fra byudvalget* [First Report of the City Committee] (Copenhagen: Indenrigministeriet).

Campbell, B. (1993) *Goliath: Britain's Dangerous Places* (London: Methuen).

Capita Ltd (1993) *Priority Estates Project Cost-Effectiveness Study: Final Report* (London: HMSO).

Castro, R. (1994) *Civilisation Urbaine ou Barbarie* (Paris: Plon).

CECODHAS (1990) *Les Organismes au logement social et la lutte contre l'exclusion dans les Pays de la CEE: principaux extraits des documents édités à l'occasion de la rencontre des Ministries du Logement de la CEE – Lille 18–19.10.89* (Brussels).

City of Cologne (1989) Report on the problems of Kölnberg (Cologne: City of Cologne).

—— (1991) Presentation to LSE European Social Housing Workshop, Cumberland Lodge, Windsor, 10–12 April.

—— (1995) *Kölnberg* (City of Cologne).

City of Cologne Adult Education Institute (1994) 'Meschenich-Kölnberg', Bestandsaufnahme und konzeptionelle Überlösungen' (Cologne City Council).

Clapham, D. and Kintrea, K. (1992) *Housing Co-operatives in Britain – Achievements and Prospects* (Southport: Pearson).

CNDSQ (Commission Nationale pour le Développement Social des Quartiers) (1987) Paris Conference Report, March 1987 (Paris: CNDSQ).

CNVDSU (Conseil National des Villes et du Développement Social Urbain) (1988) *148 Quartiers: bilan des contrats de développement social des quartiers du IXe plan 1984/88* (Paris: Datar).

Cole, I. and Furbey, R. (1994) *The Eclipse of Council Housing* (London and New York: Routledge).

Coleman, A. (1985) *Utopia on Trial: Vision and Reality in Planned Housing* (London: Hilary Shipman).

Cologne Further Education Institute (1989) September–December Programme (Cologne City Council).

—— (1991) *Report* (Cologne City Council).

Conrad, C. (1992) 'Réhabiliter ou détruire les grandes ensembles?', *Le Monde*, 17 June.

Conrad-Eybesfeld, C. (1994) 'Politique du logement: une priorité pour l'état', *Urbanisme*, June.

Cooper, S. C. (1981) *Public Housing and Private Property* (London: Gower).

Copenhagen visit to urban renewal areas, 10–15 March (1989).

Craig Gardener (1993) *An Evaluation of the Ballymun Refurbishment Report and Appendices*, for Dublin Corporation, August (Dublin: Dublin Corporation).

Créteil (1995) Information from visit, 22 May.

Dahrendorf, Sir R. (1992) Ch. 5 in Smith, D. J. (ed.) *Understanding the Underclass* (London: Policy Studies Institute), p. 57.

Danish Towns Programme (1994) (Gopenhagen: Indenrigsministeriet).

Danish Urban Renewal Unit (1989) Notes from meeting, 15 March.

Daunton, M. (ed.) (1984) *Councillors and Tenants – Local Authority Housing 1919–1939* (Leicester: Leicester University Press).

Delarue, J-M. (1991) *Banlieues en difficultés – la Rélégation*, Report to the Minister of Cities and Planning (Paris: Siros/Alternatives).

—— (1993) Paper delivered to the LSE European Social Housing Workshop Cumberland Lodge, Windsor 10–12 April.

Department of the Environment (1989) *Nature and Effectiveness of Local Housing Management*, Report to the DoE by the Centre for Housing Research, University of Glasgow (London: HMSO).

—— (1994a) 'Arm's Length Housing Companies Experimental Programme', press release (London: DoE).

—— (1994b) *Bidding Guidance – a Guide to Funding under the Single Regeneration Budget* (London: DoE).

—— (1995), *Our Future Homes* White Paper (London: HMSO).

Department of the Environment (Ireland) (Department of the Environment, Ireland) (1991), *A Plan for Social Housing* (Dublin: DOE).

D'Inguimbert, B. (1989) Notes on visit to Val de Marne, 2 September.

Dixon, J. (1995), Report on visit to Cologne, 25 March.

Donnison, D. (1980) Paper delivered to seminar on poverty, Department of the Environment, London, 24 January.

Donnison, D. and Ungerson, C. (1982) *Housing Policy*. (Harmondsworth: Penguin).

Dubedout, H. (1983), *Ensemble refaire la ville – rapport au Premier Ministre du Président de la Commission nationale pour le développement social des quartiers* (Paris: La Documentation Française).

Dublin Corporation (1991) Presentation at LSE European Social Workshop, Cumberland Lodge, Windsor, 10–12 April.

—— (1993) *Lord Mayor's Commission on Housing* (Dublin: Dublin Corporation).

—— (1994) Response to Craig Gardener Evaluation Report.

—— (1995) Written comments on Ballymun, Dublin, 20 May.

Dublin Corporation Housing Department (1991) *Remedial Works Scheme* (Dublin Corporation).

—— (1993) *Policy Statement on Housing Management and Maintenance*, adopted by Dublin City Council on 9 August 1993.

Dunleavy, P. (1981) *The Politics of Mass Housing in Britain, 1945–1975* (Oxford: Clarendon).

—— (1990) LSE Housing Lecture, January (LSE).

EC (1991) 'Towards a Europe of Solidarity: Urban Social Development, Partnerships and the Struggle against Social Exclusion', European Commission of Social Affairs Conference, at Lille, May.

Élie, C., Soubeyran, P. and Blery, J-P. (1989) *Roman d'un ZUP* (Villeurbanne: Préfecture Région Rhône-Alpes, Commission Régionale des Quartiers, Association régionale des organismes d'HLM de Rhône-Alpes).

Emms, P. F. (1990) *Social Housing – a European Dilemma* (Bristol: SAUS).

Etzioni, A. (1993), *The Spirit of Community* (New York: Touchstone).

EU (1993) *Statistics on Housing in the European Community* (Brussels: Directorate-General V Employment, Industrial Relations and Social Affairs, EU).

Ferris, J. (1972) *Participation in Urban Planning – the Barnsbury case*, Occasional Papers on Social Administration no. 46 (London: Bell).

Flynn, P. (1987) Press release issued by the Department of the Environment, Dublin.

Foth, S. (1986) *Stadtteilanalyse Ratingen West: Ansatze zur Reparatur einer Grosssiedlung*, Winter (Ratingen: Fachbereich Stadt- und Landschaftsplanung, Gesamthochschule Kassel).

Galbraith, J. K. (1962) *The Affluent Society* (London: Pelican).

— (1992) *The Culture of Contentment.* (London: Sinclair Stevenson).

Gardiner, K., Hills, J., Folkingham, J., Hechene, V. and Sutherland, H. (1995), 'The Effects of Differences in Housing and Health Care Systems on International Comparisons of Income Distribution' (London: London School of Economics , Welfare State Programme Discussion Paper 110, July).

Ghekière, L. (1988) *Housing Policies and Subsidies in France* (English trans.) (Paris: UNFOHLM).

Gibbins, O. (1988) *Grosssiedlungen, Bestandspflege und Weiterentwicklung* (München: Callwey).

Giddens, A. (1994) *Beyond Left and Right: The Future of Radical Politics* (Cambridge: Polity).

Gifford, Lord (Chairman) (1986) *The Broadwater Farm Inquiry Report: Report of the Independent Inquiry into disturbances of October 1985 at the Broadwater Farm Estate, Tottenham, chaired by Lord Gifford QC* (London Borough of Haringey).

Glasgow City Council (1985) *Inquiry into Glasgow's Housing* (Glasgow City Council).

Glennerster, H. *et al.* (1983), *Planning for Priority Groups* (Oxford: Martin Robertson).

—— (1988) 'A Requiem for the Social Administration Association', *Journal of Social Policy*, Vol. 17, 1, pp. 83–4.

Glennerster, H. and Turner, T. (1993) *Estate Based Housing Management: An Evaluation* (for the DOE) (London: HMSO).

Guenod, J-M. (1994, 1995) Information on social housing demand.

GWW (Gesamtverband der Wohnungswirtschaft) (German National Federation of Housing Associations) (1991) information received.

Handy, C. (1993) *The Empty Raincoat: Making Sense of the Future* (London: Hutchinson).

Harloe, M. (1995) *The People's Home? Social Rented Housing in Europe and America* (Oxford, UK, and Cambridge, MA: Blackwell).

Harloe, M. and Martens, A. (1990) *New Ideas for Housing. The Experience of Three countries* (London: Shelter).

Hill, O. (1883) *Homes of the London Poor* (London: Macmillan).

Hillebrand, H. (1988) *Wissenwertes über die Wohnanlage 'Kölnberg' in Köln-Meschenich*, 24 February.

Hillier, B., Kuhne-Buning, L., Rahs, R., Tsoskounoglou, H. and Marshall, C. (1987) *Problem Housing of the 60s and 70s in Britain and Germany* (Bochum: GFW; London: UAS).

Hills, J. (1993) *The Future of Welfare: A Guide to the debate* (York: Joseph Rowntree Foundation).

HLM Inser-Eco Mission du Développement Social (1993), Des Actions HLM pour le Développement de l'emploi et de l'activité économique: l'état d'avancement du programme 'Développement de l'insertion par l'économique dans les organismes HLM' au 6 janvier 1993 (Paris: UNFOHLM).

Hofmann, R. von (1989) 'Der Aufsteig ist am Kolnberg schwierig', *Küner Stadt-Anzeiger*, 15 August.

Holland, Sir Milner (Chairman) (1965) *Report of the Committee on Housing in Greater London*, Cmnd. 2605 (London: HMSO).

Holmans, A. (1995) unpublished commentary on racial issues in social housing, London, June.

Hope, T. and Foster, J. (1992) 'Conflicting Forces – Changing the Dynamics of Crime and Community on a '"Problem" Estate', *British Journal of Criminology* 32(4), Autumn.

—— (1993) *Housing, Community and Crime: The Impact of the Priority Estates Project*, Home Office Research Study No. 31 (London: HMSO).

Hulme Regeneration Ltd (1991) *Hulme City Challenge Action Plans Years 1–4* (Manchester: Human Regeneration Ltd).

Irish National Census (1991) *Population Statistics, Dublin.*

IWU (Institut Wohnung und Umweld) (1992) German articles supplied (Darmstadt: IWU).

Jacobs, J. (1987) *Cities and the Wealth of Nations: Principles of Economic Life* (New York: Random House).

Jacquier, C. (1991) *Voyage dans dix quartiers Européens en Crise* (Paris: L'Harmatten).

Jencks, C. and Peterson, P. E. (1991) *The Urban Underclass* (Washington: Brookings).

KAB (Kooperative Arbejdernes Byggeforening) Bygge-og Boligadministration (1994a) *Social Rehabilitation in Danish Social Housing Areas – Recent Developments and New Government Initiatives* (Copenhagen: KAB).

—— (1994b) *Et bedre hverdagsliv – vejledning om realisering af byudvalgets forslag til omprioritering og boligsociale initiativer*, Information leaflet, April (Copenhagen: KAB).

Kelleher, P. with the assistance of Deehan, A., McCarthy, P., Farrelly, J. and Maher, K. (researchers) (1988) *Settling in the City – The Development of an*

Integrated Strategy for Housing and Settling Homeless People in Dublin (Dublin: A Focus Point Report).

Kerner, O. (1968) *Report of the National Advisory Committee on Civil Disorders* (New York: Bantam).

Kirchner, J. and Sautter, H. (1990) *The Integration of Ethnic German Immigrants from Eastern Europe and Migrants from the GDR in the Labour and Housing Markets in the Old Federal Republic of Germany* (Darmstadt: Institut Wohnen und Umwelt).

Kleinman, M. and Piachaud, D. (1993) 'European Social Policy: Models and Rationales', *Journal of European Social Policy*, 3(1).

Konttinen, S-L. (1983) *Byker* (London: Cape).

Kreibich, V. (1995) *Commentary on Kölnberg Case Study* (University of Dortmund).

Lambert, J., Paris, C. and Blackaby, B. (1978) *Housing Policy and the State* (London: Macmillan).

Lemann, N. (1991) *The Promised Land* (New York: Knopf).

—— (1995) *The Future of Cities*, paper for 'The Myth of Community Development' seminar, St Catherine's Lodge, Windsor.

Le Monde (1995) P. Bernard, 'Un Rapport prône le retour en force de l'État dans les banlieues', 7 October; N. Herzberg, 'Le Conseil national des villes critique le plan d'intégration urbaine du gouvernement, 20 October; J. Igor, 'La mort d'un jeune au commissariat provoque des affrontements à Laval, 3 November; 'Des Lycées tentent d'enrayer la ghettoisation de quartiers sinistres', 14 November; M. Delb, 'En Préparation à HEC, au pied de la cité des Minguettes'; B. Charlot, 'La Classe de seconde est l'étape la plus sensible'.

Le Roy, M. C. (1991) 'Quartiers fragiles en Europe', in C. Jacquier, *Voyage dans dix quartiers européens en crise* (Paris: l'Harmatten).

Levy, F. (1989) *Bilan/Perspectives des contrasts de plant de dévelopement social des quartiers*, La Documentation française (Paris: DSQ).

Loi d'orientation à la ville (1992) France.

London Borough of Hackney (1994) *Comprehensive Estates Initiative* (LB Hackney).

London Borough of Haringey (1994) Meeting at Broadwater Farm with housing manager (LB Haringey).

LSE Housing (1994) Seminar on housing associations, January.

McGregor, S. (1993) *Polarisation, Social Development and Mega-cities*, paper for the Social Policy Association Conference, 'Social Policy and The City', University of Liverpool, July.

Maclennan, D. (1992) *Strategic, Multi-sector Approaches to Urban Regeneration: City Policy for the Future*, paper for joint OECD/Scottish Office seminar on 'Integrated housing Strategies: Creating Opportunities for People and Their Community', 2 October.

Martens, A. (1996) Communication on the question of *Chaos or Community*.

Mid-Tottenham Police (1985) Information given by Chief Superintendent Stainsby to the Broadwater Farm Panel, 24 March.

Ministère de la Ville (1993) *Politique de la ville* (Paris: Ministère de la Ville).

Mitterrand F. (1993) Introduction, in Ministère de la Ville.

Munchau, W. (1992), 'Counting The Cost of Being Down and Out in Paris and London', *The Daily Telegraph*, 8 July, p. 21.

Murie, A. (1995) Written commentary on estates on the edge (unpublished).

Murray, C. (1989) *Losing Ground: American Social Policy 1980–90* (New York: Basic).

Nielson, G. (1985) Information received from the National Housing Federation, Copenhagen.

—— (1995) Information received from the National Housing Federation, Copenhagen.

Nygaard, J. (1991a) Paper delivered to the LSE European Social Housing Workshop, Cumberland Lodge, Windsor, 10–12 April.

—— (1991b) *Taastrupgaard – A Social and Environmental Project Managed by the Community*, case study (Copenhagen: AKB).

—— (1995) Commentary on Danish estates (unpublished).

O'Cuinn, S. (1991) Information received from Sean O'Cuinn on Remedial Works Schemes (Dublin: DoE).

OECD (1987) *Urban Housing Finance* (Paris: OECD).

Osborne, D. and Gaebler, T. (1992) *Reinventing Government* (New York: Addison-Wesley).

Oxley, M. (1991) 'The Aims and Methods of Comparative Housing Research', *Scandinavian Housing and Planning Research* pp. 67–77.

Page, D. (1993) *Building Communities: A Study of New Housing Association Estates* (York: Joseph Rowntree Foundation).

—— (1994) *Developing Communities* (London: Sutton Hastoe Housing Trust).

Parker, T. (1983) *The People of Providence* (London: Hutchinson).

Parker, J. and Dugmore, K. (1976) *Colour and the Allocation of GLC Housing. The Report of the GLC Lettings Survey 1974–75*, Research Report 21 (Greater London Council).

Peckham Partnership (1995) *Peckham Partnership: A bid for Single Regeneration Budget Funding*, September (London: Southwark Council).

Peillon, P. (1991) paper delivered to the LSE European Social Housing Workshop, Cumberland Lodge, Windsor, 10–12 April.

—— (1995) Commentary on French case study, 25 February, CREPAH, Lyons.

PEP (Priority Estates Project) (1993) *Feasibility Report to the DoE on Broadwater Farm Tenant Management Proposals*, February (London: PEP).

Peters, T. (1987) *Thriving on Chaos – A Handbook for Management Revolution* (London: Macmillan).

Pétonnet, C. (1973) *Those People: The Subculture of a Housing Project*, trans. R. Smidt (Connecticut, Greenwood).

Pfeiffer, U. (1992) 'Observations on the German outer estates programme' (unpublished).

Pfeiffer, U., von Einem, E., Schafer, E. and Hamm, S. (1996) *Zur Neuorientierung der Städtebauforderung*, paper for seminar, January 25 (Bonn: Empirica).

Pfeiffer, U., Fritz, C. and Ammann, M. (1994) *Housing Provision of Immigrants and Refugees as a Tool of Social Integration. Survey Responses of the EU Member States*, paper presented to annual meeting of the European Housing Ministers, Greece/Germany, May (Bonn: Empirica).

Pinto, R. (1993) *The Estate Action Initiative: Council Housing Renewal, Management and Effectiveness* (Aldershot: Avebury).

Pitt, M. (1982) Notes of a visit to Mid-Tottenham Area Project, Haringey, and Broadwater Farm Estate, in particular 30 June.

Pitts, J. (1995) 'Wrong Rite of Passage', *The Guardian*, 11 December, p. 11.

Plannegruppe GmbH (1986) *Freiraum – Entwicklungsplan Ratingen West: Konzeption zur verbesserung des Wohnumfeldes und der Stadtokologischen Bedingungen in Rattingen West* (Oberhausen: Plannegruppe GmbH).

Power, A. (1979) Notes on visit to Broadwater Farm, Haringey.

—— (1984) *Local Housing Management: a Priority Estates Project survey* (London: DoE).

—— (1987a) *Property before People – The Management of Twentieth Century Council Housing* (London: Allen & Unwin).

—— (1987b) *The PEP Guide – Local Housing Management*, vols 1, 2 and 3, April (London: PEP).

—— (1991) *Running to Stand Still – Progress in Local Management on Twenty Unpopular Housing Estates* (London: Priority Estates Project).

—— (1992) *Empowering Residents*, paper for OECD Seminar, Edinburgh, 7/8 October.

—— (1993) *Hovels to High Rise – State housing in Europe Since 1850* (London and New York: Routledge).

—— (1994) *Area-based Poverty, Social Problems and Resident Empowerment*, Discussion Paper WSP/107, December (London: LSE).

Power, A. and Tunstall, R. (1995) *Swimming against the Tide: Progress and Polarisation on Twenty Unpopular Council Estates 1980–95* (York: Joseph Rowntree Foundation).

Provan, B. (1993) 'A comparative study of French and UK government programmes to tackle the physical management and social problems of postwar housing estates', PhD study of estate renewal programmes in Britain and France (University of London).

Quilliot, R. and Guerrand, R. H. (1989) *Cents Ans d'Habitat: une utopie réaliste* (Paris: Albin Michel).

Rajon, H. (1991) Personal communication from Lyons in preparation for LSE European Social Housing Workshop, Cumberland Lodge, Windsor.

Reich, R. (1993) *The Work of Nations: Preparing Ourselves for 21st Century Capitalism* (New York: Vintage).

Renaudin, G. (1991) Information received on economic initiatives.

Rodenkirchen Adult Education Institute (1987) Report of public hearing, 23 November, Kölnberg, Cologne.

Rogers, Sir R. (1991) London School of Economics Public Housing Lecture, May.

—— (1995) *Reith Lectures*, BBC Radio 4.

Rogers, R. and Fisher, M. (1992) *A New London* (Harmondsworth: Penguin).

Salicath, N. (1987) *Danish Social Housing Corporations*, vols. I and II (Copenhagen: Co-operative Building Industries with the support of the Danish Boligministieret).

SBI (Statens Byggeforskninginstitut) (1986) *Boligomraader i Krise* (Hoersholm: State Building Research Institute).

—— (1991) *Report 88* (Hoersholm: State Building Research Institute, Danish Ministry of Housing).

—— (1993) *Bedre Bebyggelser – bedre liv?* (*Better housing Estates – Quality of Life?*) – results from an evaluation project by the Danish Building Research Institute, Town Planning Report 65 (Hoersholm: State Building Research Institute, Danish Ministry of Housing).

Scarman, Lord (1986) *The Scarman Report: The Brixton Disorders of 10–12 April 1981* (Harmondsworth: Pelican).

Schmidt, S. (1995) *Commentary on Kölnberg Case Study* (City of Cologne).

Service Habitat, Rhône (1988) *Les Programmes locaux de développement social des quartiers dans l'agglomération Lyonnaise* (Rhône: Service Habitat).

Smith, D. (ed.) (1992) *Understanding the Underclass* (London: Policy Studies Institute), p. 81.

Stedman-Jones, G. (1976) *Outcast London: A Study into the Relations Between the Classes in Victorian Society* (Harmondsworth: Penguin).

Stewart, J. Kendall, E. and Coote, A. (1994) *Citizen juries* (London: Institute for Public Policy Research).

SUSS Centre (1987) *A Block of Facts – Ballymun Twenty-one Years On* (Dublin: The SUSS Centre).

Tapie, B. (1993) in Ministère de la ville.

Taylor, M. (1995) *Unleasing the Potential – Bringing Residents to the Centre of Regeneration* (York: Joseph Rowntree Foundation).

The Economist Pocket Europe (1994) (London: Hamish Hamilton in association with *The Economist*).

The European Foundation for the Improvement of Living and Working Conditions *(1989) Conditions de vie dans les villes d'Europe* (Luxembourg: Offices des Publications Officielles de Communautés Européennes).

The Guardian (1992) D. Gow, 'Tension Soars in Germany After Fire Deaths', p. 20.

—— (1993) 20 April.

—— (1994) News report, 7 August.

Thomasen, S. (1989) visit notes to Copenhagen, 10 March.

Times Atlas (1988) (London: *The Times*).

Timmins, N. (1995) 'Improvements of 1980s at Risk in 1990s', *The Independent*, 26 July, p. 4.

Toubon, J. C. and Renaudin, G. (1987) (Les politiques de réqualification du logement social Ch France), in Provan (1993).

UN (United Nations) (1994) *Monthly Bulletins of Statistics.* (New York: UN).

UNFOHLM (1989) Meeting of Directors, Paris.

—— (1993) Economic initiative proposal and reports (unpublished).

Vénissieux (1989) – Visit notes, 15 August.

Vestergaard, H. (1985) *Revitalization of Danish Post-War Public Housing in Crisis – Background, Programme, Scope and Evaluation of Effects*, lecture given at the International Research Conference on Housing Policy and Urban Innovation, Amsterdam, 27 June–1 July 1988 (Hoersholm: SBI).

—— (1992) 'The Changing Fate of Social Housing in a Small Welfare State – The Danish Case', chapter 3 in L. J. Lundqvist (ed.) *Policy, Organization, Tenure – A Comparative History of Small Welfare States*, for the Scandinavian Housing and Planning Research, supplement No. 2 (Oslo/Stockholm: Scandinavian University Press), pp. 37–45.

—— (1993) *Improvement of Problematic Housing Estates in Denmark – an Evaluation of Results/Abstract* (Hoersholm: Danish Building Research Institute).

Villadsen, S. (1989) Information from Roskilde University, March.

Wann, M. (1995) *Building Social Capital – Self Help in a Twenty-first Century Welfare State* (London: Institute for Public Policy Research).

Ward, B. (1974) *Human Settlements: Crisis and Opportunity* (Ottowa: Information Coudin).

Wassenberg, F. (1993) *Trends in Post-war Housing in the Netherlands* (Delft University).

Whelan, P. (1991) Information from Dublin Corporation records.

Wilcox, S. and Bramley, G. (1993) *Local Housing Companies: New Opportunites for Council Housing* (York: Joseph Rowntree Foundation).

Willmott, P. and Murie, A. (1988) *Polarisation and Social Housing: The British and French Experience*, Report 676: 51 (London: Policy Studies Institute).

Wilson, W. J. (1987) *The Truly Disadvantaged* (University of Chicago Press).

—— (1996) *Are ghettos emerging in Europe?*, LSE Housing Workshop, 23–27 June.

Windsor Workshop (1991) LSE European Social Housing Workshop, Cumberland Lodge, 10–12 April.

Wullkopf, V. U. (1992) 'Wohnungsprobleme in den neuen Bundesländern', *WSI Mitteilungen* no. 2, pp. 112–19.

Young, J. (1986) *Survey of Broadwater Farm prepared for Haringey Independent Panel of Inquiry – Summary of Findings* (London: Middlesex Polytechnic Centre for Criminology).

Young, M. and Willmott, P. (1962) *Family and Kinship in East London* (Harmondsworth: Penguin).

Zipfel, T. (1985) *Broadwater Farm Estate, Haringey: Background and Information Relating to the Riot on Sunday, 6th October 1985* (London: PEP).

—— (1986) 'Diagnosis of a Riot', *The Tablet*, 2 August.

Bibliography

AKB (1988) *AKB 1913–1988* (Kobenhavn: AKB).

— (1991) Information received from AKB, Taastrupgaard.

Amnesty International (1988) 'Amnesty International Questions Fairness of British Trials Resulting from Broadwater Farm Riot of 1985', press release, 19 February.

Arnold, E. and Mandle, E. (1990) 'Zukunftsmodell Seniorengenossenschaft', *Die Wohnungswirtschaft*, December.

Ashworth, G. V. and Voogd, H. (1990) *Selling the City: Marketing Approaches in Public Sector Urban Planning* (London: Belhouse).

Atkinson, A. B. (1994) 'Capabilities, exclusion, and the supply of goods' in K. Basu, P. Pattanaik and K. Suzumura (eds) *Values, Welfare and Development: essays in honour of Amartya Sen* (Oxford University Press).

Atkinson, D. (1993) *Radical Urban Alternatives* (London: Cassell).

Audit Commission (1987) *The Management of London's Authorities: Preventing the Breakdown of Services* (London: HMSO).

Ball, M., Harloe, M. and Martens, M. (1988) *Housing and Social Change in Europe and the USA* (London and New York: Routledge).

Ballymun Safety Committee (1990) *Ballymun – Make it Safe*, Newsletter, Spring.

Ballymun Task Force (1988) *Renewal of Ballymun*, report no. 2, December (Dublin: Ballymun Task Force).

—— (1992) *Evaluation Report* (Dublin: Ballymun Task Force).

Beaumont, P. (1993) 'No Money, No Jobs, No Future, No Point', *The Observer*, 3 October, pp. 12–13.

Bell, T. and PEP Consultants (1991) *Joining Forces: Estate Management Boards – A Practical Guide for Councils and Residents* (London: Priority Estates Project).

Berges, Y. G. (1985) *Le Point*, no. 654, 1 April.

Bremen Situationsbeschreibung (1987) *Revitalisierung strucktuschwacher städtischer Quartiere* (Bremen: Situationsbeschreibung).

Broadwater Farm Residents Association (1986) *Farm News*, 25 August, 19 October (London: Broadwater Farm Residents Association).

Broadwater Farm Youth Association Co-operative (1988) *Cultivating the Farm – Environmental work carried out by the Community to improve conditions of living on the Broadwater Farm Estate* (London: BWFYA Coop).

—— (1990) *Questionnaire Survey of Manston, Lympne and Kenley Blocks, Broadwater Farm Estate, July 1990* (London: BWFYA Co-op).

Burbidge, M. (1991) Notes of visit to Lundtoftegarde, Denmark, 20 December 1990.

—— (1991) Notes on tenants' influence in Swedish municipal housing.

—— (1992) *More than Bricks and Mortar – Resident Management of American Public Housing* (London: DOE).

—— Information on tenants' democracy in Denmark.

Caisse Nationale des Allocations Familiales (1981) *L'Action sociale des caisses d'allocations familiales* (Paris: CNAF).

CDP (Community Development Project) (1976) *Whatever Happened to Council Housing?* (London: Community Development Project Information and Intelligence Unit).

Christiansen, U., Kristensen, H., Prag, S. and Vestergaard, H. (1991) *Did the Buildings Become Better? Provisional Experience from the Improvement of Five Newer Storeyed Living Accommodation*, SBI Bulletin 88 (Hoersholm: State Building Research Institute).

Christiansen, U., Jensen, M. K., Kristensen, H., Lindhartsen, H., Varming, M. and Vestergaard, H. (1993) *Bedre bebyggelser – bedre liv?*, SBI Report 65 (Hoersholm: State Building Research Institute).

City of Cologne (1991) Paper delivered to the LSE European Social Housing Workshop, Cumberland Lodge, Windsor, 10–12 April.

CNVDSU (1991) (Conseil National des Villes et du Développement Social Urbain) *Média et quartiers* (Paris: CNVDSU).

—— (1992) *Bilan des 64 propositions du rapport de La commission des maires sur la securité* (Paris: CNVDSU).

Combat Poverty Agency (1993) *Planning for People – the work of the Ballymun Task Force*; contributors: Liz Hayes and Hugh Greaves; Peter Whelan; Anne Power (Dublin: Combat Poverty Agency).

Coote, A. (ed.) (1992) *The Welfare of Citizens: Developing New Social Rights* (London: Rivers Oram).

CREPAH (Crepa Habitat) (1991) Paper delivered to the LSE European Social Housing Workshop, Cumberland Lodge, Windsor, 10–12 April.

Crime Concern Conference (1992) *Family, School and Community: towards a Social Crime Prevention Agenda*, report of a conference organised by Crime Concern and Marks & Spencer, London.

Dauge, Y. (1990) Paper delivered to 'Ville et Banlieue' conference, CNIC, Paris, September.

—— (1991) *Riots and Rising Expectations in Urban Europe*, LSE Housing Annual Lecture, London School of Economics, March, trans. Anne Power (London: LSE Housing).

Département du Rhône Service Habitat (1988) *Les Programmes locaux de développement social des quartiers dans l'agglomération Lyonaise: bilan et perspectives* (Lyon: Department du Rhône).

(Department of the Environment) (1977) *Unequal city: final report of the Birmingham Inner Area Study* (London: DoE).

—— (1977) *Change and Decay: Final Report of the Liverpool Inner Area Study* (London: DoE).

—— (1977) *Inner London: Policies for dispersal and balance: Final Report of the Lambeth Inner Area Study* (London: DoE).

—— (1985) Press release on launch of Urban Housing Renewal Unit (London: DoE).

—— (1985–6) *Urban Housing Renewal Unit Annual Report* (London: DoE).

—— (1989a) *Tenants in the Lead: The Housing Cooperatives Review* (London: HMSO).

—— (1986–93) *Estate Action Annual Reports* (London: DOE).

—— (1990) *Guidelines for Section 16* (London: DOE).

—— (1993) *Estate Action Update* Issues 1–4 (London: DoE).

—— (1993) *Memorandum on the Preparation of a Statement of Policy on Housing Management* March (London: DoE).

—— (1993), 'John Gummer Announces Measures to Bring a New Localism to Improved Government Services', press release 4 November (London: DoE).

—— (1994) *The Guide to Right to Manage* (London: HMSO).

—— (1994) *Access to Local Authority and Housing Association Tenancies: A Consultation Paper* (London: DoE).

(Department of the Environment, Ireland) (1989) 'Flynn Announces Allocations for Local Authority Remdial Works Scheme', Government Information Services for the DoE Press release (Dublin: DoE).

—— (1992) Information received from Housing, Rents and Tenure Section.

Der Spiegel (1991) Interviews with East Germans, 17 November.

—— (1993) 'Viel Verstandnis für Miethaie', July.

Der Stadtdirektor der Stadt Ratingen Statistikelle (1987) *Volkszalung 1987: Erste Ergebnisse aus der Volks-, Berufs-, Gebade-und Wohnungszahlung* (Ratingen: Der Stadtdirektor der Stadt Ratingen Statistikelle).

—— (1989) *Kommunalwahl 1989: Ergebnisse der Gemeinde-und Kreistagwahl* (Ratingen: Der Stadtdirektor der Stadt Ratingen Statistikelle).

Der Tagesspiegel (1992) '5,7 Prozent weniger Sozialwohnungen', 19 August.

—— (1992) 'Umwandlung von Mietwohnung beschleunigt sich', 11 September.

Die Wohnungswirtschaft (1990) '13-Punkte-Programm des GdW zur Wohnungspolitik in Deutschland', December.

—— (1991a) 'Handlungsbedarf', February.

—— (1991b) 'Modernisierung im Genossenschaftsmodell', April.

—— (1991c), 'Engeres Zusammenrucken in Norddeutschland', April.

—— (1991d) 'Städtebauforderung ist zum wichtigsten Instrument geworden', May.

DIV (Délégation interministerièlle à la Ville et Délégation à l'Aménagement du territoire et à l'action régionale) (1990) *148 Quartiers: bilan des contrats de développement social des quartiers du IXe plan 1984/88* (Paris: DIV).

(1993a), 'Les commerces des quartiers', *Ensembles*, March.

—— (1993b) 'Politique de la ville, ceux qui la font', *Ensembles*, Juin no. 406.

—— (1994) 'La Lettre de la DIV', *Ensembles*, October no. 6.

Downes, D. (ed.) (1989), *Crime and the City* – chapter 9, 'Housing Community and Crime', by Anne Power (London: Macmillan), pp. 206–35.

Dublin Corporation Housing Department (undated) *Guide to Rent Assessment*, leaflet (Dublin Corporation).

—— (undated) *Housing Maintenance – Responsibility of Tenants* (Dublin Corporation).

English House Condition Survey (1980) 14 September (London: DoE).

Federal Research Institute for Spatial Studies and Land Use Planning for the Federal Minister for Land Use Planning, Construction and Urban

Development (1987) *Large Housing Estates in the Federal Republic of Germany*, research directed by J. Schmidt-Bartel, and H. Meuter, trans. by HA1 Division of the Department of the Environment (Bonn: Federal Research Institute).

Fitzpatrick Marketing Research (March 1994) *Ballymun Refurbishment Survey – Tabular Report*, for Dublin Corporation.

Foster, J. (1992) 'Four Gunshots Create Another Myth', *Independent on Sunday*, 12 July.

Freeman, R. B. and Katz, L. F. (1992), 'Rising Wage Inequality: the United States vs. Other Advanced countries', paper delivered to ESRC/IFS half-day conference on wage dispersion, February (London: IFS), pp. 1–25.

Fuerst, J. S. (1974) *Public Housing in Europe and America* (London: Croom Helm).

Gaudin, J-P. (1989) *Technolopis: crises urbaines et innovations municipales* (Paris: Presses Universitaires de France).

Gauldie, E. (1979) *Cruel Habitations: A History of Working-Class Housing, 1780–1918* (London: Allen & Unwin).

Gesterkamp, T. (1992) 'Wohnungsnot: Sozialer Sprengstaz für die neunziger Jahre', *Die Mitbestimmung*, July.

GGW (Gesamtverband Gemeinnütziger Wohnungsunternehem eV) (1988) *Das Neue Recht für die Gemeinnützige Wohnungswirtschaft, Vorschriften und Erläuterungen zum Steuerreformgesetz 1990*, Schriftenreihe 29.

Ghekière (1991) *Marchés et politiques du logement dans la CEE* (Paris: La Documentation Française, UNFOHLM).

Gibson, T. and Todd, L. (1993) *Danger: Opportunity A New Heart for Meadowell* (Telford: Neighbourhood Initiatives Foundation).

Gifford, Lord (Chairman) (1989) *Broadwater Farm Revisited: Second Report of the Independent Inquiry into the Disturbances of October 1985 at the Broadwater Farm Estate, Tottenham* (London: Karia Press).

Glennerster, H. (1995), *British Social Policy since 1945* (Oxford: Blackwell).

Gow, D. (1992) 'Tension Soars in Germany After Fire Deaths', *The Guardian*, 24 November, p. 20.

Greve, J. with Currie, E. (1989) *Homelessness in Britain* (York: Joseph Rowntree Foundation).

Hacker, S. and Brocker, P. (1989) *Kommunalwahl 1989*, for the Stadtdirektor der Stadt Ratingen.

Hall, P. (1992) *Cities of Tomorrow: An Intellectual History of Urban Planning and Design in the Twentieth Century* (Oxford: Blackwell).

Halsall, M. (1992) 'Caretakers' Jobs a Kind of Living Hell', *The Guardian*, 31 March.

Haringey Council (1989) 'Community Celebrates Reduction in Crime on the Farm', press release, 31 August.

Harvey-Jones, J. (1992) *Trouble Shooter*, vol. 2 (London: BBC Books).

Hayes, L. (December 1991) *Ballymun Task Force Evaluation Report* (Dublin: Ballymun Task Force).

Heagney, J. (Dublin Corporation Architect) (1990) *A Programme of Renewal for Ballymun* (Dublin Corporation).

Hill, O. (1872 to 1907) *Letters to My Fellow Workers* (London: published privately between 1872 and 1907).

Hills, J. (1995) *Income and Wealth Inquiry, vol. 2* (York: Joseph Rowntree Foundation).

Hills, J. and Mullings, B. (1990) *The State of Welfare – The Welfare State Since 1974* (Oxford: Clarendon).

Hinrichs, W. (1992) *Wohnungsversorgung in der ehemaligen DDR – Verteilungskriterien und Zugangswege* (Berlin: Wissensdaltszentrum Berlin fur Socialforschung).

HLM Aujourd'hui (1994) 'HLM et copropriéetés en difficulté', 3e trimestre, no. 35.

—— (1995) 'Logement des démunis: les chemins de l'insertion', 4e trimestre, no. 36.

Holman, B. (1992) 'Poverty is First Among Crimes', *The Guardian*, 24 June.

Hubner, F. (1990) *Sozialer Wohnungsbau in Bremen* (Bremen: Amt fur Wohnung und Stadtebauforderung).

Indenrigsministeriet (1993) *First Report from City Committee*, October (Copenhagen: Indenrigs ministeriet)

Institut National de la Statistique et des Études Économiques (1992) *INSEE Premiere*, no. 234, December.

ISH (Institut für Stadt-, Standort-, Handelsforschung-und-Beratung) (1987), *Einzelhandel, Zentrenplanung und Stadtentwicklung*, for the Stadtdirektor der Stadt Ratingen (Ratingen: Stadt Ratingen).

ITN News at Ten (1993) 'Ragworth', Focus on Britain, April.

IWU Institut Wohnung und Umweld report (Darmstadt: IWU).

Jacobs, J. (1970) *The Death and Life of Great American Cities* (London: Cape)

Karn, V. and Wolman, H. (1992) *Comparing Housing Systems: Housing Performance and Housing Policies in the United States and Britain* (Oxford University Press).

Kemp, P. (1988) *The Future of Private Renting* (Salford: University of Salford).

Kemp, P., Raynsford, N. and Donnison, D. (1984) *Housing Benefit: The Evidence: A Collection of Submissions to the Housing Benefit Review* (London: Housing Centre Trust).

Kiernan, K. and Wicks, M., (1990) *Family Change and Future Policy* (York: Joseph Rowntree Foundation).

Kinsey, R. (1992) 'Idle Chatter of Underclasses and Welfare Junkies', *The Guardian*, 24 June.

Kirkegaard, O. (1994) *Samarbejde om at bo godt – En undersogelse af samarbejdet mellem beboere, almennyttige boligafdelinger og socialforvaltningen*, SBI Report 234 (Hoersholm: State Building Research Institute).

Kjeldsen, M. (1976) *Industrialized Housing in Denmark 1965–76*. (Copenhagen: Danish Building Centre).

Klies, H. (1988) *Mitteilung zur Sitzung der Bezirksvertretung 2 – Infrastrukturelle Sanierung der Siedlung 'Am Kölnberg' TOP 5.4 der Sitzung am 14.09.1988.*

Kölner Stadt-Anzeiger (1988) 'Grillplatz, Turme und Seilzirkus', 23 February.

—— (1988) 'Täglich ein Neuanstrich', 10 May.

—— (1988) 'Die Stadt hilft dem Kölnberg', 8 June.

—— (1989) 'Der Augstieg ist am Kölnberg schwierig', 15 August.

Kristensen, H. (1989a) *Danish Post-War Housing in Trouble; Trends and Strategies, Main Trends and Discussion of some Strategies* (Hoersholm: Danish Building Research Institute).

—— (1989b) *Improvement of Post-War Multi-Storey Housing Estates* (Hoersholm: Danish Building Research Institute).

Lane, V. (1993) 'Chicago public housing reforms', seminar at the London School of Economics, March.

Layard, R. (1995) Points made at LSE Welfare State Programme Seminar on Joseph Rowntree Foundation Inquiry into Income and Wealth.

Legg, C. (1981) *Could Local Authorities Be Better Landlords?* (London: City University).

Le Roy, M. C. (1988) Notes on visit to Priority Estates Projects in London and Bradford, September.

Lewis, J. (1991) *Women and Social Action in Edwardian England* (London: Edward Elga).

Loach, K. (1993) *Raining Stones* (London: Parallax Pictures).

Logirel (1991) *Report on les Minguettes*, LSE European Social Housing Workshop, Windsor, 10–12 April.

London Borough of Camden and Hunt Thompson Associates (1988) *Maiden Lane: Feasibility Study for the London Borough of Camden* (London: Hunt Thompson Associates).

London Borough of Haringey Housing Department (1983) Information received on lettings at Broadwater Farm Estate, 1 July–31 December.

Lonsdale, S. (1991) 'Contempt and Hatred on a Sixties Estate: the Clampdown on Hotting That Has Become a Fight over Territory', *The Observer*, 8 September.

LSA (1992–3) *Quartiers en Crise News: A European Exchange Programme on the Revitalisation of Urban Areas in Decline*, nos. 6, 8, 9 (Brussels: EU).

MacFarlane, R. (1994) *Community Involvement in City Challenge* (London: National Council for Voluntary Organisations).

McGowan, Marion (1994) Notes on German unification, 3 March.

Mackinnon, I. (1992) 'From Blighted Inner Cities to the Edge of Despair', *Independent On Sunday*, 26 July.

Maclennan, D., Gibb, K. and More, A. (1990) *Paying for Britain's Housing.*(York: Joseph Rowntree Foundation Housing Finance Series, in association with National Federation of Housing Associations).

Malpass, P. and Means, R. (eds) (1993) *Implementing Housing Policy.* (Birmingham: Open University Press).

Martens, A., Bozzo, I. and Matthys, C. (1991) *Renovating by the Public Authorities: the Invisible Hand or the Iron Fist*, paper delivered to the international research conference 'European Cities: Growth and Decline', The Hague, 13–16 April.

Martens, A. and Ede, E., MV (1994) *Quartier nord, le relogement des expulsés* (Bruxelles: Editions EPO).

Meschenich Project (1988) *Arbeitskreis Soziales Meschenich* (Meschenich: Gemeinwesenprojekt Meschenich).

Mill, J. S. (1863) *Utilitarianism* (London: Dent).

Mingione, E. (1989) *Fragmented Societies* (London: Blackwell).

—— (1992) in *Les Organismes au logement social et la lutte contre l'exclusion dans les Pays de la CEE: principaux extraits des documents édités à l'occasion de la rencontre des ministries du Logement de la CEE*, May, Lille.

Ministère de l'équipment, du logement, de l'aménagement du territoire et des transports (1987) *Les Minguettes: un projet pour 30,000 habitants Année*

Internationale du Logement des Sans-Abri Monographie de projet (Paris: Ministère de l'Équipment, du Logement, de l'Aménagement du Territoire et de Transport).

Myrdal, G. (1994) *An American Dilemma: The Negro Problems and Modern Democracy* (New York: Pantheon).

NACRO (National Association for the Care and Resettlement of Offenders) (1986) *Report to Working Party on Policing Housing Estates*, March (London: NACRO).

National Federation of Danish Non-profit Housing Companies (1988) *Tenant Training Programme* (Copenhagen: National Federation of Danish Non-profit Housing Companies).

Nicholson, I., Clapham, D. and Kintrea, K. (1985), *Community Ownership in Glasgow* (Glasgow City Council).

Nygaard, J. (1993) *Do Tenant Co-operatives run the Social Housing Business in Denmark?* Is that the Answer? (Kobenhavn: AKB).

Nygaard, J. and Thomassen, S. (1989) 'Tenant Democracy in the State of Denmark', speech at Priority Estates Project Annual Conference, October, Liverpool.

OECD Conference (1992) Project group report on housing, social integration and liveable environments in cities 'Putting Crime Prevention on the Map', 24 February, Irvin Waller (Paris: OECD).

Olsen, E., MP (1987) 'Financing Housing Policies – How Denmark Brought Private Funds Into Public Housing', paper for Westminster and City Programmes two-day Conference, 29/30 April, Royal Garden Hotel, London.

Peters, T. and Waterman, R. (1987) *In Search of Excellence: Lessons from America's Best Run Companies* (New York: Harper & Row).

Pinto, R. (1992) 'Estate Action: Aims Versus Achievements', *Housing Review* 39(2), March–April, pp.45–8.

—— (forthcoming) *Innovative Management Structures and the Renovation of Council Estates: The Case of Estate Action.*

Power, A. (1981) *Report on the Tulse Hill Estate*, for the Greater London Council (London: Priority Estates Project).

—— (1982) *Priority Estates Project 1982: Improving Problem Council Estates: A Summary of Aims and Progress.* (London: DOE).

—— (1983–92) Reports to Rhondda Borough Council and Welsh Office.

—— (1987) 'Reversing the Spiral', *Architects' Journal,* 9 December 1987.

—— (1988) *Under New Management – The Experience of Thirteen Islington Co-operatives* (London: Priority Estates Project).

—— (1988) *Working Paper on Small-Scale Employment Creation on Unpopular Estates,* for the Priority Estates Project, March (London: PEP).

—— (1989) 'Housing, Community and Crime', Chapter 9 in D. Downes, (ed.), *Crime and the City* (London: Macmillan), pp. 206–351.

—— (1990) *Mass Housing Estates and Spirals of Social Breakdown in European Cities* (London: LSE Housing/CECODHAS).

Power, A. with PEP Associates (1991) *Housing Management – A Guide to Quality and Creativity* (London: Longmans).

Presse- und Informationsamt der Bundesregierung, *Das Mietrecht – Was Mieter und Vermieter wissen sollten,* Mietrecht information leaflet (Bonn).

Price Waterhouse (1993) *Evaluation of Urban Development Grant, Urban Regeneration Grant and City Grant* (London: HMSO).

Quartiers en Crise News (1992), no. 6, December.

Queen, B. (1994), Interview carried out for A. Power and R. Tunstall, *Swimming Against the Tide – Progress and Polarisation on Unpopular Estates 1980–85* (1995) (York: Joseph Rowntree Foundation).

Rainwater, L. (1971) *Behind Ghetto Walls: Black Families in a Federal Slum* (London: Allen Lane).

Raynsford, N. (1995) 'A sustainable housing policy', paper delivered to Manchester City Council Housing Conference, Manchester.

Republic of Ireland (1992) *Housing (Miscellaneous Provisions) Act 1992* (Dublin: Stationery Office).

Republic of Ireland Government Information Services (1992) 'Smith Visits Ballymun Refurbishment Project', press release, 24 July.

Reynolds, F. (1986) *The Problem Estate: An Account of Omega and its People* (Aldershot: Gower).

Robbins, G. (1992) Presentation on Jersey City (London: LSE).

Roll, J. (1992) *Lone Parent Families in the European Community: A Report to the European Commission* (London: European Family and Social Policy Unit).

Safe Neighbourhoods Unit (1993) *Crime Prevention on Council Estates*, for the Department of the Environment (London: HMSO).

SBI (undated) Documentation on worst estates: *Esbjerg – Bilag; Esbjerg – Lokalomraadeundersogelse af boligforhold og beboersammensaetning; Aalborg – Bilag; Aalborg – Lokalomraadeundersogelse af boligforhold og beboersammensaetning; Karlebo – Bilag; Karlebo – Lokalomraadeundersogelse af boligforhold og beboersammensaetning* (Hoersholm: State Building Research Institute, Danish Ministry of Housing).

— Report 234, *Cooperation for Good Housing Conditions – A Study of the Cooperation Between Tenants, Non-profit Housing Associations and Social Services* (Hoersholm: State Building Research Institute, Danish Ministry of Housing).

Schmidt-Bartel, J. and Meuter, H. (1985) *Der Wohnungsbestand in Grosssiedlungen in der Bundesrepublik Deutchland: Quantitative Eckdaten zur Einschatzung der Bedeutung von Grosssiedlungen für die Wohnungsversorgung der Bevölkerung und für zukünftige Aufgaben der Städterneurung* (Bonn: BRBS).

SCIC (Sociéte Immobilière de la Caisse des Dépots) (1995) Newsletter (Paris: SCIC).

Sheppard, Sir A. (1994) Public Lecture given at the London School of Economics, May.

SIBA (1993) *Statistisches Jahrbuch* (Bonn: BRBS).

Silberman (1964) *Crisis in Black and White* (New York: Vintage).

Stagg, E., TD (1993) speech at the launch of the estate management course at City Hall, Cork 21 September.

—— (1993) speech at the Conference on Tenant Involvement in Housing Management, November, Loughlinstown, Dublin.

Steinert, J. (1990) 'Ein Verband mit 2700 Unternehmen', *Die Wohnungswirtschaft*, November.

Stern (1993) 'Der Kampf ums Quartier', July.

Stewart, M. and Taylor, M. (1996) *Empowerment and Estate Regeneration* (Bristol: Policy Press).

Teymur, N. (1988) *Rehumanising Housing*, edited by N. Teymur, A. Markus and T. Wooley (London: Butterworth).

Thake, S. and Staubach, R. (1993) *Investing in People: Rescuing Communities from the Margin* (York: Joseph Rowntree Foundation).

The Economist (1992) 'Race and Crime: Don't Mention It', 12 September, p. 66.

—— (1994) Consultative Paper on Germany.

The Economist Surveys (1990–2), London.

The Guardian (1993) 20 April.

—— (1994) 7 August.

—— (1995) J. Meikle, 'Slaying the Giants: Squalour – Still Waiting for the New Jerusalem to be Built', 25 July.

—— (1995) R. Thomas, 'Slaying the Giants: How the Education Dream Became Divisive, Unjust and Wasteful', 28 July.

—— (1995) J. Pitts, 'Wrong Rite of Passage' 11 December, p. 11.

The Independent (1992) Press reports on British and German riots, summer 1992, 26 August.

The Irish Times (1992) 'Dublin Corporation Tender for Evaluation of Ballymun Refurbishment', 29 July.

The Observer (1992) 'Flames on Streets of LA', 13 May.

—— (1992) Press reports on British and German riots, summer 1992, 26/27 July.

—— (1995) 'New Mandarins', February.

Thompson, F. M. L. (1990) *Cambridge Social History of Britain 1750–1950*, vols 1, 2, 3 (Cambridge University Press).

Tickell, J. (1992) 'Drugs and Guns in the Sky', *Voluntary Housing*, December, pp. 26–7.

Turner, G. (1992) 'Despair and the Semtex Factor', *Daily Mail*, 27 July.

UNFOHLM (1989) 'Un Siècle d'habitat social: cent ans de progrès', *HLM Aujourd'hui*, supplement to no. 13, May.

Vestergaard, H. (1991) *Bevolkningens Bevagelser*, June (Hoersholm: SBI).

Vourch, Catherine (ed.) (1987) *Année Internationale du Logement des Sans-Abri – Monographie de projet – Les Minguettes: un projet pour 30 000 habitants* (Paris: Ministère de l'Équipement, du Logement, de l'Aménagement du Territoire et des Transports).

Waller, I. (ed.) (1992) 'Putting Crime Prevention on the Map', Project group report on housing, social integration and liveable environments in cities, OECD conference 24 February.

Webster, P. (1992) 'French Opinion Turns Against Black Africans', *The Guardian*, 2 November.

White, M. (1993) *Final Report* (London: DoE).

Whitehead, C. (ed.) (1994), *Towards a Viable Private Rented Sector* (London: LSE Housing).

Whitehead, C., Cross, D. and Kleinman, M. (1992) *Housing the Nation: Choice, Access and Priorities* (London: Royal Institute of Chartered Surveyors).

Wilson, J. and Kelling, G. (1982) 'Broken Windows', *Atlantic Monthly*, March.

Wolfe, T. (1981) *From Bauhaus to Our House* (New York: Farrar, Straus & Giroux).

WZB-Mitteilungen (1992) 'Wohnen in der DDR', September.

Young, Sir G. (1993) *Housing: the Big Issues*, LSE Housing Annual Lecture, London School of Economics (London: LSE Housing).

Young, H. (1993) 'Will Selfish Altruism Be Labour's Way?', *The Guardian*, 4 February, p. 16.

Zipfel, T. (1986) Report on Broadwater Farm Estate, Tottenham, London, delivered to the NACRO Working Party on Policing Housing Estates, March.

—— (1986) Evidence to Broadwater Farm Inquiry.

—— (1994) *On Target* (London: PEP).

—— (1992) *Crime and Policing on PEP Estates* (London: PEP).

Index